Professor Allan H. Meltzer argues that despite the centrality of Keynes's views to macroeconomics and the active controversy about Keynesian policy, his central ideas have been ignored or misstated. Attention has focused on short-term countercyclical policies, while his principal theme, concerning the types of policy rules that increase stability by lowering variability and uncertainty, has been neglected. Supporting this heterodox interpretation, the author presents a rigorous study of John Maynard Keynes's views on economic theory and policy from 1920 to 1946.

Keynes's ideas about the role and responsibility of government developed in the 1920s. His *Treatise on Money* was a flawed attempt to incorporate the effects of price variability. The *General Theory*, his second attempt, shifted the focus from prices to output. Keynes argued that variability and uncertainty lowered investment and thus the capital stock. The observed variability, he believed, was above the desired natural minimum. This excess gave rise to a risk premium in interest rates, and private market interest rates remained above the rate at which society would hold the optimal stock of capital. Keynes believed that by reducing the risk premium capital stock and output could be increased and living standards raised.

In his work on postwar policy for Britain and in his proposals for Bretton Woods, Keynes placed great weight on rules, predictability, and the reduction of uncertainty. In keeping with his theoretical work, he opposed discretionary fiscal changes and favored rules to reduce instability and increase the capital stock. These proposals are consistent with, and provide evidence for, the interpretation of Keynes's theory developed in this study.

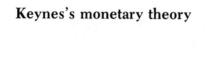

Keynes's monetary theory

Keynes's monetary theory
A different interpretation

ALLAN H. MELTZER

University Professor and
John M. Olin Professor of Political Economy and Public Policy
Carnegie Mellon University

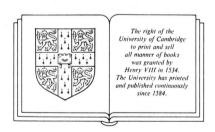

The right of the
University of Cambridge
to print and sell
all manner of books
was granted by
Henry VIII in 1534.
The University has printed
and published continuously
since 1584.

Cambridge University Press

Cambridge
New York   Port Chester   Melbourne   Sydney

Published by the Press Syndicate of the University of Cambridge
The Pitt Building, Trumpington Street, Cambridge CB2 1RP
40 West 20th Street, New York, NY 10011, USA
10 Stamford Road, Oakleigh, Melbourne 3166, Australia

First published 1988
Reprinted 1990

Printed in the United States of America

Library of Congress Cataloging-in-Publication Data
Meltzer, Allan H.
Keynes's monetary theory: a different interpretation / Allan H. Meltzer.
p.   cm.
Bibliography: p.
Includes index.
ISBN 0-521-30615-9
1. Keynes, John Maynard. 1883–1946.   General theory of employment,
interest, and money.   2. Keynesian economics.   3. Monetary policy.
I. Title.
HB99.7.K38M45   1988
332.4'01 – dc19   88-10224

British Library Cataloguing in Publication Data
Meltzer, Allan H. (Allan Harold), 1928–
Keynes's monetary theory: a different interpretation.
1. Monetary system.   Theories of Keynes, John Maynard, 1883–1946
I. Title
332.4'092'4

ISBN 0-521-30615-9 hardback

To Marilyn. Her support
and love have made all
the efforts possible.

Contents

Preface

This is a book about Keynes's theory or theories. As such, it is inevitably a work in the history of economic thought, a study of past ideas. But, perhaps more than most studies of the past, my aim is to revive interest in some of Keynes's ideas, and the vision behind them, that have been neglected. Other ideas, less important and, I believe, less faithful to Keynes's vision, have come to be regarded as Keynes's intellectual heritage.

I began this work, inadvertently, more than twenty years ago. Students in my graduate macroeconomics course lacked an understanding of the classical problems that macroeconomists address, or so I thought. One way to let them learn about the problems was to see them through the eyes of the great economists who had posed them, often in the context of their own time. Economists such as Thornton, Wicksell, Fisher, and Keynes had laid out some of the problems without always finding a solution. Problems such as the reason for unemployment, the nature and role of money, the role of the money-credit system, and inflation remain on economists' active research agenda. The great and generally helpful increase in the degree of abstraction and in the technical skills that economists now bring to these problems had the effect, at times, of obscuring rather than clarifying the nature of the problems. A few classes on the past seemed to me time well spent before turning to models and recent developments.

At the time, I would have laughed at anyone who suggested that I write a paper, let alone a book, on Keynes or any of the others. Years passed before I changed my mind. The reason was not that I failed to find differences between what I read in the *General Theory* and conventional interpretations. These differences were apparent. Standard interpretations stressed the role of public expenditure as a substitute for private expenditure during cyclical downturns. Business cycles are not a main concern of the *General Theory*, and even less is said about countercyclical government spending. The standard Keynesian model has rigid money wages. The *General Theory* spends pages discussing wage changes. But, far more important for a reader of Thornton (or Hume) was the fact that Keynes did not discover (and, I learned much later, did not claim to discover) the connection between sluggish wage changes and economic fluctuations. This was hardly a reason for a book, however.

The next step was taken by asking two questions. If not wage rigidity, what were Keynes's original contributions in the *General Theory* that made the book and the ideas so important and yet so contentious? What did people mean when they described a model as "Keynesian"? Macroeconomists use such terms as *Keynesian* or *monetarist* as both descriptive and, at times, pejorative terms. I had become convinced much earlier that the principal differences between macroeconomists were about empirical magnitudes. Later, I would add differences in assumptions about information available to policymakers and the public, different views about the aims and objectives of public officials or the degree to which personal and political objectives modify concern for the public interest, and perhaps differences in the horizon over which one looks.

One of the most puzzling aspects at the time was the difference between the popular and textbook views of Keynes as an advocate of what came to be called fiscal "fine tuning" and Keynes as a major contributor to Bretton Woods. The Bretton Woods system was a set of rules that, if followed, restricted countries' use of fiscal and monetary policy. Cyclical adjustment was facilitated by international lending and borrowing. Countries did not have to contract output and employment, as in the interwar period and under the classical gold standard. Lending and borrowing – not fiscal fine tuning – was the means Keynes had emphasized to reduce the cost of business cycles and to make the international economy more stable.

As I read more widely, I realized that there is no agreement about the Keynesian model or about Keynes's central ideas. Perhaps there never will be. I became convinced, however, that many of the interpretations were wide of the mark – influenced in some cases by a desire to develop what he "must have meant" or by a concern for a particular policy mix. I became convinced, also, that Keynes had presented a much better argument for government's role in setting policies than was usually brought out. Keynes opposed the automatic, classical gold standard and laissez-faire because he believed that there was a divergence between private and social cost. He favored rules for international borrowing and lending to reduce costs of adjustment.

What brought him to this conclusion? How did it relate to the *General Theory*, where international aspects and international monetary policy are almost absent?

A year at the Hoover Institution, 1977–8, gave me time to read and reflect on these and other questions. I began to work on permanent and transitory changes and to discuss and develop these ideas with Karl Brunner, who was at Hoover also. At the time, I thought that Keynes's different treatment of short- and long-term expectations could be formalized in a related way, but I later abandoned this approach to Keynes.

I had written a paper for Mark Perlman's first issue as editor of the *Journal of Economic Literature*. He invited me to write something for his last issue as editor. We had discussed some of my ideas about Keynes in the past. He urged me to put some of them down. Writing helps me to develop and clarify ideas, so I agreed to write the paper. The result was "Keynes's General Theory: A Different Interpretation," in the *Journal of Economic Literature* for March, 1981.

Mark Perlman sent the paper to a large number of reviewers, many of them widely regarded as "Keynesians" of various persuasions. To their surprise, I suppose, although my paper did not accept standard interpretations, it did not condemn or dismiss Keynes's ideas. To my surprise, almost all responded helpfully and even favorably. I am particularly indebted to Paul Davidson, who commented critically, but helpfully, on almost every page, and to Donald Moggridge, who sent the galley pages of volume 27 of *The Collected Works*, containing Keynes's proposals for postwar fiscal policy, particularly his exchange with James Meade. These materials showed Keynes arguing for a preannounced fiscal rule and opposed to Meade's suggestions for a more activist fiscal policy. This fit well with my interpretation, so I incorporated it in the published paper.

None of the many academic papers I have published evoked as many letters. Most of the response that I received, but not all, was favorable. Some critics published their comments in a subsequent issue of the *Journal of Economic Literature*. My reply to the criticism and an invitation to present a paper at the celebration of the Keynes centenary moved me deeper into the literature.

A feature of the *General Theory* that I found most puzzling was the absence of any discussion of the effects of permanently lowering interest rates in a single country, as Keynes urged. The reduction he proposed was a reduction in the risk premium, and he thought this could be accomplished by removing the difference between private and social cost. If everyone recognized that risk had been reduced, the fall in (real) interest rates would just offset the effect of lower risk. Misperception would lead to a capital outflow, however. Did Keynes simply neglect the capital outflow? This seemed unlikely.

The Henry Thornton lecture at the City University of London gave me an opportunity to explore Keynes's views on international economics in greater depth. Chapter 5 draws on and extends that material to trace the development of Keynes's ideas on international monetary organization from the 1920s to his death in 1946. The chapter illustrates the way in which Keynes's views about the international monetary framework evolved as his work on monetary theory developed. It also illustrates that he remained committed to some type of rule. I see this chapter as an application to policy of the ideas developed in his three books on money.

Colin Day, then the editorial director at Cambridge University Press, had urged me to extend my 1981 essay into a book. I demurred at the time. By 1984, with much more material in print, I reconsidered.

No one writes a book of this kind alone. I have received much help from friends and colleagues. I have already mentioned Mark Perlman, Paul Davidson, Karl Brunner, who perhaps heard more about Keynes than he cared to know, and Donald Moggridge, who commented extensively on Chapters 2–6, pointed out many ambiguities, and pointed me toward material that extended or altered my interpretation. I owe a special debt to Moggridge. I also owe a debt to Edward Shaw, who encouraged me to believe that I was on a right track.

James Dorn heard about my manuscript when it was about half complete. He offered to organize a conference to discuss the book. The Cato Institute and the Liberty Fund sponsored the conference. I am grateful to Edward H. Crane and William Niskanen of Cato and W. W. Hill of the Liberty Fund for sponsoring the conference and to Dorn for organizing it.

The conference, in October 1986, discussed Chapters 2–6, which were in draft at that time. David Laidler chaired the meeting and contributed many helpful suggestions. Susan Howson, John Whitaker, Donald Moggridge, Milton Friedman, Leland Yeager, and Karl Brunner led the discussion of various chapters. Friedman, in characteristic fashion, pushed all of the participants – and me – toward the central issues of economics. Axel Leijonhufvud contributed criticisms, skepticism, and helpful comments. For an author, it is a rare privilege to have so much discussion and criticism of his work by these and other participants at the conference.

Chapter 6 was presented at a session of the Eastern Economic Association. I am grateful to Robert Auerbach for organizing the session and to David Colander, Paul Davidson, and Robert Solow for their comments on that occasion. Colander also contributed by making available material from unpublished interviews with Alvin Hansen, Evsey Domar, and Abba Lerner.

I have received comments from many readers. In addition to those mentioned, already, I am grateful to John Smithin, who patiently insisted on pointing out a mistake in an early discussion of the labor market, and to Walter Salant, who pointed out some ambiguities. Naomi Perlman checked the quotations and corrected many of them.

I am grateful to Macmillan and to Cambridge University Press for permission to quote extensively from *The Collected Writings of John Maynard Keynes*, to Cambridge University Press for permission to use portions of Chapter 6 of *Keynes and the Modern World*, to the American Economic Association for permission to use portions of my papers from the *Journal of Economic Literature*, "Keynes's General Theory: A Different Interpretation" (1981) and "Interpreting Keynes" (1983), and to the City University of London for permission to use portions of my Henry Thornton Lecture, *Keynes on Monetary Reform and International Economic Order*.

Lastly, I thank Alberta Ragan, who typed and organized the material with her usual care and good spirits.

Allan H. Meltzer

Pittsburgh, January 1988

1

Introduction

Economists are inclined by training to minimize the importance of individuals and to be suspicious of explanations in which personal influence, persuasive argument, or powerful intellect have a dominant role. Impersonal forces, not persuasive individuals, shape the events that economists study. This training, and the strategy that goes with it, has proved itself repeatedly.

John Maynard Keynes is that rare exception – a man who influenced generations of economists and whose ideas and opinions affected the policies and political discussion of many countries in an important way long after his death. Keynes's ideas, and even more the ideas of those who claimed to be his intellectual heirs, dominated the textbooks and the scholarly journals for decades. His influence was strong both within and outside the areas to which he contributed directly. For example, his claim that a private economy was subject to instability encouraged research on the stability of competitive equilibrium and on the causes of business fluctuations. And his work on probability theory stimulated reconsideration of subjective probability.

Keynes died in 1946. Almost a generation later, a president of the United States, President Nixon, would declare that we are all "Keynesians" in our approach to policy. Keynes would not have been surprised. He had speculated on the role of ideas and, with his own ideas in mind, wrote:

> The ideas of economists and political philosophers, both when they are right and when they are wrong, are more powerful than is commonly understood. Indeed, the world is ruled by little else . . . I am sure that the power of vested interests is vastly exaggerated compared with the gradual encroachment of ideas. (7, p. 383)[1]

---

[1] All references to pages in Keynes's works are to *The Collected Writings of John Maynard Keynes* edited by Elizabeth Johnson and Donald Moggridge. I have adopted the convention of referring to the volume and page number without identifying references to the *Collected Writings*. Where I refer to a volume without a page reference, I use JMK followed by the volume number in parentheses.

What were the ideas? The term *Keynesian model* took on several different meanings in the textbooks, scholarly journals, and policy discussions. At a primitive level, it meant a model with a degenerate supply function for aggregate output, fixed prices, wages, and interest rates combined with an aggregate demand function dependent principally or only on income. This model was used in textbooks to demonstrate the multiplier effect on output of additional government spending, the paradox of thrift, and other Keynesian propositions. To others, the Keynesian model can be any model with sluggish adjustment of prices or money wages. At a more sophisticated level, the Keynesian model meant either the IS–LM model developed by Hicks (1937) or the related model used by Metzler (1951) and Patinkin (1965) to demonstrate the real balance effect on consumption and aggregate demand. To others, the term *Keynesian model* refers to the type of econometric model of an economy used for forecasting and policy analysis. These interpretations of the "Keynesian model" are far from exhaustive.

Keynesian policy also has several meanings. Tobin and Buiter (1976) identify the term with the proposition that countercyclical fiscal policy has a lasting effect on aggregate demand. This is a narrow interpretation though not inconsistent with the broader interpretation. On the broader interpretation, for a time, Keynesian policy meant deliberate changes in tax rates and government spending to increase government budget deficits during recessions and to achieve budget surpluses during booms. Later, greater emphasis was given to a mix of monetary and fiscal policies intended to achieve a trade-off between unemployment and inflation. But Keynesian policy also means a policy of exploiting price stickiness to achieve a temporary change in real output and employment.

Keynes's ideas had a major influence on public attitudes about the role of government. In the United States, the Employment Act of 1946 and much later the Humphrey–Hawkins Act gave the government responsibility for employment and prices. Maximum employment and purchasing power and later specific targets for unemployment became the stated policy. Large staffs were recruited at government departments and agencies to monitor details of economic life, to collect and disseminate data, and to forecast future values of prices, output, unemployment, and scores of other variables. Whether through legislation or practice, similar policies became the norm in many other countries.

Keynes and the Keynesians

Four distinguishing characteristics of Keynesian policies in the 1960s contrast with earlier policies. First, greater use was made of short-term forecasts of economic activity, prices, and interest rates. Most of the forecasts were generated by econometric models of the economy based on the Keynesian paradigm, but judgmental forecasts were used, and the two types of forecast were combined. Second, economists advised policymakers on the supposed trade-off between unemployment and inflation. A major concern of policy was to achieve maximum employment consistent with some political decision about the acceptable rate of inflation. The economists' models and forecasts took on an important, though not always decisive, role in setting the degree of stimulus. Third, greater emphasis was given in official discussions of policy to planned budget deficits as a means of implementing an economic plan and achieving target rates of inflation and unemployment annually and perhaps quarterly. Fourth, emphasis shifted from policy rules to discretionary actions based on models, judgments, political expediency, or a combination of the three.

Few economists believed that economic planning and control based on Keynesian models and policies was infallible. To supplement the general tax and spending policies and monetary actions to regulate interest rates, governments relied on incomes policies to restrict changes in individual prices and wages. In the language of the period, incomes policies were said to be useful against "cost-push" inflation. Other programs sought to restrict capital movements, to maintain fixed exchange rates under the Bretton Woods agreement, or to limit interest rates received by small savers.

After the economies of most of the developed countries experienced rates of inflation during the 1970s that were more widespread, higher, and more durable than in previous peacetime eras, the public appeal of Keynesian policies declined. By the end of the same decade in which an American president had declared that we are all Keynesians, a British prime minister concluded that countercyclical fiscal policies no longer worked. Many countries moved toward so-called medium-term strategies. Greater emphasis was given to consistency of policy and stability achieved through the maintenance of credible, long-term strategies; countercyclical actions to smooth fluctuations in output and employment had less appeal to the public and policymakers, particularly in Japan and Western Europe.

The shift in the 1950s and 1960s from the goal of price stability toward the goal of maintaining or increasing employment by increasing the rate of inflation was a major change from earlier periods. The traditional responsibility of the central bank had been maintenance of the external value of money. Under the classical gold standard a fixed exchange rate against gold became the widely accepted means of sustaining external value. The gold standard was expected also to maintain stability of the domestic price level in the long run. To achieve these goals, Britain had undertaken deliberate and sustained deflation after the Napoleonic Wars and again after World War I to restore the fixed exchange rate against gold at the historic price of gold in pounds sterling. Belief in the gold standard was so firmly held that, after World War I, policymakers in Britain and the United States thought it desirable for both countries to deflate so as to restore the prewar exchange rate of $4.86 to the pound. Any other course would have required at least one of the countries to devalue against gold. In Czechoslovakia, France, and elsewhere, governments considered or attempted even larger deflations to restore the pre-1914 gold price. In contrast, during the 1950s and 1960s, many countries devalued their currencies, some several times, rather than experience deflation.

The relation of the Keynesian policies adopted in the 1950s and 1960s to Keynes's work has never been clear. One can search through Keynes's major works on monetary theory without finding much discussion of the policies of fiscal adjustment now associated with his name. While Keynes at times preferred devaluation to deflation, he most preferred price stability. There is no basis in his analytic work for the notion of a lasting trade-off between inflation and unemployment. Indeed, Keynes opposed inflation throughout his life. A main point of his *Treatise on Money* and of his *General Theory* is that prices should remain stable. In the *General Theory* (and elsewhere) he urged that "the money wage level as a whole should be maintained as stable as possible . . . This policy will result in a fair degree of stability in the price level" (7, p. 270).

Particularly in 1929 and in the early 1930s, Keynes favored public spending, particularly investment spending, to reduce unemployment. He attacked the "Treasury view," which held that, even in an economy operating at less than full employment, additional public works spending displaced an equal amount of private spending. The policies that he advocated, then and later, were not carefully crafted, well-timed changes in money, interest rates, or government spending to stimulate expansions and retard contractions. The *General Theory* is critical of countercyclical policies that damp expansions (ibid., pp. 324–5). Keynes's preference there and in many other places is for stable policies that *maintain* price and output stability at a higher average level of output than the level that had been achieved in the past. The same section that is critical of countercyclical policy strongly favors policies to maintain investment at a higher and more stable average rate and speaks of the "prolongation of approximately full employment over a period of years" (ibid., p. 323).

Keynes is often charged with assuming that people respond to nominal rather than real values – that private decisions are subject to money illusion. This is a canard. Keynes recognized, as economists had for centuries, that changes in nominal values were accompanied by changes in relative prices; all prices did not, and do not, change equiproportionally in an immediate response to a change in money. For Keynes, however, any claim that employment could be permanently increased by increasing money is an error. He explained to Hicks, in 1937, that Hicks was wrong to attribute this view to classical economists. He had freed himself of this error: "We used formerly to admit it [that an increase in the quantity of money is capable of increasing employment] without realizing how inconsistent it was with our other premises" (14, p. 79).

Keynes does not deny – but strongly affirms – that, in the short term, changes in money increase employment. Keynes's major works, particularly the *General Theory*, are better described as opposed to short-term Keynesian policies than favoring such countercyclical policies. For Keynes, the major problem was to reduce instability, thereby lowering risk and increasing investment. The policy that Keynes recommends in the *General Theory* to increase stability is state direction of investment. On many occasions, he expressed the view that this policy should be supplemented by monetary policies that *maintained* a stable long-term rate of interest at a level below the average level that had prevailed. The point of both public investment and interest rate policy is to stabilize investment, output, and employment at a higher level than the average achieved in the past.

It is nearer the truth to say that the *General Theory* provided the analytic framework for Keynes's long-standing policy views than to conclude that the books' policy recommendations are the derived implications of his theory. Keynes favored state direction of investment from the mid-1920s. His mixture of scorn and hostility for rentiers dates from the same period or earlier. A main difference between the 1920s and the 1930s is that he did not have a model or framework to support his beliefs in the 1920s. The *General Theory* filled that gap.

There is no need to speculate about the policies he favored for the postwar period. In correspondence with James Meade and others in 1943, Keynes outlined his approach to postwar unemployment policy. He favored a more modest program than Meade, and more importantly, he wanted the main policies to be announced in advance and to aim at influencing investment, not consumption (27, pp. 319–20):

> The main task should be to *prevent* fluctuations by a stable long-term programme. If this is successful it should not be too difficult to offset small fluctuations by expediting or retarding some items in this long-term programme. (ibid., p. 322)

How could small fluctuations be offset? Keynes was skeptical about policies to stimulate consumption and opposed efforts along this line:

> I doubt if much is to be hoped for to offset unforeseen short-period fluctuations in investment by stimulating short-period changes in consumption. But I see very great attractions and practical advantage in Mr. Meade's proposal for varying social security contributions according to the state of employment. (ibid., pp. 323–4)

The proposal was for a stated policy of reducing employers' contributions when unemployment rose. Keynes quoted from a paper by Hubert Henderson favoring stable policies: "We are more likely to succeed in maintaining employment if we do not make this our sole, or even our first, aim" (ibid., p. 324).

Keynes's major effort to develop a dynamic theory of fluctuations is his *Treatise on Money*. There he devotes more space to fluctuations and to policies to damp price fluctuations than in his later work, the *General Theory*. Although the latter discusses the business cycle, it is mainly concerned with filling the gap that Keynes discovered in classical theory – that classical theory did not determine the *equilibrium level* of income around which fluctuations occur. The *General Theory* is Keynes's attempt to explain why. In his words: "This book . . . is *primarily* a study of the forces which determine changes in the *scale* of output and employment as a whole" (7, p. xxii, emphasis added). He criticized Ricardo for dismissing the issue and argued that

> the pure theory of what determine the *actual employment* of the available resources has seldom been examined in great detail . . . I mean not that the topic has been overlooked, but that the fundamental theory underlying it has been deemed so simple and obvious that it has received, at most, a bare mention. (ibid., pp. 4–5)

Classical theory (and neoclassical theories) presumes that the economy fluctuates around a level of output that is on the (dynamic) production frontier. The level of output is determined by the stocks of capital and labor and by the knowledge and skill with which they are combined. Keynes described this level as the optimum level of output. He became convinced that the principal problem of his time was that output fluctuated around an average level substantially below the optimum. Experience in the 1920s, when unemployment remained near 10 percent with exchange rates fixed and prices relatively stable, convinced him that the economy was not self-adjusting; output did not converge to equilibrium at the optimum level.

The analytical problem eventually became one of determining why the equilibrium level of output was less than the optimum level. The proximate reason he gave is that the capital stock is below the optimum. The more basic reason is uncertainty. He believed that the level of uncertainty was greater than necessary and therefore suboptimal. Excessive fluctuations in asset prices, particularly the prices quoted on the stock exchange, increased uncertainty about future returns. In the *General Theory*, Keynes considered several ways of reducing uncertainty by changing institutions. One possibility was to shut down the stock exchange. An alternative was to make investment decisions independent of stock prices and the variability of stock prices and asset values. This could be achieved, he thought, by giving the state, acting through boards of public-spirited citizens, responsibility for deciding on the level of investment. He believed that these boards would invest based on long views and would ignore fluctuations in stock prices and short-term changes in asset returns.[2]

These central ideas in Keynes's mature thought are either absent or unimportant in conventional Keynesian models and in most economic analysis. The notion of an optimum capital stock, achieved by lowering variability and uncertainty, does not have a major role and is generally neglected. The neglect of these issues, and the widespread reliance on econometric and other short-term forecasts, shifted attention from the design of economic policies and institutions to concern with current action.

In the *General Theory*, Keynes accepted a restricted version of what is now called rational expectations. As a useful approximation, he set short-term expectations equal to the realization of the relevant variables (7, pp. 50–1).[3] And he assumed, further, that short-period changes are typically small (ibid., p. 51). Given these assumptions and his concern for stability, it would have been inconsistent to insist that asset market fluctuations increased uncertainty and imposed an excess burden while urging that as a general rule government actions should create surprises – differences between actual and expected outcomes.

Keynes did not make this error. Although his public statements often recommended changes in government policy, he did not favor frequent adjustment of policy action based on econometric models or forecasts.

---

[2] Some observers attribute much of Japan's superior performance to the greater emphasis Japanese producers give to long-term results and their willingness to maintain investment during slack periods. This is done, however, without state direction of most investment. See Abegglen and Stalk (1985).

[3] This assumption is repeated several times in later writings. Long-term expectations are subject to sudden revision, so expected long-term outcomes are not the same as actual long-term outcomes.

Indeed, he was unsympathetic, even scornful, of the early econometric models of Jan Tinbergen. Many of his criticisms were aimed, not at the particular features of the model, but at the basic idea of using models to forecast and determine policy action.

Keynes's review of Tinbergen's model of investment and fluctuations in the United States raises many of the problems that have remained important (14, pp. 316–18). He mentions the problem of omitted variables and the resulting biased estimate of the weight placed on a particular factor. He is concerned about simultaneity and the proper measurement of time lags. He recognizes the critical problem of estimating coefficients that remain invariant from one sample to the next. Without invariance of the coefficients, he claims, the most that can be achieved is description of a particular period without much relevance for the future.

In correspondence with Harrod, Keynes argued against the methods of Henry Schultz and Tinbergen. He favored using data to test models but opposed their use in forecasting:

> It is of the essence of a model that one does *not* fill in real values for the variable functions. To do so would make it useless as a model . . . The object of statistical study is not so much to fill in missing variables with a view to prediction, as to test the relevance and validity of the model. (14, p. 296)

Current relevance

A wide gulf separates Keynes's views from familiar Keynesian policies and procedures. Keynes was opposed to the use of econometric models, critical about reliance on model forecasts, opposed to attempted trade-offs between prices or inflation and output or employment, and generally opposed to countercyclical policies to stimulate consumption. He favored principal reliance on rules, with strict limits on discretionary action and policy surprises. The particular rules changed from the *Tract* through his subsequent major works to the proposals for the postwar currency union or the Bretton Woods agreements. The emphasis on rules to restrict discretion remains.

These differences between Keynes and the Keynesians should be of interest to historians of economic thought and sociologists of science. How and why did Keynes's views become transmitted into the form they took in the 1950s and 1960s? It is not my aim in this book to answer these questions.[4] The book is best described as an interpre-

---

[4] The concluding chapter presents some of my speculations.

tation of Keynes's writings based on his major works between 1920 and 1946 and many of his articles, comments, letters, and notes from the same period. To bring out his views, the text and footnotes contain many quotations. This has the inevitable consequence of making the argument lengthier, thereby burdening the reader in some cases with more than one statement of Keynes's beliefs, views, or interpretations. The trade-off for this extra length is that much of the argument remains in Keynes's words. The reader has direct access to some main passages on which my interpretation relies. I believe this procedure minimizes distortion. Readers familiar with some of the more standard interpretations may find my interpretation puzzling. The many quotations from Keynes may assure them that I present a major theme – in my view the major theme – in his work.

Some persistent themes, with many variations, run through his major books and many of his papers. One of these themes is the need for institutional reform. Another is the deficiencies of laissez-faire capitalism. Others are the role of gold in the monetary system, the inadequacy of the quantity theory of money, the relation of saving to investment, the costs of variability and uncertainty, and the importance of raising living standards by increasing the capital stock.

For Keynes, a main purpose of economic policy is to remove any excess burden imposed by variability and uncertainty. In the *Tract*, this concern is expressed in a proposed monetary arrangement – or rule – to maintain domestic price stability. In the *Treatise*, Keynes makes several proposals, including an adjustable peg for gold based on a basket of commodities. The main policy proposals of the *General Theory* call for state direction of investment and stable rates of interest to reduce variability and uncertainty.

My interest in Keynes's work is heightened by its relevance to current issues in theory and policy. Keynes's emphasis on rules to reduce the excess burden of uncertainty resulting from frequent policy changes strikes me as one of the most relevant, yet one of the most neglected, aspects of his work for contemporary policy issues. Freed of the restrictions of the gold standard and freed of the discipline imposed by the belief in the necessity of annual or even cyclically balanced budgets, policies in many countries have had an inflationary bias. This bias does not produce a constant rate of inflation. The rate of inflation varies over a wide range in such countries as Mexico, Brazil, Argentina, and Israel and over a smaller, but nevertheless wide, range in more developed economies such as Italy, Britain, France, and the United States. The range does not include zero; the average rate of inflation is positive in each of these countries. Even if the optimal rate of inflation is positive, as some suggest, the variability of inflation may be

evidence of departures from optimality. The reason is that unanticipated changes in inflation induce changes in output, as is well known.
Further, to the extent that the variability of inflation causes unanticipated changes in output, variability of inflation increases uncertainty
and imposes an excess burden that society bears. Keynes believed that
the excess burden takes the form of lower investment, a smaller capital
stock, and lower output. Risk-averse investors hold more financial assets, especially money and gold, and less real capital in their portfolios.

Keynes had little interest in abstract theories developed for their
own sake. Theory was a means of obtaining implications about the
world, particularly policy propositions. Good policy depends not just
on theories showing that reliance on relative prices and endowments
to determine resource allocation produces an optimal allocation. Policy
depends also on the institution of the society in which the decisions
are made. Institutions shape the nature of the equilibrium positions
that society reaches.

He placed considerable emphasis on institutions. His interest was
not in the details of their operations, but on the policy arrangements
or rules that the institutions embodied or implemented. In the *Tract*
his proposals for monetary reform, domestic and international, are directed at the problem of reducing uncertainty by achieving price stability. Later he became convinced that stability required coordination,
and coordination was best achieved through a world monetary authority administering a set of rules, as in his later proposal for a currency union. His proposals for control of investment, particularly in
the 1920s and 1930s, called for a group of disinterested, public-spirited
individuals to allocate investment to achieve long-term benefits.

In the *General Theory*, Keynes argues that there is not a single real
rate of interest that can be called the natural rate of interest. There are
many natural rates; each corresponds to a different level of *equilibrium*
output (7, p. 242). And each level of equilibrium output reflects prevailing social or institutional arrangements. In societies with greater
risk and uncertainty, the real rate of interest is higher to reward owners
of financial assets for bearing the costs of uncertainty. As long as the
social institutions (including policy rules) remain unchanged, the risk
or uncertainty premium is expected to remain. Investors in real capital
must earn enough to cover the premium, so investment and capital
remain below their social optimum, and output is below the optimum
level.

Keynes's views on the relation of risk, uncertainty, and variability
to economic activity and welfare evolved gradually. Early in his career,
he developed his analysis of risk and uncertainty and eventually published the results in his *Treatise on Probability*. He had not yet tied

these ideas closely to his work on economic theory and policy. Both the *Tract on Monetary Reform* and the *Treatise on Money* recognize uncertainty, but the emphasis is on uncertainty about relative and absolute price changes and uncertainty about inflation. There are suggestions and hints about excess burden and concern for the effect of price variability on the size of fluctuations in output. In the *General Theory*, however, Keynes recognizes that excess burden affects the level of output. Here, at last, was a way of bringing together his longstanding wish to see the "euthanasia of the rentier" with an explanation of economic performance and his interest in reducing uncertainty and variability.

In a sense, Keynes is very much a man of his time. The interwar problems following the breakup of the Pax Britannica are high among his central concerns. Britain had provided a framework for economic stability in the nineteenth century. The gold standard, with Britain at the center, became the international monetary system in the forty years before World War I. A trading system, with Britain following a policy of free trade, contributed to economic development and welfare in Britain and elsewhere. In the realm of politics, the British naval and land forces maintained a degree of stability under which trade and finance grew and risks of expropriation remained low.

This system ended with World War I. The *Economic Consequences of the Peace* begins with Keynes's summary of the virtues of the old order and his recognition that many features of that order either were passing or had passed. The problem was to find a system of equal or greater benefit to replace the old order.

The *Economic Consequences of the Peace* is most directly concerned with the Versailles treaty, payment of reparations, and the transfer problem to which the reparations payments and the war debts gave rise. Keynes skillfully worked through the complexities of the problem to show, with great clarity, that reparations imposed on the victors the obligation to accept German imports and, therefore, to change production and resource allocation at home.

Many of the problems that concerned Keynes in the 1920s and throughout his life have returned. The international monetary system has shifted from the system of fixed but adjustable rates to a system of fluctuating rates with intervention. Occasional periods of coordinated stabilization of rates are followed by large adjustments. There is neither internal price stability nor stability of exchange rates. Keynes returned frequently to the importance of adjustable exchange rates in a world with sluggish adjustment of wages or costs of production. As in the 1920s, many so-called practical men again want to return to fixed exchange rates. The problem of adjustment in a world of sluggish wage adjustment is glossed over or often neglected. There is again a problem of repaying or servicing debts that are large relative to the volume of trade. And again measured unemployment rates have risen, particularly in Western Europe, to levels not experienced since the 1930s.

During and after World War II the United States took a major role in designing and establishing an international economic order based on the dollar as the principal currency and on tariff reduction, under the General Agreement on Tariffs and Trade, to increase trade and welfare. The United States also bore most of the cost of reestablishing and maintaining a modicum of international political stability. By the 1980s, this set of international arrangements was under stress. Restrictions on trade had grown. The power of the United States had declined relative to Western Europe and Japan, and the United States no longer seemed willing to maintain the stabilizing domestic policies that are required to keep prices or exchange rates stable or to minimize variability and uncertainty.

The transfer problem has returned also. An aftermath of the oil shocks of the 1970s is the outstanding stock of debt that must be serviced by exports from the debtor countries. This requires changes in the patterns of production and consumption in both debtor and creditor countries. The United States has shifted from the major creditor country to the world's largest debtor. These debts, too, can be serviced only if the creditor countries increase spending relative to production and the United States reduces spending relative to production.

Keynes's concern for variability, instability, and transfers is therefore relevant. The same cannot be said about many of his proposed solutions. Often these were influenced by his social views, many of which I do not share and, more importantly, that did not work as he had hoped. A main reason for the many failures of state direction of investment to achieve stability and growth lies with Keynes's error or misperception about the behavior of governments. His proposals often rest on an unsupported belief in the selflessness of political decision makers.

A sketch of the book

Keynes had an odd combination of views. He distrusted politicians and the civil service and was often critical of both. Yet, he believed that the state acting through disinterested citizens could do a better job of directing investment than private owners or managers acting in response to market signals. These beliefs were based on his personal vision and were expressed in his writing. In the 1920s, he joined parts of G. E. Moore's ethical views with the presuppositions of Harvey Road in essays setting forth his political and social views.

Chapter 2 summarizes Keynes's vision of society from his writings in the 1920s. A central theme is that ends are valued above means (9, pp. 330–1). He was an interventionist, an opponent of laissez-faire. Although he was not a socialist, he accepted large parts of the socialist vision of man and the economy. Keynes preferred a managed capitalist system, ultimately a system with freedom to choose consumption but with state direction of most investment and control of population. He never favored equalization of incomes, however, for he feared that the loss of incentives would more than offset any gain from greater egalitarianism.

In contrast to his vision, Keynes's scientific work is the work of an empirical scientist. Many of his policy discussions begin by presenting the main facts that were known or available. Much of his theoretical work, many of the issues he addressed, and the ways he addressed them reflected the facts or his perception of the facts. He believed, based on his studies of data and past experience, that the saving share was less variable than the investment share, that hourly real wages moved countercyclically, and that inflation and, more generally, price variability lowered investment and the capital stock. Chapter 2 presents some of the principal data series on which he relied and compares these data to the revised series available to us. This permits a judgment about the degree to which Keynes's conclusions may have been overly influenced by data that were incorrect or substantially revised.

The 1920s were an extraordinarily productive period for Keynes. He wrote several books, including two works on monetary theory. Chapter 3 discusses his work on monetary theory, with emphasis on his two-volume *Treatise on Money*.

The *Treatise* is a difficult work containing a plethora of terms, many of them covering the same or similar concepts, often unrelated to the analysis. Keynes's main aim was to develop a theory of the business cycle in which the relation of prices to costs of production replaced the quantity of money and velocity as the key relation. The difficulties of the book may explain why readers fail to get beyond the "fundamental equations" and often see these equations as the theory that Keynes presents. This is a mistake. The *Treatise* presents a static theory of prices and interest rates that is a forerunner of the theory of interest rates and output found in the *General Theory*. Chapter 3 develops Keynes's analysis as a model of the *Treatise* and uses the model to derive many of the conclusions Keynes reached in the book.

Many of the central ideas later found in the *General Theory* appear, often in a vestigial form, in the *Treatise*. Anticipations or expectations are quasi-rational: "Action based on inaccurate anticipations will not long survive experiences of a contrary character, so the facts will soon override anticipations, except where they agree" (5, p. 144). Keynes focused on investment. Changes in investment, resulting mainly from the changes in profits produced by changes in relative prices, generate business cycles. Saving is relatively passive. Increases in saving do not increase investment, but increases in investment lead to increased saving. More importantly, the *Treatise* introduces a stock-flow analysis combining the demand for and supply of assets and the flows of saving and investment to determine prices and interest rates. Real income is a given in this analysis, a major difference from Keynes's later work. Despite this serious shortcoming, the stock-flow analysis highlights two key decisions taken simultaneously: the decision to consume or save and the allocation of wealth between financial assets and real capital.

In the *Tract*, Keynes discusses the harmful effects of variability and uncertainty induced by inflation or deflation. The *Treatise* develops this theme more fully. Variability of prices is a major cause of business cycles. Since wages or costs of production adjust more slowly than prices, price variability affects profits and, therefore, investment.

The *Treatise* was written following Britain's return to gold in 1925 at the historic parity. Unemployment remained high throughout the decade. Keynes blamed the unemployment on the return to gold at the old, fixed parity in a system with inflexible wages. Since wages do not adjust promptly, Keynes concluded that exchange rates must be permitted to change to restore equilibrium. This experience is reflected in the policy recommendations of the *Treatise*. Keynes favored adjustment of the gold price in response to changes in the price of a basket of commodities. His proposals for fixed, but adjustable, exchange rates after World War II are an alternative solution to the same problem.

Keynes also criticized the restriction that the gold standard imposed on economic policy. The problem, as he saw it, is that under the gold standard foreign investment drives domestic investment. The reason is that costs of production change more slowly than open-market interest rates, so the trade balance changes more slowly than the capital account. The gold standard therefore achieves external stability at the expense of domestic stability. Further, efforts to stimulate production by monetary expansion lower interest rates and induce a gold outflow. To stop the gold outflow, the monetary authority must reverse course, bringing the effort to stimulate to an end.

The theoretical structure of the *Treatise* was criticized by most reviewers. Keynes accepted some of the criticism. The *General Theory* was written to correct "the outstanding fault of the theoretical parts" (7, p. xxii) of the *Treatise*.

Chapter 4 discusses the *General Theory*, its central ideas, and its relation to the *Treatise* and to Keynes's general beliefs. Of particular importance is the shift in emphasis from changes in relative prices to changes in the level of output and the reaffirmation of Keynes's long-standing belief in the relative importance of investment.

The *General Theory* is mainly about an economy in which output is not limited by factor supply, investment is not limited by saving, but output and saving are limited by investment. Keynes interpreted Say's law as implying that output is fixed at a maximum level. At that level any attempt to expand aggregate investment necessarily reduces consumption; consumption is an alternative to investment. Keynes observed that investment and consumption can, and often do, increase together. The multiplier incorporates this relation, and evidence of a positive value of the multiplier is taken as a rejection of Say's law.

A main point of the *General Theory*, in my interpretation, is the economic argument that fluctuations in output impose social costs that cannot be removed by private action. Variability imposes a premium for bearing risk or uncertainty that raises the market rate of interest above the social productivity of capital and holds the capital stock below the social optimum. Noninterventionist, laissez-faire policies therefore confine the economy to a suboptimal position. The level of output is lower, and fluctuations are larger, than attainable under alternative policy rules. Keynes main proposal follows: Let the state remove the excess burden by directing investment according to long-term benefits. This is an old theme, very much a part of his social view in the 1920s. The *General Theory* provided the theoretical framework that supported that view.

Keynes's policy recommendations in the *General Theory* and after are not calls for carefully timed changes in tax rates, spending, and interest rates. On the contrary, he favored stable interest rates and predictable policies. In wartime memos, he advocated preannounced policies to stabilize investment and opposed countercyclical actions to stimulate consumption. Although he had favored expansionist policies in the early 1930s, his emphasis in the *General Theory* and in his wartime memos is on institutional reform.

The reform to which Keynes devoted most of his attention was reform of the international monetary system. Chapter 5 traces the development of his ideas about desirable, or optimal, international monetary arrangements from the *Tract* through his proposals for a postwar clearing union and the negotiations that led to Bretton Woods.

Chapter 5 provides evidence for my interpretation of Keynes as an institutional reformer who favored rules embodied in institutional arrangements and opposed unlimited discretion. Keynes never embraced rules that were completely automatic. There was always some opportunity for adjustment within the rules, but the rules imposed constraints on policy. Keynes intended the constraints to reduce uncertainty and variability and thereby reduce the excess burden arising from bearing the costs of avoidable uncertainty.

There are many interpretations of Keynes's work, particularly of his *General Theory*. The presence of these many interpretations suggests that no single interpretation will satisfy all readers and that none is likely to supplant all others. Mine differs from others in ways that the book develops. Chapter 6 presents four prominent alternative interpretations and compares them to my interpretation.

Several of the alternative interpretations try to show how Keynes's theory, particularly the *General Theory*, can be improved or corrected by extending his analysis or changing it in a particular way. My interest is different. Although I note, at some places, that Keynes's argument is faulty or incorrect, I have not concentrated on finding errors or imprecision.

I believe that the main message that Keynes left is a correct, important, albeit neglected, message. His work, whether taken as a whole or in parts, calls attention to institutions and policy arrangements and their relation to uncertainty. Institutions and policy arrangements can augment or reduce uncertainty. A major task of economists is to find the rules and arrangements that reduce risk and uncertainty to the minimum inherent in nature. Although I do not share Keynes's belief in the desirability of the rules he proposed, I accept his view that the study of economic policy is a search for rules that reduce excess burdens. The concluding chapter develops some of these points.

2

Keynes in the 1920s: ideas, beliefs, and events

Most of the ideas that we associated with Keynes – ideas that had a lasting influence on economics – developed during the 1920s. Early in the decade, Keynes was a quantity theorist of Cambridge persuasion who differed little from his teachers and colleagues. By the end of the decade, with the *Treatise on Money* nearly complete, most of the main ideas that we think of as Keynes's distinct contributions to monetary theory were either partly formed or well developed. He was no longer a quantity theorist and believed, firmly, that the quantity theory, though not useless, provided a poor foundation for monetary analysis. He had related stocks and flows in a framework that determined, simultaneously, the price level, interest rate, saving, and investment. He had laid the groundwork for his contributions to the theories of domestic monetary and fiscal policy and of international monetary policy. The latter contribution developed, when the opportunity came, into the Bretton Woods framework. He had introduced expectations, or as he often referred to it, bearishness – a subject to which he contributed in his *Treatise on Probability* – into the theory of the demand for money. He was well along toward the development of the general equilibrium framework that became the orthodox monetary theory for generations of students.

The development was not complete. Keynes had not taken his ideas as far as he later did, and he recognized that more had to be done. The preface to *A Treatise on Money* (5, p. xvii) cautions the reader that Keynes's ideas had developed and changed in the seven years since he had started work on the book. He was aware that remnants of his past beliefs mingled with his newer views and that the old and the new were not always compatible.

Keynes's revisions reflected his intellectual development, his experience during the period, and the events that gave rise to that experience. Many of these events are known, at least in broad outline. Britain had pursued a relatively deflationary policy during the early 1920s in an effort to restore the fixed parity with gold at the prewar exchange rate. Thereafter, British prices declined about 1 percent per year. The principal continental economies, France and Germany, pursued inflationary policies that ended with the German hyperinflation of 1923 and the Poincaré stabilization of the franc in 1926–7. The latter reform restored the franc to a fixed parity with gold at a rate that enabled France to run a current-account surplus and accumulate gold. French policy increased the difficulty Britain faced in maintaining the prewar gold price. On the other side of the Atlantic, New York became a major financial center. The dollar remained tied to gold at the prewar price, but the Federal Reserve acted to moderate interest rate changes and did not permit the classical gold standard mechanism to fully determine short-term changes in money and gold.

Unemployment remained relatively high in Britain after the return to gold, but the economy experienced real growth at a rate close to its long-term average. The United States introduced major tariff increases in 1922 and again in 1930, the latter at about the time that the *Treatise* was published. The tariff changes lowered U.S. imports and added to the deflationary pressures in Britain and other countries. At the end of the decade, stock prices rose in the United States, then collapsed. The U.S. boom of the 1920s was followed by the worldwide decline in prices and output that is known as the Great Depression.

These events and others occupied Keynes. As an investor, speculator, board chairman of a leading insurance company, editor, advisor of governments, and frequent commentator on current affairs, Keynes was involved in the major events of his time. His observations of events influenced the development of his ideas about monetary theory in a number of ways. Keynes was the type of theorist who developed his theory after he had developed a sense of relative magnitudes and of the size and frequency of changes in these magnitudes. He concentrated on those magnitudes that changed most, often assuming that others remained fixed for the relevant period. Observation was a main source of his hypotheses about the principal relationships among variables that were subject to change. Major events became a testing ground for his ideas. He transferred ideas from theory to practical application, at times before he had published or circulated them outside a small circle and, at times, before they were fully developed.[1]

The application of theoretical argument to current and future events is often the most memorable part of Keynes's work. Looking back at the *Treatise* after more than fifty years, a reader is often struck by the labored argument, the relatively large amount of space taken by defi-

---

[1] The most familiar example is the use of the *Treatise* in the Macmillan committee deliberations. Less well known is his use of the analysis of the *Treatise* to discuss the stock market boom in the U.S. years before the book was completed or published.

nitions, the use of a multiplicity of terms to refer to the same (or very similar) phenomena, and the infrequent use made of many of the terms after they are defined. A formal statement of hypotheses is so rare that many readers never get beyond the "fundamental equations" to examine the theoretical structure that Keynes developed and applied. Keynes's analysis is no worse and often more explicit and less turgid than famed contemporaries such as Robertson, Hawtrey, or Pigou, but it is in his applications that one sees most clearly the source of his unrivaled reputation among his academic contemporaries and men of affairs.

At times, Keynes described himself as a Cassandra because his predictions during the 1920s were most often warnings about problems, failures, and impending disasters. He believed that most of these problems were remediable or avoidable if governments based policies on his analysis and proposals. Some of these warnings or predictions influenced his later theoretical work, and many of them eventually enhanced his reputation with the public and policymakers.[2] Four are of particular interest because of their relation to his basic views and their influence on his future work.

First, Keynes foresaw that the plan to make Germany pay large reparations would fail because the plan had been developed with scarcely any thought about Germany's capacity to pay. *The Economic Consequences of the Peace* (JMK 2) is an often emotional description of the 1919 peace conference containing an astute analysis of Germany's capacity to pay (2, p. 118), and a strong defense of price stability and opposition to inflation (ibid., pp. 148–50). Keynes foresaw that Germany could not pay the amounts demanded out of its potential production without a substantial and improbably large change in the terms of trade. He saw also that the attempt to enforce payment would require the creditors to accept imports – the transfer problem – that would damage competing firms in the payees' countries. Within a few

---

[2] He also made significant errors. In World War I, he believed Britain faced exhaustion of resources. His estimates of Britain's economic position after World War II were extremely pessimistic prior to the negotiation of the U.S. loan to Britain. Vaizey quotes Lord Annan as follows:

> He really did believe that on the whole the view expressed by intelligent members of the Establishment was completely right. Of course, he never held such a view where anything to do with economics was concerned . . .
>
> But it was on politics that he was curiously naive. I am speaking of the period after the First World War, and all his Bloomsbury friends (to say nothing of a good number of enemies in the City) can quote numerous cases where Maynard made totally false prophecies about what was going to happen. (1969, in Wood 1, p. 180)

years, many of Keynes's critics recognized that the reparations would not be paid.[3]

Second, Keynes offered scathing criticisms of French financial policy in the early 1920s. In a series on the reconstruction of Europe for the *Manchester Guardian* (JMK 17), which Keynes organized and edited and to which he contributed, he predicted, correctly, that the franc would be devalued. Several of his articles for this series are republished, along with the prediction, in *A Tract on Monetary Reform* (JMK 4). His prediction follows from his analysis of the fiscal and monetary system and the position of France. Keynes saw that an attempt by France to restore the prewar exchange rate of francs for gold, as promised by the French government, would raise the real value of the debt and transfer wealth to the owners of government bonds. He concluded that the implied service of the debt was too great to admit this outcome as a practical solution.[4] The main alternatives were inflation or devaluation. Keynes opposed inflation, argued that devaluation was the wiser course, and urged the French to devalue sooner rather than later. By the time the French edition of *Tract* was published (1924), depreciation of the franc had been accepted. Somewhat later the franc was stabilized following Poincaré's fiscal reform. St. Etienne (1984) has a recent discussion of the reform.

Third, less well known is Keynes's prediction that the rise in U.S. stock prices would be followed by deflation. The prediction was based in part on his belief that the Federal Reserve misinterpreted the rise in stock prices as a sign of inflation. Keynes interpreted the rise in stock prices as an increase in the real return to investment in both new and existing assets – a view that he refined later in the concept of the marginal efficiency of capital (7, p. 151, n. 1). In a 1928 memo sent to Benjamin Strong, Carl Snyder, and W. Randolph Burgess at the Federal Reserve and to others elsewhere, Keynes (13, pp. 52–9) argued that the Federal Reserve policy of restricting member bank borrowing was based on a mistaken belief that the rise in stock prices was inflationary. The reduction in member bank borrowing that the Federal Reserve sought "would mean that the demand deposits of the member

---

[3] JMK (17) contains these assessments and Keynes's responses to several of them. *A Revision of the Treaty* (JMK 3) puts forward his recommendations. Keynes remained skeptical even after reparations were reduced, but he recognized that Germany could delay default only by borrowing or otherwise arranging a capital transfer (17, p. 245). Keynes's views on the treaty, reparations, and their consequences for Europe remained controversial. Mantoux (1946) makes a detailed criticism of Keynes's arguments and points out that Germany in the 1930s was able to spend on armaments more than would have been required to transfer as reparations under the treaty.

[4] "The service of this debt will shortly absorb . . . almost the entire yield of taxation . . . the yield of taxation must be increased permanently by 30 percent" (4, pp. 58–9).

banks would have to fall . . . to a figure which certainly would not finance the present income of the United States or anything like it" (ibid., p. 59). His general line of argument was, he replied to Carl Snyder, based on his analysis in the *Treatise*. Snyder had found the analysis "somewhat alien" because unlike Keynes, he viewed the rise in stock prices as one reflection of an overly rapid expansion of bank credit that encouraged speculation (ibid., pp. 60–2, and Keynes's reply, pp. 62–5).[5]

Fourth, at home, Keynes argued against the return to gold at the prewar exchange rate, and he predicted that the deflationary effects of the return would continue long after the prewar parity was established in the financial market. Lengthy sections of his *Tract* and *Treatise* analyze the working of the gold standard and the costs and consequences of the deflation required to restore the gold standard by adjusting prices, the trade balance, and wages.

Keynes's assessment of the costs of returning to the historic parity is famous, but his most critical comments came after the return. Before the fact, his remarks are more temperate. An essay written at the time of the 1922 Genoa conference comments that "all currencies should become exchangeable against gold at a fixed rate as soon as possible" (17, pp. 361–2). At the time, Keynes favored a gold bullion standard under which gold would be held by central banks and exchanged only in amounts of £50,000 or more (ibid.). He wanted the pound to be fixed at about $4.30 ± 5 percent (ibid., p. 368), not the historic $4.86, but to accommodate those who wished to restore the prewar parity, he would permit appreciation to $4.86 at a rate not to exceed one half percent per month (ibid., p. 367).[6] Although he later modified the details of his proposal, his main criticisms of the official position were the timing of the return to a fixed parity and the exchange rate at which the pound became convertible. He does not seem to have recognized anywhere that if his 1922 plan had been adopted, the pound would have reached its prewar parity by 1925.

After the fact, in "The Economic Consequences of Mr. Churchill"

[5] Keynes later revised his view: "Whilst there was probably no material inflation up to the end of 1927, a genuine profit inflation developed some time between that date and the summer of 1929" (6, p. 170). He blamed his "mistake" on his use of the wholesale price index. By a profit inflation, he meant that prices rose relative to wages and other costs of production. Despite his prediction, he did not foresee the worldwide decline in stock prices in 1930. Keynes's investment results are given in the *Collected Writings* (12, p. 113). His personal net assets, base 100 in 1922, which were at 204 in 1927, fell to 36 in 1929 before beginning to rise. Investments of King's College show smaller fluctuations, but their "Chest" portfolio also fell more than 50 percent from 1929 to 1931. Clark (1977, p. 87) reports that Keynes's insurance company had heavy losses to the delight of many in the City of London, where Keynes was not popular.
[6] His proposal would have brought the pound to its old parity in 1924–5.

(9, pp. 207–30), he argued that the pound was overvalued by about 10 percent against the dollar, so the fixed exchange rate required a 10 percent reduction in prices and a fall in money wages and costs of production (ibid., pp. 209–11). But, he notes that his argument was not "against the gold standard as such . . . If Mr. Churchill had restored gold by fixing the parity lower than the pre-war figure, or if he had waited until our money values were adjusted to the pre-war parity, then these particular arguments would have no force" (ibid., p. 212). The problems of overvaluation, he believed, were of three kinds. First were the interest payments to the rentiers. Second was the increase in the real value of the debt – the burden of the debt. Third, and most important, was the depression in the export industries and the spread of unemployment to other industries. Unemployment is the mechanism by which prices and wages are reduced (ibid., pp. 213–4). The only policy for the Bank of England was to restrict credit: "The policy can only attain its end by intensifying unemployment without limit, until the workers are ready to accept the necessary reduction of money wages under the pressure of hard facts" (ibid., p. 218).

Here, long before the *General Theory* or the *Treatise*, Keynes argues that money wages are slow to adjust downward. Keynes, in his classical or Marshallian period, firmly believed that monetary restriction causes unemployment during the interval between the start of the policy and the adjustment of prices and wages (ibid., pp. 219–20). Once the price and wage adjustment is complete, "we should each of us have nearly the same real income as before" (ibid., p. 213).

Businesspeople, bankers, and high public officials rarely look at the analysis underlying a prediction. They often have limited knowledge of economics and little confidence in economists. Their confidence goes, first, to those who support their own preconceptions and, later, to those who, against the crowd, predict correctly. Keynes's arguments about the costs of restoring prewar parity, though correct, were not popular. His predictions of high, persistent unemployment enhanced his reputation as a prophet when unemployment remained high. As his reputation rose, his economic theories came to be accepted, particularly in Britain but elsewhere also, as the proper basis for policy. Further, his experience strengthened some of his basic beliefs, particularly his opposition to laissez-faire.[7]

The interplay between ideas and events is basic to an understanding

[7] Keynes's reputation among economists and government officials was based on his earlier work including books on Indian finance, memos written as a Treasury official during World War I, and the oral tradition at Cambridge. These were not well known to the public, however. Cambridge fellows and professors would have known his work on probability theory also.

of Keynes's development from the *Tract* to the *Treatise* and beyond. Both books and Keynes's articles in the popular press contain the time series he used to "test" his theories and to form judgments about relationships. The following section summarizes some of the data for the 1920s and compares the data now available to the data on which Keynes relied. Then, I trace the development of his ideas, summarizing some of his main ideas and beliefs and one of the intellectual influences important in forming or firming these ideas and beliefs.

The data and their interpretation

At the end of the long and costly war in 1918, real output in Britain was 7 percent above the level of 1913, but consumer prices were 210 percent higher than their 1913 level.[8] Prices continued to rise in 1919 and 1920 to a peak two and a half times the prewar level, but the sharp decline in output that started in 1919 was followed by an even sharper decline in prices. The price level fell by almost one-third in the next three years. The decline eliminated the postwar rise in prices but left the wartime rise. At the trough of the recession, in 1921–2, real output was 19 percent below the level of 1913 whereas the price deflator was only 18 percent below the 1919 level.

During the rest of the decade, Britain experienced alternating periods of expansion and contraction, with a particularly sharp recession in 1926 at the time of the general strike. On average, the years 1922–9 were a period of real growth, at a rate of 2.5 percent compounded starting from the low level of 1922. Prices remained in a narrow range from 1923 to 1926, then declined for the rest of the decade and during the early 1930s.

The wartime price increase, base 1913, exceeds the wartime increase in money stock, so real balances declined slightly and velocity rose. Real balances rose during the recession and continued to increase, on average, during the rest of the decade, but monetary velocity rose also. The rise in measured M_1 velocity is about 2.25 percent per year compounded from 1922 or 1923 to 1929, slightly below the average rate at which output increased.

The data used for these comparisons, shown in Table 2.1A, were not available at the time. Fortunately, Keynes published the principal data on which he either relied or used to make judgments after the

---

[8] Unless contrary indication is made, all data used in this section come from Capie and Webber (1985), Mitchell (1976), or JMK (6), as noted in the sources to Tables 2.1A and 2.1B. Keynes's data is used to show what Keynes knew at the time. Where there is doubt about which source I use, indication will be given.

Table 2.1A *Revised Data*
(1924 = 100)

Year	M_3	M_1	V_1	Base money	Real GNP	Prices	
						Deflator	Retail
1918	45	n.a.	n.a.	42	110	54	59
1919	105	n.a.	n.a.	112	107	117	123
1920	118	n.a.	n.a.	120	95	142	142
1921	118	n.a.	n.a.	112	91	126	129
1922	109	106	97	106	94	109	104
1923	101	101	98	99	97	102	99
1924	100	100	100	100	100	100	100
1925	99	98	108	101	105	100	100
1926	99	97	103	100	101	99	98
1927	100	97	108	100	108	97	95
1928	102	98	108	101	110	96	95
1929	104	96	113	102	112	95	94
1930	104	95	112	101	112	94	90
1931	103	95	103	100	107	92	84
1932	105	92	103	99	106	90	82

Source: Data for money are from Capie and Webber (1985), Tables I(9), III(12). Real GNP and the deflator are from Mitchell (1976, p. 790) based on Feinstein. Data are annual averages except monetary base taken at end of second quarter.

fact. These are shown in Table 2.1B. Comparison of the two tables permits us to reach some conclusions about the extent to which Keynes may have been misled by the limited data available to him.

The price series are broadly similar. Both tables show a steep price decline from 1920 to 1923–4 followed by a short period of stability and a gradual decline for the rest of the decade. Keynes's series on wholesale prices fluctuates over a wider range, but he was aware of the greater fluctuation of wholesale prices and commented on it at length (5, pp. 50–4, 59–62).

Despite his reservations about wholesale prices, Keynes used the wholesale price as the numerator of the ratio he called "profit inflation." To Keynes, profit inflation meant a rise in prices relative to costs of production. For the denominator Keynes used MV/production, where M is cash deposits from Table 2.1B. The profit inflation ratio was an, admittedly crude, attempt to relate costs of production (wholesale prices) to prices received by (nonfarm) producers. The basic idea is straightforward. We can think of the denominator as a measure of the average or expected price at which output will sell. If this price level is unchanged, a rise in the cost of raw materials, relative to the expected selling price of finished goods, reduces profits. In the *Treatise*, a decline in profits reduces investment of all kinds, including working capital (raw material). When the ratio is above unity, the nominal cost of producing output is above nominal expenditure (MV). In Keynes's terms, costs increased relative to selling prices, so Keynes expected investment and output to fall. In his terms, profits were low or negative and (inventory accumulation) investment was discouraged. A fall in costs (wholesale prices) relative to (selling) prices increased profits and stimulated business investment in inventories and durable capital. If we substitute the deflator (Feinstein index) for Keynes's measure (MV/production) in the denominator, the new measure is similar to Keynes's measure. The principal difference is that the rise in the index in 1927 is eliminated.

Some differences appear when we compare Keynes's measures of production or employment to the index of real GNP. Keynes's measures show increases of 11 and 6 percent between 1924 and 1929, whereas the Feinstein measure of reported real GNP rises 12 percent. The picture of the period changes slightly. On Keynes's measures, much of the rise in real output for the decade is a one-time rise in 1929; real GNP (Feinstein) shows a steadier rate of increase. The newer data might have changed Keynes's opinion about the slow "progress" following the return to the gold standard, but it is doubtful that it would have changed his policy recommendations. Unemployment in Britain

Table 2.1B *Keynes's data*
(1924 = 100)

Year	Total deposits	Cash deposits	V	Production	Employment	Profit inflation	Prices Consumer	Prices Wholesale
1919	90	106	n.a.	n.a.	n.a.	127	n.a.	n.a.
1920	100	111	137	104	103	98	150	186
1921	108	108	93	82	89.5	91	132	120
1922	106	106	91	91.5	93.5	94	106	96
1923	100	102	94	94	97	94	99	96
1924	100	100	101	100	100	100	100	100
1925	99	97	104	101	101	96	101	96
1926	100	96	97	93	95.5	89	98	89
1927	103	99	99	107	104.5	94.5	96	86
1928	106	100	98	106.5	104.5	94.5	95	85
1929	108	100	98	111	106	93	94	82

Source: JMK 6, pp. 9, 35, 77, 79, 80.

remained high despite the growth of real output, as in the 1980s.[9] Keynes and many others used unemployment as a measure of performance, and in the *General Theory* he made this standard explicit.

The *Treatise* assigns an important role to monetary factors in the business cycle. Keynes emphasizes changes in money, changes in the demand for money, and changes in the composition of deposits. He treats shifts from total deposits to "cash" deposits, or sometimes shifts between the "industrial circulation" and the "financial circulation," as important for his theory of investment, so he computed a series on cash deposits from the small amount of data available. In current jargon Keynes's hypothesis is that intermediation – shifts from time to demand deposits – are negatively related to shifts from investment to consumption.[10] His data do not lend much support; there are only two years in which his two series move in opposite directions. Total deposits rise relative to cash deposits over the period as a whole, but Keynes's argument is not about trends. Nor is there support in the more recently published data. Between 1922 and 1929, the ratio of M_3 to M_1 varies between 1.68 and 1.76, less than 5 percent. The ratio rises, steadily, throughout the period. Keynes's hypothesis receives more support after the period ended; the ratio of M_3 to M_1 rises by 9 percent in the next three years, reflecting the decline in demand deposits during the early 1930s. Both investment and consumption spending declined, but investment declined relative to consumption.

The *Treatise* partly anticipates the *General Theory* in its discussion of shifts in the demand for money. Many quantity theorists had mentioned, and as far back as Thornton (1802) some had carefully discussed, the effect of "confidence" on velocity. These early suggestions of a theory relating anticipations to the demand for money remained incomplete; confidence was treated as an independent force not explicitly related to events in the economy.

The Cambridge tradition, developed by Marshall and carried on by Pigou, Lavington, and others, shifted emphasis from velocity to the demand for money – average cash balances held. Robertson's (1926)

---

[9] Keynes was aware of the unemployment and discusses its causes, but he does not report a series for unemployment, so unemployment is not reported in the tables. Clark (1977, p. 88) remarks that in 1930 he showed Keynes data suggesting that productivity had increased in the 1920s. Clark reports that Keynes was interested, but I have not found any reference to these data. The *Treatise* (6, p. 159) assumes that efficiency increased about 1 percent per year from 1919 to 1924 but gives no basis for the assumption. Later, Keynes surmised (13, p. 179) that real wages rose during the 1920s at about the growth rate of output.

[10] Keynes used the data on time and demand deposits for the United States. For Britain, he would have liked to include unused overdrafts, but no data were available (5, pp. 32–8).

discussion of hoarding as a shift in desired money holdings and his effort to relate such shifts to saving, economic activity, and prices influenced Keynes. We know from their extensive correspondence, notes, and comments (JMK 13) and from Robertson's introduction to one of his books (1926, p. 5) that both men were thinking about these relations and trying to formulate useful definitions of saving, "hoarding," and different types of investment from the mid-1920s on.

The velocity measure (V) that Keynes computed from the scanty data on bank debits shows ample reason for rejecting constant velocity. Bank debits show a two-year decline of more than 30 percent from the 1920 peak. This is followed by a 14 percent rise over the next three years, then a further decline. The revised annual data (Table 2.1A) begin in 1922. These data show larger changes in the middle years of the decade and a much larger increase at the end. On either measure, the variations in velocity are larger than the variations in money. Given these data, Keynes had two choices. He could reformulate the theory of demand for average cash balances, or he could dismiss the theory and develop an alternative. Keynes chose the latter course.

The constant-velocity hypothesis is not firmly held even in the *Tract*, where Keynes (4, pp. 61–5) uses the quantity equation in cash balance form and, quoting Marshall (1923, Chapter 4), relates average cash balance to wealth and income. He follows the quotation from Marshall with the claim that average cash balances are not constant, except perhaps in the long run. Then, immediately, he adds the famous remark: "*In the long run* we are all dead" (4, p. 65).

The basis for his claim about velocity, repeated in this section of the *Tract*, is his earlier discussion (ibid., pp. 42–3) of the effect of inflation on velocity. In these pages, Keynes presents a concise analysis of the inflation tax[11] on cash balances and, using data on velocity in countries with hyperinflation, concludes that if it were not for the decline in average cash balances, "there would be no limit to the sums which the government could extract from the public by means of inflation" (ibid., p. 42).

There are two innovations in the *Treatise* relative to the *Tract*. First, Keynes rejects the idea of treating cyclical changes in velocity as a minor departure from the trend set by income and wealth. His observations for Germany, Austria, and Britain are not consistent with that view. Second, he concludes that velocity is not a useful construct and

---

[11] Keynes uses the term *inflation tax* and compares the tax to a highway toll. The use of money can be taxed, but money is so convenient that "only a very high levy will completely stop all traffic" (4, p. 43).

shifts from velocity to an analysis of the demand for money.[12] This shift was based on observations such as those in Table 2.1B.

The data on which Keynes relied give a distorted picture of the variability relevant for decisions. People have opinions or forecasts about future events and intuition about the range of fluctuations even when data are sparse. They use whatever clues are available to judge future events, and particularly when there are major changes in the environment, some act on these clues instead of waiting for better data or doing nothing. For many decisions, the difference between expected and actual changes is far more relevant than the numbers in Tables 2.1A and 2.1B. There is, of course, no way to recapture the forecasts, beliefs, and opinions held at the time. The best one can do is use a reliable and relatively efficient forecasting scheme to compute errors of forecast (differences between actual and predicted events). Table 2.2 compares errors of forecast for the period after the return to gold to the errors of forecast for longer periods. The forecast errors are computed by means of a multistate Kalman filter that uses only past information on the particular series to forecast one period ahead.[13] Table 2.2 compares mean absolute errors of forecast for each series to errors made after the return to gold, April 28, 1925.

Forecasts of the monetary base, money, and the deflator are at least as accurate following the return to gold as in the longer periods for which data are available. Consistent quarterly data for the monetary base are available, so it is possible to compare forecast errors for the eighteen quarters before and after the return to gold. These show a slight decline in forecast error following formal resumption. Forecasts for other variables are higher for 1925–9, and the difference is particularly large for nominal GNP. A main reason for these larger errors appears to be the general strike of 1926. In the year of the strike, forecast errors for nominal and real GNP are -8 and -11.7 percent, respectively, more than one-third of the cumulative error for the period. Even if we omit this error, the averages for the period remain above the long-term average errors of forecast. These data suggest that the trends we observe looking back from 1929 give a very different impression about uncertainty than the forecast errors. If the latter are representative, there was considerable uncertainty about real output looking ahead at the time. To a lesser extent, there was heightened uncertainty about velocity also.

---

[12] His arguments are presented in what follows.
[13] The procedure is described in Bomhoff (1983, Appendix). I am indebted to Eduard Bomhoff and Clemens Kool for these calculations.

Table 2.2 *Errors of forecast one period ahead*

Variable	Frequency	Period	Mean absolute error percentage of annual rates
Monetary base	quarterly	1870/1–1982/4	2.12
		1920/4–1925/1	1.78
		1925/2–1929/3	1.62
M_1	quarterly	1922/1–1982/4	2.40
		1925/2–1929/3	1.55
V_1	annual	1922–69	3.80
		1925–29	4.54
V_3	annual	1871–1969	3.98
		1925–29	4.30
GNP	annual	1870–1980	3.87
		1925–29	6.21
Real GNP	annual	1870–1965	3.18
		1925–29	4.55
Deflator	annual	1870–1965	3.49
		1925–29	2.78
Retail prices	quarterly	1914/3–1982/4	1.45
		1925/2–1929/3	2.44

Source: Same as Table 2.1. Data for money are from Capie and Webber (1985). Tables I(9), III(12). Real GNP and the deflator are from Mitchell (1976, p. 790) based on Feinstein.

Although changes in interest rates are important for Keynes's discussion in the *Treatise*, levels of interest rates and exchange rates, not annual fluctuations, receive most of his attention. Both short- and long-term rates are relatively stable from year to year. Prior to the return to gold, short- and long-term rates declined from their peaks of 6.4 and 5.3 percent, respectively, in 1920, when prices rose between 15 and 20 percent, to 2.6 and 4.4 percent in 1922. From 1922 to 1929, long-term rates (on consols) remained between 4.3 and 4.6 percent. Short-term rates (on three-month bills) are slightly more variable; their range is 2.6–5.3 percent, but the last rate is for 1929, and Keynes attributed that increase in rates to events in the United States. Since prices fell during the period, ex post real rates were above these nominal rates.[14]

[14] Interest rate data are from Friedman and Schwartz (1982, Table 4.9). Keynes estimated that after-tax nominal rates in 1923 were about equal to 1913 rates (19, p. 78). He believed rates were relatively high after the return to gold to maintain the fixed parity, and he blamed the high unemployment rate on this policy.

The return to gold fixed the exchange rate at the prewar parity, the gold equivalent of $4.86 to the pound. To restore this parity, Britain revalued the pound by 33 percent (from $3.66) between 1920 and 1925. The policy had been recommended as early as 1918 by the Cunliffe committee and had been accepted as policy by Labour and Conservative governments during the early 1920s. Appreciation occurred under both governments. The direction of change could not have been unanticipated, although the movements from year to year were uncertain.

The *Treatise* was published several years after the return to gold, so Keynes's interest there is mainly in the consequences of a fixed exchange rate. The *Tract*, written before the return to gold, discusses exchange rate volatility. In the *Tract* Keynes offers two reasons for skepticism about purchasing power parity as an explanation of actual exchange rate movements (4, pp. 73–5). Tariffs and the terms of trade change, disrupting calculations of parities. Also, the theory applies to the prices of traded goods, and these prices differ from the price index numbers available for computation of parities. He repeats this argument at greater length in the *Treatise*. Despite these reservations, he relied on purchasing power comparisons to estimate the degree to which the pound was overvalued at its prewar parity.[15] One reason is that his comparison of purchasing power parities and exchange rate changes for several countries led him to conclude that the theory "has worked passably well" (ibid., p. 86).

The exchange rate relevant for production and employment is the real exchange rate – the nominal or market exchange rate adjusted for differences in the price levels in Britain and in the leading gold standard country, the United States. In 1984 DeGrauwe, Janssens, and Leliaert (unpublished) analyzed monthly ex post real exchange rates for the period 1921–5. They found evidence of a cycle with a frequency of about two years but no evidence of the seasonality Keynes claimed to find (4, p. 91).[16] The sample period is short, so great weight cannot be placed on this finding. The difference may arise from the use of real rates in place of the nominal rates that Keynes discussed. DeGrauwe

---

[15] Seasonal fluctuations are a source of disturbance, however. These movements, Keynes believed, are not entirely regular, but he finds persistent seasonals in the dollar exchange rates for the pound, the franc, and the lira (4, p. 91). He concludes that seasonal changes are an important source of deviations from purchasing power parity. Keynes regarded purchasing power parity as a truism if applied only to the prices of traded goods (4, p. 75).

[16] The authors use spectral analysis. They find the same two- or two-and-a-half-year cycle for the United Kingdom for the period 1973–7 but not for 1978–82. The standard deviation of monthly changes in U.K. nominal exchange rates is about the same in the 1920s and the 1970s (DeGrauwe, Janssens, and Leliaert, p. 14).

et al. (1984, p. 13) report that wholesale price changes and real exchange rate changes are correlated during the period, but changes in real and nominal rates are not. Hence, during the period in which Britain prepared to return to gold, real exchange rates rose and fell with prices, while nominal exchange rates for the pound typically appreciated as required to restore the prewar parity.

The restoration of the gold parity in 1925 occurred at a real exchange rate not very different from the real rate achieved in late 1922 and 1923. The real exchange rate, on the data in DeGrauwe et al. (1984, p. 5) and using wholesale prices similar to the data available to Keynes, shows modest fluctuations and no trend under the gold standard until 1929, when the rate appreciated modestly. During this period it appears that changes in the value of the pound were no greater source of fluctuations in output than in the 1970s, when unemployment rates were very different.

Estimates of real exchange rates by Friedman and Schwartz (1982) using GNP price deflators do not support Keynes's belief that resumption of the gold standard in 1925 overvalued the pound. They find an advantage in favor of Britain, but the advantage is within the range of errors in purchasing power parity (PPP) calculations.[17] This measure of the British advantage is smaller in 1925 than in 1913 because the British deflator increased 83 percent and the U.S. deflator increased 62 percent from 1913 to 1925. In this sense, the pound was overvalued in 1925 relative to 1913, as Keynes claimed.[18] Use of 1913 as a base year possibly biases the result, however. Friedman and Schwartz's (1982, p. 291) calculations show 1913 as one of the most advantageous periods for British exports in the entire period 1870–1945. The Friedman and Schwartz estimates are more often above than below PPP and are therefore favorable to British exports. If we use the mean deviation for 1870–1930 as an estimate of the bias, Friedman and Schwartz's estimate of $5.50 as PPP for 1929 deviates from PPP by an amount about equal to the mean deviation. Adjusting for the bias, the pound is undervalued in 1925 by less than 5 percent and is approximately at

[17] Friedman and Schwartz (1982, pp. 289–90) estimate the 1929 PPP as $5.50 based on a careful, independent estimate of PPP in 1970 by Kravis, Heston, and Summers (1978). Friedman and Schwartz report calculations showing that from 1870 to 1932 PPP rarely falls outside 10 percent on either side of the exchange rate. Their calculations use GNP deflators, not the wholesale price indexes used by Keynes and by DeGrauwe et al. (1984).

[18] Keynes often changed his estimates of the equilibrium exchange rate. In 1922 (19, p. 56), he suggests $3.64 would have been appropriate for 1919–20, a 25 percent devaluation of the 1913 exchange rate. A week later (19, p. 61), he used a value of $4.00–$4.50 for 1920, however. And in 1922, he proposed $4.20 as the appropriate value for that year (17, p. 368).

Table 2.3 *Trade and current-account balances (selected years)*

Year	Net exports (million £)	Net exports as percentage of imports	Current account balance (million £)
1913	− 134	17	+ 235
1923	− 210	19	+ 183
1925	− 394	30	+ 52
1927	− 386	32	+ 98
1929	− 382	31	+ 96

Source: Mitchell (1976, pp. 497, 819, 826). Exports include reexports.

PPP in 1929. This is more consistent with the average or above-average growth of British output and falling price level from 1925 to 1929 than Keynes's belief. It provides no explanation of the persistent, relatively high unemployment rate of 10 percent.

The comparison of pre- and postwar exchange rates do not fully explain the changed trading and financial position of Britain after the war. Details of its trade balance with major partners show that trade deficits against Argentina, Canada, France, the Netherlands, and New Zealand more than doubled between 1913 and 1925 whereas Britain's export surplus with India declined (Mitchell 1976, p. 573). Wholesale and consumer prices were 60 percent higher, so the real value of the trade deficit increased. Table 2.3 shows the aggregate data for selected years.

The table brings out two aspects of the trade and payments problem. First, net exports rose absolutely and in real value and relative to imports, particularly after the mid-1920s. Second, Britain's real net foreign assets did not keep pace with the increase in the nominal value of imports and net exports. The net export balance and the current-account balance declined together, the former more than the latter. After the 1925 resumption, both balances remained relatively stable.

These data imply that net lending by Britain declined after the war. The on-current account balance for the period 1909–14 shows an average (nominal) surplus of £182 million (Mitchell 1976, p. 819). The surplus rises each year from 1909 to 1913 and then falls in 1914. The prewar values were the largest current-account surpluses in British history up to that time. For the period 1924–9, comparable data (but excluding southern Ireland) show an average current surplus of only £72 million with one deficit in 1926, the year of the general strike (ibid.,

p. 826). Prices had risen by approximately 50 percent, so the decline in the current balance, measured in pounds of constant value, is approximately £130 million per year on average. These data give some support to Keynes's interpretation emphasizing the rise in the cost of British output after the war.

There are three main differences between the conclusions drawn from the more complete data and the conclusions Keynes drew at the time. Real output rose after resumption at a slightly faster rate. Changes in velocity and intermediation are not as large after the postwar adjustment as he believed. And the real exchange rate gives little direct support to his main conclusions about the return to gold. This finding is consistent with the stability of prices and money wages but does not explain the persistence of unemployment at about 10 percent of the labor force.[19] To find support for Keynes's view, one must turn to the data on trade and capital movements. There, one finds evidence of the decline in Britain's ability to pay for its net imports out of its earnings on net foreign assets.

Main ideas and beliefs[20]

Keynes was greatly influenced by the philosophical ideas of G. E. Moore. In "My Early Beliefs" (10, pp. 433–50) Keynes describes the "religion" and "morals" that he got from Moore. The religion was self-centered; the morals were directed toward the outside world. The objects of life were love, beauty, truth, timeless contemplation, and the pursuit of knowledge: "We claimed the right *to judge every individual case on its merits*, and the wisdom, experience and self-control to do so successfully. This was a very important part of our faith, violently and aggressively held . . . we recognized no moral obligation on us, no inner sanction, to conform or to obey" (ibid., p. 446, emphasis added).

Moore's unworldly philosophy encouraged Keynes to seek the Ideal, a word he often used in his popular writings. The emphasis on religion, the "higher" virtues, and the Ideal led to the rejection of the Ben-

---

[19] An alternative explanation of the unemployment rate developed by Benjamin and Kochin (1979) is considered in a later chapter.

[20] On the importance of beliefs, some thoughts on the relation of Keynes's philosophic beliefs to his actions, and the source of these beliefs, see Skidelsky (1983, Chapter 6). Keynes was almost certainly influenced by his father's work and the distinction there between positive and normative. For a recent discussion of these issues see Cooter and Rapaport (1984).

thamite utilitarian calculus, with its emphasis on economic calculation of gains and losses in utility, as a guide to action. Along with his rejection of Bentham's calculus, Keynes also rejected Bentham's belief in laissez-faire and minimal state intervention.

Keynes joined Moore's philosophy to the "presuppositions of Harvey Road" according to which government "was and would continue to be in the hands of an intellectual aristocracy using the method of persuasion" (Harrod 1951, p. 192). Where individual self-interest does not produce the Ideal, Keynes wanted the state to intervene, to set boundaries and determine rules for death duties, income redistribution, regulation of money, and other aspects of economic life.

The breakdown of the prewar international order, on which Keynes commented at length in *The Economic Consequences of the Peace*, added to his belief in the desirability of state intervention. There he offered as a main justification of nineteenth-century capitalism the high rate of saving by the wealthy. This permitted a high rate of investment that sustained progress and increased living standards. Although he had not yet developed a relation between saving and investment to replace the classical model, he believed that encouraging thrift was not the way to sustain investment in the new conditions that had replaced prewar conditions.

In three essays written during the 1920s, Keynes applied his ideas to the broad issues of economics and economic policy. "Economic Possibilities for Our Grandchildren" (9, pp. 321–32), first written in 1928 but published in 1930, looks forward about 100 years to an age of abundance. "The End of Laissez-Faire" (ibid., pp. 272–94), written in 1924 and published in 1926, sets out Keynes's views on the role of the state. "Am I A Liberal?" (ibid., pp. 295–306), published in 1925, is mainly a political document but contains Keynes's criticism of doctrinaire socialists and his reasons for not joining a socialist party. These papers are supplemented by other writing and speeches that, together, give a coherent picture of the beliefs that guided his policy proposals.

Although "Economic Possibilities . . ." was published during the depression of the 1930s, Keynes is optimistic. He notes that the capital stock grew despite the problems of the 1920s. Productivity growth and capital accumulation have raised living standards; "*mankind is solving its economic problem*" (ibid., p. 325). He predicts that in the next hundred years, standards of living will rise to four or eight times the prevailing level (ibid., p. 326); this presumes a growth rate of at least 3 percent compounded annually, slightly above Britain's long-term experience. The pace at which "economic bliss" (ibid., p. 331) is achieved depends on four things: controlling population growth, preventing wars, trusting in science to solve scientific questions, and continuing the accumulation of capital by producing more than is consumed.[21]

The problem of the future will be how to use leisure. Old ideas will have to be replaced by

> the most sure and certain principles of religion and traditional virtue – that avarice is vice, that exaction of usury is a misdemeanor, and the love of money is detestable, that those walk most truly in the paths of virtue and sane wisdom who take least thought for the morrow. We shall once more value ends above means and prefer the good to the useful. (ibid., pp. 330–1)

Here, Keynes expresses his opposition to thrift and interest payments and his belief that there is an end state, which some have already achieved, where purposive economic activity is unnecessary, saving useless, and the receipt and payment of interest undesirable. His later call for the euthanasia of the rentier reflects this view most clearly, but even in the 1920s, Keynes opposed policies that increased real interest payments and preferred partial default on debt to a deflation that raised real interest payments.

"Am I A Liberal?" and "The End of Laissez Faire" reveal Keynes as an opponent of laissez-faire. In "Am I A Liberal?" he explained that laissez-faire was right for the nineteenth century (ibid., pp. 300–1), but it was no longer applicable. In place of individualism and market coordination, Keynes favored "semi-independent corporations and organs of administration to which duties of government, new and old, will be entrusted – without, however, impairing the democratic principle or the ultimate sovereignty of Parliament" (ibid., p. 302). He wanted government to accept responsibility for birth control (to control population), the economic position of women and the family, the setting of "fair" and "reasonable" wages, and other matters (ibid., pp. 302–3). A decade later his proposal for new administrative organs returns as a recommendation for social control of investment by independent bodies set up to achieve greater stability in investment spending. At the time, Keynes favored "new policies and new instruments to adapt and control the working of economic forces, so that they do not intolerably interfere with . . . what is fit and proper in the interests of

---

[21] Keynes was both a pacifist and a proponent of population control. His views on these issues are set out in several places (e.g., 17, p. 450 ff). Later, in his 1937 Galton lecture (14, pp. 124–33), his views on population seem to have shifted to concern about a declining population. This shift was probably influenced by the low birth rates of the 1930s.

social stability and social justice" (ibid., p. 306). The first step is to control monetary policy in the interests of greater stability of prices (ibid.). Here and elsewhere, Keynes's rejection of laissez-faire is not a plea for the type of detailed bureaucratic planning that was found in many countries a generation later. He did not accept the view that market prices correctly reflected values (19, pp. 664–6), but he rejected the policy of the Labour Party because it would lead to a new tyranny by the trade unionists, "once the oppressed, now the tyrants, whose selfish and sectional pretensions need to be bravely opposed" (9, p. 309). The political problem of the time was one of harmonizing economic efficiency, social justice, and individual liberty (ibid., p. 311). The first and third require economic individualism and social liberty (ibid.). Keynes shows himself to be sympathetic to the program of the socialists but unconvinced that it is best achieved by socialist parties rather than by evolution: "The battle of Socialism against unlimited private profit is being won in detail hour by hour" (ibid., p. 290).

His own program is a bit vague. Borrowing terms from Bentham, he calls on economists to separate those tasks that are best done collectively (the agenda of government) from those best done individually (the nonagenda) (ibid., pp. 288, 291). The task of politics is to devise forms of government capable of accomplishing the collective agenda within a democracy, to do particularly those things that are not done. Keynes again mentions the "semi-autonomous bodies . . . whose criterion of action is solely the public good as they understand it, and from whose deliberations motives of private advantage are excluded" (ibid., p. 288). Elsewhere, he comments on the need for an "economic general staff" (19, p. 567).

As examples of the type of institution he intends, he mentions the Bank of England, the universities, and the railroads (ibid., p. 289). These institutions are not run for profit. The Bank of England pays a conventional dividend but ignores the rights of the shareholders. Keynes sees this as a model for other institutions (9, p. 290).

This romantic view of the possibilities of selfless action by moral individuals acting in the public interest, and the neglect of incentives that reinforce personal codes of conduct, is characteristic of much of Keynes's political thinking throughout his life. The same notions appear in his letter to Hayek in 1944, commenting on Hayek's *The Road to Serfdom*, where he stresses the importance of having decisions made by people who "wholly share your own moral position" (27, p. 387). With rising wealth, "preoccupation with the economic problem . . . is becoming ever less necessary" (ibid., p. 386). "The End of Laissez Faire" notes, approvingly, that in large railways, utilities, banks, and insurance companies, management is separated from the shareholders.

The profit motive declines in relative importance, and with the decline, there is a waning of enterprise – "the faults as well as the advantages of State Socialism" (ibid.). Nevertheless he criticizes

> doctrinaire State Socialism, not because it seeks to engage men's altruistic impulses in the service of society, or because it departs from *laissez faire*, or because it takes away from man's natural liberty to make a million, or because it has courage for bold experiments. All these things I applaud. (ibid., p. 290)

The problem with state control is that, similar to laissez-faire, it addresses problems that are no longer relevant: "The greatest economic evils of our time are the fruits of risk, uncertainty, and ignorance" (ibid., p. 291). These cause unemployment, disappointment of expectations, and reduced economic efficiency.

Keynes gives three examples of collective action to reduce risk, uncertainty, and ignorance. First is a central institution to control currency and credit and to collect and make public "all business facts which it is useful to know" (ibid., p. 292). Second is the regulation of saving and investment, including decisions about the amount to be saved, the size of capital outflows, and the uses to which saving is directed at home: "I do not think these matters should be left entirely to the chances of private judgment and private profits, as they are at present" (ibid.). Third is control of the size of population. He suggests, "the community as a whole must pay attention to the innate quality as well as to the mere numbers of its future members" (ibid.).

Keynes did not develop a scheme for population control or for improving "innate quality," but his later proposals for the control of money, the management of domestic investment, and foreign exchange controls are specific applications of his views in the 1920s.[22] Experience and the circumstances of the time modified his proposals, but he never abandoned his belief that controls on investment, foreign lending, and money were parts of the solution to the problems of instability resulting from uncertainty and ignorance. With rare exceptions, he preferred government spending on investment to spending on consumption. Even in the depth of the depression, in 1933, he did not favor consumption over investment (ibid., p. 349).

In a 1927 speech to the Liberal Party (19, pp. 638–49), Keynes outlined the types of changes that would give society "intelligent control

---

[22] Keynes's views on exchange controls developed from his vague suggestions in the 1920s to a full-blown system in wartime that he favored for the postwar. Moggridge (1986) and Chapter 5 of this volume discuss these proposals.

of its own affairs" (ibid., p. 643). He excludes, specifically, "the highly centralized system of state socialism" in favor of "the maximum degree of decentralization which is compatible with large units and regulated competition" (ibid.). His proposals include (1) collection and dissemination of industrial information, (2) preparation and planning "against every industrial misfortune" (ibid., p. 644), and (3) seeing that buyers of financial assets have reasonable information about the businesses in which they invest. He also proposed (4) to encourage, but regulate, trusts and large enterprises,[23] (5) to regulate wages to improve the position of workers, and (6) in an early form of industrial policy, to decide on labor training, the types of training to be provided, and to plan the transfer of labor from contracting to expanding industries.

The general program of government, he urged, should be to do those things for people that are not done privately. Government should not undertake tasks that individuals do for themselves "more or less satisfactorily" (ibid., p. 647). Keynes does not say how society decides what is to be done collectively, but the context suggests that political programs and elections are the means of change. The voters decide guided by the party platforms. The role of the Liberal Party is to raise issues that eventually are taken up by the larger parties.

New approaches were needed for two reasons. Old issues such as opposition to private monopoly and protectionism or promotion of personal liberty and democratic government had been largely won. New issues emerged from the changes in society such as the broadening of the franchise, the strengthening of labor unions, and the "economic transition" (ibid., p. 638). The changed conditions called for "a society which is just and a society which is efficient" (ibid., p. 639). He suggests, again, that he agrees with the Labour Party in its view about justice, but the Labour Party opposes efficiency (ibid.).

At the time, Keynes saw only two alternatives to capitalism, protectionism and Marxian socialism (9, p. 285). He opposed both, not simply because they interfered with a free society, but because they were based on "logical fallacy. Both are examples of poor thinking, of inability to analyze a process and follow it out to its conclusion . . . Marxian socialism must always remain a portent to the historians of opinion – how a doctrine so illogical and dull can have exercised so powerful and enduring an influence over the minds of men" (ibid., p. 285).

He preferred a managed, capitalist system. He wrote:

> I think that capitalism, wisely managed, can probably be made

---

[23] During this period, Keynes was actively engaged in developing and promoting a cartel of the Lancaster cotton spinners. The scheme quickly failed.

more efficient for attaining economic ends than any alternative system yet in sight, but that in itself it is in many ways extremely objectionable. Our problem is to work out a social organization which shall be as efficient as possible without offending our notions of a satisfactory way of life. (ibid., p. 294)

Earlier, in 1922, he saw the main struggle not as a struggle between Russian communism and nineteenth-century capitalism but as one between militarist, dirigiste societies and liberal states that seek peace, freedom of trade, and economic wealth. His conclusion is similar. If the battle against dirigiste systems is won, the secondary struggle is over whether the "bourgeois state or the socialist state can best promote the economic wealth of the community" (17, p. 373).

In "A Short View of Russia" (9, pp. 253–71), written after a trip to Russia in 1925, Keynes describes communism as a religion. He defines religion to include "the pursuit of an ideal life for the whole community of men" (ibid., p. 254). He is critical of Soviet practice, particularly the suppression of liberty, but he is attracted to the effort to change the nature of society, to the "tremendous innovation" (ibid., p. 261), rejection of the pursuit of money (ibid., p. 259–60), and the expanded role of the community and of responsibility toward the community (ibid., p. 260). He concludes: "Out of the cruelty and stupidity of Old Russia nothing could ever emerge, but . . . beneath the cruelty and stupidity of New Russia some speck of the ideal may lie hid" (ibid., p. 271). This was not his most accurate prediction.

The same themes reappear in the 1930s.

> I am convinced that those things which are urgently called for on practical grounds, such as the central control of investment and the distribution of income in such a way as to provide purchasing power for the enormous potential output of modern productive technique, will also tend to produce a better kind of society on ideal grounds. There is probably less opposition today between the practical aim and the ideal than there has been hitherto. (21, pp. 36–7)[24]

Austin Robinson (1947, in Wood 1, p. 124) describes Keynes as "never anti-socialist." To Keynes, socialism meant planning, and planning meant "the problem of the *general* organization of resources as

---

[24] In passing, it is worth noting the contemporary note in Keynes's concern at the time (1932). Capital and labor, which had previously been cooperative, were now competitive. His concern was that more labor would have to be employed in service industries (21, p. 38).

distinct from the *particular* problem of production and distribution which are the province of the individual business technician and engineer'' (21, p. 87). The social problem was that production had run ahead of consumption. The role of "planning is to do those things which, from the nature of the case, it is impossible for the individual to attempt" (ibid.).

Moggridge describes Keynes as a rationalist: "His whole life was a constant campaign, in his eyes, against 'madmen in authority,' 'lunatics' (a very common word in his vocabulary) and others who acted according to prejudices and rules of thumb rather than reason carefully applied to an evolving situation" (1972, p. 65). According to Moggridge, Keynes saw capitalism "as a necessary, but not permanent evil . . . a means, albeit a morally distasteful one, to an end" (ibid., p. 68).

To a late-twentieth-century reader, Keynes's views on taxation do not seem entirely consistent with his rhetoric about the appeal of the socialist program. In testimony before a 1925 commission on debt and taxation, he expresses very specific views and shows concern about the effects of a "very heavy income tax on current effort" (19, p. 842). He offers two reasons for his concern: (1) high taxes discourage risk taking and (2) they discourage saving, the larger part of which is done by those with large wealth or large income (ibid., p. 846). Prevailing tax rates did not do much harm, but in 1920 they had reached or passed the tolerable limit (ibid., p. 840). Schedules for the period (ibid., pp. 678–9) show that, in 1918–19, taxes on earned income for a married taxpayer with three children reached 50 percent at £50,000 and 42 percent at £10,000. Keynes estimates that the average tax rate in 1920 was 6 shillings to the pound, or 30 percent, and he feared that it might rise to 8 or even 10 shillings. For 1925, he puts the average tax rate at 4 shillings to the pound (ibid., p. 845). In favoring a capital levy in 1920, he "wanted to avoid . . . an income tax in excess of 6 shillings" (ibid.).

Keynes repeats, then amends, his 1925 argument in the last chapter of the *General Theory*. Progress and growth do not depend on individual saving until full employment is reached. The argument for inequality based on saving is therefore no longer relevant except in the limiting position of full employment. Further, redistribution to the poor increases consumption, Keynes said, so high taxes may stimulate, rather than retard, investment by increasing consumption (7, p. 373). Keynes did not advocate taxation to equalize income, however: "There are valuable human activities which require the motive of money making and the environment of private wealth ownership for their full fruition. Moreover, dangerous human proclivities can be canalised into comparatively harmless channels by the existence of opportunities for money-making and private wealth" (ibid., p. 374). Keynes mentions personal power and cruelty as alternatives to the pursuit of wealth when incomes are pushed toward equality.[25]

Although, Keynes's ideas and interests ranged widely, within economics, his interests were more constrained (Skidelsky 1983, p. 207). Fluctuations, the conditions for price stability, the relation of money to prices, and fluctuations in output are central themes related to these broader interests. Also related are the conditions for economic progress. Keynes's concentration on investment, money, and fluctuations reflects his belief that these topics are closely bound up with economic progress. He favored progress and price stability, and he believed that price instability hindered progress. He held strong views about income distribution, particularly about the rentiers. His views are often presented as a reason for choosing a particular policy or favoring a particular outcome. Though firmly held in the 1920s, these views were not an implication of a theoretical framework. The development of the *Treatise* and the *General Theory* was his attempt to provide the missing framework.

Conditions for progress

The connection between money and economic progress is not direct. Through much of his writing, Keynes treats money as neutral in the long run, as the development of his theories will show. The lasting importance of money arises, according to Keynes, not from the nominal quantity in circulation but from the institutions and the monetary system that determine how that quantity is determined, how it changes, and whether the changes amplify or dampen fluctuations and thus inhibit or contribute to economic progress.

In *The Economic Consequences of the Peace*, Keynes describes the conditions for progress, emphasizing the roles of population and technology (2, pp. 5–9) in much the same way that any economist trained in the neoclassical tradition might describe them.[26] Keynes emphasizes, in addition, economic organization including organization of the monetary system. Before the war, the

> delicate organization by which these people lived depended partly on factors internal to the system.
>
> The interference of frontiers and of tariffs was reduced to a

---

[25] In papers discovered on his desk after he died, we find some acceptance of a maximum tax rate of 25 percent: "Colin Clark's 25% argument – pseudo-scientific; but with some sound empirical *base*" (27, p. 414).

[26] A very similar view is expressed a decade later in the preface to *Essays in Persuasion*. There, Keynes argues that the world has the resources and technique to eliminate the economic problem but lacks the organization (9, p. xviii).

minimum . . . The various currencies, which were all maintained on a stable basis in relation to gold and to one another,
facilitated the easy flow of capital and of trade to an extent the
full value of which we only realize now, when we are deprived
of its advantages. Over this great area there was an almost
absolute security of property and of person. (ibid., p. 9)[27]

The same theme is the basis for his work developing an international
economic order for the years following World War II, and it is present
in the *Tract* and in the *Treatise* as well. Both of these books criticize
monetary arrangements, particularly the gold standard but also fluctuating exchange rates, and propose alternatives that Keynes believed
were better designed to achieve progress. The *Tract* (4, pp. 4–7) develops the importance of stability of contract under the gold standard
for saving, the accumulation of wealth, and the development of confidence in long-term values. It is confidence in the stability of values
that encourages owners of wealth to let investors use their saving to
build capital and thus increase living standards and promote economic
progress.

The *Treatise* is even more explicit. Individual decisions to save are
a necessary condition for growth, but they are not sufficient. Someone
must invest what others save (6, pp. 132–3): "It is enterprise which
builds and improves the world's possessions" (ibid., p. 132). And enterprise requires not just thrift but the expectation of profit. These
"expectations partly depend on non-monetary influences – on peace
and war, inventions, laws, race, education, population and so forth.
But . . . their power to put their projects into execution on terms which
they deem attractive, almost entirely depends on the behavior of the
banking and monetary system" (ibid., p. 133).

Many of the passages in *The Economic Consequences of the Peace*
are a polemic against the Versailles treaty, but the point of the polemic
is that the choice of economic organization affects the size of the excess
burden that society bears. Keynes's main reason for opposing the
treaty is not only that the treaty violated the agreement under which
Germany surrendered, but also that the treaty imposed harsh conditions on Germany, conditions requiring an improbable reduction in
living standards. The attempt to pay the reparations, and the insistence
on payment, would prevent the principal belligerents from adjusting

---

[27] This theme – the importance of institutional conditions and economic organization –
is a main theme of the book. [See, passim, the preface to the French and Rumanian
editions (2, pp. xix–xxiv, 62–3, 92, 143–6, and 160–89), where Keynes proposes different financial and economic arrangements for mutual benefit.]

their finances and therefore lower standards of living throughout Europe (2, pp. xx–xxi, xxiii, 2, 62–3).

The banking and monetary system is one of the principal institutions affecting economic progress. The role of monetary institutions is to provide stable monetary values. Observation of the hyperinflations in Germany, Austria, Russia, and Hungary after World War I, his role as adviser to the postwar Germany government during the period of rising inflation, the lectures and writings of his teacher Alfred Marshall, and his own analysis made Keynes a strong advocate of stable prices.[28] His belief that institutions and organization are important for progress and his concern for price stability sustained a lifetime interest in finding or designing monetary arrangements that achieve price stability with lowest social cost or greatest social benefit. One of his main criticisms of the gold standard (6, p. 268) is that an unmanaged gold standard is a socially costly and inefficient way to maintain price stability.

Inflation and price instability

Few economists have been more critical of inflation than Keynes. He believed that the modern world is not well suited to violent changes in the value of money (19, p. 60). *Economic Consequences* paraphrases Lenin on the destructive effects of inflation (2, pp. 148–50).[29] These effects occur for several reasons. Businesses hold inventories so they gain from a general increase in prices, but governments accuse them of excessive profits (19, p. 114). Inflation weakens the social position of entrepreneurs and capitalists on whom progress depends. Further, inflation transfers wealth arbitrarily from private to public hands and "all permanent relations between debtors and creditors, which form the ultimate foundation of capitalism, became . . . utterly disordered . . . and the process of wealth getting degenerates into . . . a lottery" (2, p. 149).

The *Tract* is less colorful, but not much less. Keynes repeats his warnings about the harmful effects on entrepreneurs and society of the hostility arising from the arbitrary redistribution of wealth using the

---

[28] Moggridge and Howson (1974, in Wood 1, p. 454) point out that many economists favored higher interest rates in 1920 to return to the gold standard. Keynes agreed with the recommendation, but his reason was different. He wanted to bring an end to inflation promptly, whereas others favored the rise to restore the prewar gold parity. Keynes's views are discussed in the text that follows. Eshag (1963, p. 99) contrasts Keynes's views on price stability with the greater emphases on exchange rate stability given by Lavington, Robertson, and Pigou. None wanted high inflation, but Keynes was willing to sacrifice some exchange rate stability for greater stability of prices.

[29] Fetter (1977) raises some doubt about whether Lenin ever made the statement.

argument of *Economic Consequences*. He adds some others (4, pp. 27–8). Inflation in Germany and Austria discouraged saving by reducing the wealth of those in the middle class who do the saving. Inflation distorts capital values and income so people consume part of their capital unawares. A lengthy discussion of inflation as a method of taxation (ibid., pp. 37–53) analyzes the tax on cash balances and concludes that the tax lowers the amount of real balances people hold as a store of value and as a medium of exchange. These reductions, Keynes finds, reduce efficiency, but even when carried to extremes as in Germany and Russia, inflation does not eliminate the use of money as a medium of exchange. The loss from holding money does not "counterbalance the advantages of using money rather than barter in the trifling business of daily life" (ibid., p. 44).

Elsewhere, Keynes adds to the list of consequences or repeats his earlier position. Inflation distorts relative prices (17, p. 261; 19, pp. 21–2) in part because the government is slow to adjust the prices of state services (19, p. 25). Inflation sends incorrect signals to investors in capital (9, p. 73). Deflation increases the burden of the debt (19, p. 62). This transfers wealth to rentiers.

The *Treatise* is more sober than the *Tract*. Between the *Tract* and the *Treatise*, Keynes read arguments by Robertson (1926) and Ramsey (1928) in favor of inflation as a means of stimulating investment or increasing saving and capital accumulation. Keynes discusses both arguments (5, pp. 263–8; 6, pp. 144–5) before concluding that he remains unconvinced that inflation is preferable to price stability. A main reason is his concern for the effects on the distribution of income and consumption. He recognizes, however, that if the increase in the capital stock from inflation is large enough, everyone may gain (6, p. 145). He speculates that a better way to increase society's capital stock may lie in "the rate of capital development becoming more largely an affair of state, determined by collective wisdom and long views" (ibid., p. 145). This suggestion restates his view about regulation or planning, anticipates the main policy conclusion of the *General Theory* (7, Chapter 24), and shows the directions in which Keynes was thinking long before the 1929 recession had become the Great Depression.

He was willing to pay a high price to restore price stability following World War I because he thought the costs of inflation were higher than the costs of disinflation. Howson (1973, in Wood 1, pp. 443–5) reproduces a memo to the chancellor written in 1920. Keynes favored pushing the interest rate to 7, 8, and perhaps 10 percent – the maximum rate used by the Bank during crises in the nineteenth century. [In the chancellor's account (ibid., p. 443), Keynes was willing to keep Bank rate as high as 10 percent for up to three years.] The only alternative was "discrimination" – credit allocation or rationing – which he rejected as ineffective. He closed with a warning:

> A continuance of inflationism and high prices will not only depress the exchanges but by their effect on prices will strike at the whole basis of contract, of security, and of the capitalist system generally. The new state of affairs created by persistent inflation will only be tolerable under socialistic control and this is where the present policy, if persisted in, will necessarily lead us, before probably we are really ripe for such a development. (Howson 1973, in Wood 1, p. 445)

These views may be put down as the views of an earlier Keynes, a Keynes who had not written the *General Theory*. We know that is not so. When Keynes returned to the Treasury during World War II, he was shown his 1920 memo. He wrote:

> With all the methods of control, then so unorthodox, excluded, I feel myself that I should give today exactly the same advice that I gave then, namely a swift and severe dose of dear money, sufficient to break the market, and quick enough to prevent at least some of the disastrous consequences that would otherwise ensue . . .
>
> If the vast bulk of purchasing power which must necessarily exist at the end of the war is released in psychological conditions necessarily surrounding the end of the war, the result cannot be different from what it was in 1919 to 1921. (ibid., p. 447)

Keynes favored maintaining strict controls, including rationing, credit controls, allocation, and high taxation, for at least two years after the World War II to both supplement and substitute for monetary restriction.

Keynes's commitment to price stability was not absolute. He preferred inflation to deflation, if required to risk one or the other, and in the 1920s, he favored wartime inflation as a means of taxation to other alternatives capable of reducing real consumption to the same extent (6, pp. 153–5). He was certain that voluntary saving could not be increased enough to finance World War I (ibid., p. 153), and he held the same view at the start of World War II. Financing the war by direct taxation required too high a direct tax (25 percent) on wages, and he believed the tax was inequitable. The choice was between lowering money wages and raising prices. It is "natural – and sensible – to prefer the latter" (ibid., p. 154). The *Treatise* offers several reasons for this conclusion, but the main one is that government can gain control of real resources to prosecute the war at lower cost by spending newly created money than by forcing wages to fall and taxing the profits of producers to capture the gain to firms (ibid., pp. 154–5). There is no mention of anticipations of inflation in this discussion, a surprising omission in view of Keynes's analysis of the effects of anticipations during the Austrian, Russian, and German inflations (4, pp. 42–5) and the many references to anticipations in the *Treatise*. The closest Keynes comes in these pages is his recognition that, to make the real resource transfer to government effective, prices must rise more than wages. In the end, government must tax the profits resulting from the policy (6, p. 155).[30]

The analysis has some missing steps. There is a suggestion that real wages are comparatively high, and the tax on profits higher at the same level of output, if the war is financed by inflation. This argument is in accord with Keynes's principle that the government should tax wartime profits, but it does not explain why inflation raises real wages. Keynes suggests that workers may not notice the inflation tax as much as an income tax that raises equivalent revenue. He is concerned about the effects on the distribution of income between wages and profits, but he usually assumes that inflation increases profits, at least initially, so this argument works against his preference for inflation unless the government can capture most of the gain without reducing output.

Deflation is worse than inflation, Keynes said, for two reasons, one cyclical, the other not. During the cycle, deflation is more of a depressant to production than inflation (4, pp. 3, 119; 5, p. 267; 13, p. 111; 19, pp. 114–15) because all wages and prices do not adjust simultaneously and because anticipations of lower prices delay production. Further, deflation increases the burden of the debt by transferring wealth from the productive members of society to the rentiers (4, pp. 35–6, 56, 118–19; 19, p. 62). Keynes believed that a large transfer of this kind was intolerable. To prevent the transfer, he favored a capital

---

[30] Much the same argument had been used earlier in a speech on wartime finance, (19, pp. 785–6), where Keynes argues that inflation makes businessmen tax collectors for the government. Again, anticipations of inflation are not mentioned. After the war, Keynes proposed a capital levy, and he repeats the proposal in his discussion (ibid., pp. 787–8) and later as part of his plan for World War II finance published in 1940 as *How to Pay for the War* (9, pp. 367–439). In the latter, Keynes recognizes anticipations of inflation and rejects inflation – "the most burdensome alternative" (ibid., p. 392) – as a method of war finance. The usefulness of a capital levy is a subject on which Keynes changed his mind several times. His ambivalent opposition is mainly on the ground that a capital levy is too disruptive for the amount of revenue that can be raised (19, p. 839). After World War II, he opposed a capital levy and offered an alternative for managing the debt (27, pp. 396–404).

levy to reduce the internal war debts of many countries after World War I (6, p. 156; 4, pp. 53–5).[31]

One of the main messages of the *Treatise* is that rising commodity prices increase real output. The reason is that businesses hold inventories, which rise in price during commodity inflation, so they invest, increasing inventories and capital stock (4, pp. 29–30; 5, pp. 267–8). This effect lasts as long as commodity prices rise faster than incomes.[32] Deflation reverses these effects and reduces output.[33]

Keynes's recommendation that the aim of policy should be price stability is unaffected by the qualifications. In fact, much of his discussion of deflation is written to explain why prices should not be reduced to restore the gold standard. One of the principal reasons he offers is that deflation enriches bondholders, many of whom bought their bonds at a discount. The beneficiaries are the rentiers, whereas the transfer comes at the expense of the "productive" classes. Further, he expresses his doubt that many societies will accept the rate of taxation required to pay the bondholders the prewar gold value of their principal and interest (4, pp. 117–20). At one point, he gives a quantitative estimate of the dividing line for choosing between deflation and devaluation by citing David Ricardo as favoring a return to the former gold price only if the currency is within 5 percent of its former value (ibid., p. 125).

Opposition to the gold standard

Keynes's views on the gold standard and his objections to the policy of returning to the gold standard at the 1913 gold price reflected two dominant beliefs. He favored a managed monetary system, usually a system based on gold, to an automatic gold standard. And he opposed deflation as costly. After the fact, he compared the costs of returning to the gold standard – mainly the loss of output and employment – as

---

[31] Keynes does not restrict his arguments to justice and the burden of the debt (19, pp. 46–7). He argues that a large real value of the debt and a transfer of income to the creditors increases the claims of the bondholders "beyond what is tolerable" (ibid., p. 46). The government is "certain to be forced to inflate again" (ibid.). He believed that no "community ancient or modern will tolerate more than a certain proportion" of its income being paid to the idle rentiers (ibid., p. 47).

[32] The *Treatise* tentatively reverses the judgment of the *Tract* on the behavior of real wages. In the *Tract*, Keynes argues that inflation raised real wages after World War I (4, pp. 26–7), but in the *Treatise* (6, p. 138) he accepts the opposite view for the Spanish inflation of 1519–88 (but not for the period after 1588).

[33] In passing, Keynes speculates that there may be an advantage in stabilizing at the higher price level rather than undergoing a contraction during which prices fall (5, p. 267). He does not relate this suggestion to his insistence on long-term price stability or to anticipations.

"second only in amount to those of a great war" (6, p. 302). Before the fact, he was less extreme. The *Tract* asks whether the gold standard, with its flaws, is the best means of achieving the aim of a monetary standard (4, p. 117). For Keynes, that aim is price stability or the stability of nominal values, and if a choice has to be made, as it usually must, he favored stable prices to stable exchange rates (ibid., pp. 123, 125–6).

A main argument against devaluation is based on anticipations about the credibility of the parity. A country that never devalues reinforces subjective beliefs that the parity will be defended. To the extent that a fixed gold parity contributes to long-term price stability, avoiding devaluation enhances the belief that the price level will return eventually to some prior value. Keynes does not make this "rational-expectations" argument. He based his argument against devaluation on the claim that national prestige and confidence in the currency are enhanced if the gold exchange is kept at the prewar parity. He believed the argument applied to Britain (ibid., p. 122):

> Where a country can hope to restore its pre-war parity at an early date, this argument cannot be neglected. This might be said of Great Britain, Holland . . . It is the essence of the argument that the *exact* pre-war parity should be recovered. (ibid., p. 122)

A 5–10 percent deflation to restore prewar parity is tolerable if the country prefers exchange rate stability to price stability.

The case of Germany is very different. As an adviser to the German government in 1922, Keynes favored a fixed exchange rate to stabilize the mark, but at the time, he did not favor exchange controls. A prolonged period of high interest rates, to attract and hold foreign capital, and authority to buy and sell spot and forward exchange were expected to keep the mark within a 1 percent band (19, pp. 37–8). The purpose of rigidly fixing the rate was to avoid uncertainty (ibid., p. 40).

The French franc was of continuing interest to Keynes prior to the Poincaré stabilization. Judging from his language at various time, he took pleasure in needling the French ministers for their policies, for their claim that France would not devalue, and for the failure to stabilize the value of the franc. He believed that the stabilization of the franc required (1) a return to gold at a value below the prewar gold value, (2) prompt return to a fixed gold value – at the beginning, not the end, of the reform – and (3) the use of the gold reserve to support the franc.

The recommendations to France and Britain differed mainly because prices had risen less in Britain than in France. For both countries, and ultimately for Germany, he favored a return to gold. His objections to British policy were directed mainly to the way in which the policy was discussed and, he feared, the way in which it would be implemented. His three main points are (1) the proposed standard should be managed, not automatic; (2) the proposed restoration requires a lowering of nominal values that is more costly than proponents of gold recognize; and (3) the gold standard subordinates internal-to-external stability. The bases for these judgments and beliefs influenced the development of Keynes's *Treatise* and the emphasis given there to the potential role of monetary policy as a stabilizing force.

The proponents of gold emphasized the automatic working of the gold standard. Keynes believed this was a mistake. His argument is based on the political economy of monetary systems, not on the alleged advantages of stable prices or permanently fixed exchange rates:

> If, indeed, a providence watched over gold, or if Nature had provided us with a stable standard, ready-made, I would not, in an attempt after some slight improvement, hand over the management [of money] to the possible weakness or ignorance of boards and governments. But this is not the situation. We have no ready-made standard. Experience has shown that in emergencies ministers of finance cannot be strapped down. And – most important of all – in the modern world of paper currency and bank credit there is no escape from a "managed" currency. (4, p. 136)

He saw that the standard in effect was not the prewar system. The value of gold was set by the decisions of leading central banks (ibid., p. 134–5). The Federal Reserve policy of buying and selling gold at a fixed price maintained the price of gold. The policy was costly for the United States since the government felt compelled to hold a relatively large stock of gold. And the policy could be brought to an end at any time by decision of the United States. This, Keynes believed, could not reassure other countries (ibid., pp. 135, 69, n. 1).

Keynes repeats this view in the *Treatise* (5, p. 18). There, he does not see the issue as a choice between automatic and managed money. There were, he believed, two choices: whether incomes should be deflated or the exchange rate devalued and whether prices or exchange rates should be stabilized (ibid., pp. 18–19).

The principal objection to deflating to restore the prewar gold parity is the cost of doing so. At one point, after the fact, Keynes estimated the cost as £1,000 million of lost production plus the increased burden of the domestic debt. This loss of output could have been avoided by stabilizing at the 1920 price level.[34] He estimated the increase in the burden of the debt at 50 percent (6, pp. 161–2).

He believed that the losses were the result of error. The proponents of gold understood that restoring the 1913 parity required deflation and that deflation required a reduction in money. Their error was that they considered only part of the cost – the cost arising from the deflation of wholesale prices. Once the wholesale price level had been lowered, the proponents of gold believed that the gold parity could be restored without further loss. Keynes gave two reasons for rejecting this view. The first is seasonal fluctuation. Keynes believed that the pound rose against the dollar in the spring but fell in the fall (4, pp. 89, 91, 151). In late April (1925) the pound had appreciated seasonally, not permanently.

The second reason is fundamental for the thesis of the *Treatise* and for Keynes's rejection of the quantity theory as a useful basis of a dynamic theory. Costs lag behind prices, so the fall in the price level is necessary but not sufficient for equilibrium at the fixed parity. The Bank of England adopted a deflationary policy:

> Prices duly fell. The Governor of the Bank of England felt himself able to inform the Chancellor of the Exchequer that the task was accomplished.
>
> Yet this was far from the truth. Equilibrium required that the flow of money incomes and the rate of money earnings per unit of output should be appropriately reduced. But in the first instance, the fall of prices reduced, not costs and rates of earnings, but profits . . . The entrepreneur, faced with prices falling faster than costs, had three alternatives open to him – to put up with his losses as best he could; to withdraw from his less profitable activities, thus reducing output and employment; to embark on a struggle with his employees to reduce their money earnings per unit of output – of which *only the last was capable of restoring real equilibrium* from the national point of view. (6, p. 163, emphasis added)

Those who believe that Keynes discovered the fixity of nominal wages in his *General Theory* have not paid attention to the *Treatise* or

---

[34] Keynes does not give the basis for this estimate of lost output. Elsewhere, he puts the cost "at more than £100 million per annum" for several years (6, p. 165). These estimates or guesses may be the basis for his later belief that the return to gold was as costly as a great war. (ibid., p. 302) Before the fact, in 1922, Keynes favored a return to gold with as little as a 10–15 percent depreciation ($4.00–$4.50) from the prewar price (19, p. 61). He cites the burden of the debt, arising from deflation, and the effects of appreciation on trade as principal reasons.

his arguments against the return to gold, particularly the arguments made after the fact. The theoretical section of the *Treatise* (e.g., 5, p. 186) repeats the argument just quoted. The applied section amplifies the argument by explaining that money rates of efficiency earnings are "sticky" (6, p. 183).[35] Later (1930) Keynes changed the emphasis from real wages to the terms of trade (13, p. 183). His basic point is unaffected; the return to gold at the 1913 parity required the Bank of England to hold the interest rate at a level that attracted foreign capital. At that level, exports were too low (or real wages too high) to reduce unemployment. Keynes then repeats his view that it would have been better to raise the price level and tax the rentier (ibid., p. 186). And he suggests an alternative to which he returned in his postwar planning – capital controls, "forbid foreign lending" (ibid., p. 185).[36]

One of Keynes's clearest statements of his objection to the return to the prewar parity in 1925 was written a year after the event to remind his readers that his forecast had been close to correct. Relative prices had changed and some, particularly wages, had been slow to adjust. The debt burden had increased permanently. The result was unemployment:

> If all transactions expressed in money were to be changed by 10 percent simultaneously, then no harm would be done. But in practice . . . this does not happen. Some prices, of which the wholesale prices of raw materials entering into international trade are typical, adjust themselves rapidly. Others of which the cost of living is typical, are stickier and move more slowly. Others, of which wages are typical, are stickier still. Others, of which interest on the national debt and a number of other budgetary commitments are typical . . . do not move at all. The evils arise from these differing rates of adjustment . . . Pending the adjustment, our export trades, which are producing at one level of costs and selling at another, will be seriously depressed and unemployment aggravated; whilst when the adjustment is complete the problem of the Budget will remain permanently heavier because, measured in money, the revenue

---

[35] In a 1930 memorandum (13, p. 186), Keynes argues that the reduction in money wages must be much greater than the reduction in real wages, the difference depending on the proportion of home to foreign goods in domestic consumption.

[36] The return to gold was accompanied by an embargo on foreign lending. Keynes favored the embargo and wanted it reimposed in 1926: "I think that a central control of the volume of foreign investment is a permanent necessity for Great Britain" (19, p. 573). He wanted "permanent, centralized control for the regulation of foreign investment" (ibid.).

will fall off whilst much of the expenditure is fixed. (19, p. 553)[37]

Keynes's commitment to a managed gold standard at the time reflected his strong belief in the importance of stable prices. He believed that capitalism could not survive in a world of price instability:

> Modern individualistic society, organized on lines of capitalistic industry, cannot support a violently fluctuating standard of value, whether the movement is upwards or downwards. Its arrangements presume and absolutely require a reasonably stable standard. Unless we give it such a standard, this society will be stricken with a mortal disease and will not survive . . . Only by wisely regulating the creation of currency and credit along new lines, can we protect society against the attacks and criticisms of Socialist and Communist innovators. (ibid., p. 117)

Tariffs and trade

Free trade is one issue on which Keynes is uncompromising in the 1920s. With the overstatement that characterized much of his writing, he described it as "an inflexible dogma, to which no exception is admitted" (17, p. 451). Britain should avoid protection even where there is no reciprocity. The doctrine is "a principle of international morals" (ibid.). "Formerly free trade was a desirable aid to increased wealth. It has now [1922] become a necessary and essential defense against a crushing poverty" (19, p. 3).

In his lectures to the Liberal Party and his criticisms of the Labour Party, he usually included advocacy of free trade as a distinguishing characteristic. He did not base his case on the virtues of laissez-faire, however: "I no longer believe in the political philosophy which the doctrine of free trade adorned. I believe in free trade because, in the long run and in general, it is the only policy which is technically sound and intellectually tight" (9, p. 298).

When Stanley Baldwin and the Conservative Party proposed tariffs to reduce domestic unemployment, Keynes attacked the proposal and defended free trade. The issue was a major issue in the 1923 election, with Baldwin as prime minister seeking support for a change in Britain's historic policy. Keynes attacked Baldwin's proposal using standard

---

[37] Keynes does not mention anticipations in this context. The return to gold had been announced years before, and it had been standard policy. Interest rates on the debt should have reflected the anticipation. This would reduce the burden.

economic arguments (19, pp. 147–51) and rejecting the idea that protection can reduce unemployment (ibid., pp. 153–6): "A tariff will not remedy any of the main causes of unemployment" (ibid., p. 154). Any effect on employment comes as a result of reducing wages (ibid., p. 155).

Keynes's strong beliefs did not survive much beyond the decade. Early in 1931, Keynes advocated a revenue tariff to reduce unemployment. This is an expedient policy, not a change in belief: "The emergency has arrived" (9, p. 238). His aim was to expand the domestic economy and employ idle labor. To expand production, businesses must make profits, and this requires, on the argument of the *Treatise*, that prices rise relative to costs of production (ibid., p. 232). Keynes opposed cost reduction, particularly nominal wage reduction, as a solution to unemployment on the grounds that a general reduction in costs reduces domestic demand, is socially unjust, and probably is not practical (ibid., p. 235). This left expansionist policies.

England was on the gold standard. An expansionist policy "sufficiently drastic to be useful might drive us off the gold standard" (ibid.). He feared the possibly damaging psychological reaction to a larger budget deficit while, at the same time, he favored Britain taking financial leadership in the world. For the latter reason "our exchange position should be relentlessly defended" (ibid., p. 236).

The remaining alternative, which avoided the risks of other methods of demand expansion, was a revenue tariff. Keynes favored a flat rate, or at most two rates, to raise £50 million to £75 million (ibid., pp. 236–7). The revenues would be spent to expand demand.   ·

Within a few months, Keynes changed his position (ibid., p. 242). By September 1931, he favored devaluation.[38] However, he continued to advocate a tariff as preferable to the alternative policy of reducing wages to reduce costs. In less than two weeks, Britain devalued, and Keynes was again opposed to protection (ibid., p. 243). He never returned to his earlier, unqualified opposition.

Keynes's argument for the tariff suggests that his concerns about British unemployment affected his judgment. His argument neglects any effects of retaliation and, at one point, seems to argue that the British expansion will neutralize the effect on the rest of the world: "The buying power that we take away from the rest of the world by restricting certain imports we shall restore to it with the other hand."

[38] In the addendum that Keynes drafted to the Macmillan Committee report (May 1931), devaluation by 10 percent against gold is described as "the most obvious and comprehensive method" (20, p. 295) of reducing costs of production and relative prices of domestic and foreign goods. The addendum rejects devaluation as, on balance, disadvantageous, citing "the special circumstances of Great Britain" (20, p. 296).

He adds, "Some fanatical [sic] free traders might allege that the adverse effect of import duties on our exports would neutralize all this; but it would not be true" (ibid., pp. 237–8). A few years later, in 1933, he recognized the damage done by competitive devaluation and competitive tariffs (ibid., p. 352), but he advocated only the removal of tariffs and quotas introduced "to protect the foreign balance" (ibid., p. 361). His statement seems to permit revenue tariffs and tariffs "in pursuance of permanent national policies" (ibid.), but he gives no hint about how these different tariffs can be distinguished in practice.

The role of anticipations

Anticipations, or expectations, have a large role in the *General Theory*, but they are present in the *Tract* and become more important in the *Treatise*. That anticipations affected outcomes had long been recognized. Early classical writers mention "confidence" as a factor affecting the demand for money. Thornton (1802) is an example, cited previously. Alfred Marshall stressed the role of confidence as a key element in the business cycle. In an early monograph written with his wife, we find: "The chief cause of the evil [recession] is a want of confidence . . . The revival of industry comes about through the gradual and almost simultaneous growth of confidence among the various trades" (Marshall and Marshall 1879, pp. 154–5, as quoted by Kahn 1984, pp. 12–13.) Later writers developed "psychological" theories of the business cycle. Robertson (1926, p. 3) quotes Pigou's description of the common element in these theories as a claim that "optimistic error and pessimistic error, when discovered give birth to one another in an endless chain." (See also Haberler 1946.) Although Keynes later used a phrase very similar to Pigou's to describe business cycle impulses, at the time, he scorned this class of explanations and characterized it as "Professor Pigou's somewhat mythical 'psychological errors of optimism and pessimism' on the part of the business world" (13, p. 89).

Despite his criticism of Pigou, Keynes was not averse to bringing "confidence" into his argument when he found it useful. His advocacy of a tariff in 1931 instead of favoring expansion of demand is one example. His analysis of unemployment in 1923 concludes that lack of confidence in price stability is the only presently remediable cause of unemployment (19, p. 112). Here and elsewhere, Keynes recognizes the importance of anticipations or confidence, but as was standard at the time, the determinants of confidence are left unstated, and the argument is incomplete.

In the *Tract* Keynes assigned an important role to expectations in the theory of exchange rates. The preface to the French edition of the *Tract* has a classic statement of this view:

> What, then, has determined and will determine the value of the franc? First, the quantity, present and prospective, of the francs in circulation. Second, the amount of purchasing power which it suits the public to hold in that shape . . . The first of these two elements . . . depends mainly on the loan and budgetary policies of the French Treasury. The second of them depends mainly . . . on the trust or distrust which the public feel in the prospects of the value of the franc. (4, p. xviii)

The same preface cautions the French reader to disregard statements about the role of speculators, discourses on the role of bulls and bears, and concludes that exchange controls, intended to hamper speculation, depress the value of the franc (ibid., p. xxi).

The *Tract* also introduces expectations as an influence on the demand for money. Keynes (ibid., pp. 42–3) emphasizes the importance of confidence for money holding. He relates the rise in velocity during hyperinflation to the efforts people make to reduce the inflation tax on cash balances when anticipations of inflation reduce confidence. Later, he makes a more general statement, typical of earlier monetary literature, relating average cash balance to "the mood of the public" (ibid., p. 68).

Nothing in the *Tract* or the *Treatise* ties anticipations to actual events or observables. Anticipations, or expectations, are a deus ex machina that enter or leave at convenient places. At one point, Keynes explicitly makes long-run expectations consistent with actual values, but in the short run the value of securities "depends on opinion largely uncontrolled by any present monetary factors" (5, pp. 228–9): "If everyone agrees that securities are worth more . . . there is no limit to the rise in the price of securities and no effective check arises from a shortage of money" (ibid., p. 229).[39] The rise cannot continue indefinitely, however: "As soon as the price of securities has risen high enough, relative to the short-term rate of interest, to occasion a difference of opinion as to the prospects, a 'bear' position will develop, and some people will begin to increase their savings deposits" (ibid.).

These passages show some of the changes during the 1920s in Keynes's beliefs about anticipations and their influence on the economy. Three changes are of particular importance for his later work.

First, in the *Treatise* speculators are no longer as helpful or benign

---

[39] Some self-fulfilling, temporary expectational effects are also in the *Tract* (4, p. 34). Elsewhere, he uses extrapolative expectations and herdlike behavior (19, p. 81).

as in the *Tract*. The *Tract* advises the French to remove all limitations on foreign exchange "whether for immediate or deferred delivery" (4, p. xxii).[40] Explanations that blame the fall of the franc on speculation are "not far removed, intellectually, from . . . ascription of cattle disease to the 'evil eye' . . . The successful speculator makes his profit by anticipating, not by modifying, existing economic tendencies" (ibid., p. xvii). In the *Treatise*, as we have seen, speculators can move the price of securities, for a time, away from the long-run values determined by "the amount of liquid consumption goods which the securities will, directly or indirectly, yield, modified by reference to the risk and uncertainty of this expectation" (5, p. 228).

Second, in the *Treatise*, long-run expectations are consistent with equilibrium values, but short-term expectations are volatile. The *General Theory* makes the opposite assumption (7, p. 50). Keynes's change of view may be related to the different problems addressed, but there is no doubt that Keynes changed his belief after the *Tract* and changed again in the *General Theory*. One possible reason is that while writing the *Treatise*, Keynes was greatly influenced by the rise in stock prices in New York in 1929, a rise that he believed was based on short-term anticipations.[41]

Third, the market rate of interest enters the calculations of the speculators, called bulls and bears. It is through the rate of interest that monetary policy changes the balance of forces in speculative markets. The effect is not instantaneous, in the passages quoted, but Keynes appears confident of the final effect.

Liquidity preference

The mechanism Keynes introduced in the *Treatise* to link anticipations to economic activity later became known as liquidity preference. Some main assumptions are spelled out in the *Treatise* (5, pp. 39–42). Businesses and households hold money balances for income transactions, speculative transactions, and financial transactions. Balances held for income transactions depend on the money value of output or income;

---

[40] Earlier, I noted that shortly after completing the *Treatise* Keynes considered exchange controls (and tariffs) as a solution to unemployment in Britain.

[41] In a comment on this passage, Donald Moggridge points out that Keynes's experience as an investor and speculator may have influenced his views about speculative knowledge and anticipations. Keynes explains (12, pp. 102–9) that initially he had tried to follow a "credit cycle policy" – a policy that would now be called "market timing" – buying during recessions and selling during booms. In his 1938 Post-Mortem on Investment Policy for King's College, Keynes rejects this strategy and favors buying, and holding for several years, a mixed portfolio of investments that appear cheap in relation to long-term ("intrinsic") value (ibid., p. 107).

this fraction Keynes calls k_1, and he suggests that its value, though dependent on habits of payment and subject to seasonal fluctuation, can be treated as stable (ibid., pp. 39, 43). The remaining balances – speculative and financial – are treated as a unit. The amount held is independent of current output[42] (ibid., pp. 42–3). The quantity demanded of these deposits, also called (or perhaps including) "hoards" at times, depends on the relative price of nonliquid-to-liquid assets. Keynes describes the demand curve as "the 'state or degree of bearishness.' It might be better to call it 'the propensity to hoard . . . Accordingly, the amount of 'hoards' or liquid assets which he actually holds has to be in due relation not only to his propensity to hoard, but also to the price of non-liquid assets" (ibid., p. xxvi). Here, the demand for "money" has two components: one depends on output, the other on the relative price of assets, or the rate of interest, and on expectations, called "bearishness" in the *Treatise*. When Keynes talks about bears (and bulls), he means changes in the demand for "speculative" money balances, where money includes time and saving deposits.

The speculative demand for money and the quantity of speculative balances determines the price of nonliquid assets:

> My central thesis regarding the determination of the price of non-liquid assets is that, given (a) the quantity of inactive deposits offered by the banking system, and (b) the degree of propensity to hoard or state of bearishness, then the price level of non-liquid assets must be fixed at whatever figure is required to equate the quantity of hoards which the public will desire to hold at that price level with the quantity of hoards which the banking system is creating. (ibid., p. xxvii)

The quoted passages appeared more than a year after the book, in the preface to the Japanese translation, and a very similar passsage is in Keynes's response to Robertson's review of the book in the *Economic Journal* (13, pp. 220–2). The preface refers the reader to a section of the book (5, pp. 172–6) that is less clear and relates Keynes's ideas to Wicksell's discussion of the divergence between the market rate and the natural rate. The original passage reaches the conclusion that "the market rate of interest cannot be continually held even a little below the natural rate unless the volume of bank money is being continually increased" (ibid., p. 177).

There should be no doubt that Keynes had in mind the idea that

---

[42] One of Keynes's main criticisms of the quantity theory is that income and transactions differ, and the difference reflects the allocation between income and speculative balances or, in one set of terms used in the *Treatise*, the industrial circulation and part of the financial circulation.

became liquidity preference when he wrote the *Treatise*. His analysis of the price level of investment makes that price level depend on "the sentiment of the public and the behaviour of the banking system" (ibid., p. 128), where the "sentiment of the public" refers to their bullishness or bearishness. His more complete discussion of bulls and bears analyzes the effects of changes in these positions as equivalent to changes in the quantity of money (ibid., pp. 225–6).[43]

Conclusion

Keynes's basic beliefs have a large influence on the problems he considered and the way he addressed them. In the philosophy that he learned from G. E. Moore and shared with many of his closest associates, the highest good came from states of mind – contemplation, beauty, truth, and love. Pecuniary motives were at a much lower level and the pursuit of wealth or money unattractive. This broad view of the purposes of life was joined to two others. One was the values learned as a child – the so-called presuppositions of Harvey Road – under which persuasion by an intellectual elite was to be the means of improving mankind. The duty of the intellectual elite, in this view, was to lead public opinion and shape society's rules by discussion within the elite of civil servants, intellectuals, and molders of opinion and by changing public opinion. The other influence was once again Moore, who taught that there were no fixed definitions of good and evil. "Good" depended on the circumstances in which an issue was to be decided.

Keynes applied this moral philosophy or code throughout his life. His views were not static. They changed as new problems arose and as observations altered his beliefs. He did not see the boundary between public and private action as a fixed point determined by a belief in laissez-faire or socialism. The role of the state was to do the tasks that were not done or were not well done within a framework of rules, for example, rules for monetary management or for taxation. He left to judgment and the political process in a democracy the task of deciding what should be done. And he took a leading role in the discussion both of appropriate action and of the rules with a stream of proposals

---

[43] Other hints appear in the *Treatise* (5, p. 162) and in the discussion of the demand for capital (ibid., pp. 180–2). Keynes ties the velocity of "business deposits" to the opportunity cost of holding money (ibid., p. 220), to securities prices (ibid., pp. 239–40), and to speculation on securities prices (6, p. 175). The discussion in the *Treatise* is Keynes's attempt to resolve the problem of "hoarding" and its relation to money and to saving that are a major issue in his exchanges with Robertson throughout the period.

for state action to solve current problems, to reform the system, and to remove impediments to progress.

Throughout the 1920s and beyond, he retained his interest in economic progress and his belief that progress depended on investment and capital accumulation. The role of the state was to guide investment so as to maintain progress. Progress was hampered by instability and uncertainty that increased risk and raised required real returns on investment. The cost of risk was the "most avoidable burden on production" (4, p. xiv). Price fluctuations added to risk.

Progress, for Keynes, required an end to laissez-faire, particularly, improved monetary arrangements to increase price stability and reduce risk. Although he believed that the gold standard was not ideal, he did not favor substituting discretionary policy. At the time, he preferred management constrained by rules that avoided inflation and deflation. He believed that a central bank, though constrained by rules, could use discretion to increase stability by smoothing fluctuations in the demand for money, particularly by offsetting changes in the speculative demand for money.

The quantity theory that Keynes learned from Marshall did not explain fluctuations in the demand for money. Discussions, mainly with Robertson, and his own observations convinced Keynes that the quantity theory was not a useful base on which to build a theory of fluctuations. As his interest turned from the equilibrium theory of the *Tract* to the problem of business cycles, he saw the need to develop a theory that related *price* fluctuations – which he then regarded as the source of the problem of fluctuations – to investment and the demand for money. In the 1920s, Keynes developed and set forth his basic views. He needed a framework or theory to show that the interventionist policies that he favored would improve the operation of the economy, contribute to progress, and raise welfare. The *Treatise* was his first attempt to develop that framework.

3

Theories, implications, and conjectures in the 1920s

The *Treatise on Money* is Keynes's major work on monetary theory during the 1920s. At the start of the work, he is a Cambridge quantity theorist, in the tradition of Marshall. His reservations about the quantity theory are not different in degree from those of many of his contemporaries. His basic beliefs, observations, and efforts to develop a dynamic theory led him in a different direction, one that he regarded as more useful.

The *Treatise* is a major work in more than one sense. Only a relatively small part of the book addresses the theoretical problem of fluctuations. Keynes chose to address large parts of monetary theory not closely related to his main theme. He begins by sketching his views about the nature of money and considers at length the measurement of prices by means of index numbers and the types of monetary standard. A separate volume applies the theory to historical episodes, to policy issues of his own day, and more generally to the management of money. In a fashion characteristic of much of Keynes's popular writing, he discusses and analyzes available data to bring out the main movements, to apply his theory, and to form his own and the reader's views about what is relatively fixed and what is more subject to change.

Although some parts, such as the discussion of index numbers and the analyses of events have outstanding sections, our main interest is the theory. Keynes speaks in the preface of a "process of getting rid of the ideas which I used to have and of finding my way to those which I now have" (5, p. xvii). His main ideas concern four principal topics:

1. The relation of saving and investment – the "fundamental equations" of the *Treatise* tying the price level to profits, costs, and, most importantly, to the difference between saving and investment.
2. A theory of the business cycle in which stocks and flows are related, and changes in the demand for money (or idle balances) reflect expectations.
3. A theory of monetary policy relating central bank policy to price fluctuations and to changes in investment.

61

4. The extension of the theory to an open economy
operating under the gold standard.

Keynes was not alone in his concern witih these general topics. The decade was alive with activity. He was most aware of the work at Cambridge to which Pigou (1927) and Robertson (1926) were main contributors. He was familiar to some extent with work by Hayek, Hawtrey, Cassel, Wicksell, Schumpeter, Fisher, and others who are mentioned in the *Treatise* or in his correspondence at the time. As editor of a leading journal, Keynes may have been influenced by these or others of his contemporaries. He is extremely sparing in his references, so it is difficult to know how much his reading affected his writing and thinking.[1] There is no doubt that he played a leading role in the development of the ideas, but it would be a mistake to leave the impression that he was alone in analyzing the problems he addressed. We know that the greatest influence at the time was Robertson, with whom Keynes had extensive and frequent exchanges and whose contributions are acknowledged in the preface. Aside from Pigou, whose work and comments Keynes usually treated in a negative way, there is not much evidence until the end of the 1920s of extensive discussions of a broad range of theoretical issues with his contemporaries or younger Cambridge economists. After the *Treatise*, Ralph Hawtrey, Roy Harrod, James Meade, Joan Robinson, Austin Robinson, Piero Sraffa, and particularly Richard Kahn gradually replaced Robertson and helped Keynes to revise his ideas. Of this group, only Kahn and Robertson are acknowledged in the preface to the published version qf the *Treatise*.

The fundamental equations

> We leave saving to the private investor, and we encourage him
> to place his savings mainly in titles to money. We leave the
> responsibility for setting production in motion to the business
> man, who is mainly influenced by the profits which he expects
> to accrue to himself in terms of money. (4, p. xiv)

The quotation from the preface to the *Tract* relates saving, invest-

---

[1] One of many possible examples illustrates the point. At the end of the *Treatise*, Keynes discusses commodity standards and proposes that the value of money should be tied to a basket of commodities. There is no mention of the extensive discussion of this topic by Frank Graham or of the work of Benjamin Graham.

ment, profits, and money values.[2] The *Treatise* explores these relations in an effort to show that differences between saving and investment can occur and that when the differences occur, prices and profits change. The changes in prices and profits are, in turn, related to changes in the quantity of money (or other nominal assets) and to changes in expectations that affect the demand for these assets. The relations between some of these variables Keynes called *the fundamental equations*.

What was *fundamental* about these equations? Although occasionally he tried to claim more (5, p. 141), Keynes understood that the equations are identities (ibid., p. 125) – analytic expressions that hold because of the meaning assigned to the individual terms. Their fundamental property, he thought, had two bases.

First, he claims that the equations focus attention on the factors determining deviations of the price level from the equilibrium positions at which (Marshall's normal) profits are zero and money is neutral (ibid., p. 132). One equation relates prices to costs, the other to revenues. At the time, Keynes saw price fluctuations and departures from long-run neutrality as related and central to the problem of the business cycle. And, he thought that economic fluctuations were related to economic profits and to economic progress, as in Schumpeter's theory of capitalist dynamics (6, pp. 85–6). By relating prices to revenues and costs, and thus to profits, Keynes believed he had focused on the main source of fluctuations.

The second claim is that the equations show that saving and investment can differ. A modern reader will find the second reason surprising. Everyone now "knows" that planned investment and planned saving are not identical. In the 1920s, Keynes and others were working toward the level of understanding at which the distinction between planned and actual saving became standard in macroeconomics, but they had not arrived there. In fact, Keynes believed that it was necessary to define saving as net of windfalls (profits) to avoid making saving and investment identical (13, p. 251).

The point of the fundamental equations is to show that when prices differ from costs of production, investment and saving differ, and the economy departs from long-run neutrality. Neutrality is defined as the

[2] The relation of saving, investment, and changes in money is a main subject of Keynes's correspondence and discussions with Robertson. Keynes (6, p. 90) gave credit to Robertson (1926) for pioneering work on the problem. At the time, many writers discussed the role of *overinvestment* or *underconsumption* in business cycles. Most of these discussions appealed to observation, did not offer precise definitions of terms, and did not relate stocks and flows in a general equilibrium framework that tied the stock of money and the demand for money to the flows of investment and saving.

position at which the aggregate price level π is equal to the ratio of aggregate money income (or earnings E) to real product O, the latter defined as the physical volume of output.[3] The deviation of prices from long-run equilibrium is equal to the difference between investment I and saving S per unit of real product. This adds a dynamic element to the equation

$$\pi = E/O + (I - S)/O \qquad (3.1)$$

There is a similar equation for the price level of consumption goods, denoted P. This price level is the inverse of the purchasing power of money (5, p. 122).[4] Again, Keynes introduces a dynamic consideration to show why the price level departs from its long-run value:

$$P = E/O + (I' - S)/R \qquad (3.2)$$

The definitions bring out that P differs from the general price level π for two reasons. Investment I differs from I', and O differs from R. Here, I is the value of new investment goods, I' is their cost of production, and R is the amount of real consumption goods produced. The difference $I - I'$ between the value of investment output and its cost of production is a measure of the profitability of the investment goods industry, so increases in the value of new investment goods relative to their cost of production induce changes in relative prices. Differences in relative supplies of output, R/O, also give rise to changes in relative prices.

Keynes uses equations (3.1) and (3.2) to relate the lack of coordination in a market economy to the fluctuations in the price level and in relative prices that he regarded as central to the problem of fluctuations. The act of saving is separate from the act of investing (ibid., p. 251–2), and the composition of production can differ from the composition of spending. People may choose to spend more or less on consumption goods than producers plan to produce in the form of consumption goods; I then differs from I', so the general price level π and relative prices change. The relative price changes affect resource allocation by changing profits. Keynes, then, *defines* efficiency earnings (earnings per unit of effort) as

[3] This discussion follows Keynes's (5, pp. 120–39). Since I summarize Keynes's argument, I do not give a reference for each of my statements.

[4] The *Treatise* has five chapters (5, pp. 47–107) on index numbers and the "proper" measurement of the price level. Keynes put great stress on the "proper" price level. He believed that the use of what he called secondary price levels obscures rather than clarifies the role of money.

$$W/e = E/O$$

where e is a measure of efficiency, and W is the rate of earnings of *all* productive factors.[5] Substitution of W/e in equation (3.2) shows the relation between prices and costs that Keynes sought (ibid., pp. 121–2):

$$P = W/e + (I' - S)/R \qquad (3.2')$$

The *fundamental* nature of equation (3.2') comes from the relation of prices to total costs of production, including the costs of replacing or augmenting the capital stock. The remaining equation, equation (3.1), relates prices to revenues. Together, the equations imply that when revenues differ from costs, the price levels for consumer goods and total output differ.

The fundamental equations also enabled Keynes to develop two conditions for stability of consumer prices and the purchasing power of money (ibid., pp. 122–3). First, efficiency earnings of all factors must be constant and, second, the cost of new investment (I') must equal the volume of savings. Keynes then defines the profitability of investment as the difference between cost and market value, $I - I'$, and uses his definitions to relate total profits to the difference between I and S. The next step of the argument is to define terms so that whenever $I = S$, profits are zero and conversely. Keynes *defines* income and saving to be net of windfall gains and losses.[6] All windfall gains and losses are profits Q, so $I - S = Q$ (ibid., pp. 113–14, 124). Much later, Keynes concludes that Robertson's concept of *hoarding* is equal to $-Q$, thereby resolving to his satisfaction the issues about saving, hoarding, and money holding that had occupied him throughout the period (13, p. 308).

One defense of the usefulness of these definitions is in a letter to Pigou (ibid., pp. 215–16). Pigou continued to use a type of quantity equation. Keynes's letter argues that his own equations are not contrary to the quantity theory, but they highlight changes in the relative prices of investment and consumption and changes in profits. Aggregation of E and Q into a single concept ignores effects of changes in their relative importance and therefore prevents analysis of the differ-

[5] Note that W includes more than money wages, a point emphasized in Hayek's (1931) criticism.

[6] The treatment of windfalls makes the definition of income similar to permanent income, as in Friedman (1957), but the definition of saving differs from Friedman's later usage. The transactions demand for money, discussed later, depends on income, so it is independent of windfalls, but windfalls can affect the demand for speculative balances.

ence between S and I and its relation to profits and prices. Earlier, he defended the usefulness of his definitions by claiming that the definitions are important for analysis of the demand for money. Anticipating a later discussion on the role of windfalls – or differences in permanent and transitory income, as they were later called – Keynes claimed that changes in windfalls, or profits, and income have different effects on the demand for money. An increase in profits has a smaller effect on the demand for money than an increase in income (net of profits) (5, p. 133). Hence, he thought he saw an important relation between the composition of $E + Q$ and the demand for money.[7]

A more explicit defense, also written after the book was criticized, is in the preface to the Japanese edition (ibid., pp. xxiv–xxv). There, Keynes defends his definitions as enabling him to analyze within his framework a change in the demand for securities that changes the price of securities, the quantity of money remaining unchanged. The change in the demand for securities occurs because of a shift in liquidity preference. The result is a change in the price of investment goods and, therefore, a change in investment. Changes of this type Keynes called *bearishness*. Bearishness is defined as a change in the demand curve for liquid assets (ibid., p. xxvii). In the *General Theory* (7, pp. 173–4), he relates the state of bearishness to the speculative demand for money and points out the main change from the *Treatise*. In the *Treatise*, the demand for liquid assets is a demand for money and bonds. In the *General Theory*, bonds and capital are lumped together. Hence, the margin on which the rate of interest operates in the *Treatise* is between real capital (or claims to real capital) and the sum, money plus bonds. In the *General Theory*, the margin is between money and bonds.

Saving and investment

The theoretical argument starts with definitions of a bewildering number of concepts. Most of this terminology obstructs rather than clarifies, and the confusion is made worse both by Keynes's use of different terms to refer to the same, or very similar, concepts and by his failure to stay with a term after he introduces it. The main point of the saving and investment definitions is to make these terms differ by the amount of economic profits. Income and saving are defined net of profits, so the "increment of wealth of the community is measured by savings *plus* profits" (5, p. 114). Investment is the net increment of capital –

---

[7] This argument is an early version of the hypothesis that transitory income, or windfalls, does not affect the demand for money.

"the value of the increment of capital" – and is equal to the value of saving plus profits (ibid.).

The definition of saving as net of windfalls, or profits, is opposite to the fruitful hypothesis, introduced much later in Friedman (1957), that includes all windfalls in saving. On Friedman's hypothesis, individuals smooth consumption and vary saving when current receipts exceed expected income. Windfalls are used to purchase financial assets or durables. This hypothesis retains the classical position that individuals borrow and lend, and save and dissave, from windfalls. Keynes's hypothesis differed on this point. His observations convinced him that saving was much less variable than investment.

"The business of saving is essentially a steady process . . . A disturbance will seldom or never be initiated by a sudden change in the proportion of current income which is being saved. Investment in fixed capital, on the other hand has been accustomed to proceed irregularly and by fits and starts" (5, pp. 251–2; see also p. 257). Since income is defined net of windfalls, saving is a relatively fixed proportion of permanent or expected income. The proportion depends positively on the rate of interest, but it is not very sensitive to the rate of interest (ibid., p. 180). Variability is assigned to profits. In this way, Keynes focuses attention on profits and investment, the variables that change cyclically.

The effect of the rate of interest on investment is opposite in sign and quantitatively larger than the effect on saving (ibid., p. 183).[8] The dependence of investment on interest rates is a consequence of the dependence of the output of investment goods on the relative price of such goods – that is, on the price of investment relative to the cost of production of investment goods (ibid., p. 180). The price of investment goods depends on the "estimated net prospective yield from fixed capital (estimated by the opinion of the market after such allowance as they choose to make for the uncertainty of anticipation, etc.) measured in money, and on the rate of interest at which this future yield is capitalized" (ibid.). This is, of course, an early version of the relation between the marginal efficiency of capital and the rate of interest that Keynes posited in the *General Theory* (7, p. 135). In the *Treatise*, however, investment is in nominal terms, so the anticipated yield changes "due either to a change in the real yield, its price remaining the same, or to a change in the prospective price (or money value) of the real yield" (5, p. 181). This is unattractive because it fails to sep-

[8] Keynes distinguishes between investment goods and capital goods, but the distinction should not detain us, as he notes (5, p. 180). I use investment to refer to both investment goods and capital goods.

arate changes in the market value of capital from the value of changes in the stock of capital.

Keynes recognized three means by which the central bank can affect investment, but he minimized the importance of the first two. Changes in bank rate have little influence on the anticipated real yield of (fixed) capital. Bank rate can, in principle, affect the price of the goods produced, but only for a short time and only if the change in bank rate changes anticipations "by throwing new light . . . on the policy and intentions of the currency authority" (ibid.).[9]

The principal effect of bank rate is on the "rate of interest at which the prospective money yield of fixed capital is capitalised" to arrive at its present value (ibid.). A rise in bank rate raises the rate on bonds, and the latter rise deters spending on investment and the production of investment goods. The effect of the increase in interest rates on investment is heightened by the belief that the rise is temporary. The reason is that investment in durables is postponable or can be accelerated. The effect of changes perceived to be temporary is "to cause the immediate rate of investment to fluctuate much more than would be the case if borrowers believed that the change in the rate of interest had come to stay" (ibid., p. 182). These fluctuations in investment are "the major cause of disturbance" (ibid., p. 252).

The driving force for investment is the relation of the prospective return to the rate of interest. By prospective return Keynes, following Marshall, clearly intended to introduce anticipations of future profit into the investment function. (See Eshag 1963, Chapter 3.) These anticipations are subject to sudden changes and, if widely held, can be self-fulfilling at times, "even if they have no basis outside themselves" (5, p. 144). Businessmen may act to increase or reduce activity, and these actions, by changing investment, bring on the changes that were anticipated. But, alternation of optimism and pessimism is not a major driving force in the *Treatise*. Accurate forecasting is difficult and requires more information than businesses possess, so average behavior is mainly "governed by current experience supplemented by such broad generalizations as those relating to the probable consequences of changes in bank rate, the supply of credit, and the state of the foreign exchanges" (ibid.).[10]

---

[9] The passage should be read, I believe, on the assumption that there is no sustained inflation, so the change in the price of future investment goods is a change in the relative price of these goods. Eshag (1963, p. 101) notes that, in emphasizing price changes during the cycle, Keynes adopts the type of analysis developed by Marshall.

[10] Keynes then added his judgment about anticipations. They are, in large measure, rational. "Action based on inaccurate anticipations will not long survive experiences of a contrary character, so that the facts will soon override anticipations except where they agree" (5, p. 144). There are lags, however. Keynes had noted that even in the German inflation, inflation changed real rates of interest (19, pp. 8–9).

The condition for equilibrium in the output market is $I = S$. If, in addition, $I = I'$, then the price level of consumer goods and the aggregate price level, P and π, are fixed and equal to E/O and to the efficiency wage, W/e. Equality of I and S requires that aggregate profits be zero. $I = I'$ requires that aggregate cost of production of investment goods equals the market value of such goods. Costs and revenues are equal. Profits are zero in both the production of investment goods and consumption goods, and $I' = S$ (ibid., p. 136).

We can summarize some main elements of the investment–saving relation in a few equations that eliminate details and much of the complexity but bring out the main framework Keynes constructed. Saving S depends positively on nominal income Y, defined to exclude windfalls, or profits, and positively on the rate of interest[11]:

$$S = S(r, Y) \qquad (3.3)$$

Investment depends negatively on the rate of interest and positively on expected or actual profits, Q, made from selling the product. Profits, in turn, depend positively on the expected or actual selling price of the underlying product P, so we can write nominal investment I as

$$I = I(P, r) \qquad (3.4)$$

In equilibrium, there are no windfalls; Q is zero, so $I = S$, and

$$I(P, r) - S(r, Y) = 0$$

As Keynes's critics pointed out, and Keynes finally accepted, the level of expected *real* permanent income is treated as constant. The equilibrium position of the output market (OM) is given by a curve relating P and r. Subscripts denote partial derivatives. I neglect an explicit role for anticipations or shocks that shift investment:

$$\frac{dr}{dP}\bigg|_{\text{OM}} = \frac{I_P - S_Y Y_P}{S_r - I_r}$$

The slope of the OM curve is negative if I_P is small relative to $S_Y Y_P$; the price level must have a larger effect on saving than on investment. This condition is sufficient to draw several of the implications Keynes drew from his analysis, for example, the relation between interest rates

---

[11] Alternatively, S can depend on P since real permanent income is fixed.

and prices or the importance of relative price changes as a driving force in business cycles (6, p. 90).

The paradox of thrift and the real balance effect

One implication that Keynes claimed for his theory of investment and saving is that saving increases wealth only if it leads to more investment. Increased saving by itself cannot lower the rate of interest. This proposition, known as the widow's cruse, became a main topic for discussion by the young economists of the Cambridge Circus. Later, the idea that saving is harmful returned in the *General Theory* as the paradox of thrift. There, the paradox is that attempts by savers in the aggregate to save more lowers current income and aggregate saving by reducing expenditure on consumption and aggregate demand. Both the widow's cruse and the paradox of thrift reflect Keynes's belief that investment, not saving, is the source of progress. Also, as Leijonhufvud (1968) emphasizes, the discussion of saving and investment is Keynes's way of introducing the problem of intertemporal coordination in capitalist economics and presenting his belief that relative prices either did not solve the coordination problem or did not solve it in a socially optimal way.

In the *Treatise*, income is permanent income and, if prices are stable, its equilibrium level is given. Individual attempts to save more, unmatched by changes in investment, reduce the price of consumption goods. "This fall of prices increases the purchasing power of the money incomes of the rest of the community and they are able, therefore, to increase their consumption by the amount which the saver has forgone" (5, p. 156). If others follow the initial attempt to increase saving by increasing their saving also, the decline in prices is greater. The result is a transfer of wealth

> *from* the savers to the general body of *consumers*, and . . . *to* the savers from the general body of *producers*, both total consumption and total wealth remaining unchanged. Thus, in Mr. Robertson's language, the saving has been "abortive." There is no increase of wealth in any shape or form corresponding to the increase of saving" (5, pp. 156, 202–4)

The increase in wealth occurs only if there is investment. Further, increased saving does not reduce the natural or long-term rate of interest. "It is *investment* . . . which alone increases national wealth, and can alone in the long run bring down the natural rate of interest'' (6, p. 186; see also 5, p. 283–4).[12]

This line of reasoning leads Keynes to consider the relation of saving to profits. Since individual efforts to change saving cannot affect aggregate saving, with investment unchanged, these efforts do not affect profits. If businesses use their profits to spend on consumption, the prices of the goods they buy rise by an amount equal to the increase in spending out of profits. This follows from the definition of the profits of the consumption goods industry as the difference between the cost of investment I' and S, the amount saved. A change in saving, I' unchanged, is matched by a change in profits that just offsets the initial reduction in profits to increase spending on consumption. In this way, Keynes reaches the conclusion that "profits . . .. are a widow's cruse which remains undepleted" (5, p. 125). Reductions of consumption spending, to increase saving, cannot reduce business losses in the aggregate.

Keynes's conclusion requires that costs remain fixed. With costs unchanged, the fall in prices reduces the excess of price over cost of production and lowers profits (ibid., p. 159). If businesses respond by reducing employment, aggregate spending is reduced by the same amount as the cost of production (5, pp. 159–60, 284; 17, p. 265).

Robertson's review pointed out some of the flaws in Keynes's argument and took note of the so-called real balance effect on saving (1931, p. 407–9). The main criticisms are that Keynes's argument ignores timing and assumes that income is fixed, so shifts in spending do not alter relative costs. Robertson then points out that Keynes's discussion of price changes neglected what would now be called the real balance effect. He begins his argument by noting that the government can, by raising prices, "transfer real income to itself or its nominees" (ibid., p. 408). He then notes that in addition to the effect of increased saving on the price level, discussed by Keynes, there is a second effect that Keynes ignored. The fall in the price level produces "also an increase in the real value of the aggregate of money balances as a whole" (ibid.).

Keynes's response to Robertson's criticism (13, pp. 219–36) does not discuss the real balance effect, and as we know from Patinkin's

---

[12] Keynes is responding here to Robertson's criticisms and his discussion of lacking and hoarding. Note that the redistribution of purchasing power occurs, like the real balance effect, because price changes alter the real wealth of consumers but, unlike the real balance effect, aggregate consumption is unchanged unless marginal propensities to consume differ. Keynes was familiar with the real balance effect, but he neglects net wealth transfers between government and the private sector. His reasons are discussed later.

(1965) emphasis on this point, he did not introduce a real balance effect in the *General Theory*. It is a mistake to believe that this neglect reflected lack of familiarity with the concept. Keynes discusses the real balance effect in the *Treatise* under the heading of "induced lacking" (5, pp. 268–9), a term invented by Robertson (1926). (See also 13, pp. 290–2, 302–4.) He first restates the argument. An increase in the price level redistributes income and lowers the real value of money balances.[13] Those whose balances are reduced "may, therefore, be induced to save on a greater scale than they would otherwise, in order to make good the loss which they have involuntarily suffered in the value of their stock of money" (5, p. 268). Here and elsewhere (13, pp. 285–7) Keynes dismisses the effect either as unimportant or, later, as already included in his equations (ibid.).

The asset market

The quantity equation was the traditional way of relating the stock of money to the flow of output. In Keynes's view, the quantity equation obscured the interesting stock-flow dynamics. This view is central to his criticism of the quantity equation and his attempt to develop a substitute.

A main aim of the *Treatise* is to relate saving, investment, and money or financial assets within a common framework. The definitions of saving and income to exclude economic profits reflect this aim. Keynes believed that short-period changes in profits and saving have different effects on the demand for money and other financial assets. Profits have a smaller effect on the demand for money than (permanent) income and perhaps no effect at all (5, p. 133). Business demand for deposits depends mainly on their costs of production and is independent of windfalls, or nearly so. Deposits are also held to bridge the gap between receipts and payments, as in the well-known Baumol (1952) analysis.

The *Treatise* devotes many pages to demands for various classes of deposits: financial and industrial deposits, demand and savings deposits, deposits held for contingencies and for speculation (5, pp. 29–32). Again, these details introduce complexities that make the argument difficult to follow without much effect on the substance.[14] The main

---

[13] "Those who are in possession of a stock of money also discover that this stock has less than its previous value" (5, p. 268). Note that Keynes attributes the proposition to Robertson not to Pigou. In later correspondence, Robertson attributes the point to Pigou's earlier work.

[14] Keynes shifts from one set of terms to another before finally deciding which statistics are available and most useful to collect (6, pp. 6–16).

points are that the classification of deposits into demand and savings deposits obscures the economically relevant distinction between income or transactions balances on one side and speculative balances on the other. Speculative balances change with the bearishness or bullishness of the public, and these changes in the demands for money and financial assets have a significant effect on the price level (ibid., pp. 205, 225).

Shifts in the demand for money are present in the *Tract* (4, pp. 67–8). There, Keynes computes the effect of a change in the Cambridge k on the decline in the price level between October 1920 and October 1922. The larger part of the decline he attributes to the change in k. He discusses the changes in k during hyperinflations in Russia, Germany, and elsewhere (ibid., pp. 45–50). He also calculates the revenues from the inflation tax in Germany (5, p. 50) and notes the effects of the tax on average cash balances, showing that he was aware of the effect of inflation on the demand for money.

In one of his earlier writings, he discusses the role of confidence during the German inflation. He defines confidence in terms of the Cambridge k as $\Delta k/k$, and he notes that the demand for money per unit of income falls in a hyperinflation (19, p. 14). In fact, he suggests that the decline in k has reached the point of inconvenience (ibid., pp. 14–15).

From what we know of Keynes's method of working from observations to hypotheses, his observations of the substantial changes in k or velocity must have had a lasting influence on his views about the quantity equation and the role of money in business cycles. As early as 1923 (ibid., pp. 83–6), Keynes uses the demand for financial assets to discuss intermediation and interest rates. The public's decisions are the driving force in his analysis. In a period of slow growth in the economy, with weak loan demand, if the public withdraws deposits to buy securities, the banks lose deposits, so they must sell securities. Keynes takes issue with critics who seek to explain the change in securities and interest rates as a result of banks' decisions, and he does not mention the central bank. On his interpretation, the public's demand for Treasury bills bids up the price and lowers the return. The decline in bill yields lowers the yield on long-dated securities, but, he warns his readers, the decline will not last unless there is prolonged stagnation. The absence of any discussion of the central bank's response leaves the analysis incomplete, a problem that Keynes did not fully overcome in similar analysis in the *Treatise*, as his later exchanges with Robertson show.

Keynes's analysis uses elements that had become part of the Cambridge tradition in the early 1920s. Although interest rates were typically explained by saving and investment, or by saving and investment supplemented by changes in money – along the lines of traditional loanable funds theory – there are several hints of a relation between the demand for money and interest rates (Eshag 1963, pp. 58–9). These analyses stopped short, however, of simultaneous determination of interest rates, the central banks actions affecting the stock of money under a fixed or fluctuating exchange rate, the demand for money (or financial assets), and the flows of saving and investment.

In a 1924 discussion at a meeting of the Royal Economic Society, Keynes explains the reason for the shift in emphasis from the stock of money to the demand for money, or k.

> The view used to be that k was not subject to rapid fluctuations. It would move up and down over long periods, but over short periods it did not change very much. Therefore, if you kept the quantity of currency stable, you probably kept prices reasonably stable . . . Many economists now take a different view from that. They think that k, and accordingly the quantity of real purchasing power required, is itself capable of sharp fluctuations, and in fact that it is the *leading characteristic* of booms and depressions that there should be a variation in the magnitude of k . . . *even when there is no marked change in the total volume of money.* (19, p. 207, emphasis added)

The *Treatise* introduced an explicit hypothesis about the demand for money or financial assets. The quantity of money demanded, and therefore monetary velocity, are not taken as givens or dependent on unexplained "confidence." Keynes's hypothesis attempts to relate changes in the demand for money to changes that occur as part of the cyclical process studied in the *Treatise*. Further, changes in demand for different types of deposits (time and demand, industrial, and financial) become a principal cause of fluctuations in velocity (6, pp. 37–8; 5, pp. 207–8).

The two main components of the demand for money, at one point called k_1 and k_2, behave differently. Income deposits are a stable fraction, k_1, of income (5, pp. 39, 43). The average level of the remaining (financial) deposits, k_2, is more variable, so it is misleading to represent total deposits as a stable function of aggregate money income as in the quantity equation (ibid., p. 43).[15] The financial deposits depend on the size of the "bear" position (ibid., p. 225); the demand for these deposits is a demand for speculative holdings. When the demand for speculative

---

[15] This is only one of Keynes's reasons for discarding the quantity theory. His criticisms are summarized later.

holdings changes, with the quantity of money unchanged, the amount of money available for the industrial circulation – transactions balances – must also change. Changes in speculative and transaction balances have effects on prices and other variables similar to changes in the stock of money (ibid., p. 226–7). A main effect of changes in the demand for speculative balances is on P', the price level of new investment.

The demand for money is part of a nascent general equilibrium framework in which individuals make two related decisions. They decide how much to consume or save, and they decide on the allocation of existing wealth between bank deposits and securities representing claims to capital (ibid., p. 127). The first decision concerns current flows, the second the allocation of existing assets or portfolios (ibid.); people allocate wealth between fixed capital and speculative balances or "hoards" (ibid., p. 116).[16]

Keynes then introduces the liquidity preference function of the *Treatise* and relates liquidity preference to bears and bulls. A person's desire to hold more savings deposits depends on the return on securities. Securities and "fixed capital" are, not very explicitly, combined on one side and money or saving deposits are on the other. The allocation between the two groups of assets is not fixed but depends on expected returns and interest rates.

> His distaste for other securities is not absolute and depends on his expectations of the future returns to be obtained from savings deposits and from other securities respectively, which is obviously affected by the price of the latter – and also by the rate of interest allowed on the former . . . A fall in the price level of securities [a rise in the rate of interest] is therefore an indication that the "bearishness" of the public . . . an increased preference for savings deposits as against other forms of wealth and a decreased preference for carrying securities with money borrowed from the banks – has been insufficiently offset by the creation of savings deposits by the banking system – or that the "bullishness" of the public has been more than offset by the contraction of savings deposits by the banking system. (5, pp. 127–8)

---

[16] The definition of *hoards* involves Keynes in such terminology as *nonavailable output, liquid final goods, loan capital*, and similar terms (5, p. 114–17). My text avoids these definitions, which persist but have no useful role in the analysis. I believe these terms remain because Keynes has not worked out the relation between money, saving, and hoarding. I use his alternative definition of hoarding as the decision to hold bank (saving) deposits instead of capital or securities representing claims to real capital (ibid., p. 127).

The next step is to bring together the main elements of his theory. The price level of new investment depends on the sentiment of the public and the behavior of the banking system. The former shifts the demand for savings deposits or financial balances; the latter changes the supply of such balances and the terms on which they are offered. We can, therefore let nominal wealth consist of money plus capital, where the nominal stock of money M is an inclusive definition comparable in modern parlance to some measure of liquid assets:

$$M = k_1 Y - k_2(r) \qquad (3.5)$$

The interest rate r moves inversely to the price of new investment goods (5, p. 139), and k_2 balances (financial balances) move inversely to interest rates given M and Y.

Equation (3.5) looks very much like the demand for money equation of the *General Theory*, but the terms are defined differently. Nevertheless, the equation can be used, with a given stock of money, to obtain the equilibrium condition for the asset market. This is equation (3.5) with aggregate M given.

The asset market (AM) equation directly relates r and π, since π is the price level of output. Price P is a component of π, but Keynes laid great emphasis on the importance of the differences between the two in his discussion of index numbers, his criticism of the quantity theory, and elsewhere. I have ignored this difference in equation (3.4) and continue to do so here since nothing in the schematic framework depends on the distinction:

$$\left. \frac{dr}{dP} \right|_{AM} = \frac{k_1 Y_P}{k_2} > 0$$

The AM equation is positively sloped. With the money stock and real (permanent) output fixed, a rise in consumer prices raises the demand for transaction balances. Interest rates must rise to reduce speculative balances (or savings deposits) and restore asset market equilibrium.

A model of the treatise

Figure 3.1 combines the AM and OM schedules to determine, simultaneously, (consumer) prices and the rate of interest, given the quantity of money and the level of real income. This is as close as Keynes was

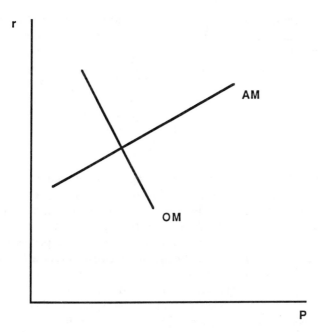

Figure 3.1   Interest rates and consumer prices.

able to come in the *Treatise* to a general equilibrium framework relating stocks and flows. We can test whether this framework captures his main ideas by comparing its implications to some main implications Keynes claimed for his theory, such as the relation between saving and hoarding or the relation between prices and interest rates or the effect of changes in bank rate.

A main failure of the model of the *Treatise* is that Keynes fails to determine real income or output, a point he eventually recognized. Real income is fixed. To establish this conclusion, we supplement equations (3.1), (3.2'), and (3.3) to (3.5) with definitions and equilibrium conditions, one of which was already used implicitly.

$$E = Y \tag{3.6}$$

$$Y = \pi O \tag{3.7}$$

$$I = S \tag{3.8}$$

There are now eight equations and twelve variables: M, W/e, I, I', P, π, R, O, Y, r, E, and S. Profits Q are defined as equal to $I - S$, so nothing is lost by omitting an explicit profits variable and an explicit equation. Keynes treats the quantity of money and the efficiency parameter, M and e, as givens despite the broad definition of M. There are no production equations, so the output variables R and O are taken as given also. For these given values, the numbered equations can determine values for I, I', P, Y, r, E, and S. The remaining variable W (or W/e) is determined only in equilibrium by imposing Keynes's restriction,

$$W/e = E/O = P$$

The simplest assumption corresponding to his procedure is to let W remain fixed. An alternative, clearly not his intention, is to let $I = I'$ and use equation (3.2') to solve for W given P (or conversely). In either case, Keynes's attempt to develop a dynamic theory of the business cycle, in which the centerpiece is the relation between prices and costs of production, is a failure. Instead, the *Treatise* offers a theory of P and r (or π and r) at full employment, equilibrium output.

When Hayek's (1931) review article made this criticism, Keynes was not ready to accept it. Richard Kahn's (1931) paper on the multiplier and discussions at the Cambridge Circus subsequently convinced Keynes that his analysis of output and employment during the business cycle does not follow from the fundamental equations of the *Treatise*.

One variable omitted from the model is the price level of investment goods, P'. Keynes assumed, at one point, that P' is inversely proportional to r, as noted earlier. He is not entirely consistent, however. For reasons that are not entirely clear, he insisted that a change in the price of consumption goods does not require a change in the price of investment goods. He recognized that this conclusion would be difficult to accept:

> A fall in the price of consumption goods due to an excess of saving over investment does not in itself – if it is unaccompanied by any change in the bearishness or bullishness of the public [k_2] or in the volume of saving deposits [$M - k_1 Y$] . . . – require any opposite change in the price of new investment goods. For I believe that this conclusion may be accepted by some readers with difficulty. (5, pp. 130–1).

As I read this paragraph, Keynes claims that the price of investment goods, P', hence the rate of interest, is independent of the change in the consumption price level P. Independence can occur only if the AM curve relating P and r is horizontal, for in that case a reduction in investment that lowers I relative to S, lowers P without changing P' or r. The idea is similar to Keynes's proposition (the widow's cruse) that changes in saving unaccompanied by changes in investment are wasted, wealth is unchanged, losses are equal to $S - I$, and only re-distribution from consumers to producers (or conversely) has occurred (ibid., p. 156). We see that we can obtain this remarkable proposition only on the assumption that real income is fixed and that the AM curve is horizontal.

Robertson's review (1931, p. 400) of the *Treatise* criticizes Keynes's conclusion and the related point that when S and I differ, business profits or losses are just equal to the difference between saving and investment. Robertson claimed that P and P' should move in opposite directions. Robertson did not dispute the fact that saving could be "wasted," since he, like most of the Marshallians, believed that "forced" saving and "abortive" or wasted saving were part of the cycle (Eshag 1963, p. 59). Robertson's objection is that, for savings to be wasted, there must be an increase in the desire to hoard – to "keep resources idle in the form of bank deposits" (1931, p. 401).

In his response to Robertson, Keynes explained how he reached his conclusion. He appears to invoke a horizontal AM line, as implied by the model of the *Treatise* on his special assumptions. He begins by establishing equilibrium:

> The price level of non-liquid assets [hence the rate of interest] must be fixed at whatever figure is required to equate the quan-tity of hoards which the public will desire to hold at that level with the quantity of hoards which the banking system is cre-ating . . .
> Accordingly, the price of non-liquid assets is not directly affected by the price of consumption goods. (13, p. 222)[17]

Keynes then explained that he reached his conclusion by assuming that it was the policy of the banking authorities to keep the quantity of hoards unchanged (ibid., p. 224). On this assumption, $M - k_1 Y$ is constant, and the AM curve of Figure 3.1 is horizontal at the level of r fixed by the monetary authority. The monetary authority matches the quantity of money supplied to hoarders to their demand for idle balances.

Keynes also tried (ibid., pp. 222–3) to explain why P and P' move in the same direction following a change in P rather than in opposite directions as Robertson claimed (1931, p. 400). This discussion is no-

---

[17] The change in terminology to "the price of non-liquid assets" is typical of his use of different terms to refer to the same or similar concepts. In Keynes's discussion of monetary policy he reaches an entirely different conclusion. Interest rates and the price of consumption goods move in opposite directions whereas P and P' move in the same direction (5, p. 187). I return to the latter point subsequently.

table for its failure to state why the initial change in *P* occurs. Shifts in OM and AM produce different answers.

Keynes reversed his position, without noticing. He devotes several pages to the Gibson paradox and to the claim that his analysis accounts for the paradox (6, p. 184). Gibson's data show that the price level moves directly with the interest rate (so *P* and *P'* move in opposite directions). Keynes often used a real theory of fluctuations, so he attributed the association to the increase in *I* relative to *S* during expansions. He claimed that the market rate *r* lags behind the natural rate, but after a delay the market rate rises during expansions and falls in contractions. The reason prices move in the same direction as rates of interest is that an autonomous increase in investment shifts the OM curve to the right along a fixed AM curve. Such a shift would occur if increased investment raises the price level with the quantity of money unchanged. The rise in the price level increases transactions demand, and the rise in interest rates releases money from "hoards."

The determination of the aggregate price level π is similar, but not identical, to the determination of *P*. The aggregate price level depends on the relation of saving to the volume of investment, so some of the forces determining *P* also affect π. However, π includes the price of new investment goods *P'*, and thus changes inversely with *r*. The relation of *P* to π is not simple. Keynes does not give an explicit solution for *P'*.[18] He concluded, however, that π and the amount of profit *Q* depend on four factors:

> (1) the rate of saving, (2) the cost of new investment, (3) the "bearishness" of the public, (4) the volume of savings deposits; or, if you like, on the two factors – (1) the excess of saving over cost of investment, and (2) such excess of bearishness on the part of the public as is unsatisfied by the creation of deposits by the banking system. (5, p. 129)[19]

These are the factors summarized in the diagram, although I have avoided the distinction between the volume of investment and its cost of production. With this exception, Figure 3.1 reproduces his argument.

A further implication that Keynes drew – and that he regarded as an advantage – is that prices can change in his model without any change in the quantity of money or the velocity of circulation (ibid., p. 132). The price change is brought about by a change in investment

---

[18] He was criticized by reviewers for not doing so. See for example Robertson's review (1931) or Hayek's review (1931).

[19] It is not difficult to see the beginnings of the IS–LM framework in this quotation. This may explain why Keynes quickly accepted Hicks's (1937) summary.

relative to saving. Suppose that, following a change in expectations, investment increases relative to saving. Let the change in investment be represented by a point on the AM schedule above its intersection with the OM schedule in Figure 3.1. At this point, the price level of consumption goods is above its equilibrium value. Profits are positive; investment exceeds saving, so π also changes. Since we are still on the AM relation and money and income are unchanged, the ratio of the two, velocity, is unchanged. The trick is that income is defined net of profits, and the claimed implication depends entirely on the definition. For, if income included profits, velocity would rise with the increase in profits, given unchanged M.

The working of the simple model illustrates some of the analysis that Keynes attempted in the *Treatise* and brings out some main implications that he drew. Prices can change if there are changes in the desired distribution of money balances between income and financial or speculative balances, with the quantity of money unchanged. A change of this kind affects k_1 and k_2 in opposite directions. These changes affect the slope and position of the AM line. Shifts in the bearishness or bullishness of the public disturb equilibrium by changing AM and thus changing the rate of interest, the price level of consumption goods, and, therefore, profitability. Windfall profits also change the relation of saving and investment and, therefore, induce cyclical changes in relative and absolute prices. These changes in relative and absolute prices and their relation to changes in investment are the features of the business cycle that Keynes stressed in the *Treatise*.

The business cycle and disequilibrium dynamics

Despite its shortcomings, Keynes's model in the *Treatise* makes an important step forward by linking stocks and flows in the determination of equilibrium values of prices and interest rates. The determination of an equilibrium position, even one in which output is not fixed, is a long way from a model of the business cycle, however. My reading of the *Treatise* turns up many hints about dynamics but no sign of how the hints can be combined in a model of the business cycle.

At the time, the business cycle was considered a disequilibrium phenomenon. Marshall, Fisher, Schumpeter, Wicksell, and others regarded cycles as three- to five-year departures from the equilibrium position. The departures were cyclical in the sense that contractions were followed by recoveries, and booms were followed by recessions. The critical questions to be answered were: How did business cycles start? What determined the movement from one phase to another? What were the regularities that caused business cycles to follow a particular, recurrent path?

Keynes's model does not answer these questions. His discussion of disequilibrium in the *Treatise* is, in the Marshallian tradition, limited to departures from positions of equilibrium and the return to equilibrium. The dynamics are a less formal version of the dynamics practiced in many classrooms and used in many journal articles, after Metzler's (1951) use of phase diagrams to show the conditions for dynamic stability. Real-time analysis and timing relations are not attempted.

The treatment in the *Treatise* is an advance. In the *Tract* Keynes attempts to use the quantity equation to discuss the business or, in the Marshallian term he used, the *credit* cycle. His treatment is entirely descriptive. There are changes in average holdings of currency (k) and deposits (k') relative to consumption. Velocity is procyclical; "k and k' . . . diminish during the boom and increase during the depression" (4, p. 67). The values of k and k' depend on "the mood of the public and the business world" (ibid., p. 68). Since attitudes, moods, or, in current terms, anticipations, are not entirely predictable, Keynes concludes that the government should manipulate the stock of money or the cash reserve ratio of the banks to offset changes in average cash balances. These actions are presumed to be stabilizing.

The analysis in the *Tract* is less developed than the analysis in Irving Fisher's *The Purchasing Power of Money* (1911, Chapter 4). Fisher recognizes the importance of real shocks, such as crop failures and inventions, in addition to monetary (gold) changes (ibid., p. 70). The main cause of the cycle, however, is not the shocks, but the lag in the adjustment of prices and interest rates to prior changes either in money (gold) or real variables. Bank lending, at rates that do not fully reflect the future rise in prices, increases domestic loans and deposits and sustains expansions. Although Fisher's description is more detailed than Keynes's *Tract*, it, too, lacks an explanation of the changes in the velocities of currency and deposits and is vague about the effect of these changes on real output.

The discussion of cyclical fluctuations in the *Treatise* fills several chapters. Keynes, applying his model, defined the cycle as "alternations of excess and defect in the cost of investment over the volume of saving and the accompanying seesaw in the purchasing power of money due to these alternations" (5, p. 249). To a modern reader, the emphasis given to price changes and the relative neglect of changes in output and employment is striking. Movements of aggregate output and employment remain in the background. To Keynes, as to many of his contemporaries, cycles meant changes in prices – usually called inflation and deflation – but the latter terms were used to refer not only to price changes but also to the changes in nominal values that cause the price changes. Keynes, for example, defines commodity inflation as the difference between the cost of investment and the volume of saving, $I' - S$, and income inflation as the rise in efficiency wages (ibid., pp. 140, 249). Thus the credit or business cycle is the sum of income inflation and commodity inflation (ibid., p. 249).

The increase in the cost of investment, I', hence the cycle, has monetary and nonmonetary causes[20]:

> It may be a new invention, or the development of a new country, or a war, or a return of "business confidence" . . . Or, the thing may start – which is more likely if it is a monetary cause which is playing the chief part – with a stock exchange boom . . . eventually affecting by sympathy the price of new capital goods. (ibid., p. 271)

The change in the expected return on investment, raises "the natural rate of interest" relative to the market rate (ibid.).[21]

Keynes, then, discusses the typical sequence of events. Output and the price of capital goods rise. Employment increases with wages unchanged at first. Increased spending by the newly employed raises consumer prices. Producers of consumer goods reap windfall profits, so they bid for factors of production by offering higher rates of remuneration. At first, the expansion is financed by reductions in average cash balance, without large increases in money (ibid., pp. 271–2). As in Fisher's earlier discussion of changes in velocity or Keynes's *Tract*, the procyclical increase in velocity (or decline in average cash balance) is the arithmetic result of changes in transactions and output relative to money. A principal difference is that the *Treatise* has an extended discussion of investment and the rise in the expected return, but there is no mention at first of liquidity preference or of a relation between the change in expected return to investment and the public's desire to hold money.

Liquidity preference, or "bear sentiment," enters later, moved by a shift in anticipations. Those who remember previous crises may see "a little further ahead than the business world or the banking world."

---

[20] Later, Keynes "unreservedly" accepts Schumpeter's explanation of major changes in investment (6, pp. 85–6). Schumpeter's explanation emphasizes real factors, such as invention and innovation of new products and new technologies, as the forces initiating changes in investment. As noted in the text, Keynes accepted monetary changes among the factors initiating the change in investment, but the *Treatise* emphasizes what would now be called real shocks.

[21] These terms were taken from Wicksell, as Keynes notes (5, p. 139). They are, of course, different from the terms Keynes used to introduce his theory.

Their bearish sentiment encourages them to hold money. This shift in anticipations by bears and the increased demand for money by transactors, not a reduction in supply, sends market rates above the natural rate (ibid., pp. 272–3).

The change in bearish sentiment is one of three sufficient conditions for an end to the expansion that Keynes mentions. The others are a decline in the attractiveness of new investment and a decline in the prices of consumption goods following the increase in the production of these goods. Only the last can be thought of as a consequence of the working of his model. The sudden change in bearish sentiment and the decline in opportunities are simply imposed or assumed.

Keynes's attempt (ibid., Chapter 20) to write down an algebraic version of his theory of the cycle does not resolve this problem. It is interesting only for its lengthy statement of the many assumptions required to complete the algebraic restatement and the confusing and rather turgid discussion of the algebraic equations. Of particular interest are two of his seven assumptions. First, wages are fixed (money costs of production constant) whereas prices change (ibid., p. 275).[22] Second, everyone currently forecasts the course of the credit cycle (ibid., p. 276). Later, he relaxes these assumptions by letting the change in wages reinforce the rise in prices and by allowing for inaccurate forecasts.

When wages are permitted to change, Keynes does not mention any effect of the higher real wage on output, and he never considers that real wages may rise cyclically. This oversight is revealing since a sufficient rise in real wages or costs of production would lower profits and abort the expansion. The most obvious explanation for the absence of this argument is that he assumed throughout that real wages and costs fall during expansions (or inflations in his terminology) and rise in contractions (deflations), that is, that costs and wages lag. This assumption is explicit in his discussion at several points and is important for his argument, based on windfall profits (5, pp. 185–6, 197, 254–5; 6, pp. 164–5; 13, pp. 109–10).

Forecasts are "certain to be imperfect, and likely, moreover, in the present state of ignorance, to have a bias in one direction" (5, p. 292). The bias comes from excessive reliance on today's spot price and its recent rate of change as an estimate of the price at which new production will sell in the future. Expectations are now extrapolative.

---

[22] The *Tract* mentions that it is "a commonplace of economic text-books that wages tend to lag behind prices" (4, p. 25). The following pages then discuss some reasons why this might not be true in a rapid inflation. There are many other references to wage rigidity or wage inflexibility in his writings during the 1920s. (See 19, p. 121, where he blames unions; see also 17, p. 429; 19, pp. 762–3, 776; 9, pp. 70–1; and 13, p. 360.)

When prices have been rising, future prices are overestimated, so output increases too much; when prices have been falling, producers are pessimistic about future prices, so they lower output. Once again there is a kind of Phillips curve, dependent on rigid wages (or costs of production) and extrapolative price expectations (ibid.).

The fundamental equations have no direct bearing on his discussion of the cycle. They are identities and remain in the background, but they influence the way in which the analysis proceeds. Keynes believed that, unlike the quantity equation, the fundamental equations focus attention on the nonmonetary factors that he regarded as most important. The equations direct attention, Keynes said, to the earnings from the production of investment and consumption goods and to the division of earnings between saving and spending on consumption (ibid., p. 121). When saving is equal to investment, the price equals the cost of producing consumer goods. Profits are zero, and the economy remains in a stationary position. When saving and investment are unequal, the fundamental equations show that the economy generates profits or losses. The framework, summarized in Figure 3.1, shows that Keynes went beyond his fundamental identities to formulate relations between prices and interest rates. I cannot find any evidence that he developed this framework into a theory of fluctuations in output and employment. In fact, he could not since real output is fixed. He was shocked, however, when Hayek (1931), in his review of the *Treatise*, argued that he had failed to produce a theory of fluctuations.[23]

Criticisms of the quantity theory

The *Tract* describes the quantity theory as "fundamental" (4, p. 61) and, immediately after, as a truism, (ibid., n. 2). As in Mill, money has no utility and is held only for its purchasing power: "The *number* of notes which the public ordinarily have on hand is determined by the amount of *purchasing power* . . . and by nothing else" (ibid., p. 62). Purchasing power depends on wealth and habits of payment. Inflation reduces the demand for money as soon as people recognize that inflation is a tax on cash balances (ibid., p. 41). These systematic influences on the demand for money reappear in the *Treatise*, where again long-run neutrality is not denied (5, p. 132).

In fact, Keynes went further. In a letter to Pigou (13, p. 217) he disavowed any claim that his equations were inconsistent with the Cambridge equation. He is more critical of the Fisher equation. The dif-

---

[23] I discuss some of these points in a later section.

ference, he explained in a response to Robertson (ibid., p. 231), is that the Fisher equation concerns the volume and price level of transactions, whereas the variables in his own equations are the volume and price level of output. He believed this was an important distinction, and it is one basis for his claim that his identities are a more useful framework. Picking up the theme of his discussion of index numbers, Keynes argues that the quantity equation does not focus on purchasing power "because the relative importance of different articles as objects of monetary transactions is not the same as their relative importance as objects of consumption" (5, p. 68). Fluctuations in the price level are accompanied by changes in relative prices:

> The failure of wages to move quickly with the wholesale standard or with the international standard over short periods and the ability of wages to have a trend of their own over long periods is, indeed, probably the largest part of the actual explanation of the failure of different price levels to move together. (ibid., p. 83)

In a footnote, (ibid., pp. 82–3), he points out that the *Tract* recognizes the relation between relative and absolute price changes, but the emphasis on relative price changes in the *Treatise* is markedly different.[24] Observation and experience in the 1920s was not the only reason for the change. The *Treatise* (6, pp. 135–65) discusses several previous, historical episodes in which studies showed that wages lagged behind prices during inflations and deflations. Principal among these are the studies by Earl J. Hamilton, particularly Hamilton's (1929) summary of the effect of gold discoveries on Spanish prices and wages. Keynes also cites the experience of France and Spain during the seventeenth century as evidence of the importance of relative price changes for economic development. The driving mechanism in progress, he concludes, is the increase in profits resulting from the increase in prices relative to wages. The rise in profits increases investment relative to saving and builds the capital stock (6, p. 141). In deflation, the opposite occurs. Saving exceeds investment and is wasted, as happened, he believed, in Britain from 1891 to 1896 (ibid., p. 150).

These and other historical episodes, including the 1920s, are used to support his criticism of the quantity theory and to show the usefulness of his theory. Further, he claims, the quantity theory does not distinguish between profit inflation and income inflation – price changes

---

[24] The much quoted statement: "*In the long run* we are all dead" appears in the *Tract* (4, p. 65) as part of Keynes's discussion of short-run nonhomogeneity in the relation of money to prices. There, Keynes develops the effect of inflation on average cash balances but not on relative prices.

resulting in changes in profits and leading, therefore, to changes in investment, and price changes resulting in changes in income, profits remaining unchanged in real terms. He wrote to Pigou:

> (i) . . . I can distinguish between price changes due to an alteration of E [nominal earnings] and those due to changes in Q [profits]. I claim that this distinction is vital. If E increases by a given amount and at the same time Q diminishes by an equal amount, according to you nothing has happened. But according to me a vital fact is disclosed. For I distinguish between price changes which correspond to changes in cost and those which do not; whereas for you they are all the same.
>
> (ii) I am enabled to arrive at an equation for P the price level of consumption . . .
>
> (iv) I can show how changes in Q are related to changes in I and S. By these means I can analyze the credit cycle. (13, pp. 215–16)

For Keynes, these differences were not matters of detail. Investment was the driving force in progress. Further, he believed that periods of profit inflation and the "short period" during which there were differences between I and S, or between rates of change of prices and wages, persisted for years not months. "A 'short period' is quite long enough to include . . . the rise and the fall of the greatness of a nation" (6, p. 141).[25]

In the *Treatise*, the quantity theory is criticized for two main faults. It does not focus attention on those factors that are central to the process by which cyclical changes occur – investment, profits, and relation of prices to costs of production. And, the standard (or price index) is an artificial construct, based on transactions, whereas the more appropriate standard is either the labor standard or the purchasing power standard (5, p. 120): "Human effort and human consumption are the ultimate matters from which alone economic transactions are capable of deriving any significance" (ibid.).

Investment and profits are the forces driving expansion, contraction, and the business cycle.[26] Based on his interpretations of the sixteenth

---

[25] Two footnotes to this passage (6, p. 141, n. 2, 3) cite Smith as allowing 90 years for adjustment of prices and 66 years for the rise in prices in England during the sixteenth and seventeenth century. Keynes estimates the period of "profit" inflation as 70 years in Spain, 100 years in England, and 170 years in France (ibid., p. 141).

[26] An early draft of the *Treatise* contains the following comment of interest for the historian of economic thought or the sociologist of science: "Even when the initiating cause [of the cycle] is of an entirely non-monetary character such as . . . Professor Pigou's somewhat, mythical [sic] 'psychological errors of optimism and pessimism' . . ." (13, p. 89).

and seventeenth centuries, Keynes might have assigned a dominant role to the increase in wealth following gold discoveries, but he did not. The critical force was investment, and this depended on profits and ultimately on the cost or wage lag. He had not yet formulated a consumption function, but he recognized that expansion also depended on the willingness of people to spend more as incomes rose. Increased spending for investment and consumption required that additions to money (gold) not be held as a "hoard" but should be used for transactions. This led Keynes to formulate hypotheses about the demand for money and changes in the demand for money.

As early as 1924, he described the *Treatise* as a study of price changes. Price changes occur "either by a change on the side of bank money (up or down) – which is what attention has been generally concentrated upon; or by a change on the side of real balances (down or up) – which may be just as important, particularly over short periods" (13, p. 21; see also, 5, p. 235). The discussion of disequilibrium lists three forces that can cause price changes. These are the supply of money, investment, and the demand for money (5, pp. 231–4).

For analytic purposes, Keynes reduced these three forces to two – oscillations about the equilibrium position and transitions from one equilibrium to another. Oscillations, he believed, arise mainly from changes in the natural rate relative to the market rate. These change investment relative to saving and are the main factor in the credit cycle. Thus, he arrived at a theory of the cycle in which real factors affecting the natural rate have a dominant role and monetary factors, although not dismissed, are either of secondary importance or a response to real factors (ibid., pp. 233, 248–9). In the business cycle theory of the *Treatise*, cycles are mainly the result of real shocks that produce windfall profits or losses and, by changing prices, investment, and interest rates, induce changes in the demand for money and in intermediation.

The *Treatise* devotes many pages to intermediation. Variations in the mix of deposits held for different purposes (income, business, and savings) are the principal source of fluctuations in velocity (6, p. 30, 38). In periods of great distrust of money – the period of inflation following World War I is his example – there is a flight from money and, therefore, a rise in velocity (ibid., pp. 40–1). At other times, Keynes believed, velocity varies with the benefits of convenience and the opportunity cost of holding money. The latter is subject to more frequent change, so the principal short-term forces affecting velocity are (1) interest rates and changes in the demand for working capital and (2) price expectations (ibid., pp. 38–9).

Keynes's criticisms of the constancy of velocity, like his criticisms of the quantity theory, are not sweeping reversals of his earlier positions. They are more in the nature of proposed advances that explore systematic relations between velocity and the sources of variability during business cycles.

The open economy

Most of the *Treatise* ignores the repercussions on exchange rates, foreign lending, and trade, but sections of the *Treatise* have much to say on these topics. Keynes regarded his work on international values as preliminary (5, p. 293), but his discussions of the gold standard, the effects of the U.S. stock market boom, and his proposals for monetary reform depend on his theory of open economy relations.

In the *Tract*, Keynes is skeptical about purchasing power parity as a short-run theory of exchange rates, but he accepted the theory, with some qualification, as a determinant of the long-run equilibrium exchange rate (4, pp. 78–80). The *Treatise* has a more developed analysis of the condition for external equilibrium. Keynes supplements the fundamental equations and modifies the definition of output and investment to take account of exports and imports and net foreign lending, respectively.

The foreign balance B is the net balance of a country's trade (net exports), and net foreign lending L is the net balance on capital account (5, pp. 118–19). Hence,

$$L = B + G \tag{3.9}$$

where G is the net gold flow. Foreign lending and gold flows supplement domestic saving as a source of financing for total investment I. There are now two equilibrium conditions, one internal and one external (ibid., p. 146). To sustain internal equilibrium,

$$I = I_1 + L - G \quad \text{and} \quad I_1 = S_1 \tag{3.10}$$

where I_1 and S_1 are home investment and home saving. To sustain external equilibrium, gold flows must be zero, so in equilibrium,

$$L = B \tag{3.11}$$

An open economy raises two relevant policy issues. The first arises from the relation between relative interest rates and relative prices at home and abroad. The central bank can alter relative prices and encourage equilibrium in the trade account by changing interest rates, thereby changing domestic investment. Second, on a gold standard or in any fixed exchange rate system, the primary obligation of the central bank is to maintain external equilibrium. Often, this requires the central bank to achieve external equilibrium at the expense of, possibly prolonged, departures from internal equilibrium.

According to Keynes, the problem lies in the sluggish adjustment of trade and production costs. In many countries, the trade balance adjusts slowly, particularly to reductions in the relative price of domestic goods. The reason is that money costs of production adjust slowly, particularly when internal equilibrium requires cost reduction. The result is that external equilibrium is achieved at the expense of lower domestic investment and higher unemployment (ibid., p. 192). This reduces progress and domestic welfare until costs fall and internal equilibrium is restored. The discussion is abstract and analytical, but there is an obvious connection to the problems faced by Britain following the return to gold:

> If the volumes of foreign lending and of the foreign balance and the internal money costs of production are all of them very susceptible to small changes in interest rates, prices and the volume of employment respectively, then the simultaneous preservation both of external and internal equilibrium will present no difficult problem. Much current theory assumes too lightly, I think, that the above conditions of susceptibility are in fact fulfilled in the present-day world. But this assumption is unsafe. In some countries (but not all) the volume of foreign lending is easily influenced, and in most countries, the money costs of production show but little resistance to an upward movement. But in many countries the volume of the foreign balance is sticky when it is a question of increasing it to meet a change in the external situation; and so are the money costs of production when it is a question of a movement downwards. (ibid., pp. 148–9)

Again, Keynes did not stop with the statement of identities or equilibrium conditions. He introduces explicit hypotheses by making L depend on relative interest rates at home and abroad, adjusted for risk, and B depend on the relative prices of domestic and foreign goods (ibid., pp. 192, 293). We can, therefore, rewrite equation (3.11) as an equilibrium condition:

$$-L(r/r^*) + B(P/P^*_{\cdot}X) = 0 \qquad (3.12)$$

where the asterisk indicates a foreign variable and X is the exchange rate. The partial derivatives of L with respect to r and of B with respect to P are negative; increases in domestic interest rates sustain higher domestic price levels and external equilibrium, and reductions in interest rates require price reductions to prevent a gold outflow.[27]

The principal implications of the analysis of external stability are for the position of monetary equilibrium and the adjustment to disequilibrium (ibid., pp. 293–5). Keynes distinguishes the effects of changes in the price level at home and abroad from the more lasting effects of changes in relative interest rates. In his references to interest rates in this discussion, Keynes clearly has in mind changes in real returns. The entire discussion concerns changes in investment abroad relative to investment at home, and, as is often true of Keynes's discussions, his concern is not limited to pure theory. The contemporary problem is the position of the United States relative to Britain in the 1920s, particularly during the stock market boom at the end of the decade.

A change in the foreign price level, under a gold standard, must eventually be matched by a change in prices at home. The adjustment occurs through an inflow or outflow of gold. There are temporary effects on interest rates and other variables but, once the change in domestic prices is completed, equilibrium is restored at unchanged real values.

A change in foreign interest rates has a permanent effect on domestic saving and investment. Suppose interest rates rise abroad under the influence of higher expected returns (ibid., p. 298). There is an outflow of loans to foreigners, L increases, and gold flows out. To restore equilibrium domestic interest rates must rise, so the central bank must raise bank rate, lowering home investment and retarding foreign lending. Following the rise in interest rates, $S > I$, so prices and profits fall. Costs and factor earnings must fall to restore equilibrium. The declines in costs, W, and in prices of domestic output resulting from $S > I$ increase the export balance, and the higher interest rate retards L. Eventually $B = L$, and the gold flow stops.

The new equilibrium following the rise in foreign interest rates differs from the old. At the new, higher interest rate, foreign lending has increased relative to domestic saving, so net exports, B, must be larger to balance the larger L. Output is diverted abroad, and domestic prices

---

[27] We can combine the internal and external conditions for the output market into a single equation, using the open-economy equilibrium condition and the definition of investment, equations (3.10) and (3.12) of the text. I suppress the subscripts on I and S and hold foreign variables and the exchange rate fixed. The slope of the OM line in Figure 3.1 becomes

$$\left.\frac{dr}{dP}\right|_{\text{OM}} = \frac{-S_Y Y_P - B_P + I_P}{S_r - I_r}$$

must be sufficiently lower than foreign prices to sustain the rise in *B*. During adjustment, the gold flow facilitates the price change by raising foreign prices and lowering domestic prices. If capital is mobile, the rate of interest must be the same in each country and equal to the natural rate (ibid., pp. 299–300).

The change in factor prices and real incomes at home depends on the gain or loss of efficiency following the diversion of resources to produce goods for export and to sustain higher net exports. Typically, Keynes reasoned, money earnings at home fall relative to earnings abroad; the terms of trade change in favor of the foreign country.[28] The home country benefits, however, from higher interest payments on foreign loans and from lower cost of the imported products produced with the new investment abroad.

The adjustment of the terms of trade can be painful. The adjustment depends on elasticities of demand, on the relative efficiency of the increased production sold abroad to raise *B* (ibid., p. 301), and on the monetary policies of the two countries (ibid., pp. 302–4). Countries can choose to allow monetary gold stocks to change or can avoid such changes. The alternative to allowing gold to flow out, thus raising prices abroad, is to lower costs at home. Allowing gold to flow in, however, requires the foreign country to adjust prices and earnings upward, in Keynes's terminology to experience "income inflation." In either case, the adjustment of prices and costs continues until the natural rate of interest is equal to the market rate in both countries.[29] The cost of the adjustment and the distribution of the cost between the domestic and foreign publics depends on whether prices must rise or fall at home and abroad.

Changes in relative interest rates have more lasting and more painful

---

[28] Keynes regarded his argument (5, pp. 296–7) as a response to Ohlin's criticism of the analysis of the transfer problem he made in *The Economic Consequences of the Peace*. He cites evidence accumulated by Taussig to support his conclusion (ibid., pp. 296, 300). His general view appears to be that long-run equilibrium is maintained because an outflow of gold induces the central bank to raise the home country interest rate, thereby changing prices, profits, and investment. Long-run equilibrium is determined by the current account and short-run position by the capital account. In a 1932 article, he writes: "Thus in the long run the influence of the income transactions wears away that of the capital transactions like drops of a waterfall upon a stone. The analogy is a good one. We can be certain that the waterfall will win in the end, but it may be a long time" (21, p. 75).

[29] Keynes then discusses the flow of lending to the United States in 1928–9. This flow did not arise, in his judgment at the time, from an increase in the natural rate. The cause was financial – an increase in the demand for money in the United States. The result was a rise in lending to the United States that was not accompanied by net imports into the United States. Hence, he said, the rest of the world did not get the stimulus of net exports and lost gold. A different version of his analysis is in his correspondence with Burgess, discussed in Chapter 2.

consequences, he concluded, than changes in relative prices that induce short-term changes in the trade balance. Lending to take advantage of increased opportunities abroad requires a country to reduce its costs of production. He clearly has the late 1920s in mind:

> If there is resistance to this fall, gold will flow, bank rate will rise and unemployment become chronic. This is particularly likely to happen if the prevalence of tariffs against manufactured goods (and a readiness to raise them when imports of such goods are increasing) renders the foreign demand for the old country's exports inelastic, whilst at the same time trade unions in the old country present great obstacles to a reduction of money wages. (ibid., p. 312)

Keynes's summary judgment in the *Treatise* is that the "troubles and inconveniences of the transition [to increased foreign lending] may be very great" (ibid., p. 311). Although much of his discussion is general, there is no reason to doubt that the circumstances in Britain following the return to gold motivate his discussion. Within a few months, his memorandum to the Economic Advisory Council (13, pp. 178–200) more openly discusses some of the advantages of forbidding foreign lending. The principal economic advantages he cites are that equilibrium real wages are higher (ibid., p. 185) and the domestic capital stock is larger, at least for a time (ibid., pp. 196, 199). Keynes's argument for some type of exchange control and his advocacy of controls repeats a theme found in his earlier (19, p. 573) and later writings.

Problems with the gold standard

The analytic basis of Keynes's criticisms of the return to gold at the prewar parity is found in the *Treatise*, particularly in his discussion of foreign lending. His criticisms and his efforts to overcome the perceived weaknesses of the gold standard are the foundation for his proposals that later became the Bretton Woods agreement.

Early in the *Treatise* Keynes explains that the principal difference between proponents and opponents of the return to the gold standard earlier in the decade was not a choice of a managed rather than an automatic standard or, in modern parlance, of limited discretion versus fixed rules. There was "no likelihood or possibility" of an unmanaged gold standard (5, p. 18).

There were two major problems. First, the proponents of gold wanted to return to the prewar gold parity without waiting for money incomes to fall to the level consistent with the prewar parity. The opponents believed it desirable either to devalue relative to gold or to wait until money values declined. Part of the difference between the two groups arose because the proponents were misled by reliance on the wholesale price index instead of an index of consumption goods (ibid., pp. 66–79). Second, the opponents of gold favored a tabular standard as an improvement over the gold standard (ibid., pp. 18–19). Later in the *Treatise*, Keynes proposed such a standard based on a basket of internationally traded commodities (6, pp. 350–4).

The specific flaws in the return to gold were the result of the failure to recognize the main point of his fundamental equations. The two conditions necessary for the price level to remain at the equilibrium required by the return to the prewar gold parity are (1) that $I = S$ and (2) that money costs of production, W, be reduced to a level consistent with the full employment price level. Money incomes had to fall by 10 percent (6, p. 162).

The Bank of England was able to bring the price level down in the traditional way. The mistake was to believe that the prewar gold parity required only that purchasing power parity be restored. In a passage very much in the spirit of his earlier criticisms, Keynes summarizes the proponents' error: "Equilibrium required that the flow of money incomes and the rate of money earnings per unit of output should be appropriately reduced. But in the first instance the fall of prices reduced, not costs and rates of earnings, but profits" (ibid., p. 163).

The efforts to reduce wages and costs of production led to a general strike. The end of the strike was not followed by a general decline in money wages. Wages fell in some industries but not in the aggregate, so adjustment to the new equilibrium was delayed until it could be brought about by an increase in efficiency.[30]

Foreign investment made the adjustment problem worse. The usual effect of a higher home cost of production is to reduce the trade balance B, but to this was added the attractiveness of foreign investment L. Keynes's analysis implied that, with slow adjustment of prices, B did not rise to finance L, so it became necessary to raise the rate of interest to reduce L and prevent a gold outflow. This had the effect of reducing home investment as well as foreign investment (ibid., p. 166). Since profits fell, home investment that would increase efficiency became less attractive. The use of tariffs by the United States and, later, the world depression added to the burden of adjustment by making it more

---

[30] Keynes cites Bowley's index of weekly wage rates to support his claim (6, pp. 164–5). He estimates the cost of the unemployment resulting from the return to gold as £100 million per annum for several years (ibid., p. 165). He suggests that Britain could have been "perhaps, just about as rich as the United States" if they had devalued gold and stabilized at the 1920 price and cost level (ibid., pp. 161–2).

difficult to increase British exports (ibid.). So investment and progress were sacrificed.

Keynes regarded this sequence as an application of his monetary theory, and he used it to support an important policy conclusion: opposition to an international system based on laissez-faire. Rejection of laissez-faire in international trade and lending was based on his judgment that (1) the British standard of living was higher than in most of the world, (2) population growth was slow, and (3) saving remained at 10 percent of income. In a closed system, the natural rate of interest would fall in these circumstances. Under the gold standard, the saving flowed abroad to finance foreign investment. Eventually, interest payments on previous investments would rise to pay for net lending. Until that happened, exports exceeded imports:

> Having regard to the tariff walls against us, to the gradual disappearance . . . of the special advantages in manufacture which used to be ours, and to the high real wages (including in this the value of social services) to which our workers are accustomed as compared with our European competitors, one cannot but feel a doubt whether the attainment of equilibrium on the line of an expanding trade surplus will in fact be practicable. (ibid., p. 169)

The best alternative, for a country faced with these problems is to achieve equilibrium in the usual way – by exporting to finance foreign lending. If that is impractical because of tariffs or other barriers, there are two alternatives. One is to adjust the rate of interest on domestic lending by subsidizing domestic investment. The other is to change the relative prices of foreign and domestic goods. Keynes clearly preferred the use of investment subsidies, including government investment at below market rates of interest (ibid., pp. 169, 337–8). The *Treatise* does not, however, dismiss tariffs or other devices to raise the cost of imported goods under the circumstances of the time (ibid., p. 169).

He considered other alternatives. One was to abandon the gold standard or make it less rigid. Keynes's *Treatise* repeats his proposal in the *Tract* (4, p. 150) to allow the central bank to vary the gold points so as to adjust prices of exports and imports (6, pp. 290–2).[31] He believed this power would enable the central bank to reduce the domestic effects of correctly anticipated, temporary changes in foreign interest

---

[31] Although the proposals are similar, the change in the argument shows a change in Keynes's thinking from concern with price stability to concern with employment. The adjustment of the gold points in the *Tract* is a means of maintaining internal and external price stability. In the *Treatise*, the adjustment of the gold price is a means of changing aggregate output and income.

rates. Although his analysis distinguishes permanent and transitory changes in interest rates and prices, his proposal makes no use of this analysis and presumes that the central bank can use the power to smooth fluctuations.

Keynes also considers fluctuating exchange rates. Fluctuating rates reduce foreign lending by introducing an element of uncertainty (5, pp. 322–5). Fluctuating rates reduce the response of output to short-term changes in foreign interest rates and eliminate the requirement to change interest rates when interest rates change abroad.

Both changes in the gold points and fluctuating exchange rates overcome the principal disadvantage of the gold exchange standard – the requirement that domestic stability be sacrificed to maintain stability of the exchange rate. The main problem of the gold standard is that "there is no possibility of rapidly altering the balance of imports and exports to correspond" to frequent changes in foreign lending (6, p. 300). In a system with rigid wages, variation of interest rates to achieve external stability places the burden on domestic investment, profits, and employment. There is, therefore, excessive and avoidable variability in employment. The emphasis is no longer on the failuire of the gold standard as a system for achieving price stability; the problem is the variability of output and employment induced by price instability.

Monetary policy under the gold standard

The classical gold standard had been abandoned in 1914, and Keynes did not expect it to return. The managed gold standard gave scope to central bank management. This scope was greater for the United States, with its relatively large stock of gold, but there were opportunities for monetary management in Britain also.

In the *Tract*, Keynes described the policy choice as a choice between stable prices or stable exchange rates (4, p. 117), and he expressed a preference for stable prices (ibid., p. 126). The job of the central bank is to vary monetary policy so as to offset changes in the public's average cash balance (ibid., p 68). In the process of writing the *Treatise*, he both modified and amplified this position, distinguishing between a policy that stabilizes prices without regard to the effect on investment in working capital and a policy that satisfies the fluctuating demand for credit without producing instability in the price level (13, p. 90).[32] He, of course, favored the latter approach, and the *Treatise* reflects

---

[32] This section is an antecedent of Keynes's later discussion of "finance." In developing this line of thought, Keynes refers to Major Douglas as an example of an unorthodox writer who emphasized the importance of credit (13, p. 91). The reference to Douglas was eliminated in later drafts.

this preference. There, the object of monetary policy is "so to fix and maintain the effective bank rate as to keep saving and investment at an approximate equality throughout. For if it were to manage the currency successfully according to [this] criterion, the credit cycle would not occur at all" (5, p. 262). The market rate and the natural rate would coincide, economic profits would be zero, and prices would be stable (ibid., p. 142).

Complete stability of prices is not possible in practice because the natural rate varies, at times by large amounts (ibid., p. 143).[33] The natural rate is the rate at which $S = I$, and the market rate is the rate that actually prevails (ibid., p. 139; 6, p. 182). The latter is a mixture of short and long rates in much of Keynes's discussion. The short rate prevailing in the market is *bank rate*; *bond rate* refers to long-term rates (5, p. 179).

According to Keynes, effective discussion of monetary policy did not begin until 1837. Prior to that date, the usury laws kept bank rate fixed. The traditional doctrine after 1837 developed the idea that changes in bank rate change the quantity of money and the price level. The change in money is brought about either by domestic bank lending or by changes in foreign lending. A rise in bank rate reduces domestic lending but also attracts foreign balances. Which dominates? The traditional view is silent on this question (ibid., pp. 168–70). And, the traditional view of Marshall and others does not explain how changes in lending are transmitted to the price level.

Keynes was searching for a policy framework based on a general equilibrium explanation of the relation between money, interest rates and prices.[34] He recognized that Wicksell, and some later Continental writers influenced by Wicksell, had attempted to develop such a theory by relating money to interest rates and interest rates to investment and saving. His own theory is similar. A change in bank rate and market rate relative to the natural rate changes investment relative to saving. The effect on saving occurs directly; saving depends positively on the rate of interest. The *price* of capital goods depends on the net prospective yield on capital and on the rate of interest at which the future yield is capitalized (ibid., pp. 180–1). The price level of investment

---

[33] An alternative, available in a socialist system but not in a capitalist system, is to change money wages (and other costs) by fiat so as to maintain zero economic profits (5, p. 141). As in the *General Theory*, the main alternative to changes in money to stabilize prices is changes in money wages or costs of production. The fundamental equations express this idea.

[34] As early as 1913, Keynes criticized quantity theorists like Fisher for failing to develop a plausible, empirically supported explanation of the relation of money to prices and interest rates. He suggests there that the connection must be through investment (13, pp. 2–5).

goods, P', changes when the market rate of interest changes relative to the prospective yield. Bank rate has little effect on the prospective yield, however. That yield depends on market anticipations, after allowance for uncertainty (ibid., p. 180). Bank rate may affect future prospects by "throwing new light . . . on the policy and intentions of the currency authority" (ibid., p. 181). Keynes discards this effect in favor of the more direct effect. Bank rate changes the bond rate or long-term rate – the rate at which prospective yields are capitalized.

The *Treatise* rejects "elasticity pessimism" (ibid.; also 29, p. 365). The effect on investment may be small for very long-lived investment but investment is postponable. By raising interest rates, the central bank lowers P' below its normal value and encourages postponement (5, p. 182). The decline in P' reduces profits in the investment goods industry and the production of investment goods, while the increase in saving reduces consumption. With $S > I$, the price of consumption goods, P, falls. Profits are lower, so firms try to reduce costs by lowering W, and they reduce employment (ibid., pp. 186–7): "A tendency will, therefore, be set up to change the prevailing rate of earnings in the same direction as P and P' and *in the opposite direction* to bank rate" (ibid., p. 187, emphasis added).

Again, Keynes analyzes fluctuations (disequilibrium) by shifting curves and considering the effects on his equilibrium position. He reaches a conclusion consistent with Figure 3.1. Bank rate (or monetary) policy shifts the AM curve along OM, so P rises as r falls, and conversely, in response to changes in bank rate. There are complications that prevent a rapid response of prices and investment to changes in bank rate, but Keynes has little doubt that the "central bank can use its powers for easing (or stiffening) the credit situation to stimulate (or retard) the rate of new investment" (6, p. 331).

The business cycle is mainly a response to real shocks, but it is a monetary event in the sense that a prompt and proper monetary response could reduce the cycle. Keynes writes: "For the mere occurrence of a credit cycle is in itself a demonstration of the fact that the banking system has failed to change the market rate so as to keep pace with changes in the natural rate" (ibid., p. 325). Some instability is unavoidable, however. To effect a permanent change in the purchasing power of money, the central bank must change the market rate relative to the natural rate. The disturbance in the market rate changes investment relative to saving. The disequilibrium, $I - S$, causes profits or losses to firms and thus increases or decreases the demand for factors of production. Changes in factor demand, ultimately, induce changes in factor prices (5, p. 188).

Keynes is aware of some of the difficulties of coordination arising from anticipations, but he does not see some major problems. He recognizes that there are lags in the production of capital, so precise coordination of saving and investment cannot be achieved unless the central bank changes bank rate in anticipation of a change in saving (ibid., p. 187). He recognizes some of the difficulties in a policy of anticipating future changes in saving. The producers of capital goods must read a reduction in bank rate as a signal to produce more, while the producers of consumption goods must read the same signal as an indication to reduce production in anticipation of the rise in saving (ibid., pp. 187–8). Keynes does not discuss how producers distinguish a change in bank rate taken in anticipation of a future increase in saving from the change in bank rate taken in response to a reduction in the natural rate. In the latter case, the aim of policy is to lower market rates enough to match the decline in the natural rate and prevent a decline in saving and investment. Apparently, Keynes had not thought carefully about this issue. The unreliability or ambiguity of interest rates as an indicator of future events is not mentioned in this context.

Keynes's views contrast with the productive credit, or real bills doctrine, that has appealed to many central and private bankers. According to the usual version of that doctrine, bank earning assets consist of *productive* and *speculative* credit. Productive credit arises from the financing of inventories or goods in process that in the normal course of business will be sold at a profit. After the sale, the borrower liquidates the loan; thus productive credit is often described as self-liquidating. Proponents of the productive credit doctrine claim that, under a gold standard, discounting real bills prevents inflation and deflation.

Keynes favored a managed gold standard, with definite rules of management, to maintain price stability. In the 1920s he favored using interest rates to control credit. His 1920 proposal called for rates as high as 10 percent to end inflation (Howson 1973, in Wood 1, p. 445). On the other hand, low market interest rates did not necessarily imply that credit was available (19, p. 97). He criticized an increase in bank rate to 4 percent in 1923 as misguided; prices were falling. The bank was trying to manage the exchange rate instead of following the policy that Keynes favored, stabilizing prices and encouraging trade (19, pp. 100–1). As early as 1921, he outlined the effect of changes in bank rate along the lines that he later developed more fully in the *Treatise* (17, pp. 263–5). He distinguishes between short- and long-term rates and between real and nominal rates. Short rates oscillate around the long rate on "permanent investments" and should "oscillate sharply in accordance with temporary conditions" (ibid., p. 264). Short-term rates are driven mainly by the demand to borrow, given the gold stock (19, p. 82–5). Long rates are more stable, determined by the real return on investment.[35]

Keynes did not believe that banking and financial markets were efficient, particularly in Britain.[36] There are two ways in which inefficiency arises. First, he remarks that the variability of asset prices is too large to be explained by the variability of the underlying prospects for enterprise: "If investors were capable of taking longer views, the fluctuations in the natural rate of interest would not be so great as they are" (6, p. 324). This view, which became a dominant theme of the *General Theory*, is a sharp change from his earlier ridicule of Pigou for suggesting that there are waves of optimism and pessimism affecting investment.[37] Second, for Britain, Keynes mentions nonprice credit rationing as part of the process by which bank rate policy becomes effective. A so-called "fringe of unsatisfied borrowers" (5, p. 190; 6, pp. 326–7) stands ready to borrow more when lenders reduce eligibility requirements and can be cut off from loans by raising eligibility requirements. This fringe group strengthens the response of investment to changes in bank rate.

Monetary policy is procyclical, reinforcing fluctuations. The central bank delays the rise in market rates during economic expansions, thereby allowing prices to rise: "Booms, I suspect, are almost always due to tardy or inadequate action" (6, p. 332). In contractions, the central bank does not lower rates rapidly enough. Keynes concluded that central banks, by their hesitant policy, encouraged the contraction.[38]

A countercyclical monetary policy could be counted upon to expand investment. The principal limitation on the effectiveness of monetary action to lower interest rates was the complication arising from an international standard (5, p. 314; 6, p. 335). If international agreement to expand money and lower interest rates was not forthcoming, "government must itself promote a programme of domestic investment" (6, p. 337).

[35] If we replace short-term rates and long-term rates by actual and expected rates, we have Keynes's position in the *General Theory*.

[36] Keynes characterized the U.S. market as "more freely competitive" (6, p. 327). He did not believe that problems of credit rationing – to which so much effort has been directed – were important for the United States.

[37] See footnote 26. The proposition that variability is excessive has been revived in the work of Shiller (1981) and has spawned a large literature.

[38] This criticism is similar to the criticisms of monetarists in the postwar period. The monetarists drew a different conclusion about policy activism, however.

Fiscal policy

In the *Treatise* Keynes proposed two kinds of fiscal action to expand output when monetary expansion, under a gold standard (or other fixed exchange rate system), produced mainly an outflow of gold with little expansion of the economy's monetary base. Government can subsidize "approved types" of domestic investment or can direct investment programs (6, p. 337). The last proposal – state direction of investment – returns as a main recommendation in the *General Theory*.[39]

Keynes began the decade as a proponent of expenditure reduction, despite prevailing unemployment (19, pp. 2–3). He considered, also, the usefulness of a capital levy to reduce the burden of the debt (ibid., pp. 48–9) and as an alternative to an increase in income tax.

By 1924, his views had changed. He favored what became known as *pump priming*. The economy needed "an impulse, a jolt, an acceleration" (ibid., p. 220). The timidity of businessmen and the immobility of labor between industries due to trade unions and wage differentials are mentioned as causes of the persistent, high level of unemployment. Government can reduce unemployment by shifting from a policy of debt reduction to a policy of "replacing unproductive debt by productive debt" (ibid., p. 222). By spending up to £100 million a year on construction of houses, roads, and electricity and by monetary reform (such as he had proposed in the *Tract*), the level of output and employment could be raised (ibid., pp. 222–3). He saw the key to his proposal as the more effective use of available saving achieved by replacing foreign investment with more productive domestic investment.

At the end of the decade Keynes was offering proposals for "national development" in which government spending for investment would increase by £100 million a year. One reason for the change was that Keynes learned some facts about investment. He estimated that by 1927 two-thirds of the capital investment in Britain was managed by state enterprises and other nonprofit units (ibid., p. 696). There was, for him, no issue about whether this was desirable. Much of the in-

[39] This is not his only reference to fiscal policy as an alternative in a slump. Keynes's discussion of the 1892–5 depression in Britain concludes with a reference to public works: "It may have been a case where nothing but strenuous measures on the part of Government could have been successful" (6, p. 151). The *Treatise* also discusses fiscal policy in World War I (ibid., pp. 152–3). Earlier (13, pp. 22–3) Keynes had discussed debt finance and concluded: "The expenditure, on the production of *fixed* capital, of public money which has been raised by borrowing, can do nothing in itself to improve matters; and it may do actual harm" (ibid., p. 23).

vestment was in roads and infrastructure, so it was regarded as a state function by most citizens.

A second reason for the change was the analysis in the *Treatise* with its concentration on profits as the moving force in private investment and of investment as the moving force in the business cycle. Since state investment did not have to await profitable opportunities, Keynes had found a policy to expand the economy, increase progress and stability, while moving toward his social goals. In the theory developed in the *Treatise*, there is no difference in efficiency of private and public investment, a point on which he was explicit at times (ibid., pp. 808–9).

The argument for investment spending to be financed by government borrowing became the main point of the Liberal Party program in the 1929 election. Lloyd George pledged that, if elected, he would reduce unemployment from about 10 percent to the normal peacetime rate. His program called for investment spending to be paid for without raising taxes. Keynes and Hubert Henderson defended the proposal in *Can Lloyd George Do It?* (9, pp. 86–125).

Since Britain was on the gold standard, interest rates were set in world markets and could be assumed unchanged. The payment for the program, Keynes and Henderson said, came from three sources. First, expenditure for unemployment relief would be lower; second, as in the *Treatise*, saving that is "wasted" would, instead, finance productive investment; and, third, there would be a reduction in foreign lending as domestic demand increased (ibid., p. 116). To get the full benefit, the Bank of England would have to support the program by expanding credit and money (ibid., p. 117).

The argument of the *Treatise*, that saving can be wasted, is a major shift from his earlier position. The burden of Keynes's 1924 argument (19, pp. 219–23, 225–31) was that if saving is diverted from foreign to domestic investment, employment will rise (or rise sooner rather than later). The 1929 argument seeks to avoid the waste of saving by increasing investment and employment. The implication that employment and income can be raised is, of course, not possible under the analysis of the *Treatise*.

There is no doubt that Keynes's view had changed. Although the concept of the multiplier had not been developed formally, Keynes and Henderson point to the secondary effects on production and consumption. Part of the increased employment is achieved by increasing demands for materials and products used in the investment program and in the transport industries that haul the products. Further, the spending of the newly employed increases incomes, increases confidence, and has a cumulative effect (9, pp. 105–7).

In the debate that followed, Keynes is more explicit about the secondary effects of increased spending on employment, (19, p. 822), and he is clear about the difference between his argument and the "Treasury view": "They use an argument which would be correct *if everyone were employed already*, but is only correct *on that assumption*" (ibid., pp. 823, 830–1). He agreed that wage reduction would be a better alternative if it could be achieved. A reduction of real efficiency wages would "operate with greater efficacy and certainty" (ibid., p. 833). However, real wage reductions are "ruled out by political and social considerations. Therefore, we have to try the only alternative"[40] (ibid.).

Criticisms and responses

The *Treatise* did not achieve what Keynes intended – an accepted, new framework for analyzing the interaction of saving, investment, money, and prices. Critics attacked the foundations and failed to see the benefits of Keynes's approach. Reviews by Robertson and Hayek raised issues about the definitions Keynes had used for several of the key variables but, more importantly, criticized the theory as an inadequate explanation of the relation between money, prices, output, investment, and the rate of interest.[41]

Keynes gave ground slowly. Under the influence of Richard Kahn, Joan Robinson, and others, Keynes became convinced that his treatment of output was inadequate and that his statements about output did not follow from his theory. This led him, finally, to abandon the fundamental equations.

There is little reason to report the details of these arguments here. Instead, I concentrate on a few main points in the criticisms by Robertson and Hayek and in Kahn's work on the multiplier that were influential in recasting the argument, in moving Keynes from the ideas of the *Treatise* to those of the *General Theory*, or in showing why he

[40] The conservatives were defeated in the election, but Lloyd George and the liberals did not get the opportunity to redeem his pledge. The new Labour Party government increased nominal spending by £32 million in 1930, about one-third of the amount Keynes mentioned. This was the highest level of spending since 1921, and the first increase since 1926. Small additional increases were made in 1931 and 1932 (Mitchell 1976, p. 702). Note that Keynes does not take the position of the *General Theory* that wage reductions are undesirable because they increase price instability.

[41] Ralph Hawtrey corresponded with Keynes extensively at the time of publication. He offered many detailed comments, but what I take to be his major criticisms are more limited in scope. He disagreed with Keynes about the causes of unemployment. He believed Keynes placed too much emphasis on prices and costs and not enough on productive activity and sales. Further, Keynes neglected expectations (13, p. 167).

discarded ideas, like the real balance effect, which later became subjects of much professional attention.

Robertson's review (1931) mentions several issues that recurred later. One is the emphasis on interest rates rather than money in Keynes's explanation of the operation of monetary policy. Robertson takes some of the positions later identified as *monetarist*. Two others are the definition of saving and the compatibility of Keynes's theory with the quantity theory. Robertson criticizes Keynes's definition of saving on the grounds that incomes that are not earned during recessions – and thus are not spent – are considered as saved (1931, p. 407). Also, Robertson, like several others, noted the constancy of output in Keynes's theory and in his discussion of the so-called widow's cruse (ibid., pp. 405–9).

Two additional points in Robertson's review are Keynes's treatment of P and P' and his neglect of the real balance effect of a change in prices on money balances. Keynes replied to both of these comments (and others) after some private exchanges of letters and notes with Robertson.

Robertson devotes several pages to the lack of clarity in Keynes's treatment of the price of investment goods, P' and the relation of P' to the price of consumption goods P and to the rate of interest. One of his main points (1931, pp. 400–1) is that analysis of the relation between P and P' (or the rate of interest) during a business cycle must involve changes in the demand for money or hoarding. Robertson also questioned Keynes's failure to separate effects on the prices and demands for new and old capital and statements by Keynes suggesting that P and P' were determined independently.

Keynes's response (13, pp. 224–5) distinguishes the behavioral equations determining P or r from the effects on P and r in the general equilibrium system. Both P and r depend, in general equilibrium, on the forces in the capital market – the excess of saving over investment and the relation of savings deposits to the propensity to hold money (hoard). Further, Keynes replies (ibid., pp. 228–9), the price of existing capital moves with the price of new capital, the size of the change depending on the shape of the "curve which measures the propensity to hoard."

This exchange brought home to Keynes that he had not succeeded in communicating his theory of interest. Shortly thereafter, in the preface to the German edition and later in the Japanese edition, he shifted away from terms like "the degree of bearishness" and presented a more explicit statement phrased in terms of a demand curve for money (5, p. xxvii).

Robertson quotes Pigou's *Economics of Welfare*, written in 1920, as an early statement of the real balance effect of a change in prices on consumption spending. According to Robertson, Pigou had written: "What they have done by not spending their money has been to reduce prices in general below what they would otherwise have been, thus making the money of other people worth more goods than it would otherwise have been worth, and thus *enabling these people to buy more goods*" (1931, p. 410, n. 1, emphasis added). In the same section (ibid., pp. 407–8), Robertson argued that Keynes had neglected the effect of price changes (called inflation) on wealth. Even if profits in Keynes's sense are always zero, "it would still be possible for the Government or the banking system, by means of inflation, to transfer real income to itself or its nominees" (ibid., p. 407). Further, Robertson notes that, according to Keynes's argument, real wealth remains unchanged if entrepreneurs spend profits on consumption. This neglects the reduction in real money balances, and therefore in wealth, that results from the price increase accompanying the increased spending (ibid., pp. 409–10).

Robertson tried to relate the real balance effect and the effect on saving to his, always complicated, discussion of hoarding and lacking. This continued an old dispute between them; they had covered similar ground in the past. As early as 1925, Keynes had denied a real balance effect on aggregate consumption.[42] An earlier version of the *Treatise* (13, p. 105) also dismisses Robertson's "induced lacking" under which saving rises to compensate (in part) for reductions in real money balances when prices rise.[43] Keynes's rejoinder to Robertson's review does not take up this issue in detail.

The exchange with Hayek is much less friendly. Hayek praises the shift in emphasis from money to interest rates, saving, and investment

---

[42] "In assuming that the public as a whole has to reduce its current consumption when inflation takes place you overlook the fact that whilst some depositors may as the result of the inflation have less real resources at the bank, other depositors have more" (Keynes to Robertson, May 1925, 13, p. 35). Keynes neglects the transfer to the government from the public, a surprising omission in the light of his earlier discussion of the inflation tax.

[43] An abbreviated version of the argument appears in the *Treatise* (5, p. 154, n. 1, p. 269). See also (13, pp. 286–7) the 1932 exchange where Keynes decides that induced lacking arises from the effect on saving of changes in windfall profits. He again (ibid., p. 288) dismisses the real balance effect as ambiguous, the ambiguity arising from Keynes's uncertainty about whether the effort to maintain living standards, following a rise in prices, raises current consumption or raises saving. Robertson's response is not entirely clarifying (ibid., pp. 291–3). Keynes's conclusion (ibid., pp. 276–7) is that all of the discussion of lacking and hoarding can be reduced to a single equation:

$$\Delta Q = \Delta I + \Delta F$$

where Q is windfall profits, I is investment, and F is the amount of money spent on consumption.

as an important break with the Cambridge tradition, but he describes Keynes's exposition as "difficult, unsystematic and obscure" (1931, p. 271). Much of Keynes's response is an attack on Hayek's *Prices and Production*, which he characterizes as "one of the most frightful muddles I have ever read," a book that demonstrates "how, starting with a mistake, a remorseless logician can end up in Bedlam" (13, p. 252).

Hayek (1931, pp. 277–8) criticized Keynes's use of aggregates such as capital, net investment, and profits and the lack of clarity in his definitions. Changes in investment and capital can mean the value of the increment of capital or the increment in the value of capital (ibid., pp. 280–1). These, and many other criticisms, reflect unresolved issues, ambiguities or errors in Keynes's definitions and shifting use of terms. Four of Hayek's many criticisms are of interest for later work.

First, Hayek's work on *Prices and Production* helps Hayek to realize that the *Treatise* lacks a theory of supply. The fact that nominal income and factor payments are equal "does not prove that the cost of *current output* need necesssarily also be the same" (1931, pp. 282–4). Hayek argues that the equality of current income and cost of production holds only in a full equilibrium and does not hold generally in a dynamic process (ibid.). He traces the problem to Keynes's definition of income and his fundamental equations (ibid., p. 287). Hayek is the first to point out that Keynes's measure of output is fixed as of some base date, the same point later made by Alvin Hansen (5, pp. 329–30).[44]

Second, Hayek notes (1931, p. 277) that Keynes's definition of W includes all costs of production (and all factor payments except windfalls). This implies that W cannot be fixed while prices and interest rates change. Changes in interest rates, for example, change the payments to lenders and thus change the cost of production. More generally, if consumption prices and the interest rate are determined simultaneously, as in Figure 3.1, all such changes necessarily affect cost of production, profits, and output.

Third, there are major differences about the theory of interest. Hayek uses a type of "loanable funds" theory in which the *change* in money, not the stocks of money and hoards, interacts with saving and investment to determine hoards (1931, pp. 290, 293). Keynes's response (13, pp. 246–50, 253) brings out some of the differences and insists that his theory is not "an embroidered version" of the old theory (ibid., p. 247).

---

[44] In his reply to Hansen, Keynes introduces a free parameter to keep the units consistent. In a dynamic theory of output, the free parameter would change, so the problem is not resolved.

Fourth, Hayek claims Keynes offers a theory of the cycle in which monetary disturbances set off changes in spending and its distribution between consumption and investment. Keynes responds that there can be nonmonetary shocks; saving and investment can differ without any change in money (ibid., p. 251). He restates his definition of saving and repeats his belief that if saving and income are defined to include profits, then "saving and the value of investment are identically the same thing." Keynes had not yet learned to distinguish between planned and actual magnitudes.

A further issue raised in Keynes's response is the interpretation of the natural rate of interest. Keynes interprets Hayek's natural rate as the rate that equals the market rate "if the prevailing relationship of capital to consumption were to be permanent" (ibid., p. 253) and everyone believed this to be true. His own "natural rate" does not require that the rate of investment remain at its permanent value. Keynes's natural rate is the rate "which would at any moment equalise saving and investment, after taking account of the existing psychology of the market, including errors of forecasting" (ibid., p. 254). This discussion reappears, with some changes, in the *General Theory* when Keynes discusses (7, pp. 183, 243) the neutral rate of interest and attacks Hayek's version of the loanable funds theory.[45]

The exchanges with Robertson and Hayek made Keynes aware of some of the deficiencies in his exposition and, possibly, in his theory.[46] An exchange of letters with Nicholas Kaldor, then a student at London, also pointed out an inconsistency in Keynes's argument (13, pp. 241–2). The most important development moving Keynes beyond the *Treatise*, however, was the argument developed by Richard Kahn in his classic 1931 paper on the multiplier.

The importance of Kahn's paper for Keynes is not confined to the algebraic and numerical demonstration of the secondary effects of investment on consumption and output. Kahn introduces a supply curve of output and establishes that, at least in the short run, when money wages are fixed (1931, p. 175–6), the supply curve of output (consumption goods) is not completely inelastic. Under most conditions, Kahn argues, the short-run supply of output is positively related to

---

[45] The discussion (7, p. 183) is reminiscent of his exchange with Hayek. Keynes even refers to the loanable funds theory as a "muddle." Hayek is not mentioned, however.
[46] Mention should also be made of comments on the assumption of fixed output by Hawtrey (13, p. 153) and Pigou (29, p. 5). Hawtrey's comment (in 1929) refers to Keynes's discussion of changes in money and not to the general framework. Keynes's response recognizes that "I am not dealing with the complete set of causes which determine the volume of output . . . It will probably be difficult in the future to prevent monetary theory and the theory of short-period supply from running together" (13, pp. 145–6). Pigou notes only that changes in bank rate do not affect output.

prices. Kahn notes that this differs from Keynes. Keynes's equations apply most accurately to the case in which "the whole of the factors of production are employed and continue to be employed" (ibid., p. 181).[47]

The positively sloped supply curve of output at less than full employment made the case for government investment in recessions "stronger than is always recognized" Kahn (ibid., p. 173). Further, Kahn's discussion (ibid., pp. 188–90) extends Keynes's analysis of saving and investment to complete the argument in *Can Lloyd George Do It?* Investment creates its own saving in a closed economy with idle resources. Public works spending finances itself by creating income and saving. This idea appealed to Keynes as a more powerful proposition than his own notion – the widow's cruse – that saving that is not used is wasted. It avoided the assumption that output is fixed. He greeted Kahn's paper with the same enthusiasm displayed by proponents of expansionist policies thirty years later following the similar discovery, known as the Phillips curve, and for much the same reason.

Keynes accepted the argument that he had kept output fixed in his theoretical work, and he recognized the need to revise his discussion of saving and income. In a letter to Ralph Hawtrey, dated June 1932, he indicated that he was planning a new version of his argument, (13, p. 172), and he earlier made a similar comment to Frank Taussig (29, p. 10). It is not entirely clear how much of his theoretical structure he intended to change. In a note to Joan Robinson, in April 1932, he complained about her criticism of his assumption of constant output, although he acknowledged that the criticism was correct:

> I think you are a little hard on me as regards the assumption of constant output. It is quite true that I have not followed out the consequences of changes in output in the earlier theoretical part. I admit that this wants doing, and I shall be doing it in my lectures; though that does not absolve me from being criticized for not having done it in my *Treatise*. . . . Surely one must be allowed at a particular stage of one's argument to make simplifying assumptions of this kind. (13, p. 270)

Earlier, in September 1931, he had started thinking through the ef-

---

[47] This was, of course, Keynes's criticism of the "Treasury view." Kahn's development of a supply curve of aggregate output that is less than perfectly inelastic at less than full employment opened the way for Keynes's assault on Say's law, a main step in moving from the *Treatise* to the *General Theory*. Keynes may have been aware of what he had done. In a response to Hawtrey, written in November 1930, Keynes wrote: "The question *how much* reduction of output is caused . . . [is] not strictly a monetary problem. I have not attempted to deal with it in my book . . . I am primarily concerned with what governs prices" (13, p. 145).

fects on output by introducing a positively sloped supply curve of output at less than maximum output. He wrote to Kahn describing the supply curve of aggregate output, distinguishing the case of full employment from less than full employment by the slope of the aggregate supply curve:

> When resources are fully employed, the supply schedule for goods as a whole is inelastic. Thus any new factor can only have reaction of two kinds – to cause changes in the proportionate division of output between consumption and investment goods, and to bid up (or down) the remuneration of the factors of production.
>
> But if the cost of production is sticky or if there is already unemployment, there is a third reaction possible, namely changes in total output . . .
>
> The bidding up of the remuneration of the factors of production is associated with increasing output until *maximum* (or zero) output is reached. (ibid., pp. 373–4, emphasis added)

Keynes recognized the implication. Equilibrium could occur at less than *maximum* output. And he phrased the conclusion just that way:

> Points of equilibrium output can be reached which fall short of maximum and zero . . . Thus if, *starting with equilibrium*, an increase of *I* [investment] makes *Q* [profits] positive, *O* [aggregate real output] increases and *S* [saving] increases but *Q/O* gradually diminishes. If *Q/O* reaches zero before *O* reaches maximum, we have "*long-period unemployment*", i.e. an *equilibrium position* short of full employment. (ibid., p. 374, emphasis added)

Keynes concluded by pointing out the policy implication. To ensure "a maximum value for *O* . . . *dI/dO* . . . should be sufficiently strongly positive when *O* is increasing . . . It is unlikely that this will occur without management" (ibid., p. 375). At last, he had reached the analytic conclusion to support his long-standing policy view. The task of bringing the supply curve into his general equilibrium framework could begin.

Much later, shortly after completing the *General Theory*, he referred to two propositions as critical to the development of his thinking (29, p. 215). The first point, concerning the supply of aggregate output, convinced Keynes that a persistent equilibrium at less than maximum output could be sustained. Although his formulation at the time related output to profits, so it was not a true supply curve, the main idea – that available productive factors do not create their own demand –

became part of his thinking and led to the rejection of Say's law.[48] The second point, he explained, was "the discovery that, as income increases, the gap between income and consumption may be expected to widen . . . This can only be filled by investment" (ibid., p. 215).

Conclusion

The *Treatise* shows a major change in Keynes's analysis. Some ideas in the *Treatise*, of course, have antecedents in the *Tract*, and in the works of Marshall, Robertson, Schumpeter, Wicksell, and others, as noted in the preceding pages, but there are major differences.

The *Tract* uses the quantity equation to explain events such as inflation and disinflation in the early 1920s. Keynes's observations later in the 1920s convinced him that a substantial part of the fluctuations in spending and income could not be explained adequately as the result of changes in money. Prices and costs changed at different rates, and fluctuations in spending and income seemed to him to be related to the difference. Further, he regarded the quantity equation as a statement about transactions, not the basis for a theory of spending and income.[49]

One means of resolving some of these problems would have been to use the quantity equation as an equilibrium condition and to introduce a demand for cash balances and a theory of the distribution of nominal output between prices and real output using the supply curve of output that, he recognized after Kahn's (1931) paper, was required to complete his analysis. A theory of the demand for money had started to develop at Cambridge, but there is no sign that Keynes ever considered com-

[48] Keynes (13, pp. 368, 372) uses the terms *supply curve* and *supply curve for industry as a whole* in his lecture and discussions in Chicago in June 1931. Keynes's supply curve relates aggregate output to aggregate profits, where profits are defined as the excess of receipts over prime costs. Prime cost is defined by Marshall (1920, p. 360) as variable cost – the money cost of raw materials, the extra wear and tear on the plant, and the (hourly) wages paid to produce the output. At the same meeting, Henry Schultz claimed that he had developed a similar concept of short-run aggregate supply (13, p. 372). W. B. Reddaway recalls that in his tutorial with Keynes in October 1932, Keynes had shifted from price movements to output movements. See the comment by Reddaway in Harcourt (1985, p. 60).

[49] He expressed these views much later in a 1933 letter to Dennis Robertson where he forgets the applications he made in the *Tract* and how convinced of their value he was at the time:

I doubt that either version of the Cambridge equation is of any serious utility, and I can't remember that I have ever come across a case of anyone ever using either of them for practical purposes of interpretation . . . All the versions of the quantity theory, which make no distinction between swops and intermediate transactions, and genuine production-consumption transactions, seem to me to tell one nothing. (29, p. 18).

bining this work with the quantity equation. Instead, he took a different approach.

The *Treatise* was Keynes's first attempt to implement his approach. Although the book was unsuccessful as theory, it was an important step in the development of his analysis. Many of the ideas and much of the analytic framework that eventually became the *General Theory of Employment Interest and Money* are found in the *Treatise*. The central idea, which Keynes retained but later gave much less emphasis, is that prices and costs change at different rates cyclically. Prices rise relative to costs of production in expansions, and prices fall relative to costs of production in recessions. Hence, profits rise and fall procyclically. The fundamental equations were his attempt to express this central idea.

The relative movement of prices and costs depends on an explicit empirical hypothesis – that prices are more flexible than costs of production. In the language that later became familiar, wages or costs of production are "sticky." Without this hypothesis, the theoretical core of the *Treatise*, represented by the fundamental equations, makes no prediction about the cyclical relation between investment and profits.[50] Further, Keynes main criticism of the return to gold at the prewar parity is based on the same empirical proposition – that costs and wages would fall to restore equilibrium only after prolonged and severe unemployment convinced workers and firms to reduce money wages and costs of production. The *Treatise* can be looked upon, without injustice, as Keynes's effort to develop a framework capable of analyzing the return to gold at the prewar parity and showing that the unemployment of the late 1920s was a direct consequence of that costly mistake. The reasoning is more general, and Keynes makes other applications. These are intended to show that the problems experienced after the return to gold were of a general character.

The theoretical structure of the *Treatise* is not limited to the fundamental equations. Keynes recognizes that people make two, separate allocation decisions – the allocation of earned income between consumption and saving and the allocation of existing assets between financial assets and real capital. Others had recognized that the latter decision, as well as the former, depends on the interest rate. The *Trea-*

---

[50] Perhaps because output is fixed, Keynes never considered the possibility that the procyclical movement of profits reflected changes in real output and did not require a specific assumption about the relation of wages or costs to prices. The idea that costs or wages lag prices, as he later explained in his reply to Dunlop and Tarshis (7, pp. 395–8), was based on Marshall. The idea was carried over to the *General Theory* as the proposition, maintained through most of the first half of the book, that money wages are fixed.

tise advances the analysis by recognizing that the interest rate is determined as part of a simultaneous, general equilibrium solution to the two allocation decisions. This was an important advance.

The analysis of the *Treatise* introduces the key ideas that became familiar as the IS–LM model, following Hicks's (1937) classic paper. The basic idea is present – a solution for the interest rate from a stock-flow analysis. There are major differences, however. The equations of the *Treatise* determine the interest rate and the price level, given the level of income or output. The asset demand function lumps money and bonds together. Keynes changed his mind and his theoretical framework in the years that followed, but despite harsh criticism of his interest rate theory, he retained the stock-flow framework.

The *Treatise* also lays the foundation for government action to smooth investment spending. Keynes does not distinguish formally between private and public spending, but he was aware that most investment in Britain was made by public or quasi-public bodies. The *Treatise* insists on a positive relation between private investment, profits, and prices, but Keynes believed at the time that the *Treatise* had shown also that increases in investment raised output and reduced unemployment. It was a small step, and one easily taken, to conclude that government action to increase investment would raise output and reduce unemployment. By 1929, with the *Treatise* on its way to completion, Keynes and Hubert Henderson vigorously defended Lloyd George's program to reduce unemployment by increasing public investment in roads, railways, and other infrastructure. While he referred to Pigou and others when he supported his case, much of the analytic argument comes from the then unpublished *Treatise*.

There are other ways in which the *Treatise* anticipates the *General Theory*. Real shocks that affect investment are the main impulses generating business cycles. Keynes explicitly adopts Schumpeter's view that innovations and other influences on investment are most important, although he does not rule out monetary shocks, as causes of fluctuations. Anticipations play a less important role than in the *General Theory*, however. Most of the discussion of anticipations and uncertainty concerns the effects of bearishness and bullishness on the demand for financial assets. Effects on investment, and the concept that became the marginal efficiency of capital, are either missing or of minor significance. Profits and prices, not the expectations of profits and prices, are the variables on which Keynes focuses in the *Treatise*. And, although Keynes comments on the rise in the U.S. stock market in 1928–9, the role of the stock exchange as a casino producing fluctuations in the expected return to investment becomes prominent in Keynes's work only after the *Treatise*.

Although many of the main ideas used to construct the *General Theory* are present in the *Treatise*, there are major differences. Some key elements are missing, and Keynes changed his mind about major points. I have already mentioned that expectations and uncertainty are less closely tied to investment and that the demand for financial assets in the *Treatise* became the demand for money in the *General Theory*.

One of the most important changes concerns the relative roles of output and prices. Although the *Treatise* has lengthy discussions of changes in output and employment, these discussions are unrelated to the theory. The main part of the analysis concerns prices. The first eighteen chapters of the *General Theory* go to the opposite extreme, this time deliberately and as a matter of exposition. Prices are fixed, and real output varies. In the *Treatise* one of the main ideas is that output fluctuates in response to price changes acting on profits. In contrast, the main conclusions of the *General Theory* do not depend on the relation of price and output changes. This is a major change from Keynes's earlier emphasis on price variability as the main source of instability and represents a departure from his Marshallian heritage.

A second, important change is the shift from an analysis of disequilibrium, with emphasis on cyclical fluctuations, to a static theory of equilibrium at less than full employment. Much of the *Treatise* is about positions at which profits, defined as transitory windfalls, are not zero. Consequently, investment and saving (as defined in the *Treatise*) are unequal and prices adjust. In contrast, discussion of the business cycle comes late in the *General Theory* and is used mainly to illustrate the workings of the theory.

Keynes made other, less far-reaching changes. He shifted from the nominal values of the *Treatise* to variables defined in wage units. He ignored the open economy, perhaps because most of the world had left the gold standard, perhaps because the open economy analysis of the *Treatise* did not change main conclusions. He eliminated many of the cumbersome definitions. He redefined variables like saving and income, and he eliminated the emphasis given to changes in the relative prices of consumption and investment goods. These changes took six years. They required Keynes to rework the entire framework and to develop the principal relations on which his later analyses rest – the marginal efficiency of capital schedule, the propensity to consume schedule, and the liquidity preference schedule – and to combine these relations with the heightened role assigned to anticipations and uncertainty.

His concerns remained much the same. He wanted a theory that explained the facts, or his perception of the facts, and that was consistent with his basic beliefs. In both of his major works, investment

– for Keynes the driving force in economic progress – plays a central role. Both books conclude with major recommendations for institutional changes that, Keynes believed, would increase stability. And both were intended to show that it was not optimal to rely on laissez-faire capitalism to maintain stability and progress. Control of the monetary system and costs of production are critical elements for maintaining stability. In the *Treatise*, Keynes concludes:

> If we have complete control both of the earnings (or wages) system and of the currency system, so that we can alter the rate of earnings by *fiat*, can accommodate the supply of money to the rate of earnings which we have decreed, and can control the rate of investment, then we can afford to follow our fancy as to what we stabilize – the purchasing power of money, its labour power, or anything else – without running the risk of setting up social and economic frictions or of causing waste. (5, pp. 151–2).

This passage could appear as well in the *General Theory* or in Keynes's statements of his basic beliefs.

4

The General Theory: *a different perspective*

A fledgling economist approaching Keynes's *General Theory* for the first time expects to find the policy recommendations derived from a theory that everyone knows to be "Keynesian." Although much of the thought and apparatus identified as Keynesian is there – underemployment equilibrium, liquidity trap, spending multiplier, downward wage "rigidity" – there is little about pump priming, tax cuts, and carefully timed changes in government spending or tax rates to spur recovery. To find this type of fiscal policy recommended in Keynes's work one must look to Keynes's popular writings, many of them written before the *General Theory*. Keynes of the *Treatise on Money*, who had not yet succeeded in the "long struggle of escape" from "habitual modes of thought and expression" (7, p. xxiii), gives at least as much attention to fiscal policy as Keynes of the *General Theory*, who mentions public works spending in a few passages of the chapter on the multiplier (ibid., Chapter 10) but neglects to mention public works in his "Notes on the Trade Cycle" (ibid., Chapter 22). There, as in other parts of the book, Keynes's main recommendation is for social management of investment.

The *General Theory* is addressed to economists (ibid., p. xxi). Its purpose is to correct "the outstanding fault of the theoretical parts of that work [the *Treatise*] . . . My so-called fundamental equations were an instantaneous picture taken on the assumption of a given output . . . the dynamic development, as distinct from the instantaneous picture, was left incomplete and extremely confused. This book, on the other hand, has evolved into what is primarily a study of the forces which determine changes in the scale of output and employment as a whole" (ibid., p. xxii).

Thus, Keynes acknowledged that the major flaw in the *Treatise* required him to make a new effort to analyze the determination of aggregate income. This time, however, much of the monetary detail was pushed into the background: "A monetary economy, we shall find, is essentially one in which changing views about the future are capable of influencing the quantity of employment and not merely its direction" (ibid.). The new book, freed of the major mistake in the *Treatise*, focused on the forces determining the scale of aggregate output. Keynes regarded this as a new departure and, in his more hopeful moments, believed that his book would revolutionize economics.

The main theme of the *General Theory* is familiar; the classical theory does not explain involuntary unemployment and cannot do so without violating its postulates. Chapter 1 takes less than a page to name the classical theorists and to state Keynes's theme: "I shall argue that the postulates of the classical theory are applicable to a special case . . . the situation which it assumed being a *limiting point* of the possible positions of *equilibrium*" (ibid., p. 3, emphasis added). Chapter 2 leaves no doubt about the postulate Keynes has in mind: "We need to throw over the second postulate of the classical doctrine and to work out the behaviour of a system in which involuntary unemployment in the strict sense is possible" (ibid., pp. 16–17).

Keynes makes clear that the classical proposition that he has in mind is Say's law: "The classical economists have taught that supply creates its own demand; meaning by this in some significant, but not clearly defined, sense that the whole of the costs of production must necessarily be spent in the aggregate, directly or indirectly, on purchasing the product" (ibid., p. 18). Keynes had given much time and thought to the meaning of "hoarding" in his correspondence with Dennis Robertson and, doubtless, in their many conversations from the mid-1920s on. At least from the time of writing *The Economic Consequences of the Peace* (JMK 2), he was on record as believing that investment, not saving, was the factor limiting output. The *Treatise* developed this argument in elaborate detail, verbally, but had used special definitions and, more importantly, had failed analytically. The new attempt tried to restate these ideas in a new way – one that differed from the classical emphasis on conditions of supply (or Say's law) as the principal determinant of the position of equilibrium output at full employment of resources.

The classical theory, according to Chapter 2 of the *General Theory*, depends on three assumptions: (1) equality of the marginal disutility of employment and the real wage; (2) the absence of *involuntary unemployment*; and (3) equality of the aggregate demand price and aggregate supply price at all levels of output and employment. "These three assumptions, however, all amount to the same thing . . . any one of them logically involving the other two" (ibid., p. 22, emphasis added).

What I take to be key words – *limiting point, equilibrium*, and *involuntary unemployment* – are in italics. The main problem in interpreting the *General Theory* is to understand what Keynes meant by these words.

Keynes believed that the notion of involuntary unemployment, the description of the classical theory as a special case – a *limiting position* of equilibrium that the economic system does not generally reach – and the policy recommendations that he made are linked in a consistent framework. The equilibrium level of employment does not rise and the equilibrium rate of interest and the equilibrium level of the money wage do not fall to the values consistent with full-employment equilibrium. The *General Theory* is Keynes's attempt to explain why this is so and to offer a remedy.

Some have interpreted Keynes's comments on unemployment as a statement about money illusion in the labor market. Modigliani (1944) presents this argument among others. Keynes, however, is clear that – far from endorsing money illusion or nonneutrality of money – he wished to rid economic theory of this error. He wrote to Hicks, commenting on Hicks's classic article (Hicks 1937). In his letter, Keynes distinguishes between the "pure classical doctrine" and the "much more confused state of mind" that had developed into "an inconsistent hotch-potch" (14, p. 79):

> The inconsistency creeps in, I suggest, as soon as it comes to be generally agreed that the increase in the quantity of money is capable of increasing employment. A strictly brought-up classical economist would not, I should say, admit that. We used to admit it without realizing how inconsistent it was with our other premises. (ibid.)

Classical and neoclassical theories of production and employment deny that the levels of output and employment depend on nominal values. Changes in nominal values (money or money wages) do not change real wages, so they cannot *permanently* change the equilibrium levels of employment and output. Keynes did not deny that changes in money or money wages could temporarily change output, but as his reply to Hicks shows, he did not believe that *equilibrium* output could be changed solely by changing nominal values.[1]

---

[1] I have not found any place in the *General Theory* where Keynes relies on money illusion to sustain underemployment equilibrium. The closest he comes to that position are statements that distinguish between the effects of changes in relative wages and changes in the price level. Keynes argues (7, pp. 14–15) that workers resist changes in their relative wages much more than the changes in their real wages brought about by a rise in the price level. This argument is about distribution, as he notes when he makes the argument. In a letter to Gottfried Haberler (29, pp. 272–3) Keynes compares reductions in money wages to changes in real money balances (money in wage units). An increase in real balances can, in principle, reduce unemployment by lowering the rate of interest. Classical economists, and Keynes in the *Treatise*, emphasized the effect of wage reduction on costs and profits. The same points are made in the *General Theory* and are discussed more fully in what follows here.

The *General Theory* does not challenge the classical proposition that the equilibrium levels of real output and employment can only be changed permanently by permanently changing some real variable. On the contrary, by raising investment and the capital stock, equilibrium output and employment can be moved close to the *limiting point* of equilibrium emphasized in classical theories. In the *General Theory*, Keynes attempts to explain why state direction can do what unaided private action cannot do – permanently increase the capital stock, employment, and output. The *General Theory* is correctly described as Keynes's restatement, using economic analysis, of his often repeated criticisms of laissez-faire capitalism.[2]

The classical proposition that Keynes challenged is the impossibility of what he called involuntary unemployment. For Keynes *full employment* means the level of employment reached when the economy is, in modern terms, on the (dynamic) production frontier or, as Keynes described it, at an optimum position (13, p. 406) or a maximum level (7, p. 30). At full employment, the economy produces the maximum output that available labor, capital, and technology permit; the real wage equals the marginal disutility of labor; people work the number of hours they regard as optimal. In keeping with Keynes's usage, I refer to this level of output and the associated level of employment as *maximum employment* and maximum output to distinguish Keynes's definition from other definitions of full employment.

Keynes's involuntary unemployment is the difference between maximum employment and equilibrium employment. Keynes believed that private decisions produce an equilibrium rate of investment that is lower and an equilibrium capital stock that is smaller than the social optimum. Because the privately chosen capital stock is less than the socially optimum capital stock, equilibrium output is less than the social optimum. Because investment is lower on average than the rate required for maximum output, aggregate demand is deficient – that is, less than the amount required to *maintain* full (maximum) employment. Nothing in the market economy adjusts. The equilibrium position is stable; everyone expects the equilibrium to persist. The problem is *not* that people do not know and cannot learn the equilibrium values of the money wage, the rate of interest, and the level of investment. The problem is that they know these values and cannot change them.

The idea that an economy can fluctuate around an equilibrium level of income that is below full employment is one of the major changes between the *Treatise* and the *General Theory*. Although the model in

---

[2] References supporting the interpretation in these and the following introductory paragraphs are given in the text and footnotes that follow.

the *Treatise* failed to deliver the implication, there is no doubt that price fluctuations were the main cause of output fluctuations in Keynes's thinking during the 1920s. The importance of price stability and policies to achieve price stability is a dominant theme in both the *Tract* and the *Treatise*. In contrast, price changes fade into the background of the *General Theory*; prices are held constant for more than half of the book. When price fluctuations are introduced, they remain capable of increasing uncertainty and variability, but they are no longer the principal cause.

Keynes leaves no doubt that involuntary unemployment is the concept that gives an analytic foundation for his revised beliefs. Equality between the price of aggregate output and its cost of production restores the classical theory by removing the divergence between private and social costs. Once this divergence is removed, the rest of the classical conclusions follow: "the social advantages of private and national thrift, . . . the quantity theory of money, the unqualified advantages of laissez-faire in respect of foreign trade" (7, p. 21).

This passage and Keynes's definition of full employment describe full employment as the limiting point at which Keynes's theory no longer holds. Full employment is "the point at which the supply of output as a whole ceases to be elastic, i.e., where a further increase in the value of the effective demand will no longer be accompanied by any increase in output" (ibid., p. 26). At this point "the marginal disutility of labour sets an upper limit" to output (ibid.).[3]

The "long struggle of escape" (ibid., p. xxiii) did not lead to the complete rejection of the quantity theory. The quantity theory (classical theory) remains as a special case (ibid., p. xxiii). What Keynes escaped from was the set of beliefs, which he described as classical theory, according to which fluctuations cause departures from equilibrium but eventually the economy returns to the position of full employment. In this world the simple quantity theory holds; the equilibrium price level is proportional to the stock of money; and the equilibrium real wage is equal to the marginal disutility of labor. The position of full-employment equilibrium is determined, in classical theory, by supply, and supply is fixed by capital and labor. Marshall, in particular, and English and American economists as a group never

---

[3] These passages (and others in the chapter on prices) should make clear why the search for Keynes's theory of inflation does not produce support for incomes policies and other proposals of his later followers. Once full employment is reached, Keynes believed that the quantity theory was the relevant theory of prices. Keynes was not always clear about how to interpret parts of the classical theory (29, pp. 256, 258). On many occasions, he challenged his critics to state the classical position or refer him to a statement.

separately developed a theory of aggregate output and consumption (ibid., pp. xxv, xxxi). They did not show that the economy reached the equilibrium that was socially optimal. They assumed that the only equilibrium was at full (maximum) employment, that there was no difference between the level of equilibrium output resulting from private decisions and the attainable, socially optimum level.

What Keynes escaped to is a theory in which aggregate demand determines the level of output until full employment is reached: "The actual level of output and employment depends, not on the capacity to produce or on the pre-existing level of incomes, but on current decisions to produce which depend in turn on current decisions to invest and on present expectations of current and prospective consumption" (ibid., p. xxxiii). In particular, he had made his "final escape from the confusions of the Quantity Theory" (ibid., p. xxxiv). The price level is not determined directly by the quantity of money but depends on technical conditions and the level of money wages just as in the theory of product prices (ibid.).

The second major change from the *Treatise* is the increased emphasis Keynes gives to uncertainty. Keynes's views on probability and uncertainty were not new. They were first developed in his prize-winning fellowship dissertation of 1908 and revised and published in his *Treatise on Probability* (JMK 8) in 1921. In the 1920s, they have a relatively minor role in his analysis. Not so in the *General Theory*. There, uncertainty is the major reason that the rate of investment is suboptimal.

The bulls and bears appear in the *Treatise*, but their role is heightened in the *General Theory*. Price fluctuations on the stock exchange are now a main source of uncertainty about long-term values. The reason for this change in emphasis is never stated. We know that Keynes was concerned about the fluctuations on the New York Stock Exchange in the late 1920s. We know that he lost (and subsequently more than recovered) a substantial fraction of his personal wealth (net assets) between 1927 and 1929 (12, p. 11) and a smaller, but not inconsiderable, fraction of the portfolio of King's College and the National Mutual Insurance Company between 1928 and 1931 (ibid., pp. 91, 96). We know, also, that he changed his investment strategy after these experiences. He ceased trying to predict the general movements in the stock market arising from the credit cycle and adopted a policy of buying stock based on "intrinsic value" (ibid., p. 107). We do not know whether his losses and the losses of others on which he comments (ibid., pp. 100–1) convinced him that the stock exchanges overreacted to changes in economic conditions. The *General Theory* decries the failure of investors in stocks to consider long-term values; the stock market is "a casino" dominated by professionals "concerned, not with what an investment is really worth to a man who buys it 'for keeps,' but with what the market will value it at, under the influence of mass psychology, three months or a year hence" (7, pp. 154–5). It is consistent with Keynes's approach to a problem that he would criticize severely those who continued to pursue the portfolio strategy that he once considered promising but now had abandoned.

What matters for his analysis is that investors shift from owning claims to capital to holding money. This shift drives down the prices of assets and drives up the real rate of interest. The cause of this shift into money is uncertainty – avoidable uncertainty; the result of the uncertainty is that investment and aggregate demand are too low to sustain full employment.

Although the *General Theory* was written during the period known as the Great Depression, the book, unlike the *Tract* and the *Treatise*, has few specific references to contemporary problems.[4] This is misleading. Keynes had little interest in pure theory. His concerns are to explain the failure of unemployment to fall during the interwar period, particularly after the return to gold, and to develop an analysis that would show the causes of persistent unemployment and point to a solution. He regarded the problem as a general problem, requiring a general theory that determines the actual level of output. Those who read the book as "depression economics" are, I believe, mistaken.[5] Keynes's problem is not to explain why output has deviated temporarily from full employment. The problem is to explain why "full employment is of rare and short-lived occurrence" (ibid., p. 250). The effect of uncertainty on investment is a key element in the explanation.

The third major change is in the analytic structure, his solutions to technical problems that would remove the defects of the *Treatise* and

---

[4] There are exceptions. Keynes discusses the causes of the depression and offers a monetary explanation similar to the explanation used in his letter to Burgess, discussed in Chapter 2 of this volume. He attributes to U.S. monetary policy a more important role in starting the depression than was given later by Friedman and Schwartz (1963a). In Keynes's view, U.S. monetary policy in the 1920s started the slump. The boom in the United States was driven by investment. The high rate of investment, maintained for several years, lowered the marginal efficiency of capital while the Federal Reserve maintained a high rate of interest. At the prevailing rate only very speculative investments could be considered profitable by investors (7, p. 323). Compatible explanations of the depression are given in the 1931 Harris lectures (13, pp. 345, 352) and *The Means to Prosperity*, written in 1933. Both of the latter put more emphasis on the international aspects. The high rate of interest in the United States relative to the rest of the world brought gold to the United States and reduced lending by the United States to the rest of the world (9, p. 352).

[5] Keynes says very little about inflation, so his theory may be said to lack generality in that respect. He is explicit, however, that the quantity theory is the relevant theory for "true inflation."

express his new ideas. There is no doubt about his view of these problems.

In a letter to Harrod (14, pp. 84–6) commenting on Harrod's essay on his book, Keynes cites the three main analytic problems that he had to solve to make the transition from his classical heritage. The first is the theory of effective demand, including the multiplier with its implication that investment and consumption can increase together. The second is interest as "being the measure of liquidity preference" (ibid., p. 85). This required Keynes to revise his analysis of the demand for money in the *Treatise* where he confuses the effects of changes in the rate of interest and changes in the marginal efficiency of capital (7, pp. 173–4). The last is the proper definition of the marginal efficiency of capital. This change brought risk and uncertainty into the framework. The first two factors are emphasized again, almost three years later, in the preface to the French edition (ibid., p. xxxiv). A notable feature of Keynes's explanations and his restatements of the *General Theory* in the book (ibid., Chapter 18) and in the *Quarterly Journal of Economics* (14, pp. 109–23) is his failure to emphasize the part of the *General Theory* that received most attention, particularly in recent decades – the theory of the labor market. A by-product of my interpretation is the explanation it offers for this lack of emphasis.

This chapter offers an interpretation of the *General Theory* that, I believe, is more consistent with Keynes's theory and policy recommendations than other more familiar interpretations. The *General Theory* and many of Keynes's letters leave no doubt that he recognized the need to reexamine old ideas and to harmonize his views on policy with the theory he had developed. Although he insisted on the main implications of his theory, he remained open to suggestions about the way in which the theory was presented and the policy implemented (ibid., pp. 121–3). He thought that the main idea – the existence of involuntary unemployment – was simple and that, once the idea was understood, it could be expressed in alternative ways.

No single set of statements is *the* correct restatement of the *General Theory*. There is, however, considerable difference in the degree to which different interpretations are consistent with the points that Keynes stressed in the *General Theory* and in the papers he published subsequently and restated in his correspondence. There is, perhaps, a greater difference between the policies Keynes favored in the decade following publication and the activist, countercyclical policies usually described as Keynesian.

The following section elaborates Keynes's central thesis: The economy reaches a stable equilibrium that is below full employment. Then, I consider the main building blocks that Keynes used to develop this thesis and their relation to Say's law. I put the main building blocks into a model and use the model to obtain some of the main implications that Keynes claimed or that he obtained with the help of his theory.[6] A test of my interpretation is given by the ability of the model to generate implications that Keynes claimed for his theory. Quotations present much of the argument in his own words. For this reason and to avoid lengthy discussion of the ways his ideas changed, I rely mainly on material included in the *General Theory* or written following publication.

The central thesis

It was an important moment in the development of my own thought when I realized that the classical theory had given no attention at all to the problem at what point the supply of output as a whole and the demand for it would be in equilibrium. When one is trying to discover the volume of output and employment, it must be *this point of equilibrium for which one is searching.* I attach importance to this point because whereas the earlier classical economists were quite consciously believing in something of the nature of Say's Law, more recently the whole matter has slipped out of sight. (29, p. 215, emphasis added)

You go on to say that . . . you do not understand my doctrine of involuntary unemployment or full employment. But, heavens, my doctrine of full employment is what the whole of my book is about! Everything else is a side issue to that. (14, p. 24)

The central thesis of the *General Theory* is that a capitalist economy operating on the principles of laissez-faire fluctuates around a stable equilibrium at which there is less than full use of resources. Keynes's letters to Abba Lerner in June and to Ralph Hawtrey in April 1936 and quoted here make this point. The *General Theory* is Keynes's attempt to explain why the effective demand for output fails to reach equilibrium at the *maximum* output attainable with available technology and given population and labor supply.

A secondary but closely related thesis restates his earlier Marshallian view. Business cycles are mainly real, not monetary, events. Fluctuations, or cycles, are the result of unpredictable private actions that are not reversed quickly but cumulate for a time. The level around which

[6] Chapter 6 discusses some of the alternative interpretations of the *General Theory*.

fluctuations occur is below the average level of output and employment that could be achieved with a higher but attainable rate of investment. Although Keynes favored redistribution of income to increase consumer spending (7, pp. 321, 324–5; 14, pp. 16–17, 270–1), he preferred to increase investment until the stock of capital "ceases to be scarce" (7, p. 325; 29, pp. 210–11; 14, p. 190). The central points of the theory can be developed if we, like Keynes, center attention on investment rather than consumption.

There are periods of three to five years duration, according to Keynes (7, p. 317), in which the demand for investment remains below its long-term average. These periods follow a collapse of private investment – the schedule of the marginal efficiency of capital. The consequences of the collapse are discussed in detail (ibid., pp. 315–20), but the main reason given for the collapse of investment modifies an old theme. Fluctuations are mainly the result of "a fickle and highly unstable marginal efficiency of capital" (ibid., p. 204) itself the result of destabilizing speculation by "purchasers largely ignorant of what they are buying" (ibid., p. 316). Market changes influenced by speculators are used by entrepreneurs to estimate the return on investment. When the prices of assets fall, capital losses reduce returns and asset values, so investment declines until expected returns rise.

Fluctuations occur around a position that is below the system's potential. In his words:

> It is an outstanding characteristic of the economic system in which we live that, whilst it is subject to severe fluctuations in respect to output and employment, it is not violently unstable. Indeed it seems capable of remaining in *a chronic condition of sub-normal activity* for a considerable period without any marked tendency either towards recovery or towards complete collapse . . . [But,] full, or even approximately *full employment is of rare and short-lived occurrence*. (ibid., pp. 249–50, emphasis added)[7]

Keynes gives three principal reasons:
1. The multiplier is greater than unity but not very large. If this were not so, he wrote, "a given change in the rate of investment would involve a great change (limited only by full or zero employment) in the rate of consumption."
2. "Moderate changes in the prospective yield of capital or

---

[7] Keynes describes these observations as "the facts of experience" (7, p. 250). A better description would be strongly held beliefs, as the discussion of money wages in what follows suggests. The task of the *General Theory* was to develop "psychological propensities of the modern world . . . to produce these results" (ibid.).

in the rate of interest will not be associated with very
great changes in the rate of investment.'' Rising marginal
cost of production limits the response of investment and
output to inventions or improvements in business
psychology (anticipations).
3. ''Moderate changes in employment are not associated
with very great changes in money wages.'' This
condition, Keynes said, keeps the price level stable when
the money stock is constant (ibid., pp. 250–4).

As a result of these conditions, ''we oscillate, avoiding the gravest
extremes of fluctuations in employment and prices in both directions,
round an intermediate position *appreciably below full employment* and
appreciably above the minimum employment a decline below which
would endanger life'' (ibid., p. 254, emphasis added).[8]

These themes, restating Keynes's central thesis, are repeated many
times. In contrast to the *Treatise*, there is no attempt at a dynamic
theory of adjustment toward equilibrium at full employment. Fluctuations may at times bring output near to full employment, but the conditions sustaining equilibrium at full (maximum) employment are not
present in the economic system.

Notable in these statements is the absence of the principal assumption required by the familiar Keynesian special case. Neither absolute
liquidity preference (the liquidity trap) nor absolute wage rigidity appear in these statements, and they do not appear in the summary of
the *General Theory* (Chapter 18). Keynes's 1937 restatement (14, p.
121) mentions the social factors that influence the money wage, but he
dismisses these factors as of secondary importance for the theory of
output and employment. In articles for the *Times* published in the winter of 1937, Keynes is entirely clear that wages and prices change during
periods of expansion and contraction. Price changes during cyclical
expansions are distinguished from inflation in much the same way that
he had tried to distinguish income and profit inflation in the *Treatise*.
At the same time, he repeats the classical view of inflation and discusses that theory as the relevant theory once full employment is
achieved:

[A] rising tendency for prices and wages inevitably, and for
obvious reasons, accompanies any revival of activity. An im-

---

[8] Keynes introduces a fourth ''condition'' but indicates that it ''provides not so much
for the stability [sic] of the system as for the tendency of a fluctuation in one direction
to reverse itself in due course'' (7, p. 251). The fourth condition is that the marginal
efficiency of capital is inversely related to the capital stock. Low investment reduces
the capital stock and eventually raises the marginal efficiency of capital. Sustained
investment lowers the marginal efficiency (7, pp. 253–4).

provement in demand tends to carry with it an increase in output and employment and, at the same time, a rise in prices and wages. It is when increased demand is no longer capable of materially raising output and employment and mainly spends itself in raising prices that it is properly called inflation. When this point is reached, the new demand merely competes with the existing demand for the use of resources which are already employed to the utmost. (21, pp. 404–5)[9]

Keynes's principal analytic difference from what he called classical theory is reflected in his definition of involuntary unemployment. He believed that the average level of employment and output could be raised permanently by increasing the rate of investment. Involuntary unemployment is the difference between the average, actual level of employment and the level of employment that would be achieved with a higher and more stable rate of investment. The actual level of employment reflects current expectations and risks. These hold the level of investment, on average, below the social optimum. Elimination of this risk – this excess burden on the economy – would raise the average level of investment and therefore increase the level of output. Since saving and investment are equal in equilibrium, the higher level of investment would be financed by the additional saving induced by the higher level of income. The multiplier is the mechanism that brings forth the additional saving. With greater stability of investment, risk would be lower, so people would part with liquidity, reducing the demand for money and lowering the rate of interest. Further, by damping cyclical fluctuations, any cyclical component in involuntary unemployment would be reduced. On my interpretation, cyclical unemployment is of lesser importance in Keynes's analysis. The central thesis concerns the suboptimal equilibrium position, not the cyclical component. Although Keynes believed that the level of employment could be raised by institutional changes that reduced the variability of investment and employment, the key was to reduce uncertainty and variability. These are the same general concerns Keynes had expressed in the 1920s, but his emphasis shifted from price fluctuations to fluctuations in output and the expected returns to capital. Of course, he continued to believe that improvements could be made: "The unimpeded rule of the above conditions [fluctuations around a position

---

[9] The article, written with unemployment above 12 percent, goes on to consider whether proposed defense and rearmament expenditure of £80 million will achieve full employment and bring on inflation. Keynes's conclusion, after allowing for the multiplier effects, was that there was danger of inflation but inflation would be avoided with proper policies.

that is below full employment] is a fact of observation concerning the world as it is or has been, and not a necessary principle which cannot be changed'' (7, p. 254).

What were the reasons behind the fact, and what could be done to change them? Keynes summarized the causal factors under three headings (ibid., pp. 246–7). The first is the expectations of wealthowners. Here, Keynes included the consumption function, the demand function for money,[10] and the marginal efficiency of capital. The second factor is the money wage, and the third is the quantity of money. Keynes called the three factors ''ultimate independent variables'' (ibid., pp. 246–7). Though he acknowledged that the three factors could be analyzed further and listed the main forces on which they depend, he argued that further analysis is not necessary for the determination of real income (in wage units) and employment.

There is no reason why we should not take Keynes at his word and accept as his proximate determinants of current employment the three factors he labeled ultimate independent variables and used in the very next paragraphs to explain the determination of output and employment. The problem is that a few pages later, in a famous passage, Keynes seems to dismiss two of the three ultimate factors:

> There is, therefore, no ground for the belief that a flexible wage policy is capable of *maintaining* a state of *continuous* full employment, any more than for the belief that open-market monetary policy is capable, *unaided* of achieving this result. The economic system cannot be made self-adjusting along these lines. (ibid., p. 267, emphasis added)[11]

Does this passage imply that there is no real value of money in wage units for which the system reaches and maintains full employment? Keynes's answer is a qualified yes, but his affirmative answer applies only to the ability of the private sector in a laissez-faire economy to maintain full employment as he defined the term. Unless anticipations of a higher future return to real capital shift the schedule of the marginal efficiency of capital, reductions in money wages or increases in the quantity of money do not maintain full (maximum) employment. Reduction of money wages may, for a time, increase employment, but the higher level will not persist unless the reduction in money wages raises the expected return to capital or permanently lowers the ex-

[10] Actually, Keynes refers to the psychological attitude to liquidity. Following (7, p. 168) I interpret this as the demand for money.
[11] The emphasis on ''unaided'' in the quotation points up Keynes's belief that state management of investment would raise employment to a permanently higher level.

pected rate of interest. Nominal changes cannot permanently change the real equilibrium.

Keynes reaches exactly the same conclusion about increases in money and for the same reason. Here, again, Keynes insists that an increase in the stock of money can, in principle, temporarily raise the level of output, but unless there is a change in expected output, the stock of capital will not increase permanently. An increase in money or a reduction in money wages lowers the short-term rate of interest. The long-term rate is a conventional value, governed by anticipations about long-term real returns, so it responds very little to monetary or money wages changes. Reducing the risk premium would lower the long-term rate decisively, but a reduction in the risk premium cannot be achieved under laissez-faire. Hence, changes in money and in money wages can produce temporary changes in investment and output, but they cannot sustain the higher level of investment required to increase the capital stock, so full (maximum) employment cannot be sustained by changes in money or money wages. (See 14, pp. 103, 131, 161, 222, 232–3.) Keynes's claim is that in a particular and fundamental sense – not previously emphasized – output is a real variable that cannot be changed permanently by increasing money even if *equilibrium* output is less than full (maximum) employment output.[12]

The problem is that, under private decision making or laissez-faire, the schedule of the marginal efficiency of capital settles below the level required for full employment. To explain why, Keynes distinguishes between the schedule of the marginal efficiency of capital and the prevailing rate of interest. There are, he believes, three ambiguities about the marginal efficiency schedule, but the "main cause of confusion" is the failure to distinguish "between the increment of value obtainable by using an additional quantity of capital in the *existing* situation, and

---

[12] Earlier, Keynes had discussed the real balance, or Pigou, effect with Robertson, as noted in Chapter 3 of this volume. We know from that discussion that he chose to disregard the real balance effect as unimportant. More surprising is his neglect of the inflation tax. His correct analysis of the effect of inflation on the demand for money, presented in Chapter 2 of this volume, shows that he understood that the demand for money and the real rate of interest could be reduced by inflation. Yet, he never mentions this possibility. I cannot explain this important omission. It is noteworthy, however, that none of his critics make this point. Even Jacob Viner, who sharply criticized the emphasis on liquidity preference and emphasized the inflationary consequences of Keynes's proposals, does not point out that the inflation tax would lower the real rate and bring the economy to equilibrium with higher employment. Keynes gives three reasons why money wage changes are unlikely to maintain full employment (7, pp. 232–3). First, reductions may give rise to further reductions – extrapolative expectations. Second, if money wages were flexible, this would increase instability "with unfavorable reactions on the marginal efficiency of capital" (ibid., p. 232). Third, beyond some point, increases in real balances have small effects on the rate of interest. This is related to the liquidity trap, but the trap is not absolute.

the series of increments which it is expected to obtain *over the whole life* of the additional capital asset'' (7, p. 138). Others had seen that returns are not received instantly; they had neglected the role of uncertainty. Three pages later (p. 141), Keynes restates the principal confusion as the failure to see that the position of the marginal efficiency schedule depends on the *"prospective* yield of capital, and not merely on its current yield.'' Once again, he emphasizes expectations and uncertainty.

Keynes makes a similar point, emphasizing expectations, in a letter to Hicks responding to Hicks's (1937) classic interpretation of the *General Theory.* Keynes criticized Hicks for failing to distinguish between actual and expected income in the investment function. According to Keynes:

> At one time I tried the equations as you have done, with *I* [income] in all of them. The objection to this is that it overemphasises current income. In the case of the inducement to invest, expected income for the period of the investment is the relevant variable . . . My own feeling is that present income has a predominant effect in determining liquidity preference and saving which it does not possess in its influence over the inducement to invest. (14, pp. 80–1)[13]

Changes in the rate of interest by monetary or wage policy can change the amount of investment and thereby increase income and employment. But, to *maintain* full employment, the capital stock must increase. To sustain an increase requires either a change in expectations about the stream of future returns or (7, pp. 203–4) a sustained reduction in the *expected,* effective interest rate. Keynes did not believe either change would occur without a reduction in actual and perceived risk.

There are three types of risk (ibid., pp. 144–5). The first arises from uncertainties inherent in nature. In an uncertain world, actual and anticipated returns differ. This risk must be borne, according to Keynes, in every society and cannot be eliminated. A second risk is the risk of capital losses arising from changes in the real value of financial assets. This risk, Keynes said, ''renders a money-loan . . . less secure than a

[13] Note the changes from the *Treatise* where profits (windfalls) drive investment but do not affect money. Hicks (14, p. 82) responded from the perspective of general equilibrium theory. Although he acknowledged the importance of expected income, he insisted on retaining current income in the investment equation. A generation of economists followed him and, I believe, missed one of Keynes's main points. Later, Hicks (1977, p. 146, n. 14) was skeptical of Keynes's claim to have ''tried the equations'' in their Hicksian form. In his early draft, we now know that Keynes used expected values of some variables (13, pp. 420, 441).

real asset; though all or most of this [risk] should be already reflected, and therefore absorbed, in the price of durable assets'' (ibid., p. 144). The remaining risk, to which he attached particular importance, he called "lender's risk." This risk arises because borrowers default, voluntarily or involuntarily, "due either to *moral hazard*, i.e. voluntary default or other means of escape, possibly lawful, from the fulfilment of the obligation or . . . due to the disappointment of expectation" (ibid.).[14] This risk "is a pure addition to the cost of investment which would not exist if the borrower and the lender were the same person" (ibid.). Moreover, Keynes said, the cost for this risk is added twice, once by the lender and once by the borrower. In his role as investor, the borrower requires compensation for the risk to induce him to invest in high-risk projects, and the lender in the ordinary case seeks compensation for the risk of default. Unless there is excellent security, the lender will be concerned that the borrower will elect to default if the project does not succeed so he will charge a premium. The lender's and borrower's premiums fluctuate, however. In periods of expansion, the evaluation of this risk is biased downward; "both borrower's risk and lender's risk, is apt to become unusually and imprudently low" (ibid., p. 145). This leads to a boom caused by a rate of investment that is not sustained in a market economy.

The last point is crucial for Keynes. The risk that is most subject to change – to bullish and bearish sentiments and to cumulative waves of optimism and pessimism – can be eliminated entirely by social direction of investment. Social direction, he believed, would provide a steady rate of investment, thereby lowering risk. Investment by public bodies would eliminate moral hazard and, therefore, lender's risk. With lower risk, the required rate of return would be lower and investment higher. The difference between the social and the private rate of return would fall toward zero, so output would approach its maximum.

Keynes explains more fully how full employment can be achieved and fluctuations reduced. After discoursing on the baneful influence of speculators who greatly influence the prices of real capital quoted on financial markets, he explains why speculators

> inevitably exert a decisive [sic] influence on the rate of current investment. For there is no sense in building up a new enterprise at a cost greater than that at which a similar existing enterprise can be purchased; whilst there is an inducement to spend on a new project what may seem an extravagant sum,

---

[14] Later, Keynes refers to the third type of risk as "moral risk" (7, p. 208). John Whitaker has pointed out to me that Marshall (1920, p. 590) refers to this risk as "personal risk."

if it can be floated off on the Stock Exchange at an immediate profit. (ibid., p. 151)

Chapter 12 attempts to explain why short-term speculators have great and growing influence on quoted asset prices and thus on investment, but the main point of the argument does not change: "There is no clear evidence from experience that the investment policy which is socially advantageous coincides with that which is most profitable" (ibid., p. 157). Management of investment by the state, Keynes suggests, based on long views, can eliminate the additional cost of unanticipated default and possibly bring the equilibrium marginal efficiency of capital to zero in a generation. This, of course, had been Keynes's belief since the 1920s, as discussed in Chapter 2.

In correspondence with J. A. Hobson, Keynes set out criteria for judging when investment is socially advantageous but not privately profitable. In a passage that anticipates later work on optimal money growth, he calls once again for reducing the interest rate to zero: "I cannot agree that investment has ceased to be socially profitable as long as it yields any return at all . . . investment has only reached saturation point when capital is so abundant that it yields no more over a period of time than its cost of production without any surplus" (29, p. 211). Keynes makes a similar point elsewhere (29, p. 210; 7, p. 376).

Keynes does not have in mind the optimum quantity of money. For him, the best way to achieve a zero rate of interest is to satiate the capital stock by state action to encourage investment. He wrote:

It is not quite correct that I attach primary importance to the rate of interest. What I attach primary importance to is the scale of investment and [I] am interested in the low interest rate as one of the elements furthering this. But I should regard state intervention to encourage investment as probably a more important factor than low rates of interest taken in isolation.

The question then arises why I should prefer rather a heavy scale of investment to increasing consumption. My main reason for this is that I do not think we have yet reached anything like the point of capital saturation . . . After twenty years of large-scale investment I should expect to have to change my mind. (27, p. 350)[15]

---

[15] A similar statement is in Keynes's Harris lecture of 1931. The main policy recommendation is not a temporary program to expand consumption and reduce unemployment:

The central idea that I wish to leave with you is the vital necessity for a society, living in the phase in which we are living today, to bring down the long-term rate of interest at a pace appropriate to the underlying facts . . . Thus we need

These are not isolated thoughts. They are the theme of the book and a central point of Keynes's long-standing beliefs. The point they make is repeated in Keynes's correspondence with Hicks and in three 1937 papers: "The Theory of the Rate of Interest" (14, pp. 101–8), "The General Theory of Employment" (ibid., pp. 109–23), and his Galton lecture, "Some Economic Consequences of a Declining Population" (ibid., pp. 124–33). In the first of the three papers, Keynes distinguishes his theory from the classical theory of interest on two grounds. First, the demand for money in wage units depends, inter alia, on the quantity of money because in the short run the rate of interest depends on the stock of money.[16] Second, investment reaches its equilibrium rate before "the elasticity of supply of output as a whole has fallen to zero" (ibid., p. 104). To Keynes, this means that aggregate output can be pushed to a higher level than can be achieved under laissez-faire. Keynes then notes that his reason for calling his theory a general theory is a direct consequence of the treatment of expectations. In the second of the three papers, he backs away from his policy recommendations[17] but repeats the two "main grounds of my departure" from classical

> to pay constant conscious attention to the long-term rate of interest for fear that our vast resources may be running to waste . . . and that this running to waste may interfere with that beneficial operation of compound interest which should, if everything was proceeding smoothly in a well-governed society, lead us within a few generations to the complete abolition of oppressive economic want. (13, pp. 366–7)

Keynes was applying the arguments of the *Treatise*. By his reference to wasted resources, he means that saving exceeds investment, so on the argument of the *Treatise*, it is wasted.

[16] The statement Keynes makes appears in the *Collected Writings* (14, pp. 103–4). Keynes talks about the marginal efficiency of money, not the demand for money. Paul Davidson has called my attention to the term *money* in this sentence. In the original draft, I referred to money as "real balances" to represent the marginal efficiency of money in terms of itself. Davidson argues that this is not what Keynes said, and he suggested *nominal money* be used instead. I am not persuaded. The ambiguity arises because in the first half of the *General Theory* prices and money wages are held fixed, so it is often difficult to judge from the context when Keynes means nominal money and when he means money in wage units. In an exchange with Henderson (29, p. 221), Keynes writes, "the absolute quantity of money has no enduring effect on the rate of interest, I do not admit that the quantity of money measured in wage units has no enduring effect." On the following page, he repeats the point: "The rate of interest still depends on the interaction of liquidity preference and the quantity of money in terms of wage units."

[17] Keynes states:

> "I consider that my suggestions for a cure, which, avowedly, are not worked out completely, are on a different plane from the diagnosis. They are not meant to be definitive; they are subject to all sorts of special assumptions and are necessarily related to the particular conditions of the time. But my main reasons for departing from the traditional theory go much deeper than this. They are of a highly general character and are meant to be definitive [sic]. (14, p. 122)

He then discusses the two issues, expectations and full employment.

theory. Again, these are the treatment of expectations and the meaning of full employment. In his Galton lecture, Keynes discusses long-term growth and expresses, not doubt but, strong conviction that the depression will end and that investment will rise relative to output "in the near future up to the best standard we have ever experienced in any previous decade" (ibid., p. 130).

The similarity of these papers lies not only in what is said but in what is omitted. Rigid wages, liquidity traps, disequilibrium (in the current or conventional sense), elasticity pessimism, irrational expectations, denial of gross substitution, none of these common interpretations of the main point of the *General Theory* is prominent in the argument and most are not present.[18] That this is not an accident is shown not only by the repetition of his main point but also by his response to Hicks following Hicks's review of the *General Theory* in the *Economic Journal*.

Keynes (ibid., p. 71) began by discussing whether he must assume, as Hicks claimed, that the price elasticity of the supply of consumption goods must be high. Keynes responded that a high elasticity is not required. All that is required is that the price elasticity of the supply of output is not *zero*, as classical theorists believed. He then redefined full employment in terms of the price elasticity of supply:

If I were writing again, I should indeed feel disposed to define full employment as being reached at the same moment at which the supply of output in general becomes inelastic. It is perfectly true that a great part of my theory ceases to be required when the supply of output as a whole is inelastic. (ibid., p. 71)[19]

Hicks's response withdrew the point about "high" elasticity and added:

I do not want to give up my substantial point, that output may have reached a short-period maximum, even when there are a considerable number of unemployed specialised to the investment goods industries. But I take it you would now accept this and redefine full employment to cover this case. (ibid., p. 73)

Keynes neither granted Hicks's point nor conceded much. He agreed that the economy can reach a short-period maximum with workers unemployed: "The definition I gave in my previous letter is formally

---

[18] Alternative interpretations are discussed in Chapter 6.
[19] In fact, he gives a similar but not identically worded definition in Chapter 3 (see 7, p. 26).

equivalent, I think, with that which I gave in my book" (ibid., p. 75).[20] Hicks appears to have missed the point about underemployment equilibrium. What Hicks calls "a short-period maximum" is close to what Keynes means by underemployment equilibrium. The difference is mainly that for Keynes the position does not depend on the presence of specialized workers. It is the position expected to be reached in an economy operating under the institutional arrangement he described as laissez-faire.

The development of Hicks's (1937) IS–LM model without expectations submerged Keynes's central thesis directly, by eliminating expectations, and indirectly, by eliminating the distinction between actual and expected rates of interest. The crucial problem for Keynes is that the conventional or expected rate of interest, the rate relevant for investment, can be made to fluctuate but cannot be reduced permanently by changes in nominal values. Hence, the discrepancy between actual equilibrium income and full-employment (maximum) income cannot be reduced by increasing money or reducing money wages. There is excess supply in the sense that the equilibrium rate of investment is less than full-employment saving. Once again, potential saving is wasted. Since the rate of interest does not fall, the economy fluctuates around a low-level equilibrium. If investment increased permanently, the multiplier would assure that saving (and consumption) increased to sustain equilibrium at the higher level – the full-employment (maximum) value of income.

Keynes links expectations to uncertainty and uncertainty to the excess burden borne by a society in which private investors choose the level of investment spending. The cost of investment, as viewed by private investors, includes a risk premium to cover lender's risk. This risk arises because the possibility of default creates a "moral hazard" (7, p. 144). The cost associated with lender's risk is not part of the social cost of investment. It is avoidable if investment is directed by public bodies that internalize the risk of default by acting as lenders and borrowers. Hence, Keynes concluded, society is not at a Pareto optimum; investment and output are too low.

Society is capable of reaching a classical stationary state within a

---

[20] Compare the similar statement from Chapter 20 of the *General Theory*:
> We have shown that when effective demand is deficient there is under employment of labour in the sense that there are men unemployed who would be willing to work at less than the existing real wage. Consequently, as effective demand increases, employment increases, though at a real wage equal to or less than the existing one, until a point comes at which there is no surplus labour available at the then existing real wage. (7, p. 289)

Hicks (1977, p. 144, n. 12) was convinced only that Keynes was correct on Keynes's assumption.

generation if the excess burden can be eliminated. Each period capital would depreciate and be replaced, so gross investment would remain positive in the stationary state, but net investment would be zero. The capital stock would be satiated, and the marginal product of capital would be zero. Since capital depreciates, the actual capital output ratio would fall below the desired ratio but would be pulled back to equilibrium by the replacement demand for capital.[21]

There are, then, two major themes in Keynes's central thesis. First, in the prevailing circumstances of the 1930s or the 1920s, income and employment could be increased by increasing investment. Increases in investment, if maintained at a higher rate, would raise consumption and income. The slump could be ended. Second, if investment remained at the higher rate, the capital stock would increase, and within a generation, the demand for capital would be satiated and the rate of interest brought to (or near) zero. As Keynes had long believed, it is investment, not saving, that determines the outcome for society. The *General Theory* is Keynes's attempt to develop a theory that yielded this implication.

The building blocks

Keynes developed his argument in two ways. He attacked classical theory, which, he recognized, he had taught along with Marshall, Pigou, and others; and he both developed new concepts and used older ideas in new ways. The attack on classical theory centers on Say's law. Many of the new concepts that seemed so strange to Keynes's contemporaries – concepts such as effective demand, the equality of saving, and investment or liquidity preference – have long since become familiar. Before we bring together the major ideas in a formal model of the *General Theory*, this section considers the main point of Keynes's criticism of classical theory and presents his ideas about some of the building blocks of his theory.

Say's law

Keynes's central thesis is that equilibrium output is less than full (maximum) output and employment. If equilibrium output can be raised, it

---

[21] I am indebted to Milton Friedman for making this point and suggesting that I tie the argument about saturation more clearly to the zero rate of interest and the classical stationary state. (See Friedman 1962.) Keynes had edited and commented on Ramsey's (1928) article on optimum saving, so he was familiar with the formal argument (12, pp. 784–9).

becomes possible to increase investment and consumption together. One is not a substitute for the other; there is no need to sacrifice current consumption to achieve more future consumption. Increases in investment, if sustained, increase both consumption and saving. The theory of the multiplier is one application of this idea. The general idea is the core of Keynes's criticism of Say's law.

Keynes expressed the idea in this way on several occasions. The preface to the French edition is one of the clearest. There, he recognizes that Say's law had been abandoned by most economists, but the fallacy lives on – that "demand is created by supply. Say was implicitly assuming that the economic system was always operating up to its full capacity, so that a new activity was always in substitution for, and never in addition to, some other activity" (7, p. xxxv). In 1933, Keynes told a radio audience, "spending and saving are in very truth complementary activities" (21, p. 154), so we can be sure that the idea predates publication of the *General Theory*.

Keynes's 1929 pamphlet Can Lloyd George Do It? written with Hubert Henderson made the case for additional government spending on grounds that the spending could be financed without raising taxes. Surprisingly, in 1933 Henderson criticized Keynes's *Means to Prosperity* using as an argument against public spending that "it's quite conceivable that the reduction in the number of houses built by private enterprise will be more than 100 percent of the houses your corporation will build in practice" (ibid., p. 164–5). Henderson added that Keynes's proposal for public works may "by raising rates of interest, disturbing confidence, etc., diminish the volume of general industrial activity" (ibid., p. 166).

Arguments of this kind, including the so-called Treasury view, convinced Keynes that the prevalent and perhaps dominant belief among economists was that any increase in government spending was a substitute for private spending. This proposition was believed to be true independent of the level of employment.[22] In his public speeches and

---

[22] Corry (1978, pp. 30–1, n. 1) provides a clear statement of the Treasury view written in an official document dated May 1929:

> The additional £125m a year required for new state or local authority borrowing cannot be found without impinging on the supply of capital or other home requirements . . . The large loans, if they are not to involve inflation, must draw on existing capital resources. These resources are, on the whole, utilized at present in varying degrees of active employment; and the great bulk is utilized for home investment/commercial purposes. The extent to which any additional employment could be given by altering the direction of investment is, therefore, at the best strictly limited. But the direction of investment can only be altered if we are prepared to offer sufficiently high money rates to counteract the attractions offered. If, however, we do so, the damage done to home trade and employment by the imposition of such high rates would undoubtedly be much greater than any benefit they could obtain from the funds that could thereby be diverted from foreign investment.

writing, Keynes attacked the Treasury view, but in the *General Theory*, he substituted Say's law as the more general statement on which the Treasury view was based.

Early in 1932, Keynes is particularly clear about the proposition he wished to deny:

> There are also, I should admit, forces which one might fairly well call "automatic" which operate under any normal monetary system in the direction of restoring a long-period equilibrium between saving and investment. The point on which I cast doubt – though the contrary is generally believed – is whether these "automatic" forces will, in the absence of deliberate management, tend to bring about not only an equilibrium between saving and investment but also an optimum level of production. (13, p. 395)

This early passage is notable for the distinction between stable (or long-period) equilibrium and optimum (full-employment) output. (See also 29, p. 91.) For Keynes, this difference became "involuntary unemployment" that cannot be reduced without intervention. However, the passage does not appear in the *General Theory*. There, Say's law is defined as "the proposition that there is no obstacle to full employment" (7, p. 26). With Say's law effective, aggregate output is inelastic with respect to an increase in aggregate demand, so increases in investment necessarily reduce consumption.

Kahn's (1931) paper developing the theory of the multiplier strengthened Keynes's case by demonstrating that the investment multiplier is greater than 1. Keynes's subsequent (1933) restatement of the multiplier (21, pp. 171–8) argues that the size of the multiplier changes with the level of output. As employment increases, more of the additions to demand take the form of higher prices and wages, so the increment to output is smaller (ibid., p. 175). He stresses that contrary to his interpretation of Say's law, the average or maintained level of output responds to demand as long as resources are idle – involuntarily unemployed.

Keynes attributed the failure to accept the idea of the multiplier to

> the fact that all our ideas about economics . . . are, whether we are conscious of it or not, soaked with theoretical pre-suppositions which are only applicable to a society which is in equilibrium, with all its productive resources already employed. Many people are trying to solve the problem of unemployment with a theory which is based on the assumption that there is no unemployment . . . these ideas, perfectly valid in their proper setting, are inapplicable to present circumstances. (ibid., p. 178)

Keynes cites Hobson and Malthus as precursors who saw that saving, or refraining from consumption, could lead to lower, not higher, output (7, pp. 362–70). Perhaps because Keynes had failed in the *Treatise* to make a valid argument that saving could be "wasted," he seems eager to praise these authors despite the flaws that he recognizes in their arguments. Malthus is particularly singled out for "the first explicit statement of the fact that capital is brought into existence not by the propensity to save but in response to the demand resulting from actual and prospective consumption" (ibid., p. 368). In other words, it is not capital and labor that limits output as in neoclassical growth theory; it is the demand for current and future consumption. This proposition is true, in general, only if we are always below the limiting point at which the supply of output becomes vertical.

My interpretation of Say's law differs from the usual statements such as those found in the works of Patinkin, Leijonhufvud, or Lange. Patinkin (1965, pp. 355–9) interprets Say's identity as the statements that (1) aggregate demand intersects the aggregate supply curve at full employment and (2) there can never be a shift in aggregate demand to disturb the equilibrium. The second statement denies fluctuations in aggregate demand. Keynes did *not* attribute any such proposition to early classical writers nor to Marshall, Pigou, or himself in the 1920s.[23] Since these are the authors identified repeatedly as the people he has in mind, we can be certain that, whatever its merits, this is not the meaning Keynes gave to Say's law or identity. Leijonhufvud properly rejects Lange's (1942) overly formal discussion of Say's law but substitutes failures of market coordination (Leijonhufvud 1968, pp. 68, 280). I find no firm basis for this interpretation, and Leijonhufvud does not make a strong claim to this effect.[24] Keynes's writings make clear that the point he has in mind is both simple and closely related to the arguments raised against his efforts to get the government to expand aggregate demand in 1930–2.

Expectations and aggregate demand

One of the main innovations in the *General Theory* is the explicit role given to expectations and uncertainty in the theory of aggregate de-

---

[23] Patinkin (1965, p. 359) also claims that Say's identity applies only in a barter economy. Keynes certainly did not intend this interpretation of those, including himself at an earlier stage, whom he identified as classical economists.

[24] Much of Hansen's (1953) discussion of Say's law is unclear. He suggests (1953, pp. 20, 27) that Keynes substituted the consumption function for Say's law. Later, (p. 130) he makes a clearer statement that Say's law implies automatic adjustment toward full employment. The earlier reference to the consumption function is puzzling. A plausible interpretation is that in the *General Theory* output is determined by demand, not by available resources as in classical and neoclassical theories. The puzzling aspect is that Hansen emphasizes consumption, not aggregate demand.

mand and money. The importance of expectations had been recognized much earlier. Classical writers often referred to "confidence" as a factor affecting the demand for money or to explain fluctuations in cash balances and monetary velocity. Alfred Marshall's discussions of fluctuations and cycles introduce confidence and other terms that present-day economists have no difficulty interpreting as anticipations or expectations (Eshag 1963, pp. 78–82).

Keynes used waves of optimism and other expectational notions to explain the boom after World War I.[25] A few years later (1923), he described lack of confidence as the only remediable cause of current unemployment (19, pp. 112, 115). His *Tract* (4, pp. 39–42) discusses the inflation tax as a consequence of the slow formation of expectations and explains the rise in the interest rate as the eventual adjustment of interest rates to expectations of inflation. The *Treatise* invokes expectations as a determinant of the demand for liquid assets.

Keynes's reliance on expectations is not surprising. His works on probability antedates most of his work in economics. In the *Treatise on Probability* (JMK 8), he developed the idea that is now called subjective expectations, distinguished between ideas such as risk and uncertainty, and applied his ideas on expectations to many types of personal and social decisions. His ideas about risk and uncertainty are similar to the ideas published by Knight at about the same time (1921).

Keynes wrote that the "importance of probability can only be derived from the judgment that it is *rational* to be guided by it in action . . . in action we *ought* to act to take some account of it" (8, p. 356). He introduced the notion of "weight" (ibid., Chapter 6) and used the notion to discuss the relevance of an argument. He related the ideas of weight and relevance to a priori probability where "the weight of an argument is at its lowest . . . The evidential weight of an argument rises, though its probability may either rise or fall, with every accession of relevant evidence" (ibid., p. 78).

In the *General Theory*, Keynes introduces very similar ideas when he distinguishes between the "best estimates we can make of probabilities and the confidence with which we make them" (7, p. 240). The distinction is used at one point to explain the difference between a risk premium and a liquidity premium. He maintains the distinction between

---

[25] Skidelsky (1983, pp. 207–8) quotes from a letter Keynes wrote to his father in 1910 commenting on "irrational waves of optimism and pessimism." See also Hutchinson (1978, p. 204), who notes that Keynes held these views as early as 1910. Keynes favored a sharp rise in the rate of interest to break the speculative boom after World War I. See Moggridge and Howson (1974, in Wood 1, pp. 453–4) and Howson (1973, in Wood 1, p. 443). Recall from Chapter 3, however, that Keynes was critical of Pigou's use of this explanation of fluctuations.

low weight ("very uncertain") and low probability ("very improbable") (ibid., p. 148), on which he dwelt in his work on probability, and he refers to the earlier discussion of the "weight" of a probability to develop his notion of uncertainty.

The discussion of uncertainty and expectations leads Keynes to the issue of variability and instability. There is

> instability due to speculation, [and] there is the instability due to the characteristic of human nature that a large proportion of our positive activities depend on spontaneous optimism rather than on a mathematical expectation, whether moral or hedonistic or economic. Most, probably, of our decisions to do something positive, the full consequences of which will be drawn out over many days to come, can only be taken as a result of animal spirits – of a spontaneous urge to action rather than inaction, and not as the outcome of a weighted average of quantitative benefits multiplied by quantitative probabilities. (ibid., p. 161)

This view, based on his earlier work on probability, is repeated in different words at several places. It is a main theme in his 1937 restatement of the *General Theory* (14, pp. 121–3). He returns to it again when he expresses his belief that not only economic reward but "habit, instinct, preference, desire, will, etc." affect every decision (29, p. 294):

> Human decisions affecting the future, whether personal or political or economic, cannot depend on strict mathematical expectation, since the basis for making such calculation does not exist; and that it is our innate urge to activity which makes the wheels go round, our rational [sic] selves choosing between the alternatives as best we are able, calculating where we can, but often falling back for our motive on whim or sentiment or chance. (7, pp. 162–3)

The problem of forming accurate expectations is more difficult for long-term than for short-term decisions. In both cases, people use information as best they can. They act rationally: "We should not conclude . . . that everything depends on waves of irrational psychology. On the contrary, the state of long-term expectations is often steady" (ibid., p. 162). It is rational to use expectations or "equivalent certainties" when making decisions (29, pp. 288–9; 8, p. 356). We often have limited information, and for this reason, long-term expectations are at times subject to large, discrete changes and depend on the actions of others. People try to find out what others are doing or saying and then do the same (7, pp. 155–7); dominant opinion may change violently in response to relatively small changes in prices, economic activity, or other variables (ibid., p. 154); and future gains are discounted at a very high rate (ibid., p. 157). At times, expectations are extrapolative; a small change in money wages or interest rates generates expectations that additional changes in the same direction will occur. At another time, a large change in the same variables or a particular level of the variable may give rise to regressive expectations.

Keynes believed that probabilities are *not* numerical values (e.g., 29, p. 289; 7, p. 148; 8, p. 344) but men must act as if they are. His statements about "animal spirits," casinos, and "bulls and bears" reflect his belief that relatively large changes in expected values can occur quickly and that risk and uncertainty must be distinguished (29, p. 258).

Keynes's comments on volatility are often repeated. Less often repeated are his statements about expectations in Chapter 5 of the *General Theory* and his definition of expectations. He defines a person's sales expectation, in a way that should appeal to rational expectationists, as the "expectation of proceeds which, if it were held with certainty, would lead to the same behavior as does the bundle of vague and more various possibilities which actually makes up his state of expectation when he reaches his decision" (7, p. 24, n. 3). This definition and the more orderly and customary influence of expectations is developed in Chapter 5. There, Keynes distinguishes short- and long-period expectations. The former are orderly and revised slowly. They can be taken as given (7, p. 51): "Knowledge of the factors which will govern the yield of an investment some years hence is usually very slight" (ibid., p. 149). Long-term expectations are at times subject to sudden change. A succinct statement of his position – that people act as if the future is calculable when it is not – appears in an often repeated quotation from his 1937 article in the *Quarterly Journal*. The last part of his comment is often omitted, however:

> By "uncertain" knowledge, let me explain, I do not mean merely to distinguish what is known for certain from what is only probable. The game of roulette is not subject, in this sense, to uncertainty; nor is the prospect of a Victory Bond being drawn . . . The sense in which I am using the term is that in which the prospect of a European war is uncertain . . . or the possition of private wealth-owners in the social system in 1970. About these matters there is no scientific basis on which to form any capable probability whatever. We simply do not know. Nevertheless, the necessity for action and for decision compels us as practical men to do our best to overlook this

awkward fact and to behave exactly as we should if we had behind us a good Benthamite calculation of a series of prospective advantages and disadvantages, each multiplied by its appropriate probability, waiting to be summed. (14, pp. 113–44)[26]

I interpret this paragraph as one of several that justifies the use of expected values derived from his theory while asserting that decisions taken in this way are subject to large, persistent errors. The best one can do in an uncertain world is to compute expected values using current and past observations while remembering that permanent or persistent changes in expected values rarely can be predicted.

Despite the emphasis on expectations, Keynes's theory is a static theory. He is explicit in his 1937 lecture notes (ibid., pp. 181–2), where he makes three relevant points. First, "the theory of effective demand is substantially the same if we assume that short-period expectations are always fulfilled." Second, he discusses the theories of Robertson, Hawtrey, and the Swedish theorists as examples of disequilibrium, where "the whole explanation [lies] in the *differences* between effective demand and income . . . they do not notice that in my treatment this is *not* so." Third, "The main point is to distinguish the forces determining the position of equilibrium from the technique of trial and error by means of which the entrepreneur discovers where the position is." Keynes's main interest is in the statics, not the adjustment.

Fluctuations in aggregate demand occur around the equilibrium value. Equilibrium is defined in terms of expectations; it is the position at which actual and expected values are equal. The position of equilibrium is not fixed by conditions of supply, as in Say's law and the classical theory; it is conditional on the state of expectations affecting

---

[26] Compare the much earlier formulation in the *Treatise on Probability* where Keynes criticizes G. E. Moore's discussion of probability as a guide to action.

> We must sum for each course of action a series of terms made up of the amounts of good which may attach to each of its possible consequences, each multiplied by its appropriate probability.
>
> The first assumption, that quantities of goodness are duly subject to the laws of arithmetic, appears to me to be open to a certain amount of doubt . . . The second assumption, however, that degrees of probability are wholly subject to the laws of arithmetic, runs directly counter to the view which has been advocated in Part I of this treatise. Lastly . . . the doctrine that "mathematical expectations" of alternative courses of action are the proper measures of our degrees of preference is open to doubt on two grounds. (8, p. 344)

Keynes discusses the two grounds. One is the *weight* of the argument (the evidence on which the assigned probability is based); the other is the neglect of risk. Keynes's conclusion on the latter recognizes risk aversion (8, pp. 347–8).

demand[27]: "The steady level of employment thus attained may be called the long-period employment corresponding to that state of expectation . . . Every state of expectation has its definite corresponding level of long-period employment" (7, p. 48).[28]

The discussion of equilibrium and short-term expectations reaches the conclusion that current employment (and aggregate demand) depend on expectations and the capital stock (ibid., p. 50). In an earlier draft of the *General Theory* (13, pp. 441–2) Keynes summarized his theory of aggregate demand in two equations, the consumption and investment functions, as follows:

$$C/W = f_1(N, r, E)$$

and

$$I/W = f_2(N, r, E)$$

where C, I, and W are nominal values of consumption, investment, and the money wage; N is the volume of employment; r is the rate of interest; and E is the state of long-term expectations. This corresponds closely to the IS curve used in Meltzer (1981) with Y/W, nominal income in wage units, used in place of N. My formulation was[29]

$$Y/W = A(Y/W, r, E)$$

As Keynes notes in the passage just cited and elsewhere (7, pp. 315–16), the capital stock properly belongs in the equation even though it is fixed in the *General Theory*. With this change, the IS curve becomes

[27] In what follows, I discuss the meaning of Keynes's equilibrium for the labor market. There is an *underemployment equilibrium* in the labor market, as Keynes used the term. In reading the quotation in the text that follows, it is useful to recall that Keynes treats employment as proportional to real output. He notes that the level need not be constant.

[28] Changes in expectations set off oscillations that have the characteristics of business cycles. Keynes refers to the price–cost–profits of the *Treatise* (7, p. 49).

[29] At the time, I avoided reading the earlier drafts of the *General Theory* in vol. 13, so I did not find Keynes's equations until much later. The material from volume 13 confirms Keynes's statement to Hicks cited in the preceding and supports his statements to Hicks about Hicks's failure to distinguish between actual and expected income (14, pp. 80–1). Keynes's early formulation makes clear that he regarded expectations as more important for investment than for consumption. By using expected income in the IS curve and current income in the LM curve, Keynes sought to overcome the problem of specifying the period to which the equilibrium position applies, a problem to which Hicks gave considerable attention elsewhere (Hicks 1982, pp. 325–30).

$$\text{IS:} \qquad Y/W = A(Y/W, r, E; K) \qquad (4.1)$$

The IS curve is one of three equations in the model used to derive some of the implications Keynes claimed for his theory.[30]

Equation (4.1) seeks to capture the considerable emphasis Keynes gave to expectations as a driving force moving the economy from one equilibrium to another or, more often, keeping it at the prevailing underemployment equilibrium. Changes in expectations – animal spirits, waves of optimism, and pessimism – are the principal shocks causing cyclical fluctuations. Keynes believed that a principal error in the economic theory of his day was the failure to recognize that decisions to invest in real capital depend on the whole stream of returns, not just the immediate prospect (ibid., pp. 138, 141). In his account of changes in investment, prospective future returns are the driving force. These returns, and the expectation of these returns, are often stable but are subject to sudden change. The changes have two effects. They shift the IS curve, and they increase the variability of returns. The former causes fluctuations. The latter adds to the risk premium in interest rates and thus raises the rate of interest and lowers the average rate of investment and the size of the capital stock.

The emphasis on expectations and uncertainty was submerged or omitted in the Hicks (1937), Metzler (1951), and Patinkin (1965) interpretations that dominated macroeconomic theory until the late 1960s. Although some of this literature mentions expectations and uncertainty and expectations are a central element in Friedman's (1957) permanent income theory, a revival of interest in the analysis of expectations and their influence came with concern about inflation in the mid-1960s. Price and inflation expectations became of increased importance for the analysis of interest rates, prices, and wages. From these developments came the major role now assigned to expectations by the rational-expectations hypothesis (e.g., Lucas 1972).

Most of the rational-expectations literature does not address the issue of major concern to Keynes. In the rational-expectations literature, expectations are typically certain and widely shared. Keynes's discussion of long-term expectations emphasizes uncertainty, bulls and bears, and sudden changes in belief as well as habits, conventions, and persistent beliefs. Alchian (1969, 1977), Brunner and Meltzer (1971), and Leijonhufvud (1968) bring these notions into the theory of employment or money by appealing to costs of acquiring information and

---

[30] Comparison with equations (3.3) and (3.4) of my summary of the *Treatise* shows the important changes in Keynes's thinking. Investment, saving, and consumption are now in real (wage unit) terms. Expectations enter explicitly, and real income is not taken as given.

diffuse knowledge of future states. Gertler and Grinols (1982) develop an explicit model in which the random behavior of the money stock affects investment by changing the distribution of asset returns. Increased variance of money growth and inflation lowers investment and the demand for capital. In Gertler and Grinols (1982, pp. 255–6), increased uncertainty about money growth moves the economy to a balanced growth path along which investment is lower and consumption is higher.[31]

Keynes anticipates the rational expectationists in his discussion of changes in short- but not long-term values. He remarks that "the existing market valuation, however arrived at, is uniquely *correct* in relation to our existing knowledge of the facts" (7, p. 152). Given this convention, "an investor can legitimately encourage himself with the idea *over the near future* . . . and he need not lose his sleep merely because he has not any notion what his investment will be worth ten years hence" (ibid., pp. 152–3). However, daily "fluctuations in the profits of existing investments, which are obviously of an ephemeral and nonsignificant character, tend to have an altogether excessive, and even absurd, influence on the market" (ibid., pp. 153–4).[32]

Generally statisticians and economists have not accepted the Keynes–Knight distinction between risk and uncertainty. A main reason is that these terms do not have independent meaning in modern theories of statistical decision making. I believe the Keynes–Knight notion is dismissed too readily. The distinction between risk and un-

---

[31] Fischer and Merton (1984) discuss the role of stock prices in macroeconomics, particularly for the theory of investment. They argue that changes in the uncertainty component in interest rates can at times dominate the effect of changes in risk-free real rates, so investment may be driven in the direction given by the uncertainty component. Fischer and Merton also consider Keynes's notion of the stock market as a casino and its relation to recent work, following Shiller (1981), on excessive volatility of stock prices. At a more abstract level, Jordan (1983) shows that where the distribution of asset returns is not normal, equilibrium asset prices are generally inconsistent with the strong form of the efficient market hypothesis under which asset prices reveal all relevant information about future states to the public. Variability matters in Jordan's model, as does the type of risk aversion and differences in the type of risk aversion. This work captures some of Keynes's ideas. Discrete jumps in beliefs can produce nonnormal distributions of errors.

[32] Why do not informed traders take advantage of the long-run gains by buying securities when they fall below their long-term value and selling them in the contrary case? Keynes's answer is that profits can be earned only if their influence can predominate (7, p. 156–7). This argument is not correct. A patient holder who buys on a wave of pessimism and sells on a wave of optimism profits from his speculation. Further, if he profits, others are likely to copy his strategy. Keynes does not pursue his argument but, instead, shifts to the assumption of a high discount rate (ibid., p. 157). Once again, the conclusion drawn is very close to the conclusion Keynes reaches about his own efforts to time purchases and sales of securities to take advantage of the "credit cycle" (12, pp. 102–9). I am indebted to Donald Moggridge for suggesting the last point.

certainty can be treated as a difference in the (subjective) probability distribution and the information that people use when making decisions. Uncertainty can be represented by a very diffuse prior probability distribution assigned to the returns that will be earned and the states in which they will be earned in the distant future. Risk can refer to near-term prospects where the probability distribution is much less diffuse. As Keynes said in the preceding passage, the only near-term risk is that the news will change, and he added that the change is "unlikely to be very large" (ibid., p. 153). Much less is known, according to Keynes, about long-term prospects. Since people must make decisions, they act as if they know the probabilties or the distribution of returns when, in truth, the (subjective) prior probability assigned to any particular outcome in the distant future is small and the probability distribution is diffuse. Diffuse uncertainty about long-term events would be nondiversifiable and therefore noninsurable by the owners of a firm. Hence, it fits the criteria for uncertainty in the Keynes–Knight terminology.

Keynes offers no reason for his belief that short-term changes are "unlikely to be very large" (ibid., p. 153). I believe this misstates an important distinction. It is not only the size of changes but also uncertainty about persistence that is troublesome to investors. Large, transitory changes around an unchanging mean increase variability and risk. When transitory variability becomes sufficiently large, skilled professionals create methods of shifting the risk of transitory fluctuations to those willing to bear it. Large permanent or persistent changes in expected value often are more difficult to shift. Recent experience with oil shocks and sudden changes from inflationary to disinflationary policy suggests that uncertainty about the persistence of observed changes can be a major cause of losses. The reason is that misinterpretation of infrequent, relatively large, persistent shocks gives rise to major mistakes.[33]

A major problem with Keynes's theory of expectations is that he says very little about the determinants of changes in expectations. Expectations change, suddenly at times, but Keynes does not commit himself to even the rudiments of any particular dynamic theory of the mutual interdependence of actual and expected values. This permits him to treat some expectations as extrapolative, others as regressive, or to shift, when convenient for his argument, from one to the other.[34]

---

[33] A model of fluctuations in which uncertainty about persistence has a large role is Brunner, Cukierman, and Meltzer (1983). (See also Cukierman 1984.)

[34] He even proposes a type of distributed lag at one point (7, pp. 47–9). His discussion mentions some of the factors affecting the speed of adjustment and ends by referring to his discussion in the *Treatise* of the adjustment of working capital.

Uncertainty and money

There are two possible effects of uncertainty on economic activity. People may respond to uncertainty by increasing saving and the ownership of capital to improve their prospects of achieving their goals. Or, they may choose to hold less capital and more, relatively safe, financial assets.

Keynes has no doubt about which effect dominates. Uncertainty increases the demand for money and raises the interest rate. This conclusion may have had an analytic foundation in his analysis of uncertainty, but most likely it was based on observations, particularly his observations of inflation in Europe in the early 1920s. These experiences reinforced his belief that "the modern capitalist world is even less suited in my opinion for violent fluctuations in the value of money upwards than it is for violent fluctuations in the value of money downwards. Either form of action is very ill advised, and ought never to be undertaken on purpose" (19, p. 60). A decade later, in 1932, Keynes commented on the effects of an increased demand for money during deflation:

> The risk of carrying assets with borrowed money is so great that there is a competitive panic to get liquid. And each individual who succeeds in getting more liquid forces down the price of assets in the process of getting liquid, with the result that the margins of other individuals are impaired and their courage undermined. (21, p. 40)

The principal effect of changes in anticipations is on the rate of interest:

> The shift in the rate of interest is usually the most prominent part of the reaction to a change in the news. The movement in bond-prices is, as the newspapers are accustomed to say, "out of all proportion to the activity of dealing" . . . which is as it should be, in view of individuals being much more similar than they are dissimilar in their reaction to news. (7, p. 199)[35]

Keynes introduces liquidity preference by restating the theme he developed in the *Treatise*. There are "two distinct sets of decisions" (ibid., p. 166). The first is the decision about how much to consume

---

[35] Notice that Keynes explains high volatility by invoking common beliefs and the arrival of "news." The news results in a change in the expected value. Note also that he does not invoke bulls and bears – differences in belief or differences in information. Differences in belief can have the effect of stabilizing the rate of interest or reducing fluctuations.

today. The second is the decision about the form in which claims to future consumption are held. The latter decision involves a choice about liquidity preference – "a schedule of the amounts of his resources . . . which he will wish to retain in the form of money in different sets of circumstances" (ibid., p. 166). By choosing to hold money, a person chooses to have immediate command over goods. He sacrifices interest, "the reward for parting with liquidity for a specified period" (ibid., p. 167).

The necessary condition for the existence of liquidity preference is "*uncertainty* as to the future of the rate of interest, i.e. as to the complex of rates of interest for varying maturities which will rule at future dates" (ibid., p. 168).[36] By uncertainty, Keynes means matters about which useful information is lacking, events to which, in his terms, investors attach low weight or, in my terms, circumstances in which prior probabilities are diffuse. The owner of an income yielding asset must accept that the return he anticipates may become a capital loss if he finds it necessary to sell the asset before it reaches maturity. "The actuarial profit or mathematical expectation of gain calculated in accordance with the existing probabilities – if it can be so calculated, which is doubtful – must be sufficient to compensate for the risk of disappointment" (ibid., p. 169).

Keynes also mentions differences in expectations as a reason for holding money – the "bulls and bears" of the *Treatise* (ibid.). Elsewhere (29, pp. 293–4), Keynes repeats the distinction between probability and "weight" and relates these terms to the difference between risk and liquidity premiums. Then, he adds:

> A risk premium is expected to be rewarded on the average by an increased return at the end of the period. A liquidity premium . . . is not even expected to be so rewarded. It is a payment, not for the expectation of increased tangible income at

---

[36] The insufficiency of Keynes's argument when there are short-term government securities is the subject of Tobin's (1958) classic paper. (See also Viner 1936, reprinted in Wood 2, pp. 90, 92–3.) Viner also points out that the transactions demand for cash has "equal influence on the rate of interest" (ibid., p. 93). Keynes elaborates on the reason for holding money instead of securities. He begins by recognizing that, to use his term, it is "insane" in a classical economy:

> For it is a recognized characteristic of money as a store of wealth that it is barren; . . . Why should anyone outside a lunatic asylum wish to use money as a store of wealth? . . .

> [O]ur desire to hold money as a store of wealth is a barometer of the degree of our distrust of our own calculations and conventions concerning the future. . . . The possession of actual money lulls our disquietude; and the premium which we require to make us part with money is the measure of the degree of our disquietude. (14, pp. 115–16)

the end of the period, but for an increased sense of comfort
and confidence during the period. (ibid.)

The liquidity premium defined in this way is a forerunner of the non-pecuniary return to money in contemporary economics.

The role of money in the *General Theory* is closely tied to Keynes's rejection of his version of classical economics and Say's law. In classical theory, an increase in saving reduces current consumption. Prices and interest rates fall, investment increases, and the full employment position is maintained, possibly after some adjustment (7, pp. 210–11).

Keynes rejects this conclusion and calls "absurd" the belief that an increased desire to save has indirectly the same effect on aggregate demand as the direct effect of an increase in consumption. The fallacy reflects the mistaken belief that "an increased desire to hold wealth, being much the same thing as an increased desire to hold investments, must, by increasing the demand for investments, provide a stimulus to their production; so that current investment is promoted by individual saving to the same extent as present consumption is diminished" (ibid., p. 211). The fallacy arises, Keynes says, because an act of saving, though it transfers wealth to the saver, does not require the creation of new wealth. The creation of new wealth (for society) is a separate decision that depends on a comparison of the return on new wealth to the rate of interest (ibid., p. 212). And modifying his position in the *Treatise*,

the current rate of interest depends . . . not on the strength of
the desire to hold wealth, but on the strengths of the desires
to hold it in liquid and in illiquid forms respectively, coupled
with the amount of the supply of wealth in the one form relatively to the supply of it in the other. (ibid., p. 213)

Here and in many other places (e.g., 7, p. 181), Keynes gives the misleading impression that the demand for and supply of money determine the rate of interest independently of the saving and investment schedules. He may have been confused on this point. He often wrote as if he were, but he also accepted without comment on this point Hicks's (1937) simultaneous determination of interest rates and income, and in the *Treatise*, interest rates are determined simultaneously by stock and flow equilibrium positions. I will accept the latter as his intention, relying in part on statements implying that the rate of interest depends not only on monetary factors but on the marginal efficiency schedule and the propensity to save. (See, e.g., 7, pp. 178–9.)

One confusion from which he freed himself concerned hoarding. In the *General Theory*, Keynes abandons the idea that hoarding is in some way related to saving and comes close to abandoning the concept: "Hoarding may be regarded as a first approximation to the concept of *liquidity-preference*" (ibid., p. 174). Hoarding is therefore a schedule, so the amount of hoards depends on the rate of interest. The nominal quantity of hoards cannot change unless there is a change in the quantity of money or in the transactions demand for money, but changes in the demand to hoard change the rate of interest (ibid.).

The same ideas are repeated in Keynes's "Alternative Theories of the Rate of Interest," (14, pp. 213–14) and in his response to Viner (ibid., pp. 110–11, 118). Viner (1936, reprinted in Wood 2, p. 92) called the importance Keynes attributed to hoarding "a fatal flaw" on two grounds. First, the demand for hoards is small (ibid., p. 93). Second, people demand money mainly to spend (ibid., p. 151). Keynes's reply suggests that he thinks Viner missed his point. The importance of hoarding arises from the effect on the interest rate. The "rate of interest . . . [is] the inducement *not* to hoard . . . Liquidity preference mainly operates by increasing the rate of interest" (14, p. 110). Later, he added:

> A rise in the rate of interest is a means *alternative* to an increase of hoards for satisfying an increased liquidity preference . . .
> The mischief is done when the rate of interest corresponding to the degree of liquidity of a given asset leads to a market-capitalization of that asset which is less than its cost of production., (ibid., p. 111)

An increase in the demand for hoards or liquidity balances raises the rate of interest and thus sets a floor below which the rate of interest on less certain claims does not fall. Further, the rise in the rate of interest lowers capital values. Wealth is reduced. During a slump, if some values fall below cost of production, pessimism grows.

The central issue for Keynes, as for Viner, is whether there is a mechanism in the economic system (under laissez-faire, Keynes would say) to restore the interest rate to its previous level following an increase in the demand for money (liquidity balances). Keynes's answer is no; there is no automatic mechanism that can be relied upon to lower the interest rate under these circumstances. Hence, he concludes, investment and output are reduced. The public holds more real balances and less real capital. They are poorer and, he claims, the equilibrium level of employment is lower.

The demand for money is a demand for real balances in wage units. Demand depends on the interest rate r, on real income (in wage units) Y/W, and on the interest rate expected to prevail in equilibrium, r^e. This rate is the long-term rate (29, p. 266) and depends on the degree of uncertainty u about the future; the greater the degree of uncertainty about the future, the higher the expected equilibrium rate of interest:

$$M/W = L(r, r^e(u); Y/W)$$

The stock of money, M, is one of the variables Keynes takes as given in the *General Theory*. The money market equilibrium relation, or LM curve, is then obtained by equating actual and desired money balances and solving for real output in wage units:

$$\text{LM:} \qquad Y/W = L(r, r^e(u), M/W) \qquad (4.2)$$

The market rate today, given by r, may differ from r^e, but in equilibrium, whether underemployment or full employment equilibrium, actual and expected interest rates are equal. The minimum expected rate of interest in a community with money but with no uncertainty could be as low as zero. Keynes takes this as a theoretical possibility but of no practical interest. In practice, there are administrative costs of borrowing and lending and costs arising from uncertainty about the future rate of interest. Under laissez-faire, these costs set a minimum that he estimates may be 2–2.5 percent. This rate of interest may be too high, he notes, to satiate the capital stock (7, pp. 218–19). By implication, income is then not at full (maximum) output.

Since the expected rate is a given, or a datum, that depends on the degree of uncertainty, the model determines only one rate, r. Keynes confuses the reader by discussing many different rates, rates that differ by maturity and rates on bonds and returns to equity. If new and existing capital earn the same rate of return, the return is given by the marginal efficiency of capital, which is to say by expectations of the future. In equilibrium the return on capital is equal to the rate of interest. Presumably, the equilibrium rate that is determined by the model is the rate for assets with minimum risk. Other assets receive returns that compensate for the additional risk, but although these premiums are discussed, they are not determined by his model.[37]

---

[37] I see no way to determine the term structure of future rates that Keynes discusses (7, p. 168) except by invoking premiums for uncertainty that increase the expected rate for that maturity relative to other maturities. Keynes's treatment of many rates in a system that determines only one rate has been criticized by Kahn (1978, in Wood 1, pp. 551–2). Kahn claims that Keynes confused the returns to equity holders with the returns to capital in the *Treatise* and did not provide for the determination of returns to capital in the *General Theory*. His point is correct if he means that expectations are not determined. The only point at which we know the return to capital is when it is equal to the long-term rate of interest. Keynes says very little. At one point, he notes that in the *Treatise* he combined real assets and debts. This was a mistake, he points out, because it combined the effects of changes in the rate of interest with the effects of changes in the marginal efficiency of capital (7, pp. 173–4).

In an important passage, Keynes discusses the relation between the rate of interest in his model and the neutral and natural rates of interest. In the *Treatise*, he had followed Wicksell in using the term *natural rate* to refer to the equilibrium interest rate at which saving equals investment: "I had not then understood that . . . the system could be in equilibrium with less than full employment" (ibid., p. 243).

In the *General Theory*, there can be many possible equilibrium positions and many possible equilibrium rates of interest. There is

> a *different* natural rate of interest for each hypothetical level of employment. And, similarly, for every rate of interest there is a level of employment for which that rate is the "natural" rate, in the sense that the system will be in equilibrium with that rate of interest and that level of employment. (ibid., p. 242)

These positions of underemployment equilibrium differ from the position of full employment, and the equilibrium rate differs from what Keynes calls the neutral rate "though this rate may be better described, perhaps, as the *optimum* rate" (ibid., p. 243).

On my interpretation, the term *optimum* is not casual usage. The optimum rate is the rate which keeps society on the production frontier. Keynes does not say this, but he defines the neutral or optimum rate as "the rate of interest which prevails in equilibrium when output and employment are such that the elasticity of employment as a whole is zero" (ibid., p. 243). This is the position he defined as full (maximum) employment. Further, he distinguishes his theory from the classical theory by pointing out that in the classical theory "the actual rate of interest is always equal to the neutral rate of interest" (ibid.). Keynes was aware that Marshall and Pigou discussed fluctuations, so his statement is not intended as a denial that fluctuations arise in classical theories. Rather, Keynes's statement should be seen as a reference to the differences in the (stable) equilibrium position around which fluctuations occur. He attributed the difference between the equilibrium rate and the neutral rate to a failure of the equilibrium interest rate to decline to the neutral or optimum rate.

This interpretation is consistent with Keynes's conclusion from a comparison of his theory with the classical theory of interest (ibid., Chapter 14). He accepts the classical position that saving and investment depend on the rate of interest (ibid., pp. 177–8). Error creeps in, however, and the classical theory becomes "nonsense" (ibid., p. 179) when it assumes that income is constant at full employment. On Keynes's interpretation, the classical position introduces Say's law when it claims that an increase in saving leads to an increase in investment at an unchanged equilibrium level of income. If this were so, changes in investment and consumption would be negatively related. In Keynes's theory, a permanent increase in investment triggers the multiplier and raises the equilibrium levels of income and consumption until full employment is reached. Investment and consumption are positively related; the aggregate supply curve is not completely inelastic.

The reason for the error in classical theory is that "the classical theory has not been alive . . . to the possibility of the level of income being actually a function of the rate of investment" (ibid., p. 180). Keynes then presents a diagram showing several possible positions of equilibrium between saving and investment and uses the diagram to argue that one cannot determine the equilibrium rate of interest until the level of income is known. To determine the rate of interest and the level of income simultaneously requires the propensity to consume, the marginal efficiency schedule, liquidity preference, and the quantity of money.

Keynes's insistence on the relation between interest rates and money has been supported by a large number of empirical studies for many countries and time periods. Of interest, however, is the finding that there is often better support for the years after he wrote than for the interwar period or earlier periods. One reason may be that the magnitude of the response of interest rates to fluctuations has increased. Cagan (1966) finds that the size of cyclical changes in interest rates is relatively small in the interwar period.

Recent estimates of the effect of variability in money growth tend to support Keynes's conjecture. Bomhoff (1983) and Mascaro and Meltzer (1983) report evidence of positive effects of increased monetary variability on rates of interest in a general equilibrium framework. Tatom (1985) finds that increased variability reduces output and raises prices, presumably by reducing investment. The issue remains open, however, in large part because of the limited amount of work that has been done.

The labor market and aggregate supply

In a comment (13, p. 406) that Moggridge dates as probably written in 1932, Keynes leaves no doubt that (1) by involuntary employment he means that output is less than the optimal level and (2) involuntary unemployment is the norm:

> For a modern community one may say that it is a *normal* thing, except in times of war and at the height of booms, for output to be below the *optimum* level . . . The maintenance of output,

and hence of real income, at the optimum level, in the sense of *everyone being able to obtain as much employment as he desires* for a reward equal to the *real wage he would get with output in equilibrium at an optimum* level should be the primary object of policy . . . whenever output is below the optimum level, i.e. whenever there is *involuntary unemployment*, we may be sure that an increase in investment will, so to speak, "finance itself." (ibid., p. 407, emphasis added)

As Keynes turned from the *Treatise* to write what became the *General Theory*,[38] he faced the problem of explaining why a system based on laissez-faire principles experienced a period of sustained unemployment in the 1920s and early 1930s. His 1932 definition of involuntary unemployment distinguishes between the actual position the economy achieves and the position Keynes described as an optimum position of equilibrium. Classical theory assumes, as in Say's law, that the only position of equilibrium is an optimum position on the community's production frontier. In Keynes's words:

> The orthodox equilibrium theory of economics has assumed . . . that there are natural forces tending to bring the volume of the community's output, and hence its real income, back to the *optimum* level whenever temporary forces have led it to depart from this level. But we have seen . . . that the equilibrium level toward which output tends to return . . . *is not necessarily the optimum level.* (ibid., p. 406, emphasis added)

The same ideas reappear in the *General Theory* where Keynes describes full employment as a special case:

> The effective demand associated with full employment is a special case, only realized when the propensity to consume and the inducement to invest stand in a particular relationship to one another. This particular relationship, which corresponds to the assumptions of the classical theory, is in a sense an optimum relationship. (7, p. 28)

Again,

> On the classical theory . . . the volume of employment is in neutral equilibrium . . . the forces of competition between entrepreneurs may be expected to push it to this maximum value.

---

[38] Earlier, Keynes had used the notation of the *Treatise* to conjecture that if profit per unit of output reaches zero before output reaches its maximum, "we have 'long-period unemployment'" (13, p. 374). The note, written to Richard Kahn, did not get a coherent response (ibid., p. 375).

Only at this point, on the classical theory, can there be stable equilibrium. (ibid., p. 29)

In his theory, this is not so:

The volume of employment is not determined by the marginal disutility of labor measured in terms of real wages, except in so far as the supply of labor available at a given real wage sets a *maximum* level to employment . . . If the propensity to consume and the rate of new investment result in a deficient effective demand, the actual level of employment will fall short of the supply of labor potentially available at the existing real wage, and the equilibrium real wage will be *greater* than the marginal disutility of the equilibrium level of employment. (ibid., p. 30)

And, again he comments that the rate of interest

may fluctuate *for decades* about a level which is chronically too high for full employment . . . the failure of employment to obtain an *optimum* level being in no way associated, in the minds either of the public or of authority, with the prevalence of an inappropriate range of rates of interest. (ibid., p. 204, emphasis added)

These passages and others are the basis of my interpretation of involuntary unemployment as the difference between maximum employment, achieved when the economy is on the production frontier with full use made of capital and labor, and an interior point of equilibrium employment. At the position of full (maximum) employment, the real wage equals the marginal disutility of labor. Maximum employment is the limiting position that, in Keynes's words, is rarely achieved persistently other than in wartime. Full employment is achieved, temporarily, in a boom, but it is not sustained. Typically, the economy fluctuates for decades[39] around an equilibrium level that is below the full-employment level.

Keynes leaves no doubt that involuntary unemployment includes more than the unemployment that occurs during a business cycle. He responded to Beveridge's criticism by noting that "cyclical employment is only a part of involuntary unemployment" (14, p. 56). Economic activity rises during cyclical expansions above the maintained equilibrium. Employment rises toward maximum employment, so according to Keynes, part of involuntary unemployment is reduced. The

---

[39] This certainly means longer than a business cycle, since Keynes described the typical business cycle as having a duration of three to five years (7, p. 317).

reduction is temporary if nothing is done to permanently change the equilibrium level.[40]

The multiplier is the mechanism by which additional investment generates additional consumption, employment, and output. If the economy is at full employment, the elasticity of the supply of output is zero, so the multiplier is zero. Investment and consumption are substitutes, as implied by Keynes's interpretation of Say's law. This is the classical world in which involuntary unemployment cannot occur (7, pp. 21–2).

Traditional interpretations

Gottfried Haberler, Bertil Ohlin, Dennis Robertson, and A. C. Pigou were among the first to comment on Keynes's theory of unemployment.[41] Several of these explanations continue to appear both as explanations of unemployment and as interpretations of Keynes. Keynes's responses make clear that he did not wholly accept any of these interpretations, and he rejected some completely.

Gottfried Haberler proposed some common recurring explanations of wage rigidity and unemployment based on monopoly or monopolistic competition. Haberler asked:

> Would you agree that an equilibrium with involuntary unemployment is incompatible with perfect competition in the labor market? If . . . competition there were perfect, money wages would fall all the time so long as unemployment existed . . . If that could be agreed upon . . . most classical economists would agree with you, because nobody denies that unemployment can persist, if money wages are rigid. (29, p. 272)

Keynes rejected Haberler's argument and challenged him to cite a reference to a classical writer who presented a theory of wages similar to his own. He responded to the substantive point by insisting that a critical difference between his theory and the classical theory is that in his theory changes in money wages affect the level of employment by changing the rate of interest, whereas in the classical theory changes in money wages affect output by changing costs of production (ibid., pp. 272–3). Keynes did not reject the notion that money wages adjust slowly; he rejected the argument that full employment could be restored by reducing costs of production. Money wage changes are similar to

---

[40] Modern theories of employment that emphasize search have no bearing for Keynes's involuntary unemployment. Keynes includes search as part of voluntary unemployment. In his words, "in a non-static society, a proportion of resources [is] unemployed 'between jobs'" (7, p. 6).

[41] Hicks is also an early commentator. His changing views are discussed in Chapter 6.

changes in the quantity of money; to increase employment permanently, there must be a permanent reduction in the rate of interest. In
Keynes's theory, the reduction is achieved by increasing real money
balances – the supply of money in wage units. He told Haberler:

> If a decline in employment is associated with an increase in
> the quantity of money in terms of wage units . . . a compen-
> satory factor comes into force . . . If classical economists have
> always meant that a sufficient increase of money in terms of
> wage units would be a compensatory element, well and good.
> (ibid., p. 272)

A year earlier, in correspondence with Ohlin, Keynes rejected the
idea of monopoly elements in the labor market. Ohlin (1) accused
Keynes of not being "radical enough in freeing himself from the conventional assumptions" (14 p. 196) and (2) expressed his view that
"long-lasting unemployment may be due simply to the fact that wages
in investment trades are 'too high' compared with the rest of the price
system" (ibid., p. 197). Ohlin's reference to Joan Robinson's work on
imperfect competition as part of the explanation of unemployment, a
theme revisited by Kaldor (1983) and Tobin (1983), brought the following response. The "reference to imperfect competition is very per-
plexing. I cannot see how on earth it comes in. Mrs. Robinson, I may
mention, read my proof without discovering any connection" (ibid.,
p. 190).[42]

Involuntary unemployment is not the result of money illusion.
Keynes forcefully rejected nonneutrality of money in a letter to Hicks.
He distinguished the "pure classical doctrine" and the "much more
confused state of mind" that had developed "an inconsistent hotch-
potch" (ibid., 79):

> The inconsistency creeps in, I suggest, as soon as it becomes
> generally agreed that the increase in the quantity of money is
> capable of increasing employment. A strictly brought-up clas-
> sical economist would not, I should say, admit that. We used
> to admit it without realizing how inconsistent it was with our
> other premises. (ibid., p. 79)

Dennis Robertson correctly saw that involuntary unemployment

---

[42] Keynes was, of course, familiar with the Robinson book and had served as reader of
the manuscript for the publisher. Although he recommended publication, he was unen-
thusiastic about Robinson's own contribution, referring to the book as "predominantly
a discussion of the development of ideas which have been started by others" (12, p.
866). In the *General Theory* (7, p. 8) Keynes includes unemployment arising from the
monopoly power of trade unions as part of voluntary unemployment.

meant a "chronic failure to get up to a norm," not "fluctuations around a norm" (13, p. 500). He expressed skepticism, but as was often the case, he could see some merit in Keynes's idea. The main reason for his skepticism at the time (1935) was that he could not reconcile Keynes's argument with rational behavior in a competitive market. He read Keynes's argument as implying that people are available and willing to work at money wages below the money value of their marginal product (ibid.). Keynes responded that *he had not made this error*. In his theory, the amount of employment is determined by demand given the conditions determining the position of the supply curve. An increase in demand for labor that lowers the marginal product of labor and the real wage "will not, in general, be interfered with by labour withdrawing its services" (ibid., p. 516).

In correspondence (and most likely discussion) over several years with Robertson, Hawtrey, Kahn, Shove, and others, Keynes tried to develop what he called the classical theory of the labor market and its implications for unemployment. He complained, frequently, that he could not find a clear account of the classical theory of employment.[43] The principal sources to which he turned were Marshall and Pigou, the latter because he had written books on fluctuations and employment.

Keynes found very little in Marshall that altered his view that classical writers had a positively sloped supply curve of labor relating employment to the real wage as the usual case.[44] He attempted to read this interpretation into Pigou (ibid., p. 316; 14, p. 36) despite strong objections from Robertson (13, pp. 318–19) and later Hawtrey (14, p. 29). Hawtrey argued that Keynes's discussion of Pigou in Chapter 2 and the Appendix to Chapter 19 was wrong. After many exchanges, Keynes sent Hawtrey's interpretation to Pigou, who responded that his supply curve of labor is a reverse *L*, as in textbook versions of *Keynesian* theory (ibid., p. 54). According to Pigou, unemployment is the difference between the number of available workers, a fixed quantity, and the quantity of labor demanded (ibid.). In other words, just as in the traditional rendering of the *General Theory*, the demand for

---

[43] Keynes does not mention Hicks's *Theory of Wages*, published in 1932. We know that Keynes had read Hicks's book as referee for the publisher and had commented that he did not like the method of analysis. A specific complaint is that "prices are fixed independently of wages, so that whatever happens to money wages may be assumed to happen, more or less to the same extent, to real wages" (12, p. 861).

[44] He refers (14, p. 35) to Marshall (1920, pp. 141–2, 525–8). In the first reference, Marshall develops the theory of supply as a schedule and its relation to the theory of labor supply based on the (usually) increasing disutility of an additional hour of work. The second reference discusses the theory of income distribution. Marshall (p. 528) discusses the slope of the labor supply function and concludes that it may be either positively sloped or backward bending.

labor determines employment until the supply of labor becomes vertical.

Keynes did not have the benefit of Pigou's comment when he wrote the Appendix to Chapter 19, and he does not appear to have asked for his criticism. The Appendix and Chapter 2 set out to show that Pigou, taken as the representative of classical economics, does not have a theory of unemployment. The main criticism is that since the supply of labor depends on the real wage and the labor market is competitive, there is no way to determine the money wage, the price level, and the volume of employment from equations for the demand and supply for labor. Keynes observes that workers bargain for their money wage: "The classical school have tacitly assumed that this would involve no significant change in their theory. But this is not so" (7, p. 8). Price and wage changes can have different effects on employment. Failure to separate these effects leaves the level of employment indeterminate; there is no classical theory of unemployment.

For current purposes, the relevant point is Keynes's conclusion about the properties of the labor supply function. If labor bargains in terms of the money wage, the supply function depends on the price level (the price of wage goods) as well as the money wage, not on the real wage (ibid., pp. 275–6). Aggregate supply increases with the price level until full (maximum) employment is reached. Keynes conjectures that workers may accept reductions in real wages brought about by price increases more readily than reductions requiring them to accept lower money wages. The former reduces all real wages proportionally; the latter may change relative wages in a system of multimarket wage bargains.

The Appendix to Chapter 19 has one of Keynes's clearest statements about rigid money wages. Using the observation that money wages varied by 6 percent while real wages varied by 20 percent during the years 1924–34, Keynes comments that "we are . . . one equation short." A "provisional assumption of a rigidity of money-wages, rather than of real wages . . . would bring our theory nearest to the facts" (ibid., p. 276). This discussion is notable for two reasons. First, Keynes fails to mention that money wages peaked in 1929 and were *lower* in 1934 than in 1924, whereas real wages *rose* each year from 1924 to 1935. Money wages rose during the expansion to 1929 and fell during the contraction to 1933, as shown in Table 4.1. Second, the discussion of rigid money wages is a main basis for the reverse-L-shaped supply curve of labor used in traditional Keynesian models.

Keynes explicitly rejects the reverse-L-shaped supply curve of output. After stating the conditions (ibid., p. 295) under which the aggregate supply curve has a reverse L-shape, Keynes notes that these con-

Table 4.1. *Interwar wages, prices, and unemployment*

Year	Weekly money wage	Price index	Real wage	Unemployment rate
1921	62.2	138	45.1	17.0
1922	49.7	112	44.4	14.3
1923	49.7	106	46.9	14.3
1924	45.4	107	42.4	10.3
1925	45.9	107	42.9	11.3
1926	45.8	105	43.6	12.5
1927	46.0	102	45.1	9.7
1928	45.8	101	45.4	10.8
1929	46.2	100	46.2	10.4
1930	45.5	96	47.4	16.1
1931	44.5	90	49.4	21.3
1932	43.7	88	49.7	22.1
1933	43.6	85	51.3	19.9
1934	44.4	86	51.6	16.7
1935	45.1	87	51.8	15.5
1936	46.0	90	51.1	13.1

Sources: Matthews (1985, p. 5); Mitchell (1976, p. 746).

ditions are not satisfied in practice. Among the reasons he gives are diminishing returns as employment increases, increases in money wages before full employment is reached, and differences in the slope of the supply curve of different commodities (ibid., p. 296). Of particular interest is his denial that the money wage is constant up to full employment (ibid., pp. 296, 301).

In contrast to Keynes's problem of understanding Pigou, Pigou had no difficulty understanding the relevant parts of Keynes's theory of employment. He recognized Keynes's definition of full employment as "maximum possible employment," and he recognized, more fully than Keynes, that a policy to achieve maximum employment was likely to produce rising money wages and prices.[45] (See Pigou 1936, in Wood 2, pp. 29–30.) Further, Pigou saw, as many later writers did not, that Keynes's main policy prescription was to permanently raise the level of investment to avoid what Pigou called "the day of judgment" (ibid., p. 28), a position with low investment.

[45] Richard Kahn apparently shares this view for he describes Keynes's analysis of money wages as "unsystematic and unsatisfactory" (1978, in Wood 1, p. 556). The reason appears to be the failure to recognize the inflationary consequences of a full-employment policy. (See also Viner 1936, in Wood 2, p. 86.)

Interwar experience

One remarkable aspect of the labor supply discussion in the light of later emphasis is that there is very little discussion of wage rigidity in the many exchanges about the labor market. The principal reason is that few, possibly none, of Keynes's correspondents doubted that money wages adjust more slowly than prices. The idea was very old, and Keynes had used the argument throughout the 1920s. The basis of his position against returning to gold in 1925 at the prewar parity, it will be recalled, was that the prewar parity could be maintained only if money wages were reduced. He interpreted the 1926 strike as a part of the costly effort to reduce money wages and as an unavoidable consequence of the 1925 decision. He compared the cost of bringing about wage adjustment to the costs of a great war.[46] He often commented on the slow adjustment of money wages (e.g., 19, pp. 762–3; 9, pp. 70–1). In the *Tract*, he wrote: "It has been a commonplace of economic textbooks that wages tend to lag behind prices" (4, p. 25). The same view reappears as a central idea of the *Treatise*, where Keynes attempted to use changes in prices relative to costs of production (or efficiency wages) to explain changes in profits and output. In all of the discussion of his ideas and in the reviews of his books, there is no criticism of the idea that wages and prices adjust at different rates. Critics attacked the analytic basis for Keynes's claim, however.

Keynes favored using hourly earnings instead of the weekly earnings in Table 4.1, but the differences in the series do not change the main conclusion.[47] Real wages rose at about the same rate from 1929 to 1935 as they had from 1925 to 1929. The compound annual rates of increase are 1.8 and 1.9 in the two periods. The periods differ mainly in the response of money wages. Money wages are almost constant from 1925 to 1929; almost the entire change in real wages is the result of the decline in prices. The period 1929–33 shows a somewhat steeper average annual decline in prices and a small average rate of decline in

[46] These arguments and the appropriate references are in Chapter 3.
[47] Hicks (1974, p. 67) apparently relied on data comparable to those in Table 4.1 to reach the conclusion that money wages fell no more than 5 percent from 1926 to 1933. He notes that the data are not very reliable. The data on which Keynes based his conclusions about interwar changes in real and money wages also must have been similar to the data in Table 4.1. He tells us (7, p. 276) that between 1924 and 1934, money wages "were stable within a range of 6 percent, whereas real wages fluctuated by more than 20 percent." For the data in Table 4.1, the comparable percentages are 5.5 and 22 percent. The explanation of unemployment and its relation to real wages and other variables continues to be a subject of dispute. Benjamin and Kochin (1979) find that the real value of unemployment compensation benefits, which rose with falling prices, explain 5–8 percentage points of unemployment. Their findings have been challenged in several papers but also supported, for example, in Matthews (1985).

money wages. For the period 1929 to 1935 or 1936, price reductions account for almost all of the increase in real wages.

The choice of units

The *Treatise* devotes considerable space to the problem of measuring the price level. Keynes's basic view, there, is that price index numbers are not reliable measures of purchasing power. The measure of costs used in the *Treatise* is efficiency earnings W or money cost of production adjusted for the efficiency of productive units (5, p. 122).

The *General Theory* discards some of the complexity of the early discussion but remains faithful to the main idea. Keynes objected to aggregation of output since this reduced nonhomogeneous output to a common unit (7, p. 38), but he believed that labor units could be aggregated if each worker is weighted by his marginal product. In a competitive market, the wage equals the marginal product, so Keynes chose wage units to reduce nominal values to real units and to retain the idea of efficiency units.

The labor market

The demand side of Keynes's labor market does not differ from the classical theory of the labor market. The demand for labor is derived from the production function, and the wage is set equal to the marginal product of labor (7, p. 5).[48] Output (in units of employment) depends on given technology, the given stock of capital K, and the number employed N:

$$Y/W = F(K, N)$$

The demand for labor is then obtained from the first-order condition

$$N^d = f(W/p; K), \qquad f_1 < 0$$

where W/p is the real wage, or in Keynes's terms, the money wage received by labor measured in units of wage goods.[49] Increases in the real wage reduce the number of hours of labor demanded by employers, and reductions in the real wage increase the number of hours demanded.

---

[48] See also his comments on Pigou's derivation where he finds no significant difference from his own (7, p. 273).

[49] The absence of any discussion of a general price level reflects Keynes''s dislike of this concept, a subject developed in detail in the *Treatise*.

Keynes's discussion of the labor market makes two points that are critical for his argument. The first concerns the effect of money wage reductions on employment. The second is the social benefit of wage inflexibility.

Chapter 19 has a rather lengthy discussion of possible effects of reducing money wages. The argument shows Keynes as skeptical about the possibility of increasing employment in this way. The conclusion he reaches is *not* that money wage reductions cannot increase employment: "It is . . . on the effect of a falling wage and price level on the demand for money that those who believe in the self-adjusting quality of the economic system must rest the weight of their argument; though I am not aware that they have done so" (ibid., p. 266). In fact, he makes no effort to establish that wage reductions cannot increase employment: "A reduction in money-wages is quite capable in certain circumstances of affording a stimulus to output, as the classical theory supposes. My difference from this theory is primarily a difference of analysis" (ibid., p. 257). The classical theory assumed that the system is self-adjusting, so one can rely on the market to eliminate unemployment. Keynes, of course, did not believe that in practice involuntary unemployment could be eliminated permanently by lowering money wages unless the reduction in the money wage reduced the interest rate by increasing M/W.

A principal reason is given at the outset. Far from asserting that there is money illusion, Keynes opts for homogeneity: "Thus if money-wages change, one would have expected the classical school to argue that prices would change in almost the same proportion, leaving the real wage and the level of unemployment practically the same as before" (ibid., p. 12). A footnote to this passage notes that this argument contains "a large element of truth" (ibid.). The reason for his agreement is that, for him, money wages are a principal determinant of money prices.

The importance of wage inflexibility lies elsewhere. Wage inflexibility is a sufficient condition for price stability in Keynes's system. This condition recalls the argument of the *Treatise*, with wages now taking the place of costs of production in one of the fundamental equations determining prices (5, p. 122). Keynes maintains his view that price stability is desirable, and price instability is harmful. Since prices depend on wages, wage inflexibility contributes to price stability but does not guarantee it: "It is true that, if there are, nevertheless, large fluctuations in employment, substantial fluctuations in the price level will accompany them. But the fluctuations will be less . . . than with a flexible wage policy" (7, p. 271).

I defer to Chapter 6 additional discussion of wage rigidity and of authors who see wage rigidity as the key to understanding the *General Theory*. For the purpose of specifying Keynes's theory, three comments are required.

First, at the start of the *General Theory*, wages are fixed, and since prices depend on wages, prices change only as productivity changes. These assumptions are provisional and "introduced solely to facilitate the exposition" (ibid., p. 27).

Second, the complete argument has money wages changing. Often the changes are discrete jumps, particularly in a closed economy:

> In addition to the final critical point of full employment at which money-wages have to rise, in response to an increasing effective demand in terms of money, fully in proportion to the rise in the prices of wage-goods, we have a succession of earlier semi-critical points at which an increasing effective demand tends to raise money-wages though not fully in proportion to the rise in the price of wage-goods; and similarly in the case of decreasing effective demand. (ibid., p. 301)

Keynes distinguishes these price level changes from the changes that characterize inflation.

Third, the main propositions of the *General Theory* do not depend on wage rigidity. This is the reason that Keynes can hold prices and wages fixed through most of his discussion in the first eighteen chapters. Wage changes are not irrelevant, but the main conclusions about involuntary unemployment are unaffected.

Keynes's clearest statements about the supply of labor appear to make labor supply depend separately on the money wage and the price level (ibid., pp. 275–6). Despite the difficulties that this introduces, I follow Keynes and write the labor supply function as a function of wages and prices separately up to full employment and as a function of the real wage W/p once full employment is reached:

$$N^s = g(W, p), \qquad g_1 > 0, \qquad g_2 < 0$$

For given capital stock and technology, the production function and the labor demand and labor supply equations form a system of three equations in four variables, Y, N, W, and p. The two labor market equations have three variables, N, W, and p. Hence, the level of employment cannot be determined from the production and labor equations without specifying the level of aggregate demand and equating aggregate demand and output. This is the main point of Keynes's criticism of the classical theory of employment found in Marshall and Pigou (ibid., pp. 274–6). The argument does not depend on wage rigidity. It depends, however, on the denial of equality between the marginal disutility of labor and the real wage. Without that assumption, the supply of labor would depend on the real wage, not on money wages and prices separately. In that case, Keynes says, involuntary unemployment would be impossible (ibid., pp. 273–4).

Involuntary unemployment

Keynes's definition of involuntary unemployment is one of the most frequently quoted passages in the book:[50]

> Men are involuntarily unemployed if, in the event of a small rise in the price of wage-goods relatively to the money-wage, both the aggregate supply of labor willing to work for the current money-wage and the aggregate demand for it at that wage would be greater than the existing volume of employment. (7, p. 15, emphasis deleted)

He then added that he had in mind an alternative definition "which amounts, however, to the same thing." The second definition is a definition of full employment, not of involuntary unemployment. Full employment is "a situation in which aggregate employment is inelastic in response to an increase in the effective demand for its output" (ibid., p. 26). If the second definition applied everywhere, Keynes adds, Say's law would be true, and there would be no obstacle to full employment.

Later, in response to criticism from Jacob Viner, Keynes (14, p. 110) backed away from his first definition and accepted Viner's criticism. Viner (1936, in Wood 2, p. 86) describes Keynes's involuntary unemployment as unemployment that disappears "if real wages were to be reduced by a rise in the prices of wage-goods, money wages remaining the same or rising in less proportion, *but not falling*" (ibid.). This led Viner to conclude:

> In a world organized in accordance with Keynes' specifications there would be a constant race between the printing press and the business agents of the trade unions, with the problem of unemployment largely solved if the printing press could maintain a constant lead and if only volume of employment, irrespective of quality, is considered important. (ibid., pp. 86–7)

The main reason for Keynes's involuntary unemployment, Viner rec-

---

[50] Professor J. N. Smithin in correspondence has pointed out an error in the discussion of labor supply (in Meltzer 1983), where *I* permitted the labor market to clear at less than full employment. (See also Smithin 1985.)

ognized, is not the failure to print money but "lies with the persistence of interest rates at levels too high to induce employers to bid for all the labor available at the prevailing money rates of wages . . . high liquidity preferences of savers, an excessive disposition to save and a low marginal productivity of investment are responsible" for the absence of full employment (ibid., p. 88).

Keynes responded that his definition and treatment of involuntary unemployment "is particularly open to criticism." He believed the section could be improved and "when I do so, Professor Viner will feel more content" (14, p. 110).

We do not know the particular changes Keynes intended. His outline of *Footnotes to the General Theory* (ibid., pp. 133–4) prepared in August 1936 does not mention unemployment. The only alternative definition of involuntary unemployment I have found is in an August 1936 letter to Hicks where involuntary unemployment arises when "the reward [a worker] could earn . . . remains *greater than his minimum terms*" (ibid., p. 71, emphasis added).[51] This language suggests a very standard definition of unemployment in which the real wage is higher than the equilibrium wage.

My definition of involuntary unemployment does not depend on whether the labor supply curve is horizontal at the given money wage until full employment or is generally upward sloping, as suggested by Keynes's rejection of the reverse-L-shaped curve. Involuntary unemployment is the difference between the point at which the supply curve of labor becomes vertical and any *equilibrium* position at a lower level of employment. At full employment, the supply of output – output supplied as a function of the price level – becomes inelastic and involuntary unemployment is zero.

Keynes's assumption that real wages move countercyclically is, of course, a different version of the key assumption of the *Treatise* where the relation between costs, prices, and profits is emphasized. Most subsequent research has shown Keynes to be wrong about cyclical changes in real wages. Contemporaneous correlation between real

---

[51] However, Keynes's 1939 reply to Dunlop and Tarshis refers to Chapter 2 as the "portion of my book which most needs to be revised" (7, p. 401, n. 1). The reply also modifies Keynes's discussion of the relation of real and money wages but does not concede much substance. For current purposes, the most important change is Keynes's statement that if real wages rise during periods of economic expansion (instead of falling as he assumed), the conclusions he had reached would be strengthened. It would be possible to increase real wages while reducing involuntary unemployment (ibid., pp. 400–1). He was hesitant to accept this conclusion, however. Earlier, he described the fall in real wages when employment and output rise as "one of the best established of statistical conclusions" (14, p. 190). He repeated a similar view in correspondence with Dunlop (29, pp. 284–5).

wages and measures of economic activity have generally been non-negative. Bils (1985), Bodkin (1969), Dunlop (1938), and Tarshis (1938) are examples using different data sets and time periods. Moreover, Bils claims that studies that do not find procyclical movements in real wages typically neglect overtime compensation.

Aggregate supply

The labor market clears only at full employment, so the equilibrium condition of the labor market is

$$N = N^d \quad \text{for } N < N^*$$

and

$$N^d = N^s \quad \text{for } N \geq N^*$$

where N^* is full employment – the level of employment at which the supply curve of output becomes completely inelastic. By combining the production function, the demand and supply equations for labor, and the equilibrium condition for the labor market, we obtain the supply curve[52]

$$Y/W = F[N(W, p); K] \tag{4.3}$$

With appropriate manipulation, we can rewrite (4.3) as a price-setting function, and using SS to denote the aggregate supply function, we have

$$\text{SS:} \quad p = Z(W, Y/W; K) \tag{4.3'}$$

The SS equation is Keynes's "final escape from the confusions of the quantity theory" (7, p. xxxiv). The price level now depends on the money wage and the technical conditions of production and not directly on the money stock.

The model

Keynes describes the "main grounds of my departure" from classical theory as follows:

[52] At full employment, (4.3) specializes to $Y/W = F[N(W/p); K]$.

In a system in which the level of money income is capable of fluctuating, the orthodox theory is one equation short of what is required to give a solution. Undoubtedly, the reason why the orthodox system has failed to discover this discrepancy, is because it has always tacitly assumed that income *is* given, namely at the level corresponding to the employment of all the available resources. In other words it is tacitly assuming that the monetary policy is such as to maintain the rate of interest at that level which is compatible with full employment. (14, pp. 122–3)

This section presents a condensed restatement of Keynes's theory using the equilibrium equations developed in the preceding sections. I have kept the restatement close to conventional models, so the differences become apparent, and their influence can be seen. The test of the model is its ability to generate many of the implications Keynes drew from his theory. These implications concern the working of the model, the role of business cycles, and the policies that, Keynes believed, would raise the level of employment permanently.

In the markets for money and goods, the principal difference between Keynes and many of his predecessors is the explicit treatment of expectations and the insistence on treating money as an asset. Equation (4.1) is an IS curve representing alternative positions of equilibrium for the goods market.[53] Expected income E appears in the investment function. Keynes's letter to Hicks (14, pp. 80–1) cited earlier suggests that E is most appropriately defined as expected income in wage units. Equation (4.2) is an LM curve written with the expected rate of interest r^e in addition to the current rate of interest and income. A fall in the expected rate of interest reduces the demand for money. The *General Theory* has many statements interpreting r^e as the currently expected long-term rate. The use of deflated values for money and income in equations (4.1) and (4.2) is based on the principle of homogeneity of degree 1 of nominal values in the money and goods markets and is supported by Keynes's letter to Henderson (29, pp. 221–2):

$$\text{IS:} \qquad Y/W = A'(r, E; K) \qquad (4.1)$$

$$\text{LM:} \qquad Y/W = L(r, r^e(u), M/W) \qquad (4.2)$$

[53] Keynes also mentions the effect of wealth on consumption, citing U.S. experience as an example of the effect of a rising or falling stock market on consumption (7, p. 319). The passage makes clear that for Keynes, consumption does not depend solely on current income. This passage and the effect of the capital stock on investment (ibid., p. 316) introduce capital or wealth into the IS relation.

SS: $p = Z(W, Y/W; K)$ (4.3′)

Keynes's main innovation on the supply side is a claim that the economy reaches *equilibrium* at less than the maximum output attainable with the available labor force, tastes, and customs. This proposition takes several forms that I have cited repeatedly. These include Keynes's statements about the positive slope of the supply curve, his claim that an increase in the rate of investment for twenty years would satiate the capital stock and raise output to the full-employment level, and his criticism of Say's law and the classical tradition that, he claimed, accepted Say's law as applicable to the interwar economy.

The three equations are an equilibrium model in the restricted sense that the IS, LM, and SS equations are equilibrium relations that determine equilibrium values of Y/W, r, and p. The labor market does not clear, however; the number of man-hours supplied exceeds the number demanded except at full employment. The number of manhours employed, N, is demand determined, where demand is derived from the product market.

The SS relation does not interact with IS and LM to determine the economy's equilibrium output. Keynes uses this feature to suppress the SS relation by ignoring price and wage changes for many chapters. The SS relation is introduced only when Keynes wants to show that his system determines prices as well as interest rates and output.

Some readers have tried to interpret the *General Theory* as a dynamic system.[54] Nothing in the *General Theory* clearly points in that direction. In fact, Keynes recognized (7, Chapter 5) that a dynamic theory requires a theory of expectations in place of his assumption that short-period expectations can be taken as given. His 1937 lectures compare his system to work by Robertson, Hawtrey, and the Swedish economists (14, pp. 181–3). He is critical of Robertson's one-period lag between consumption and income because it is backward, not forward, looking. Hawtrey is too concerned with short-term dynamics, which Keynes described as the higgling of the market, and he fails to explain what determines the equilibrium position. Keynes dismisses the Swedish economists' notion of ex ante saving and writes: "I'm more classical than the Swedes, for I am still discussing the conditions of short-period *equilibrium*. Let us suppose identity of *ex post* and *ex ante*, my theory remains" (ibid., p. 183, emphasis added). The equality of ex ante and ex post rules out differences between actual and expected. Keynes recognizes this point, and he accepts it: "I now feel that if I were writing the book again I should begin by setting forth my theory on the as-

---

[54] See Chapter 6 for references and further discussion.

sumption that short-period expectations were always fulfilled" (ibid., p. 181). His reason for this choice is that "the theory of effective demand is substantially the same if we assume that short-period expectations are always fulfilled (ibid.).

The three equilibrium equations could be expanded to capture other interactions Keynes mentions. For example, the distribution of income could be entered in the saving function to correspond with Keynes's stated views. My purpose is not to replicate detail but to reach Keynes's main conclusions. To do so, we follow Keynes (7, p. 245) and take as given the skill and quantity of available labor and capital, techniques of production, tastes for consumption and leisure, the distribution of income, and institutional arrangements. The "ultimate independent variables" (ibid., pp. 246–7) are the expectations and functions or propensities, the money wage, and the stock of money. These variables determine "the volume of employment and the national income . . . measured in wage-units" (ibid., p. 245).

A few pages later (pp. 249, 253), Keynes suggests that the model or framework also determines the price level. His reason for excluding the price level from the earlier discussion is that the price level, the money wage, and the rate of interest (p. 250) are subject to moderate changes. He adds that these moderate changes are not matters of "logical necessity" (ibid.); they are some of the factors keeping the system stable for given expectations of long-term values.[55]

Equations (4.1)–(4.3′) contain eight variables. Keynes presets at least five variables: the two expectations, M, W, and K. With these assumptions and given uncertainty, we can solve for Y/W, p, and r. The solution for p, given W, determines the real wage, demand for labor, and level of employment under all conditions except full (maximum) employment.[56] The labor supply affects the outcome only at full employment, a temporary and unusual circumstance in the *General Theory*.[57]

In the more restricted solution, with the price level constant through most of the first seventeen chapters, IS and LM determine Y/W and

---

[55] Recall Keynes's belief that price stability was a condition of economic stability. This position is carried over from the *Treatise* and before.

[56] "Hence the volume of employment in equilibrium depends on (i) the aggregate supply function . . . (ii) the propensity to consume . . . and (iii) the volume of investment . . . This is the essence of the General Theory of Employment" (7, p. 29).

[57] The dichotomy that keeps the determination of Y/W independent of p would be broken if Keynes included a real balance effect, M/p, in the aggregate demand function. We know from his discussions of the *Treatise* that he dismissed the importance of the real balance effect. (See Chapter 3 this volume, the section on Criticisms and responses. Also, he preferred wage units to price units, so he is unlikely to have broken the dichotomy by including M/p.

r, just as in the more general case. The supply equation SS becomes a fixed relation between the price level and employment that depends only on technology, or in Keynes's words "the physical conditions of supply" (ibid., p. 89). The demand for labor sets the level of employment required to produce a level of output equal to aggregate demand. Since both W and p are taken as given in this case, the real wage is constant.

To show that the model corresponds to the discussion in Keynes's Chapter 3, replace Y/W with the symbols Keynes used, D for aggregate demand and Z for aggregate supply. For given K and on the assumption that both W and p are fixed, the supply function (4.3) becomes

$$Z = \phi(N)$$

For the special case of a fixed price level, N is independent of p and depends only on aggregate demand. Labor demand specializes to

$$N = n(D)$$

Keynes returns to the ϕ and n functions in his discussion of the price elasticity of supply and the employment function (7, p. 280 and Chapter 20). The supply function with a variable price level is

$$Z = \phi[N(p)]$$

the particular form of (4.3') that corresponds to Keynes's discussion.[58]

We can investigate the implications of the three equilibrium relations and compare the implications to Keynes's statements using a two-quadrant diagram. The upper quadrant shows the IS and LM curves, equations (4.1) and (4.2). The position of the IS curve depends on the stock of capital K, and expected output E, and the position of the LM curve depends on M/W and r^e and thus on the degree of uncertainty. The lower quadrant shows the SS curve, equation (4.3'). The price level rises with Y/W. The position of SS depends on K and W. With fixed money wages and prices, the supply curve is horizontal up to full employment; then it becomes vertical. In general, the SS curve has a

---

[58] In February 1935, Keynes responded to Robertson's criticisms by noting:
There is only one value of N for which [aggregate demand] $D = D'$ [aggregate supply] and . . . this may have a lower value than the N given by the classical theory. In this case actual employment is given by the lower value. . . . The employment function $D' = F(N)$ can be derived from the ordinary supply function. . . . Nor do I spend much time on D' . . . since it is only a re-concoction of our old friend the supply function. (13, p. 513)

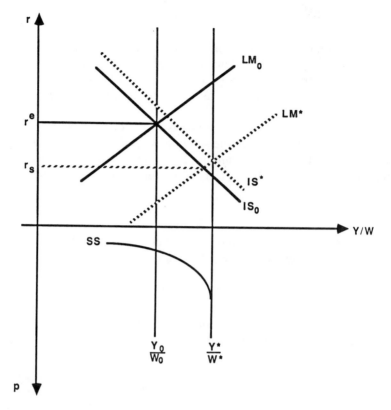

Figure 4.1

positive slope to reflect Keynes's belief, discussed earlier, that prices rise before full employment is reached. The IS, LM, and SS curves are shown in Figure 4.1.

On average, Keynes's economy achieves a level of output that is less than full employment. The actual level of output depends on the degree of uncertainty present in the economy since it is the degree of uncertainty that determines how wealthowners allocate assets between real money balances M/W and real capital. The (long-term) rate of interest depends on this allocation; the greater is uncertainty, the more wealthowners desire to hold money. Since the stocks of money and capital are fixed, an increased demand for real balances raises the expected actual rate of interest r^e and r. In Figure 4.1, the LM curve moves to the left, and if the degree of uncertainty persists, the rate of interest is higher and real output is lower.

There is no mistaking Keynes's insistence on this meaning of equilibrium. The only diagram printed in the *General Theory* relates saving, investment, and rate of interest and is used to show why the classical theory of interest is incomplete (ibid., p. 180). Keynes's explanation is that the position of equilibrium investment and output is indeterminate until we know the rate of interest, and we cannot know the rate of interest until we introduce the demand for money (liquidity preference) and the stock of money. In his words,

> The functions used by the classical theory . . . do not furnish material for a theory of the rate of interest; but they could be used to tell us what the level of income will be, given (from some other source) the rate of interest; and, alternatively, what the rate of interest will have to be, if the level of income is to be maintained at a given figure. (ibid., p. 181)[59]

Later Keynes states, "We oscillate . . . round on intermediate position appreciably below full employment" (ibid., p. 254). Output rises toward full employment in expansions and falls below the *equilibrium* at less than full employment during recessions or slumps. Let E_0 denote the level around which the economy fluctuates.[60] When the position of the output and money markets is given by IS_0 and LM_0 in Figure 4.1, output is Y_0/W_0, and the price level is at the intersection of SS and Y_0/W_0. When output falls below Y_0/W_0, prices fall and real wages rise. With output above Y_0/W_0, prices rise and real wages fall. For given money wages, capital, and technology, real wages move inversely to prices, rising in recessions and falling in expansions, as Keynes said.

The level of full-employment output is Y^*/W^*. At Y^*/W^*, we find all of Keynes's descriptions of full employment. The price elasticity of output is infinite; no additions to output are obtainable. Keynes's version of Say's law holds; increases in investment are matched by

---

[59] The diagram was added to the text in September 1935 at the suggestion of Roy Harrod (13, p. 557). Keynes had claimed that Harrod did not understand his theory. Harrod restated the theory (ibid., p. 553) and sent the diagram to help Keynes express his ideas to others. Keynes replied that Harrod's restatement "could not be stated better" (ibid., p. 557). Harrod's restatement and many of Keynes's responses can be read as a denial of simultaneous determination of interest rates, output, saving, investment, and real balances. Hansen (1953, pp. 147, 154–5) criticizes Keynes's theory of interest for sequential rather than simultaneous determination. Keynes is certainly open to this charge; e.g., see the passage at the top of p. 213, vol. 7, where Keynes seems to deny an effect of increased saving on the rate of interest. Other passages in the same volume are more ambiguous, e.g., p. 181. As I noted earlier, Keynes used a model of simultaneous determination in the *Treatise*, and he accepted simultaneous determination without a quibble when he read Hicks's (1937) paper.

[60] My reason for treating the equilibrium value as an expected value is developed in what follows.

reductions in consumption and conversely. Employment is at the intersection of the demand-and-supply curves for labor, $N^s = N^d$, and the marginal disutility of labor equals the real wage. Prices and money wages rise together.

Keynes refers to positions above IS* as absolute inflation to distinguish permanent increases in prices and money wages from cyclical fluctuations around given average levels. Increases in money wages raise prices in Figure 4.1 by shifting the SS curve without changing the slope of the curve. In the *Tract*, inflation increases real wages (4, p. 29). Keynes does not restate this view in the *General Theory*.[61]

Involuntary unemployment is the difference between Y^*/W^* and Y_0/W_0. Workers cannot permanently reduce this level of unemployment by reducing money (and real) wages. A reduction in money wages (or an increase in money) changes the position of the LM curve in Figure 4.1. Starting from LM_0, a reduction in W (or an increase in M) moves LM toward LM*, raising output and lowering the rate of interest. If the degree of uncertainty is unchanged, the investment schedule and the IS schedule are unchanged; the expected rate of interest r^e remains above the actual rate r. The risk premium remains in long-term rates, and is expected to remain, so nothing has happened to permanently change the level of income around which the economy fluctuates. Changes in nominal values are capable of temporarily changing the actual level of output, but they do not change the average or expected value of output unless they change the expectations that dominate r^e and the equilibrium level of output. On the contrary, frequent changes in W may raise r^e by increasing price level volatility (7, pp. 267, 269).

The key to the problem is r^e. The level around which interest rates fluctuate, in an economy with private direction of investment, is the minimum rate set by the liquidity premium on money. This premium differs from the pecuniary risk premium earned on investment or the risk premium on loans paid by borrowers. The liquidity premium is a nonpecuniary return received in the form of increased safety and the confidence that wealth held as money will be maintained (29, pp. 293–4).

For a given degree of uncertainty and given values of K, M, and W, the IS and LM curves solve for equilibrium values of r and Y/W. The value of r, for example, is

$$r = r(M/W, r^e(u), E)$$

[61] Real wages fall as the economy moves toward Y^*/W^*. I have not found a suggestion in Keynes that SS shifts to restore the real wages received at the underemployment equilibrium Y_0/W_0. Keynes did not dispute Viner's (1936) criticism that his system would produce inflation, but there is also no evidence that he agreed with Viner.

To determine r^e, we treat r as a random variable and take the expected value. The expected long-term rate, when expected output is $E_0 = Y_0/W_0$ and $(M/W)^e$ is the expected value of real money balances, is

$$r^e = r[(M/W)^e; E_0] \qquad (4.4)$$

Equation (4.4) is consistent with many of Keynes's statements about long-term interest rates. The "actual value [of the rate of interest] is largely governed by the prevailing view as to what its value is expected to be. *Any* level of interest which is accepted with sufficient conviction as *likely* to be durable *will* be durable" (7, p. 203). Changes in the quantity of money or changes in money wages do not change the long-term real rate unless expected M/W changes (29, pp. 221–2). Monetary policy and wage policy are symmetric in their effect, as Keynes insisted. The key to changing long-term interest rates is the expected or average level of income. This level of income is

$$E_0 = E[(M/W)^e; r^e] \qquad (4.5)$$

The stock of money is fixed (or given by monetary arrangements). Keynes relied on conventions or customs to set the money wage, but he defined conventions in terms of expectations (7, p. 152), so he would not have objected to treating W as the wage paid on average. On this interpretation, expected and actual money wages coincide at Y_0/W_0; W_0 is the wage expected to be paid on average; $W_0 = W^e$ in equations (4.4) and (4.5).

Equations (4.4) and (4.5) derive expected values from the equilibrium position of the model, as a rational expectationist would do. Keynes believed it was rational to use expectations or "equivalent certainties" when making decisions (29, p. 289), but his treatment of expectations differs from current versions of rational expectations in at least two respects. The first is based on his observations. For Keynes, individual's expectations change in discrete jumps that are not entirely independent. People try to find out what others are doing. Dominant opinion can change violently in response to relatively small changes in prices, economic activity, or other variables. Second, Keynes believed that probabilities are *not* numerical values, but to make decisions, men must act as if they are (7, p. 169; 14, p. 122; 29, p. 289). His statements about animal spirits, casinos, and bulls and bears reflects his long-standing belief that relatively large, sudden changes in expected values occur quickly at times.

The expected value of the interest rate is the equilibrium rate around which short-term changes occur under laissez-faire. Equation (4.4) is consistent with Keynes's distinction between the natural and the neutral rates of interest and with a main conclusion Keynes draws. Ruminating on the differences between his *Treatise* and the *General Theory*, Keynes writes that he tried in the *Treatise* to develop Wicksell's "natural" rate as the rate that equates saving and investment and maintains a stable price level. What he overlooked, Keynes says, is the relation between employment or output and the rate of interest. The "natural" rate is not unique but "is merely the rate of interest that will preserve the *status quo*" (7, p. 243). The notion of a natural rate in the *Treatise* is not useful. If any rate is "unique and significant," it is "the *neutral* rate of interest, namely the natural rate in the above sense which is consistent with *full* employment . . . though this rate might be better described, perhaps, as the *optimum* rate" (ibid.).

Keynes continues: "The neutral rate of interest can be more strictly defined as the rate of interest which prevails in equilibrium when output and employment are such that the elasticity of employment as a whole is zero" (ibid.). This rate is, of course, the long-term rate at which $E = Y^*/W^*$; in Figure 4.1, the "neutral" rate lies at the intersection of IS* and LM* and is denoted r_s. It is r_s, Keynes says, that classical economists expected because their theory did not recognize the role of liquidity preference and money in the determination of interest rates and the level of equilibrium output.

The distinction between the neutral rate r_s and r^e, the equilibrium rate expected to prevail under laissez-faire, takes us to the heart of Keynes's theory. The neutral rate is the rate at which investment and the capital stock are optimal. Society is on the production frontier; r_s is the social rate of return that keeps investment and capital at their optimum values.

The difference $r^e - r_s$ is the cost of avoidable uncertainty. There are risks that society must bear – risks inherent in nature and in trading arrangements. These are included in r_s. In addition, there is "lender's risk," a risk "due either to moral hazard . . . or to . . . involuntary default due to the disappointment of expectation" (ibid., p. 144). This risk introduces a premium into the conventional or expected rate, r^e, that must be borne in a system with private investment decisions and private financing of investment. Lender's risk "is a pure addition to the cost of investment which would not exist if the borrower and the lender were the same person" (ibid.).

The problem, then, is to lower the expected rate of interest r^e until it approaches the social rate of return r_s. Keynes considers two ways to make the change. One is monetary (or banking) policy; the other is state direction of investment. He rejects the first and opts for the second:

It seems unlikely that the influence of banking policy on the rate of interest will be sufficient by itself to determine an *optimum* rate of investment. I conceive, therefore, that somewhat comprehensive socialisation of investment will prove *the only means* of securing an approximation to full employment. (ibid., p. 378, emphasis added)

There are two reasons behind this conclusion corresponding to the two ways of driving r^e down to r_s. First, increase nominal money or reduce money wages to raise M/W and shift the LM curve to the right until the interest rate reaches r_s. Second, eliminate lending risk and moral hazard so that the demand for money falls and the interest rate falls to r_s.

Keynes rejects the first solution. Changes in money or in the nominal wage can change the short-term rate; they can cause fluctuations in r^e; but they cannot eliminate moral hazard, disappointed expectations, and lender's risk so they cannot drive r^e down to r_s. Keynes does not consider an inflation tax, and he dismisses the real balance effect as a means of lowering the demand for real balances or increasing spending, as noted earlier. He denies that the economy can be made to fluctuate around the neutral rate, the full employment rate r_s, by simply changing the scale. That is the meaning of the often-quoted conclusion:

There is, therefore, no ground for the belief that a flexible wage policy is capable of maintaining a state of continuous full employment; any more than for the belief that an open-market monetary policy is capable, unaided, of achieving this result. The economic system cannot be made self-adjusting along these lines. (ibid., p. 267)

Eliminating moral hazard, disappointed expectations, and lender's risk reduces uncertainty. With reduced uncertainty, people hold less money, so the demand for real money balances shifts to LM* in Figure 4.1, and the equilibrium interest rate falls to r_s. The economy reaches a Pareto optimum. At the optimum the only uncertainty remaining is unavoidable uncertainty about the future.

In a barter economy, the real wage is the only wage, and there is no money. Neither M/W nor the properties of the liquidity preference function can affect the rate of interest. The expected rate r^e is the *neutral* rate determined by saving and investment, as the classical economists believed (29, pp. 66–7). Further, there are no fluctuations in aggregate output; real output is always at full employment. Keynes suggests that in a barter economy, output would be higher and would fluctuate less. His conjectures about barter and money (discussed in

7, Chapter 17) are not fully developed to say the least, but they are consistent with the interpretation of his theory presented here.

Keynes makes clear that he does not envisage a multitude of potential solutions or a large number of equilibrium positions:

> The only alternative position of equilibrium would be given by a situation in which a stock of capital sufficiently great to have a marginal efficiency of zero also represents an amount of wealth sufficiently great to satiate to the full the aggregate desire on the part of the public to make provision for the future, even with full employment, in circumstances where no bonus is obtainable in the form of interest. (ibid., p. 218)

The rate of interest – actual and expected – must be reduced toward zero.[62]

Although Keynes's argument seems fanciful, he applies the argument to the experience of Great Britain and the United States where the "marginal efficiency has fallen more rapidly than the rate of interest can fall in the face of the prevailing institutional and psychological factors" (7, p. 219). The way out, he proposes at this point, is to control investment *and* consumption in the social interest. As a last resort, holes can be dug and refilled. It is only if saving continues at a rate that prevents full employment when all productive investments have been made that he recommends such nonproductive activity (ibid., pp. 219–20).

Involuntary unemployment is not the result of misperceptions of the price level as in the theories of Friedman (1968) and Lucas (1972). Involuntary unemployment occurs because investment is too small to achieve and maintain the socially optimal stock of capital. If the rate of investment could be increased and held at the level corresponding to IS* in Figure 4.1, aggregate demand would sustain full-employment output. This cannot happen. Under laissez-faire, investment depends on the decisions of "purchasers largely ignorant of what they are buying and of speculators who are more concerned with forecasting the next shift of market sentiment than with a reasonable estimate of the future yield of capital-assets" (ibid., p. 316). If the rate of investment could

---

[62] These passages from pp. 217–18 are part of the basis for the stagnationist interpretation of Keynes. Other passages supporting that interpretation are from vol. 7, pp. 31–2, 164, 219–21, 308–9, and 347–8. Pigou was an early critic of this argument on the grounds that Keynes confused average and marginal returns. Also, Pigou notes that Keynes's argument against downward wage adjustments fails. Keynes's main argument is that reductions in money wages are extrapolated and expected to continue. Pigou notes that in the circumstances Keynes describes, there would be no reason to expect further wage reductions in the future or to use this as a reason for postponing money wage reductions. (See Pigou 1936, in Wood 2, pp. 28–9.)

be stabilized at a higher level by reducing risk to the minimum inherent in nature, the marginal efficiency of capital could be reduced to a minimum (zero) within a generation or two. Under laissez-faire with asset prices driven by speculators, expectations are often disappointed, so the risk premium remains.

Keynes's proposed solutions, to increase the role of the state in the direction of investment and to drive the rate of interest to zero, do not take account of the effect of lower interest rates on capital flows. The *General Theory* is almost entirely about a closed economy, but Keynes was always interested in practice. It seems implausible that he would neglect capital flight.

Three explanations come to mind. Keynes may have assumed, without saying so, that the decline in actual and expected interest rates is entirely the result of a decline in risk premiums. This seems an unlikely presumption about fortuitous timing. Second, he may have intended the theory to apply in a system of fluctuating exchange rates or some variant of the managed system of the 1930s. Keynes was never a proponent of freely fluctuating exchange rates, and there is no reason to believe that he favored them when he prepared the *General Theory*. Third, he may have expected countries to prevent capital flows by imposing exchange controls. He had proposed capital controls in the past, and his plans for postwar policy envisaged controls.[63] There is no way to be certain about what he had in mind. The absence of any clue leaves the theory incomplete.

Business cycles

Keynes wrote the chapter on the trade or business cycle to apply his theory. The title of the chapter, "Notes on the Trade Cycle," conveys its tentative character, and the opening sentence of the chapter stresses that his object is not to introduce new material but to apply the theory of employment developed in earlier chapters (7, pp. 313, 315).

Keynes's theory of the cycle is a real theory. For periods lasting three to five years, the demand for investment remains below its long-term average. These periods follow a collapse of the marginal-efficiency-of-capital schedule. One consequence of the collapse is a rise in liquidity preference, which raises the rate of interest and aggravates the slump. Keynes is explicit, however, about causation: "Liquidity

---

[63] See Chapter 6 of this volume and Keynes's discussion of a very similar point in the *Treatise*. In the latter he chooses exchange controls – "differentiated rates for home and foreign lending" (6, p. 169) after considering alternatives such as tariffs.

preference . . . does not increase until *after* the collapse of the marginal efficiency of capital" (ibid., p. 316).[64]

The reason for the collapse is "a fickle and highly unstable marginal efficiency of capital" (ibid., p. 204) dominated by speculators and ill-informed buyers of claims to capital (ibid., p. 316). The marginal-efficiency schedule depends on the current stock of capital, the cost of producing capital goods, and expected future returns. The last is most important. Expectations of future returns, "being based on shifting and unreliable evidence . . . are subject to sudden and violent changes" (ibid., p. 315). Since expected returns change with the price quotations on the stock exchange, a fall in asset prices and lower expected future returns reduce investment (ibid., pp. 315–16).

The business cycle is the result of mistaken expectations, the same problem that keeps the long-term rate higher than the social rate of return. Businessmen make systematic errors, overestimating the long-term return to investment during expansions and underestimating returns during contractions. Keynes speaks of the "error of pessimism," a "misguided state of expectation," and "the illusions of the boom" (ibid., 321–2).[65]

Once started, business downturns persist. Keynes suggests that the duration of the cycle is nearly fixed and cannot be affected much by a reduction in interest rates: "An interval of time of particular order of magnitude must usually elapse before recovery beings" (ibid., p. 317). He gives two reasons: Time is required to depreciate exisitng capital, and time is required to reduce excessive inventories of finished and unfinished goods (ibid., pp. 317–18).[66] He repeats the same ideas in correspondence with Harrod the following year (14, pp. 177–8).

The almost mechanical treatment of the cycle is one of the least impressive features of his discussion of the business cycle. Forgotten

---

[64] Keynes qualifies this statement. Speculators may increase their liquidity preference. With the exception of this aside, the implication is that interest rates decline at first, then rise under the influence of liquidity preference. Keynes clearly speaks of a rise in interest rates, not a decline, in the early stages of the slump, but he may have intended a rise relative to the marginal efficiency of capital. The discussion follows an explicit statement about the role of interest rates: "The predominant explanation of the crisis is, not primarily a rise in the rate of interest, but a sudden collapse in the marginal efficiency of capital" (7, p. 315). The emphasis on real factors was common to many writers at the time. Robertson, in particular, worked on real business cycle theory. (See Wilson 1983.)

[65] Keynes uses his analysis to explain events in the United States in 1928–9 as an example of faulty expectations: "Correct foresight would have brought down the marginal efficiency of capital to an unprecedentedly low figure" (7, p. 323). Instead, interest rates were raised.

[66] Brunner et al. (1983) discuss the factors affecting the duration of business cycles. In addition to the factors mentioned in the text, the slope of the demand for money with respect to interest rates also affects the duration of the business cycle in their model.

is the effect of a reduction of wages on interest rates and liquidity preference, perhaps because Keynes considered the effect on wage and price expectations as unhelpful for his argument. A decline in real interest would also affect the intertemporal allocation of labor, a topic Keynes neglects.

In contrast to his earlier repeated emphasis on lower interest rates, lower taxes, and more spending to stimulate the economy (21, pp. 114, 116, 126, 141, and elsewhere), the *General Theory* does not strongly advocate either fiscal or monetary stimulus in the chapter on business cycles or, for that matter, elsewhere in the book. On the contrary, Keynes's discussion of monetary policy in his chapter on business cycles retains his almost mechanistic view of duration: "If a reduction in the rate of interest was capable of proving an effective remedy by itself, it might be possible to achieve a recovery without the elapse of any considerable interval of time . . . But, in fact, this is not usually the case" (7, pp. 316–17). The same thought is repeated three pages later and leads Keynes to conclude "that the duty of ordering the current volume of investment cannot safely be left in private hands" (p. 320).

The reference is to the "conditions of laissez-faire" that prevent markets from stabilizing the rate of investment. The main remedies considered by Keynes are of two kinds. One, countercyclical policy, prevents the slump by preventing the boom. This policy calls on the central bank to raise interest rates and reduce investment during the boom. The other features "a socially controlled rate of investment with a view to a progressive decline in the marginal efficiency of capital (ibid., p. 325). Keynes clearly favors the latter.[67] The idea of using monetary policy to prevent booms so as to prevent slumps is "dangerously and unnecessarily defeatist. It recommends . . . for permanent acceptance too much that is defective in our existing economic scheme" (ibid., p. 327).[68] Keynes does not say what is defective, but the section suggests that the use of monetary policy to control booms disappoints expectations and therefore drives a wedge between social and private returns. Later (29, p. 227) he comments on this passage and remarks that the system for controlling booms is defective. The system creates fluctuations, increases uncertainty, raises the rate of

---

[67] A third proposal, to increase consumption, is recommended only when the capital stock is satiated (7, pp. 324, 325).

[68] See also vol. 7, pp. 164, 320. In 1932, Keynes strongly favored debt management policies to lower the long-term rate of interest by refinancing some outstanding long-term debt at lower rates. The operation is known as the Conversion Loan. At the time, he made strong claims about the benefits of the operation (21, pp. 112, 114, 116). His views on the effects of refunding on interest rates are challenged in Capie, Mills, and Wood (1982).

interest by a risk premium, and keeps average output below maximum output.

Policies and recommendations

Alvin Hansen gives the conventional interpretation of Keynes's policy views: "Thus it is that modern countries place primary emphasis on fiscal policy in whose service monetary policy is relegated to the subsidiary role of a useful but necessary handmaiden" (1953, p. 203). The *General Theory* makes no statement of this kind. Keynes's main policy recommendation is for public direction of investment. The *General Theory*, like the *Treatise*, argues for stability and against variability. Keynes believed that greater stability of investment required a change in the process by which investment decisions are made.

Hansen, like many others, dismisses Keynes's recommendations in Chapter 24 of the *General Theory* as Keynes "flying his kite," allowing "his fancy to roam in an irresponsible manner" and seeking utopia (Hansen 1953, p. 215). Keynes believed that his main recommendations were policy implications drawn from his theory. His principal recommendation – public direction of investment – is repeated several times in the *General Theory* and was not a new idea. Keynes had made a similar but less explicit recommendation in "The End of Laissez Faire" (9, pp. 290, 292), and his view that investment, not saving, is the basis of economic progress is strongly stated in *The Economic Consequences of the Peace.*[69]

The views Keynes expressed in the 1920s closely parallel the views expressed in Chapter 24. The key difference is that Keynes believed that the *General Theory* provided the analytic foundation that his earlier proposals lacked. Readers of Keynes's earlier work should not be surprised at his calling for the euthanasia of the rentier (7, pp. 221, 376). He had held this view for years. After the *General Theory*, Keynes believed that the recommendation was based on his analysis and was part of a valid program to achieve full (maximum) employment.

Keynes told G. B. Shaw that the *General Theory* is a book that "will largely revolutionise . . . the way the world thinks about economic problems . . . the Ricardian foundations of Marxism will be knocked away" (13, pp. 492–3). This was not intended as a statement about the particular way in which he developed the analysis or about the details of his model. Keynes saw the revolutionary aspect of his theory in his solution to the problem of persistent unemployment. Full employment did not have to wait on the decisions of private savers or depend on

---

[69] Chapter 2 in this volume develops this theme.

the rewards to rentiers. It could be achieved by increasing the stock of capital until capital is no longer a scarce resource.[70]

The relation of the policy recommendations to the theoretical chapters becomes clearer if we read Keynes's theoretical argument as the hypothesis that uncertainty imposes an excess burden on the economy. Uncertainty raises the demand for real money balances and reduces the demand for investment relative to the social optimum. The equilibrium rate of interest is higher, and the equilibrium stock of capital lower, than is consistent with that optimum. The equilibrium is stable and is expected to persist. But, at the equilibrium that is reached, output and capital are too small, and unemployment is too high and persistent. Hence, Keynes said, reform the institutional structure to remove or reduce the excess burden that society bears.

The point is made repeatedly, at times in the colorful language that Keynes the polemicist seems to have enjoyed. The excess burden arises "when enterprise becomes the bubble on a whirlpool of speculation . . . the capital development of a country becomes a by-product of the activities of a casino" (7, p. 159). The central problem in the way of achieving and maintaining full (maximum) employment is to reduce the excessive uncertainty resulting from the operation of financial markets.

To solve this central problem, Keynes offered three proposals but then rejected two of them.[71] First, to reduce speculation, particularly in the United States, he considered either a substantial transfer tax on purchases and sales of securities or an edict preventing the sale of securities except at time of death (or for "other grave cause"), (ibid., p. 160). He rejected this proposal because it would make securities less liquid for individual investors and thus reduce the demand for capital and increase the demand for money. Second, he proposed requiring people to spend either for consumption or investment (ibid., p. 161). It is not clear who would be permitted to save or how the rule would be enforced. Third, "I expect to see the State, which is in a position to calculate the marginal efficiency of capital-goods on long views and on the basis of the general social advantage, taking an ever

---

[70] The problem with the classical theory is not "logical flaws in its analysis." Its "tacit assumptions are seldom or never satisfied," so it "cannot solve the economic problems of the actual world" (7, p. 378).

[71] Keynes was skeptical about the possibility of reducing the average level of unemployment by monetary means. His analysis should have concluded that the relevant rate of interest is a real rate that cannot be reduced unless the demand for money is reduced, particularly by reducing uncertainty. He makes this argument but at times draws a wrong conclusion. After subtracting taxes, costs of uncertainty, and other real costs to reach what he calls the "net yield," he concludes that this rate may be too low ("infinitesimal") to be reduced by monetary expansion (7, p. 309). His analysis should have told him that in a system with stable prices the net yield is a real variable independent of the quantity of money.

greater responsibility for directly organising investment'' (ibid., p. 164). This proposal, long favored by Keynes, became the main recommendation of his book.[72]

In the 1920s he had distinguished between the tasks that are well done and can be left to the private sector and those that require reforms. He called the latter the agenda. The *General Theory* makes a similar distinction. Decisions about the use of labor lead to an efficient allocation of employed workers, so they can be left in private hands: ''There are, of course, errors of foresight; but these would not be avoided by centralising decisions . . . It is in determining the volume not the direction, of actual employment that the existing system has broken down'' (ibid., p. 379).

The problem of variability was part of the agenda. The *Treatise* tried to show that unemployment, instability, and fluctuations were caused by price variability. The required reforms, according to Keynes, were mainly changes in domestic and international monetary arrangements to reduce instability from the monetary side. In the *General Theory*, Keynes still views the central problem as excessive variability, but the main problem is now the excess burden the economy bears because uncertainty increases the demand for money and raises the real (risk included) rate of interest above the social productivity of capital. He did not abandon his interest in monetary reform, as his later proposals leading to Bretton Woods show, but his principal concern in the *General Theory* is for policies to increase investment and the capital stock toward the social optimum.

Proposed reforms

Keynes favored intervention and opposed nonintervention – which he called laissez-faire – whenever he believed that the state could increase output or stabilize prices. He had long favored planning of investment by public bodies. He thought that his *General Theory* not only provided an analytic case for state direction of investment but also showed that

---

[72] In correspondence with President Franklin Roosevelt, Keynes distinguished policies for reform from policies for recovery (21, p. 290). The recommendations in the *Treatise* and the *General Theory* are proposals for reform. Keynes the concerned activist often was not content to wait for reforms and did not restrict his proposals to reforms based on his theory. The fact that he does not recommend policies for recovery in the *General Theory* does not mean that he did not at times favor such policies. He saw his theoretical work as ''definitive'' (14, p. 122) and his recommendations as a means of achieving structural reform. In practice, when structural reforms could not be achieved, he proposed solutions that he regarded as helpful in the prevailing circumstances.

accumulation and progress do not depend on saving and the rentier[73]: "Our argument leads to the conclusion that in contemporary conditions, the growth of wealth, so far from being dependent on the abstinence of the rich, as is commonly supposed, is more likely to be impeded by it" (ibid., p. 373). Further, he had shown that there was no reason for concern that low interest rates would prevent progress by deterring saving:

> We have shown that the extent of effective saving is necessarily determined by the scale of investment and that the scale of investment is promoted by a *low* rate of interest, provided that we do not attempt to stimulate it in this way beyond the point which corresponds to full employment. (ibid., p. 375)

Capital would cease to be scarce (ibid., p. 376). There would still be a price and a return, but the return would cover (1) wastage and obsolescence, (2) risk (but not uncertainty about the rate of interest), and (3) a payment for the exercise of skill and judgment (ibid., p. 375). There would be no payment of interest as a reward for thrift. The "rentier aspect of capitalism . . . will disappear" (ibid., p. 376).

Keynes makes the same proposal elsewhere. He describes the process of capital "saturation" (ibid., p. 220) as relatively easy and as a sensible way of "gradually getting rid of many of the objectionable features of capitalism" (ibid., p. 221). The problem of satiating the capital stock arises under laissez-faire because of costs of "bringing the borrower and the ultimate lender together, and the allowance for risk, especially for moral risk, which the lender requires" (ibid., p. 208). Allowing the state to determine investment removes this excess burden. Uncertainty is reduced. The demand for money falls; the payments for uncertainty, lenders and borrowers risk, and coordination are no longer required. When the rate of interest falls to zero, the capital stock increases until its marginal efficiency is zero or even negative (ibid., p. 221).

To show that these recommendations were completely misunderstood and the main implications of the *General Theory* discarded, we can turn to Alvin Hansen, one of the leading proponents of so-called Keynesian policy. Hansen refers to the sections of the *General Theory* just discussed as "a kind of 'free wheeling' detour by Keynes in his less responsible moments" or as a throwback to the "utopian St. Simonians of the early nineteenth century" (Hansen 1953, pp. 158–9).

---

[73] His notion of progress includes increased per capita income, as discussed in Chapter 2 of this volume. It includes, also, a role for the state to make a person (1936, p. 35) "finer, more gifted, more splendid, more care-free than he can be by himself." To accomplish these other objectives, Keynes favored programs in the arts.

In fact, Keynes had made a very similar proposal in the *Treatise* (6, p. 145), where he describes the "ultimate solution" to the problem of accumulation as one of "the rate of capital development becoming more largely an affair of state, determined by collective wisdom and long views" (ibid., p. 145). He repeats this conclusion in a 1932 article, "The Dilemma of Modern Socialism" (21, p. 36), and in a 1939 discussion where he remarks that "we need, if we are to enjoy prosperity and profits, so much more central planning that the reform of the economic system needs as much urgent attention if we have war as if we avoid it" (ibid., p. 492).

In correspondence with J. A. Hobson, Keynes set out criteria for judging when investment is socially advantageous but not privately profitable: "I cannot agree that investment has ceased to be socially profitable as long as it yields any return at all . . . investment has only reached saturation point when capital is so abundant that it yields no more over a period of time than its cost of production without any surplus" (29, p. 211). Keynes makes a similar point (ibid., p. 210).[74]

Many of the countercyclical fiscal policies commonly called Keynesian attempt to smooth the business cycle by changing government spending for consumption or by changing taxes to increase private consumption. Keynes's wartime memos on postwar policy oppose policies of this kind. He favored policies to stabilize investment and opposed policies to increase consumption on grounds consistent with my interpretation of the main implication of the *General Theory* – income can be raised permanently by increasing and stabilizing investment.

His wartime memos to Meade read as if he accepted Friedman's permanent-income theory:

> I doubt if it is wise to put too much stress on devices for causing the volume of consumption to fluctuate in preference to devices for varying the volume of investment . . .
>
> People have established standards of life. Nothing will upset them more than to be subject to pressure constantly to vary them up and down. A *remission of taxation* on which people could only rely *for an indefinitely short period might have very limited effects* in stimulating their consumption . . . On this particular tack your proposal about varying the insurance contribution seems to me much the most practicable, partly be-

---

[74] A year after the *General Theory*, he wrote to Harrod commenting on an early version of Harrod's growth model: "The maintenance of steady growth is at all times an inherent improbability in conditions of *laissez faire*" (14, p. 173). The letter gives the reason. The multiplier and the capital output ratio are not constant. Slight changes in either disturb steady growth. Keynes suggests that if a choice must be made, he prefers higher employment to more stable growth.

cause it could be *associated with a formula* . . . This seems to
me quite enough as a beginning. I should much deprecate . . .
dealing with income-tax, where there is a huge time lag and
short-run changes [are] most inconvenient . . .

Moreover, the very reason that capital expenditure is capable of paying for itself makes it much better budgetwise and
does not involve the progressive increase of budgetary difficulties, which deficit budgeting for the sake of consumption
may bring about. (27, pp. 319–20, emphasis added)

A month later, May 1943, Keynes again urged Meade to avoid proposals that depend on short-term changes in consumer spending. His
letter also makes clear that Keynes's stabilization proposal did not
depend on prompt changes in the amount of public works. Keynes
wanted to *prevent* fluctuations, and he believed that "if the bulk of
investment is under public or semi-public control and we go in for a
stable long-term programme, serious fluctuations are enormously less
likely to occur" (ibid., p. 326).

In addition to his interest in public direction of investment and his
advocacy of procedural changes to achieve stability of government
investment, Keynes favored Meade's proposal to provide a formula
for reducing social security taxes paid by firms when the unemployment
rate rose above 8 percent. (See 27, pp. 206–8, 312, 319). He believed
that if a 5 percent unemployment rate is the "minimum practicable rate
of unemployment" (ibid., p. 208), tax rates should not decline until
unemployment reaches 8 percent.[75]

Throughout the spring and summer of 1943, he pressed on the chancellor his view of the central importance of a policy to stabilize postwar
investment by *stabilizing* and controlling investment (ibid., pp. 352–
61). He continued to follow the discussion of postwar employment
policy while on a trip to the United States, and on his return again took
as active a role as his responsibility for postwar international economic
policy permitted. Keynes's familiar themes are repeated.[76] When the

[75] It is not clear how he chose the numbers. He was aware of an empirical study by
Beveridge (1936) showing that minimum unemployment was between 6 and 8 percent.
He estimates "800,000 men unemployed (or a somewhat larger aggregate of men and
women together, 10 women reckoning [for cost calculations] as the equivalent of 7
men)" (27, p. 281). The 800,000 figure is about 5 percent of the labor force.

[76] Keynes favored control of consumption spending to increase saving during the transition from war to peace. He expected the transition to last about five years, and he
believed that controls would ease the transition. If a crisis occurred, he was prepared
to accept autarky as a "last resort" (27, p. 404, n. 18). But, he supported forcefully
Lionel Robbins's statement on the importance of preserving "the liberty, the initiative
and . . . the idiosyncrasy of the individual in a framework serving the public good"
(27, p. 369).

1944 White Paper on Employment Policy appeared, he accepted the main points but opposed a section that suggested cyclical variation in interest rates as a countercyclical policy on the grounds that such a policy is "unworkable": "If it relates to the short-term rate of interest I am very doubtful how much it will help. If it relates to the long-term rate of interest, then the practical and fiscal difficulties in the way of significant fluctuations over a short period . . . are, in fact, overwhelming" (ibid., p. 377).

In Chapter 22 of the *General Theory* Keynes discusses the use of monetary policy to dampen the business cycle. There he asserts that most people prefer increased income to increased leisure (7, p. 326), insists that his definition of full employment is not the usual definition but is "a higher level" (ibid., p. 325), and contrasts his definition with that of D. H. Robertson, "who assumes . . . that full employment is an impracticable ideal and that the best we can hope for is [a] level of employment much more stable than at present and averaging, perhaps, a little higher" (ibid., p. 327). Keynes then compares two alternatives, social control of investment and reliance on a countercyclical policy that permits interest rates to rise in a boom. He concludes, tentatively, that allowing interest rates to rise might deter "even the most misguided optimists" (ibid.). However, Keynes rejects the use of monetary, or, as he would say, banking, policy. His reason for rejection is relevant and contradicts those who identify the Keynesian case with the liquidity trap. He does not assert that monetary policy cannot work or that money is not a substitute for capital. Reliance on monetary policy is "dangerously and unnecessarily defeatist. It recommends . . . for permanent acceptance too much that is defective in our existing economic scheme" (ibid.).[77]

The main exception in the *General Theory* to the emphasis on investment is in Keynes's discussion of the underconsumptionist view (ibid., pp. 324–6). There, he points out that under prevailing conditions, with investment highly variable and determined by private judgment, the only way to increase income is to increase consumption. He then criticizes the underconsumptionists for "neglecting the fact that there are *two* ways to expand output" (ibid., p. 325). His judgment is that there are "great social advantages of increasing the capital stock until it ceases to be scarce" (ibid.). But, he concludes that "there is room . . . for both policies to operate together" (ibid.). The goal should be

---

[77] In vol. 29, p. 227, Keynes comments on this paragraph and interprets the statement to mean that the methods of controlling booms are deficient. The reference is to the use of monetary policy. The context suggests that the use of monetary policy increases uncertainty.

a higher level of per capita income.[78] The same argument is made in his Galton lecture (14, p. 131).

The meaning of planning

At one point (27, p. 322), Keynes makes a specific reference to the share of investment that the state should carry out or influence to achieve maximum employment. His proposal is for two-thirds to three-fourths of total investment to "be influenced by public or semi-public bodies" (ibid.). Keynes did not favor state ownership, as shown by his exchange with Durbin (29, pp. 233–5) and his use of a quotation from Hubert Henderson favoring "an arrangement under which the State would fill the vacant post of entrepreneur-in-chief, while not interfering with the ownership or management of particular businesses, or rather only doing so on the merits of the case and not at the behests of dogma" (27, p. 324).

What did Keynes mean by these vague references to planning? His writings in the 1930s provide a few more clues than his earlier work but remain indefinite and imprecise. As in the 1920s, he accepted much of the socialist program, but he stopped short of becoming a socialist. The common element with the socialists is his opposition to laissez-faire. In its place, he wanted "a system where we can act as an organized community for common purposes and to promote social and economic justice, while respecting and protecting the individual – his freedom of choice, his faith, his mind and its expression, his enterprise and his property" (21, p. 500). Profits would continue, and the wage system would remain (ibid., p. 88).

The problem is not a temporary problem of the slump. It is part of the agenda for collective action, and the words recall his 1920 essays.

> Let us mean by planning . . . the problem of the *general* organization of resources . . . We suffer a chronic failure to live up to the opportunities of our technical capacity to produce material goods.
> To remedy this failure is the problem of planning. The problem of planning is to do those things which, from the nature

---

[78] Keynes also discusses tax changes to redistribute income, but he does not reach any clear conclusion, and he does not stress tax changes in his other writing to the same degree as state control of investment. He is uncertain about the effects of progressive taxes and death duties (7, pp. 372–3). He favors, on balance, higher death duties (ibid., p. 373). But he also favors smaller but "significant inequalities of incomes and wealth" (ibid., p. 374). The main reason is political or social. The pursuit of wealth channels aggression away from "the reckless pursuit of personal power and authority" (ibid., 374).

of the case, it is impossible for the individual to attempt. (ibid., p. 87)

Keynes gives some examples of planning. He mentions taxes, tariffs, management of the exchange rate, regulation of transport, emigration, and immigration. Most important is the mitigation of industrial slumps (ibid., p. 89). Again, he proposes not countercyclical policies to increase consumption but that the state maintain "the general average of industrial production and activity at the optimum level" (ibid., p. 90).

The planners would be nonelected government officials, just as under an autocratic government. The difference would be that elected officials would act as "judges." They would not supervise "in detail," but they would be available when "grave mistakes had been made" (ibid., p. 92).

Keynes does not say what would be regarded as a mistake, but he did compare autocratic and democratic planning (ibid., p. 91). Autocratic planning is easier, he thought, but it loses the consent of the public.[79]

By 1945, Keynes had changed his views on the best arrangement for planning. He no longer proposed a national investment board operating as a semiautonomous agency. In its place, he proposed to give responsibility to the government of the day. His reason is tactical. Part of the government's full-employment policy calls for "some authority . . . charged with the duty of examining and reporting on the state of the Public Capital Budget as a whole, not merely after the event but also prospectively" (27, p. 408).

Keynes's case for planning rests on the alleged advantages of collective action. In his 1926 essay, "The End of Laissez Faire" (9, pp. 272–94), he had argued forcefully that economists had never made a case for complete laissez-faire. Economists chose the hypothesis "because it is the simplest, and not because it is nearest to the facts" (ibid., p. 282).

The poor quality of alternatives to laissez-faire helped to make the popular case for laissez-faire. In the 1920s, Keynes saw the main alternatives as protectionism and Marxism (ibid., p. 85). This may explain why in the early 1930s he turned toward protectionism and, in his essay "National Self-Sufficiency" (21, pp. 233–46), argues against free trade. Although the rhetoric he uses sounds, at times, like the

---

[79] In the 1920s, he had spoken of independent boards, but these are not mentioned in the radio address on which most of this section is based. An interesting response to Keynes's advocacy of state planning is the message of praise received from Harold Macmillan, later to be a Conservative prime minister (21, p. 93).

beginnings of a call for revolution,[80] the recommendations are for planning (ibid., p. 238) and for experimentation (ibid., pp. 240, 243). The problem, as he sees it at the time, is that the rate of interest cannot be reduced enough to permit society to benefit from technical advances (ibid., p. 240).

Keynes believed that personal freedom was compatible with the enlarged role of the state. He never gave up his attachment to personal freedom, but neither did he explain how to reconcile freedom with some of the restrictions he proposed, particularly exchange controls and investment planning. Even the essay on self-sufficiency strongly criticizes Stalin as a "terrifying example" (ibid., p. 246) and insists on the importance of open criticism. The *General Theory* and his later work contain many statements praising individual freedom, personal liberty, and decentralized decision making. He defended the increased power of the state that he favored "as the only practicable means of avoiding the destruction of existing economic forms in their entirety and as the conditions of the successful functioning of individual initiative" (7, p. 380).

Keynes could praise Hayek's *Road to Serfdom* as a "grand book" and declare himself "morally and philosophically" in agreement while disagreeing with Hayek's program. He told Hayek:

> I should say that what we want is not no planning, or even less planning, indeed I should say that we almost certainly want more. But the planning should take place in a community in which as many people as possible, both leaders and followers, wholly share your own moral position. Moderate planning will be safe if those carrying it out are rightly oriented in their own minds and hearts to the moral issue . . .
>
> I accuse you of perhaps confusing a little bit the moral and the material issues. Dangerous acts can be done safely in a community which thinks and feels rightly which would be the way to hell if they were executed by those who think and feel wrongly. (27, pp. 387–8)

Keynes believed that the power of the state would be checked by public criticism, elections, and elected officials serving as "judges." He was able to convince himself, and he tried to persuade others, that the increase in living standards from state planning and direction of investment would more than compensate for the inefficiency and pos-

---

[80] The polemics against capitalism in this essay are unusual even for Keynes. Later in the essay, Keynes explains his method: "Words ought to be a little wild, for they are the assault of thoughts on the unthinking" (21, p. 244).

sible corruption that it would bring.[81] Although he favored intervention, his proposed reforms were rules. Examples are his wartime proposal for precommitment to tax changes in postwar recessions and his proposals for limits on the size of balance-of-payments deficits and surpluses. Keynes's major books do not advocate the kinds of discretionary monetary or fiscal policies that have become known everywhere as "Keynesian policies."

Joan Robinson (1979, p. 27) summarizes his attitude from her perspective. He was[82]

> somewhat skeptical about the possibility of achieving permanent full employment . . . It was his British disciples, rather than he, who drafted the white paper in 1944 which proclaimed that it is the responsibility of government to maintain a high and stable level of employment. Keynes said: you can promise to be good but you cannot promise to be clever.

Econometric policy models

The *General Theory* stimulated construction of multiequation econometric models to forecast economic activity and to estimate policy responses. Keynes was very critical of these models and of the econometric work of Henry Schultz. He showed little enthusiasm for further work (14, pp. 296, 299, 307, 320).

He makes most of the criticisms that have since been made many times. His main objection is "the apparent lack of any adequate degree of uniformity in the environment" (ibid., p. 316). This criticism refers to the replication of events in time, the stability of the coefficients in different samples, and the extent to which different researchers using the same data would reach the same conclusion (ibid., pp. 316–20).

[81] Clark (1977, p. 89) reports on a conversation with Keynes about protectionism. Clark argued that protection would lead to corruption. Keynes was unimpressed; he was sure the level of corruption would be low. Clark quotes Keynes as saying, "no great harm would be done."

[82] Robinson (1979, p. 27) also reports on a conversation between Keynes and Austin Robinson in which Keynes, after a meeting with "his converts," told Robinson: "I was the only non-Keynesian there." The meeting to which she refers may have been the meeting described by Abba Lerner, Alvin Hansen, and Evsey Domar, discussed in Chapter 6 of this volume, at which Keynes was skeptical about the use of countercyclical deficits and of functional finance as a policy. Moggridge (1976, p. 24) quotes some of Keynes's cautious statements about the applicability of functional finance. An early version of the *General Theory* (29, p. 95) written in late 1933 has a statement favoring countercyclical spending policies that did not survive.

Keynes is alert to the problem of testing models and is perceptive that by appropriate choice of lags, different hypotheses can be rendered compatible with the same data.

Keynes did not claim that nothing could be learned, although he was skeptical about the method and about the degree to which coefficients estimated from one sample would be applicable to another. Coefficients are not constant. The marginal propensity to consume and the multiplier vary with the level of real income. There are more basic problems also. He comes close to describing the problem now called a change in regime when he expresses doubt about the stability of coefficients estimated from pre-1914 data (ibid., p. 316). He concludes that the method is "singularly unpromising" for the study of business cycles (ibid., p. 317).[83]

In a letter to Harrod (ibid., pp. 295–7), Keynes expressed his views about useful methods in economics. He was not opposed to empirical work. He strongly supported data collection and computation of relative magnitudes. He favored model building, but he saw no benefit in estimating multiequation models. The coefficient estimates have "no value" (ibid., p. 307), and they make the model "useless":

> It is of the essence of a model that one does *not* fill in real values for the variable functions. To do so would make it useless as a model. For as soon as this is done, the model loses its generality . . . That is why Clapham with his empty boxes was barking up the wrong tree and why Schultz's results, if he ever gets any, are not very interesting (for we know beforehand that they will not be applicable to future cases). The object of statistical study is *not so much to fill in missing variables with a view to prediction*, as to test the relevance and validity of the model.
>
> Economics is a science of thinking in terms of models joined to the art of choosing models which are relevant to the contemporary world . . . The object of a model is to segregate the semi-permanent or relatively constant factors from those which are transitory or fluctuating so as to develop a logical way of thinking about the latter . . .
>
> Good economists are scarce because the gift for using 'vigilant observation' to choose good models . . . appears to be a very rare one. (ibid., pp. 296–7, emphasis added)

[83] In a letter to Richard Kahn, he described Tinbergen's work as "hocus," a "mess of unintelligible figurings" (14, p. 289).

The activist Keynes

There are two sides to Keynes. One, most often found in his books and scholarly papers, proposes reforms. These call for new rules to achieve an optimum, or what Keynes often called an ideal. The other, most often found is his letters to editors, pamphlets, and newspaper columns, proposed solutions to problems he regarded as pressing.

When problems arose, Keynes proposed remedies based on his judgment, intuition, computations, or hunch if no theory was available. This explains why we find much discussion of expansionary fiscal policy before Keynes completed the *General Theory*. "Can Lloyd George Do It?" (9, pp. 86–125) and "The Means to Prosperity" (ibid., pp. 335–66), with prescriptions for the slump and the depression, antedate the work in which Keynes is alleged to have discovered fiscal policy. To the extent that he relied on economic analysis for these proposals and for the fiscal policy recommendations of the Macmillan report, it was the flawed analysis of the *Treatise*. Although Kahn's (1931) paper helped Keynes to understand the multiplier and the supply curve of aggregate output, it was not the source of his belief that increased government spending would expand output. The opposite is more nearly true. Kahn tried to work out the economic analysis underlying Keynes's intuition after it became clear that the *Treatise* did not provide the foundation.

At the depth of the depression, in 1932, Keynes urged remedial action. He attacked the popular response – we cannot spend more than we earn – pointing out that for the community as a whole, "it would be much truer to say that we cannot earn more than we spend" (21, p. 126). He favored open-market operations to prevent deficit finance from raising the rate of interest and to bring down the long-term rate (ibid., p. 200). And he met his critics with gusto: "Can America spend its way into recovery? Why, obviously . . . No one of common sense could doubt it, unless his mind had been muddled by a 'sound' financier or an 'orthodox' economist" (ibid., p. 334).

These strong statements that Keynes the polemicist seemed to relish do not appear in his scholarly work.[84] Countercyclical fiscal policy (called loan expenditure) is recommended as an alternative "if the education of our statesmen on principles of the classical economics *stands in the way of anything better*" (7, p. 129, emphasis added). Later,

---

[84] Nor do they appear to have been based on it. In a 1935 letter to Arthur Salter (21, pp. 354–5), Keynes explained that he agreed with Salter's program calling for more planning, greater public control of the Bank of England, etc., but he would not endorse the program. He believed it was more important to base the program on a "fundamental diagnosis," which was lacking.

Keynes repeats his preference for what he regarded as "reform" over programs aiming at recovery (ibid., pp. 219–20).

In his 1937 proposals "How to Avoid a Slump" (21, pp. 384–95) written for the *Times*, Keynes is a proponent of reforms intended to prevent another slump without setting off a boom. The circumstances were very different: "We have entirely freed ourselves . . . from the philosophy of the *laissez-faire* state" (ibid., p. 384).

Keynes's main recommendations call, again, for a board of public investment to plan future investment projects (ibid., p. 394) and for tax changes that increase consumption by redistributing income toward the poor (ibid., pp. 393–4). Although the unemployment rate was above 11 percent in 1937, Keynes did not propose that expansive measures be taken at once. His emphasis is on achieving stability, achieving the *optimum* rate of investment, avoiding a boom, and planning actions that avoid a slump by relying to a modest degree on countercyclical investment.[85]

He opposed changes in interest rates. His argument is not that changes in interest rates are ineffective – the elasticity pessimism that became prominent in later discussion. The problem he sees is very different. Variability of interest rates creates uncertainty and inhibits investment:

> A low enough long-term rate of interest cannot be achieved if we allow it to be believed that better terms will be obtainable from time to time by those who keep their resources liquid. The long-term rate of interest must be kept *continuously* as near as possible to what we believe to be the long-term optimum. It is not suitable to be used as a short-period weapon. (ibid., p. 389)

Again, Keynes uses extrapolative expectations where it serves his argument. He made a similar argument in a letter to E. F. M. Durbin, the reviewer of his book in *Labour*. Keynes complained that Durbin had represented the *General Theory* as saying that "to cure unemployment it is, therefore, only necessary to force the rate of interest sufficiently low and maintain it there" (29, p. 232). This was not his belief. He told Durbin:

---

[85] He recognizes (21, pp. 386–7) that maintaining investment in the "right proportion" is difficult: "The best that we can hope to achieve . . . is to . . . preserve as much stability of aggregate investment as we can manage." Despite the persistence of unemployment, Keynes suggests slower investment "to keep our more easily available ammunition in hand for when it is more required" (21, p. 387). Countercyclical public investment, but not consumption, is recommended again (ibid., p. 390), and Keynes adds countercyclical changes in tariffs (p. 391).

There are many passages in the book devoted to proving that attacks on the rate of interest by themselves are likely to prove an inadequate solution except perhaps temporarily. I, therefore, advocate measures designed to increase the propensity to consume, and also public investment independent of the rate of interest . . . investment is a matter which cannot be left solely to private decisions. (ibid.)

Durbin's reply (ibid., pp. 232–4) emphasized two points. Keynes did not favor state ownership of the means of production; Durbin, who later became a Labour member of Parliament, did. Durbin believed that financing investment with increased money caused inflation. Keynes replied that he would not expand when the economy is near full employment but would "relax my expansionist measures a little before technical full employment had actually been reached" (ibid., p. 235). His optimism appears to foreshadow the views of those who believed that forecasting accuracy or judgment could be used to increase stability, but he probably had in mind an unemployment rate of 5 percent.[86]

Conclusion

Among the many contributions Keynes made to economics, none is more lasting than the stimulus he gave to the development of the theory of output and employment within a general equilibrium framework. "Keynes stirred the stale economic frog pond to its depth," Haberler (1962, p. 269) wrote, but many writers including Hicks (1937) and Modigliani (1944) found the *General Theory* less novel than it at first appeared.

Keynes believed that the *General Theory* was both novel and revolutionary. The classical theory, he claimed, was based on Say's law; equilibrium could occur only at full employment. Frictional unemployment could arise when workers looked for new jobs or during a business cycle, but the major British problem of the interwar period was not of that kind. In the 1920s, unemployment persisted at a rate well above previous norms, then rose again in the 1930s and remained high by past standards. The classical theory had no explanation for the kind of persistent unemployment that occurs when an apparently stable equilibrium is reached at a level of output less than the maximum at-

---

[86] Despite Keynes's emphasis on stability, he often recommended changes in tariffs in the 1930s. See, e.g., vol. 21, pp. 207–10. At times, Keynes also favored commodity price stabilization schemes.

tainable output. What he regarded as the major problem of Britain in the interwar period seemed inconsistent with existing theory.

Keynes called the difference between maximum employment and equilibrium employment involuntary unemployment. In extensive correspondence with economists and in several papers published after the *General Theory*, he repeated many of the same points. The classical theory assumes Say's law, does not explain unemployment, neglects the differences between barter and monetary economies, ignores expectations, and assumes that the price elasticity of the supply of aggregate output is zero. Contrary to the usual identification of Keynes's unique contribution with the so-called Keynesian special case, Keynes did not emphasize either the inflexibility of money wages or money illusion or absolute liquidity preference – the liquidity trap – when responding to critics or restating his argument.

In the *General Theory* (7, p. 24) Keynes suggested an empirical investigation of the relation of real and money wages during business cycles. Published results appeared to reject his hypothesis that money wages are inflexible. Although Keynes did not accept the evidence as sufficiently compelling to abandon the hypothesis, he indicated that abandoning the postulate of money wage inflexibility would simplify his hypothesis. He makes clear that his book would have been simpler if real, rather than money, wages are inflexible during cycles. And, Keynes insisted, for "my own theory this conclusion [inflexible money wages] was inconvenient, since it had a tendency to offset the influence of the main forces which I was discussing" (ibid., p. 400).[87]

What were the main forces? The many quotations in the text reproduce the answer Keynes gave repeatedly: The economic system is stable, but employment is subject to fluctuations around an average level that is less than full (maximum) employment. The important point for Keynes is that the *expected* levels of output and employment are below full employment. The problem is manifested in the labor market, but it does not arise in the labor market. The central problem is uncertainty which, by increasing the demand for money, puts a premium in interest rates, thereby raising the required return to private investment above the social marginal product of capital. This wedge between private and social returns lowers investment and the stock of capital and therefore lowers the level of equilibrium output. My analysis shows

---

[87] Keynes's statement should not be interpreted as a claim that the implications of the theory would be unchanged. The implications for the paths followed by some principal variables during cycles would, indeed, differ. The implications for involuntary unemployment, on my interpretation of that term, are unchanged. Uncertainty would not be affected, so the expected rate of interest and liquidity preference would sustain the same equilibrium, and the excess burden would not be removed.

that his conclusions do not depend on the properties of the labor supply function or on wage setting, so he is correct in his claim that his main policy conclusions would not be affected if empirical evidence rejected the inflexibility of money wages (ibid., p. 401).

At a position of permanent full employment, the economy has the "optimum rate of interest" (ibid., p. 243). Keynes believed that the way to raise the economy's average output to the optimum level was to reduce the uncertainty premium in interest rates by increasing state direction of investment. He believed that state direction would raise the rate of investment and either reduce or eliminate the amplitude of cyclical fluctuations in investment. He identified volatile expectations of future returns as the principal cause of uncertainty. Volatility gives rise to default risk in loans and therefore to a risk premium to compensate the lender. The state can eliminate this risk – and reduce the excess burden – by combining the functions of lender and borrower. Further, by stabilizing the rate of investment, the state stabilizes output. With lower uncertainty, the public willingly reduces its desired money balances, thereby reducing the expected and actual rate of interest to the social optimum.

Keynes discusses two ways to increase investment. One way is to lower the long-term rate of interest by monetary or wage policy. The other is to eliminate the baneful influence of private speculators and the volatility of expectations, thereby reducing uncertainty premiums and (within a generation) increasing the capital stock until capital ceases to be scarce. This is the social optimum.

He rejects the first solution as infeasible or unlikely. Neither monetary expansion nor a reduction of money wages is likely to lower the long-term interest rate permanently. Keynes's reason is that these actions do not eliminate the uncertainty premium and do not change the expected level of real income. Expansive monetary (or wage) policy is not a solution; these actions can increase output temporarily, but the level around which output fluctuates and the amplitude of fluctuations remain unchanged.

His discussion of the effects of wage reduction is tentative and, to a degree, inconclusive. He does not claim that wage reductions *cannot* raise real money balances and lower interest rates. His claim is that frequent changes in wages increase volatility and therefore increase price instability and uncertainty. This *raises* the demand for money and raises the equilibrium interest rate (ibid., p. 232). On the other hand, money wage reductions that do not give rise to expectations of further reductions are expansive; real balances rise, and the equilibrium real (long) rate falls (ibid.).[88]

---

[88] Keynes's experience in the 1920s, particularly after the general strike of 1926, probably reinforced his view that money wages were inflexible. This was the standard view.

Having rejected a market solution as unlikely, Keynes proposed to solve the employment problem by state management of investment (ibid., pp. 378–9). He believed that the state would take a long view and would not be influenced by short-term changes in economic activity. State management or direction of investment would remove the externality – the risk premium paid to risk-averse lenders by risk-averse investors – that holds the expected rate on private investment above the social rate of return.

The *General Theory* stimulated development of the theory of fluctuations, but it is not primarily a theory of cyclical fluctuations.[89] It is more aptly described as a static theory in which the effects of fluctuations – avoidable fluctuations – have a critical role. Keynes's applications to the business cycle are an afterthought intended to demonstrate the important role played by expectations and the marginal efficiency of capital during a cycle.

Keynes's views of expectations reflect his early writing on probability theory. In his *Treatise on Probability* and in the *General Theory*, Keynes expresses the view that the best one can do in an uncertain world is to act as if the future can be known while recognizing that the important future events are unknown and cannot be foreseen. There is neither conflict nor contradiction when he writes that the long-term interest rate and the level of output around which the economy fluctuates are constant but the future is uncertain and the levels of output and interest rates are subject to violent change. Constancy refers to the average level around which fluctuations occur. The size of the fluctuations affect the average, however, through their effect on uncertainty.

It is often remarked that the *General Theory* is an untidy book, full of asides, speculations, comments, and conjectures unrelated to the main theme. No less common is the belief that Keynes frequently changed his opinion. There is some truth to these statements but less than is commonly believed. The statements presume that one of the several conventional interpretations of his work is correct.

The *General Theory* is broadly consistent with the beliefs Keynes expressed in the 1920s. The opposition to laissez-faire, the importance of state planning, the concern for progress, and the relation of investment to progress are all present. Savers are not very important, and rentiers are not important at all. By directing investment, saving can, in most circumstances, be brought to its equilibrium value. The principal differences are that the beliefs and conjectures of the 1920s were now reflected in a theory of aggregate output, and many of the earlier conjectures are now claimed to be implications of a theory. There are,

---

[89] Salant (1985, p. 1181), a student of Keynes, shares this view.

of course, differences in detail. Some are important. Fluctuations are no longer caused by a mixture of real and monetary shocks. The dominant impulses are real; the business cycle is driven by expectations of returns to capital, the latter dominated by speculators on the stock exchange. Monetary policy remains important; countercyclical changes in interest rates increase uncertainty and thus lower the average level of output.

My interpretation of the *General Theory* ties many of the chapters – on long-run expectations, business cycles, changes in money wages, interest rates, liquidity, and mercantilism – to the main theme and to his earlier work. It explains why Keynes regarded the concluding chapter, speculating on social philosophy and proposing reforms, as an implication of his analysis. It explains, also, why Keynes – a practical man with a keen sense of theory, history, policy, and practice – assumes throughout that the economy is closed. His principal concern is to reduce the gap between average and maximum output. To analyze the causes of that gap, the damping effects of countercyclical fluctuations in the trade balance are of little moment, so where necessary, Keynes recognizes and quickly dismisses these changes, as in his discussion of money wages.

Keynes's wartime memos on the role of fiscal and monetary policies in the postwar economy (JMK 27) were written by a man who favored rules and was against discretionary policies and countercyclical changes in consumption. These memos are consistent with his long-standing interest in policies to raise living standards by gradually satiating the capital stock. A main concern in the *General Theory* and after is to reduce the instability of the economy by eliminating fluctuations in the most volatile elements, not to substitute one source of variability for another. Variability introduced by a well-intentioned government attempting to smooth the economy is as likely a source of error and disappointed expectations as private decisions. His wartime discussions of postwar policy therefore favor a limited range of preannounced changes in business taxes, not activist fiscal policies.[90] Although he favored income redistribution on the belief that redistribution increases spending, in his wartime memos he opposed policies to increase consumption. He preferred to increase investment and believed that stimulating consumption was less desirable than investment in housing, utilities, and productive capital. Although Keynes pressed for lower interest rates in the early 1930s, his wartime memos and his

---

[90] Deficit spending is a *last resort*: "If for one reason or another, the volume of planned [mainly state] investment fails to produce equilibrium, the lack of balance would be met by unbalancing one way or the other the current Budget. Admittedly, this would be a last resort" (27, p. 352).

letters emphasize stable interest rates and state investment.[91] In his words, "I should regard State intervention to encourage investment as probably a more important factor than low rates of interest taken in isolation" (27, p. 350).

I have tried to highlight the dominant role of expectations in the *General Theory* and, to a lesser degree, to contrast Keynes's views on probability theory and expectations with the currently prominent view known as rational expectations. I have not tried to emphasize places where Keynes's argument is faulty or incomplete.[92] His theory is not remembered for the careful, step-by-step craftsmanship of the argument. It is his general framework and his vision, not his detailed analysis, that has had a lasting impact.

Four puzzling aspects should not escape comment, however. These are the treatment of expectations, the neglect of inflation, the problem of capital flight, and the conclusions about unemployment.

First, Keynes's treatment of expectations is unsatisfactory. Expectations are extrapolative where that is useful for his argument, as in some of his discussion of wage and interest changes. Expectations are also regressive when that serves his purpose, as in the explanation that falling interest rates give rise to a belief that rates will return to their mean.

Second, Keynes rarely mentions the inflationary consequences of his full-employment policy. Respected critics such as Jacob Viner (1936, in Wood 2, pp. 86–7) pointed to these consequences early in the discussion. Keynes never responded fully.[93] He was aware that inflation could occur at full employment, since he made the supply curve of aggregate output vertical at that point. He even defined the point at which the supply curve becomes vertical as both the position of full employment (7, p. 26) and as the position at which true inflation starts (ibid., p. 303). Yet, his only response to critics who saw his policy as

---

[91] In the 1930s, he remarks that an interest rate of 3.5 percent is too high for full employment. For 1835–1914, he puts the average return on government bonds at 3 percent. For 1934, the equilibrium rate is below 2.5 percent (21, pp. 315–16). In the *General Theory*, he mentions 2–2.5 percent as the lower limit under laissez-faire (7, pp. 218–19).

[92] Keynes is never completely clear about whether the interest rate is determined by IS and LM or only by the monetary sector. At times, he treats the equilibrium of saving and investment as an identity. The properties of his aggregate supply function are obscure.

[93] Kahn (1978, in Wood 1, p. 559) cites similar comments by Benjamin and Frank Graham to which Keynes replied that he was aware of the risk. There are a few references to inflation in Keynes's wartime memos about postwar policy. He recognized inflation as a problem in the immediate postwar period, and he favored continuing price controls to minimize the effect (27, p. 322). He believed that the greater risk was "too much rather than too little control" (ibid., p. 358).

inflationary was that *he* would "relax my expansionist measures a little before technical full employment had actually been reached" (29, p. 235).

Would others do the same? Would his argument be persuasive? Keynes does not say. One of his leading disciples, Richard Kahn concluded that the *General Theory* was "designed for an economy in a state of depression" (1978, in Wood 1, p. 557). A principal reason Kahn gives is that Keynes's analysis of money wages is unsatisfactory (ibid., p. 556).[94]

A related problem arises in Keynes's treatment of monetary policy. Since he believed that the public desired to hold money balances for reasons of safety and security, the central bank could satiate the demand for money by printing money. In the *Tract*, Keynes discusses the inflation tax, so he was aware of the effect of inflation on the demand for money. He never proposes (or even mentions) this solution to the problem of involuntary unemployment. On the contrary, he insists on the neutrality of money – the independence of the real equilibrium position from the quantity of money.[95]

Third, Keynes never mentions capital flight and does not explain how a single country can drive the rate of interest to zero by eliminating the uncertainty premium. Rapid or instantaneous adjustment of antic-

[94] In the same section, Kahn tries to interpret Keynes as a proponent of cost-push inflation. He cites Keynes's distinction in the *Treatise* between income inflation and profit inflation (Kahn 1978, in Wood 1, p. 553). This is misleading. It is true that prices depend on money wages, as in my model of the *General Theory*. However, Keynes does not say that wages rise under the influence of trade union pressure independent of aggregate demand and money. Keynes is explicit that prices begin to rise before full employment is reached and rise in proportion to money once full employment is reached (7, pp. 295–6). At full employment, he expected the quantity theory to hold because the supply of output is vertical. Harrod's efforts to cite a passage where Keynes said something about "cost-push" inflation produced nothing except his thought that there might be such a passage though he could not find it (Harrod 1972, pp. 8–9). What Hicks later called the wage theorem relating prices to money wages is already found in the *Treatise* both in the fundamental equations relating costs (mainly wages) to prices and in Keynes's application of the theory to historical episodes (e.g., 6, pp. 145–51). Further, Keynes assumes competition. Oligopolistic price setting, commonly invoked in cost-push theories, never enters his discussion. He retains competitive pricing.

[95] Kaldor (1983, p. 21) and other Cambridge economists raise the issue of endogenous money supply. Keynes has much to say about the monetary process in the *Treatise*, but he says very little in the *General Theory* and after. In a 1934 article he discussed the issue in a way entirely consistent with his work in the *Treatise*: "It is hard to see how the effect [of expenditure] can be altered if the money spent by the government comes from banks rather than the public" (21, p. 335). The point made by Kaldor about endogeneity would gain relevance if either the interest elasticity of the supply function for money was negative and large relative to the (negative) interest elasticity of the demand for money or the income elasticity of supply was positive and large relative to the income or (wealth) elasticity of demand. There is no evidence that either problem arises.

ipations to entirely new and unique arrangements seems most unlikely. Yet some assumption of this kind, or capital controls, would be required to prevent capital flight.

Fourth, the *General Theory* does not adequately explain persistent unemployment. The moral hazard that raises the private return above the social return can, at best, explain why investment is lower than the optimum rate. The cumulative effect of persistent, suboptimal investment is a suboptimal stock of capital and a level of income below the level that could be achieved if moral hazard is reduced. Under these conditions, the country is poorer, but there is no reason for persistent unemployment.

Further, Keynes's main explanation is unconvincing. During a business cycle, a decline in money wages may give rise to the extrapolative expectations of further declines, which in Keynes's theory increase price instability, uncertainty, the demand for money, and the risk premium in interest rates. After years of relatively high unemployment, why are money wage reductions extrapolated? Keynes does not explain; indeed, he does not claim that they will be extrapolated. His claim is more modest. He recognizes two conditions (in a closed economy) under which wage reduction are most likely to increase employment (7, p. 265); and he concludes that a sufficient reduction would in fact raise employment (ibid., p. 266). He decides, however, that "a moderate reduction in money-wages *may* [sic] prove inadequate, whilst an immoderate reduction *might* [sic] shatter confidence even if it were practicable" (ibid., p. 267, emphasis added).

I believe that the *General Theory* and Keynes's subsequent writings offer an explanation of suboptimal output but not of persistent unemployment. It is possible that Keynes mistakenly went from his assumption that output is a measure of employment to the conclusion that suboptimal output gives rise to suboptimal employment. This would be true if the capital–labor ratio is fixed. Keynes does not make that assumption.

In his response to Viner (14, p. 110) and his reply to Dunlop and Tarshis (7, p. 401, n. 1), Keynes recognizes that his labor market analysis is unsatisfactory. On my interpretation, this is an understatement. I believe Keynes failed to deliver an explanation of persistent unemployment as an implication of his analysis. He is not alone in his failure. Generations of economists before and after Keynes have not provided an explanation of British unemployment in the interwar period and other episodes of sustained unemployment that is consistent with received price theory. Like our intellectual ancestors long before Keynes, we continue to assume sluggish wage or price adjustment.

The anomaly is that the novel and important part of Keynes's analysis in the *General Theory* was lost, and Keynes's contribution came to be identified with wage rigidity in textbooks and in much professional writing. The emphasis he gave to expectations, variability, and the excess burden created by excessive variability all but disappeared from economics for thirty years. The principal policy recommendations – smooth investment and raise its level – were wrongly reinterpreted as an argument for more variable government monetary and fiscal policies.

Time has not dealt kindly with Keynes's conjectures about government management of investment. Where governments have controlled the rate of investment, they have often directed resources toward declining industries, where the expected return is low or negative – to space shots, supersonic aircraft, road building in the Amazon, state-owned airlines, and other "prestige" projects. These projects often have low rates of return, but that was not the way Keynes expected to bring the marginal efficiency of capital to zero in a generation. Keynes favored wasteful projects only if other alternatives were not available or had failed. Often, governments have favored consumption and transfers and reduced investment when growth of spending was reduced. This, too, is contrary to Keynes's program. The precepts of Harvey Road, and his confidence that he and others like him would influence policy, misled him.

5

Monetary reform and international economic order

> Never in history was there a method devised of setting each country's advantage at variance with its neighbours' as the international gold . . . standard . . . The part played by orthodox economists . . . has been disastrous . . . For when in their blind struggle for an escape, some countries have thrown off the obligations which had previously rendered impossible an autonomous rate of interest, these economists have taught that a restoration of the former shackles is a necessary first step to a general recovery. (7, p. 349)

Keynes rarely overlooked an opportunity to criticize the classical gold standard. The main point of his criticism changed, however, in parallel with the development of his ideas. The mature Keynes, as in this quotation, gave two main reasons why the gold standard is not a welfare maximizing arrangement. First, countries cannot reduce unemployment by expanding domestic demand. They must compete for exports to acquire gold and increase money. Their gain is at the expense of another country (or other countries) that loses gold and must contract. Second, the classical gold standard prevents a country from independently lowering its interest rate. Keynes often wanted a zero rate of interest, and certainly a permanently lower rate of interest, to increase investment, the capital stock, and per capita income.

The association of Keynes with closed-economy macroeconomics, in which money "does not matter," is one of the great anomalies in the history of economics. Throughout his life, Keynes gave great importance to monetary arrangements and the rules governing monetary policy. From his first book to his last effort, he developed and promoted programs of monetary reform.

His first book, *Indian Currency and Finance* (JMK 1), analyzes and describes the problem of monetary management in an open, developing country maintaining a gold exchange standard. The policy issue, at the time, was the circulation of gold coins. Keynes opposed gold coins on the Ricardian argument that centralization of the gold reserve economized on gold and lowered the cost of the standard. Keynes found the gold exchange standard "the ideal currency of the future," but the objective he chose for the standard was maintenance of confidence in the reserve not stability of prices or output.

His last major professional activity, planning for postwar economic reconstruction and development, led to the establishment of the postwar international financial arrangements through the Bretton Woods agreement. Gold continues to have a role, but its role is much less important than it had been in the interwar period. Keynes's main concerns are to prevent surplus countries from accumulating large reserves of gold and foreign exchange and to remove the external diseconomy arising from the requirement on deficit countries to contract output. Keynes believed that if the size and frequency of contractions could be reduced, uncertainty would be lower; output would be more stable and predictable; investment, capital per worker, and per capita income would be higher; and welfare would increase.[1]

The three decades that span Keynes's professional career as an economist were years of frequent international monetary disturbance and experimentation. Keynes participated as theorist, critic, policy adviser, and prominent citizen in discussions of the monetary reconstruction that followed the two major wars, the problem of German reparations, Britain's return to the gold standard in 1925 at the traditional parity, the world depression of the 1930s, and the financing of Britain's contribution to World War II. Each of these events brought forth letters to the editor, memos to officials, newspaper columns, and journal articles, often including proposals for monetary reform or a change in monetary management. Although Keynes saw business cycles mainly as the result of real shocks, the level of output or the variability of prices – his principal concerns in his major works – depended on monetary arrangements.

In the 1920s, Keynes thought monetary reform would reduce uncertainty by increasing price stability. As his ideas evolved, he became convinced that by increasing price stability society can reduce the variability of investment and real income. This view appears in the *Tract*, but it becomes a dominant theme in the *Treatise on Money*, where Keynes's principal concern is with policies to maintain price stability

---

[1] Keynes would have been pleased by the greater stability of postwar output and the higher growth in the early postwar years. Most likely, he would have been tempted to claim some of the improvement as evidence of the correctness of his ideas about monetary arrangements. Variability remained low and in some countries variability declined after the Bretton Woods system ended, however. Meltzer (1986a) presents evidence on the variability of unanticipated output and prices in the United States for different monetary regimes in the pre- and postwar years. Meltzer (1985, 1986b) compares the variability of unanticipated prices and output for major countries during the Bretton Woods and post–Bretton Woods periods.

as a means of achieving economic stability. His belief that variability of investment and income affects the average level of aggregate income emerges most clearly in the *General Theory* and the letters and papers that followed. There, increased variability and uncertainty lower the level of equilibrium output by increasing the demand for money. People hold gold (or currency) in their portfolios in place of capital, so the capital stock and output are smaller. The resulting excess welfare burden is greater under laissez-faire, the term Keynes used to refer to the prewar gold standard with complete freedom of trade and capital movements. The excess burden could be lowered, he believed. Once he had drawn this conclusion from his theory, Keynes had an economic rationale for the illiberal policies he had long favored – state intervention to direct investment and to control (or prevent) capital movements.

Although Keynes changed his views about the details of monetary arrangements many times, four principal changes of opinion stand out in the mass of material. The four changes reflect the development of his thinking about the sources, costs, and consequences of variability and the means of reducing these costs.

First, Keynes came to believe that institutional arrangements are not simply a means by which societies allocate resources and achieve full employment and price stability or some set of micro- and macroeconomic objectives. Institutional arrangements constrict or expand the set of feasible outcomes and, in this way, condition and perhaps determine what a nation, or the world economy, can achieve. In the *General Theory* variability of asset prices, unanticipated events, and the separation of borrowing and lending introduce an excess burden in the form of a risk premium in interest rates. Internationally the excess burden arises because gold flows and capital movements disturb prices and output. Under fixed exchange rates, deficit countries must raise interest rates and contract output and employment to maintain fixed rates and reverse gold outflows. Keynes produced several plans to reduce this source of variability. The postwar proposals that became the Bretton Woods system reduce the burden borne by deficit countries in two ways (25, pp. 27–30). Surplus countries share the adjustment (1) by expanding and (2) by lending to deficit countries. Keynes expected the system of lending and borrowing to reduce fluctuations in interest rates, investment, output, and employment, thereby reducing the risk premium in interest rates, increasing the capital stock, and raising the level of world income.

Second, Keynes opposed the classical gold standard with its commitment to permanently fixed exchange rates and noninterventionist policy in the 1920s, but he also opposed freely fluctuating rates. Generally, he favored a managed monetary system operating under rules that would reduce fluctuations in prices and output. Keynes saw changes in the demand for gold (or money) as a destabilizing element. In a crisis or when people became uncertain about the future, they held gold or money, thereby raising interest rates and lowering investment. As Keynes's proposals evolved, the role of gold in the international monetary system declined.

Third, from the mid-1920s on, he favored restrictions on capital movements to gain control of foreign investment. As his ideas developed, the emphasis on capital controls grew until he favored an extensive system of exchange controls to support a system of fixed, but adjustable, exchange rates.

Fourth, wage inflexibility was part of Keynes's Marshallian heritage. With wage inflexibility, a reduction in money falls most heavily in the short-run "on those particular factors which are in the weakest bargaining position or have the shortest contracts governing their rate of money earnings" (5, p. 243). Exchange rate changes removed some of the burden of adjustment from money wages. Hence, Keynes favored flexibility in exchange rates, crawling pegs, and finally an international system of adjustable pegs with rules restricting the adjustment.

These changes in his views reflected his experience, and his interpretation of that experience, in the turbulent period through which he lived. By the 1920s, New York had become a more important competitor of the London financial market, and the United States had become a relatively larger holder of gold.[2] Keynes came to believe that the movement of speculative balances between London and New York exacerbated Britain's problem. Efforts to expand activity lowered interest rates, produced a gold outflow, a loss of reserves, and encouraged or forced the Bank of England to defend the parity by raising interest rates. The United States did not follow the rules for a major financial center. Although it was a substantial gold importer in the 1920s, the United States raised tariffs substantially in 1922 and 1929. Particularly during the stock market boom of 1928–9, the United States drew capital from the rest of the world and added to its gold stock, thereby imposing deflation and short-term contraction on the rest of the world. Friedman and Schwartz (1963b, p. 297) point out that the Federal Reserve sterilized gold movements during the 1920s, producing an inverse correlation between gold movements and the monetary base instead of the classical positive association. During the contraction

---

[2] From 1890 to 1930, U.S. gold holdings rose at a 4.5 percent compound annual rate. World gold stocks rose at a 2.5 percent rate. The U.S. share of world gold stocks rose from 8.8 percent in 1890 to 12.3 percent in 1910 and 20.6 percent in 1925. Data are from Commission on the Role of Gold in the Domestic and International Monetary System (1982, pp. 196, 203, 205).

after 1929, the United States drew gold from the rest of the world, spreading the deflation instead of losing gold and encouraging expansion abroad.[3] In the 1930s, the United States joined others in the use of beggar-thy-neighbor policies. Despite a large and growing gold stock, tariffs, though reduced, remained high, and the United States did not lend abroad substantially. A sizable net gold inflow again imposed deflation on gold standard countries and failed to provide stimulus to the rest of the world. From 1934 to the end of 1940, the U.S. share of the world's gold stock rose from 20.3 to 45.5 percent, but much of the inflow was sterilized, so it could not contribute to expansion.

The interwar policies of the United States had a major influence on Keynes's postwar plans. At first, Keynes did not trust the United States to avoid repetition of the deflationary experience of the interwar period. Although he became convinced later that U.S. policy had changed, his concerns about the postwar financial system remained more heavily weighted toward avoiding deflation than preventing inflation. His weighting was not unique. Most of the architects of postwar policy arrangements were anxious to avoid a return to the interwar experience. No one in authority seems to have imagined that the United States would produce the high rates of inflation that destroyed the Bretton Woods system.

Although the policies and actions of the United States were an important influence on the world and on Keynes, they were not the only influence. Keynes had witnessed the German inflation of the early 1920s at close range, and he was familiar with many of the details of inflation in Austria, Hungary, Italy, and France. These observations, and his interest in maintaining price stability, may have contributed to his reluctance to abandon all connections between money and gold. For Keynes the problem of devising a system in which gold had a role was to avoid the excess burdens of contraction and variability.

Even in *Indian Currency* Keynes predicted that Britain would not "leave permanently the most intimate adjustments of our economic organism at the mercy of a lucky prospector, a new chemical process, or a change of ideas in Asia" (1, p. 71). In the *Tract* and the *Treatise*, he had concluded, as he noted in 1933, that gold should retain a place in the monetary system but that

> (1) the parities between national standards and gold should not
> be rigid, (2) . . . there should be a wider margin than in the
> past between the gold points, and (3) . . . if possible some

---

[3] Nurkse (1944) points out that many countries failed to follow the rules of the international gold standard. The United States was a principal, and for much of the period the principal, gold standard country.

> international control should be formed with a view to regulating
> the commodity value of gold within certain limits. (21, p. 186)

These proposals prescribed the range within which Keynes searched for alternatives for the next twenty years.

Keynes's discussions of monetary arrangements are of interest for reasons that go beyond the specific recommendations he made or his reasons for making them. First, his theoretical work and his proposals for an International Clearing Union led him to consider the principal functions that a monetary system performs and its potential for increasing the social productivity of exchange arrangements (money). He understood that the postwar monetary system could be either risk absorbing or risk augmenting, and he believed that the postwar standard of living in Britain and elsewhere depended on the outcome. Second, in the course of his writings, he analyzed not only the reasons for choosing an internal or an external standard, but he also considered various ways of achieving what he often called "ideal" combinations of the two. Third, Keynes discusses specific issues that are relevant for the contemporary world economy. Among these issues are the transfer of resources from debtor to creditor countries, and the restrictions on the domestic policies of debtors and creditors that the transfers impose. For Keynes, the latter problem arose in the context of Germany's reparations in the 1920s, but many similar issues returned in the 1970s and 1980s with the transfer of resources to OPEC and the payment of interest and principal on the debts incurred by developing countries. Fourth, Keynes's proposals for the postwar era gave him an opportunity to apply to the world economy any applicable principles developed in his *General Theory*. From his choices we can infer what Keynes would have preserved if he had extended his *General Theory* to an open economy with fixed exchange rates. A main issue left open in the *General Theory* is how to reduce the rate of interest to an equilibrium at zero without inducing capital flight. From Keynes's postwar plans, we can infer how he proposed to deal with the problem of capital flight.

In the remaining sections, I follow mainly an evolutionary course, tracing the development of Keynes's treatment of international monetary arrangements from the *Tract* to the Clearing Union. The relation of the proposed Clearing Union to the system that emerged at Bretton Woods and after is a tale that has been told by others, so I do not repeat it. My main concern is with the development of Keynes's ideas and their relation to his theory and to my interpretation. The proposals for the Clearing Union, in fact all of his proposals, show Keynes as a proponent of monetary rules intended to restrict discretionary policy and reduce uncertainty without eliminating short-term policy responses. For Keynes, rules acted as general guides to action and restrictions that provide stability and reduce uncertainty. Rules did not prevent discretionary action by well-intentioned policymakers acting in what they judged to be the public interest.

The *Tract*

A Tract on Monetary Reform (JMK 4) first appeared as part of a series on postwar reconstruction in 1922–3. The *Tract* raises issues of social choice that concerned Keynes for the rest of his life, and properly so, because the issues are of highest importance and are not easily resolved analytically. The basic choice is between internal price stability and external stability, stability of the exchange rate. The issue arises because a country, acting alone, cannot provide both and, as we have learned, may sacrifice both.

Viewed in one way, the choice is between a monopoly central bank, restricted to control the money stock so as to achieve domestic price stability, and a fixed price or exchange rate, sustained by a government guarantee of convertibility into such units as gold, commodity bundles, or other currencies. The former requires the exchange rate to change, so external stability is sacrificed. The latter surrenders control of money and the domestic price level. Economic theory generally does not support price-fixing arrangements and supports the case for monopoly only in particular circumstances that must be established, so there is a presumption that neither fixed exchange rates nor a monopoly central bank is likely to be demonstrably superior on first principles. This suggests the reason why the choice between monetary and exchange rate control has not been resolved by applying general principles of economic analysis to the choice of monetary standard. The costs and benefits of each standard differ with the circumstances of the country, the arrangements in other countries, the risks that must be borne, and attitudes toward risk bearing.

Keynes ignores the resource costs of alternative standards and bases his choice on the level of risk that society must bear. The *Tract* leaves no doubt that the proper objective is internal price stability. The problem is not what should be chosen but whether the objective can be achieved:

> There does seem to be in almost every case a presumption in
> favour of the stability of prices, if only it can be achieved.
> Stability of exchange is in the nature of a convenience which

adds to the efficiency and prosperity of those who are engaged in foreign trade. Stability of prices, on the other hand, is profoundly important. (4, p. 126)

The importance of price stability is discussed at length, but the main point is made early in the book and repeated frequently. Price stability encourages saving and, thus, increases investment (ibid., p. 16): "The individualistic capitalism of today, precisely because it entrusts saving to the individual investor and production to the individual employer, *presumes* a stable measuring-rod of value, and cannot be efficient – perhaps cannot survive – without one" (ibid., p. 36).[4] And on a previous page: "The provision of adequate facilities for the carrying of this risk [relative and absolute price changes] is one of the greatest of the problems of modern economic life" (ibid., p. 33).

The core of his argument is that price stability shifts resources from current to future consumption, while inflation breaks down habits of thrift. Keynes refers to the experience in Germany to make his argument.[5] Price instability reduces investment by increasing risk, induces fluctuations in relative prices, and thus makes trade, particularly international trade, less attractive, and therefore smaller (ibid., p. 32).

The role of risk as an influence on investment and output and the influence of institutional arrangements in augmenting or diminishing risk are basic themes in Keynes's writings. These themes are clearly stated in the *Tract*. He writes:

The *fact* of falling prices injures entrepreneurs; consequently the *fear* of falling prices causes them to protect themselves by curtailing their operations; yet it is upon the aggregate of their individual estimations of the risk, and their willingness to run the risk, that the activity of production and of employment mainly depends. (ibid., p. 34)

And, he offers a remedy:

[4] "Inflation is unjust and deflation is inexpedient" (4, p. 36). Deflation is worse, Keynes thought, because it provokes unemployment via the lag of money wages and, in his view, it is worse to increase unemployment than to disappoint rentiers.

[5] Keynes's discussion of the German inflation comments on the inflation tax on cash balances. During periods of inflation, the government relies increasingly on revenues from inflation, but this leads to abandonment of legal tender money, so the "inflationary tax" ceases to be productive (4, p. 52): "What is raised by printing notes is just as much taken from the public as is a beer duty or an income tax" (ibid.). At the time, Keynes believed that an increase in saving raises investment, so his concern with the effect of inflation on saving reflects his lifelong interest in progress. Later, he abandoned the idea that increased saving raises investment, but he did not favor inflation. The effect of inflation is to reduce investment and increase consumption.

One of the objects of this book is to urge that the best way to cure this mortal disease of individualism is to provide that there shall never exist any confident expectation either that prices generally are going to fall or that they are going to rise; and also that there shall be no serious risk that a movement, if it does occur, will be a big one. If, unexpectedly and accidentally, a moderate movement were to occur, wealth, though it might be redistributed, would not be diminished thereby . . .

The remedy would lie . . . in so controlling the standard of value that, whenever something occurred which, left to itself, would create an expectation of a change in the general level of prices, the controlling authority should take steps to counteract this expectation by setting in motion some factor of a contrary tendency. (ibid., p. 35)

A similar point is made in the opening paragraphs of the preface. There, Keynes argues that the cost of risk bearing is part of the cost of production. He introduces a theme that remains important in all his subsequent work. The cost of risk bearing can be most easily reduced by institutional change: "Currency reforms, which led to the adoption by this country and the world at large of sound monetary principles, would diminish the wastes of *risk*, which consume at present too much of our estate" (ibid., p. xiv).

What are the "sound monetary principles"? Keynes rejects both freely fluctuating exchange rates and a return to the prewar gold standard. And he rejects the argument that exchange rates will remain stable if policies are stabilizing. While it is true that "budgetary deficits covered by a progressive inflation of the currency render the stabilization of a country's exchange impossible" (ibid., p. 88), the converse does not follow, at least not in any precise way. The fact that a country's budget, currency, foreign trade, and internal and external price levels are properly adjusted may assure that the exchange rate changes little from year to year, but it does not maintain stability within the year.

Freely fluctuating exchange rates increase risk and the cost of risk bearing above the attainable minimum. The *Tract* discusses some reasons why the social cost of risk bearing increases under fluctuating exchange rates even when policies are stabilizing. Much of his discussion concerns seasonal movements. Keynes presents data showing that speculators do not remove all seasonal influences from exchange rates. He concludes[6]:

[6] The context suggests that "never come to an equilibrium" refers to seasonal fluctuations around an equilibrium level.

If, therefore, the exchanges are not stabilized by policy, they will never come to an equilibrium of themselves. As time goes on and experience accumulates, the oscillations may be smaller than at present. Speculators may come in a little sooner, and importers may make greater efforts to spread their requirements more evenly over the year. But even so, there must be a substantial difference of rates between the busy season and the slack season, until the business world knows for certain at what level the exchanges in question are going to settle down. Thus a seasonal fluctuation of the exchanges (including the sterling–dollar exchange) is inevitable, even in the absence of any decided long-period tendency of an exchange to rise or to fall, unless the central authority, by a guarantee of convertibility or otherwise, takes special steps to provide against it. (ibid., p. 93)

The argument is of interest for five reasons. First, it appears in a book that contains one of the earliest discussions of forward exchange markets, yet Keynes makes no effort to compare the costs of private hedging in the forward market with the social costs of smoothing under fixed, but adjustable, rates maintained by a central bank. He is clearly aware of the issue, for he writes:

A free forward market, from which speculative transactions are not excluded, will give by far the best facilities for the trader, who does not wish to speculate, to avoid doing so. The same sort of advantages will be secured for merchants generally . . . Where risk is unavoidably present, it is much better that it should be carried by those who are qualified or are desirous to bear it. (ibid., p. 113)

One of his main recommendations, discussed later, is for the central bank to speculate on the forward gold market.[7] Second, in contrast to the later Keynes who warned about destabilizing speculation, the *Tract* is explicitly on the opposite side. Speculators stabilize prices. In the preface to the French edition, Keynes advises the French, who often tried to prevent speculation on the franc, that "the successful speculator makes his profit by anticipating, not by modifying, existing economic tendencies . . . Superstitions about speculation can only exist in an atmosphere of ignorance concerning the veritable influences that fix the level of the exchanges" (ibid., p. xvii).

---

[7] The earlier version, published in the *Manchester Guardian Commericial*, mentions that the cost of risk bearing may be high and the supply of the service inadequate. (See 4, p. 113, n. 2.)

Third, and most important for his later work, Keynes considers the cost of risk bearing as a main element affecting the choice of a monetary standard, and he relates risk bearing to variability and variability to the choice of monetary standard. He accepts the quantity theory and purchasing power parity (ibid., p. 86) as theories of the level of prices and exchange rates, but he regards these theories as incomplete. They provide no explanation of variability and give no hint about how much variability can be reduced. Later, the liquidity preference theory of interest and the marginal efficiency of capital schedule brought these elements – risk and uncertainty – into his theory of interest and output.

Fourth, Keynes opposed exchange controls as a solution to the problem of exchange rate fluctuations: "The threat of interference with the freedom of exchange dealings invariably operates to depress the value of the currency" (ibid., p. xxi). This is his last major work to express this view.

Fifth, Keynes's calculations showing seasonal variation use nominal exchange rates. Recent work fails to find a seasonal in real exchange rates – market exchange rates adjusted for price level changes at home and abroad – for the period Keynes discussed.[8]

Keynes's main criticism of fluctuating exchange rates extends the argument about seasonal fluctuations and adds an additional element, the difficulty in distinguishing the causes of permanent and transitory changes in relative prices:

> The fault of the postwar regime . . . is that it is too rapid in its effect and oversensitive, with the result that it may act violently for merely transitory causes . . . Relative prices can be knocked about by the most fleeting influences of politics and of sentiment, and by the periodic pressure of seasonal trades . . . The postwar method is [also] a most rapid and powerful corrective of real disequilibria in the balance of international payments arising from whatever causes, and a wonderful preventive in the way of countries which are inclined to spend abroad beyond their resources. (ibid., pp. 129–30).

The point of the critical remark appears to be that speculators adjust prices promptly to new information, but they may misinterpret transitory changes (in politics, sentiment, or seasonal factors) as permanent changes. This increases volatility and imposes a burden. Keynes does not argue that the central bank or government can reduce the burden or lower the cost of bearing it. Neither does he argue that government

[8] See the discussion of this issue in the Section "The Data and Its Interpretation" in Chapter 2, earlier.

can avoid errors of judgment. His recommendations take for granted that the government has an advantage, however.

At the time, Keynes rejected a return to the prewar gold standard on two grounds. First, the gold standard requires adjustment of the internal price level to external influences. Second, the value of gold is no longer set by the combined action of many central banks. Gold's value is uncertain. A third argument, emphasized in Keynes's criticism of Churchill (9, pp. 207–30), is that the gold standard requires adjustment of money wages to the price level required by the international standard. This increases unemployment if money wages must fall to restore equilibrium.[9]

In his discussion of the adjustment to external events, Keynes argues that price adjustment is "too slow and insensitive in its mode of operation . . . The adjustment even before the war might be imperfect" (4, pp. 129–30). Again, the problem is that confusion of permanent and transitory changes increases risk, including the risk that a country may be able to borrow "for a considerable time at the risk of ultimate default" (ibid., p. 130).[10]

The prewar gold standard did not depend "on the policy or the decisions of a single body of men" (ibid., p. 133), whereas the postwar system depends on the policy of the United States. The United States must be "foolish enough to go on accepting gold which it does not want, and wise enough, having accepted it, to maintain it at a fixed value" (ibid., p. 135). The argument that the gold standard provides stability of international values is based on prewar experience that cannot be repeated. Further, central banks do not wish to repeat it. They are more interested in maintaining the "stability of business, prices, and employment" (ibid., p. 138). But, the restoration of gold "can only give us complete stability of the external exchanges if all other countries also restore the gold standard" (ibid., p. 132).[11]

He does not see complete discretion as a solution. It is not ideal to

---

[9] A possible reason for his not stating this argument at this point is that he is not discussing a return to the prewar parity, only a return to the prewar system.

[10] We have since become aware that this risk is not removed when countries are not on the gold standard.

[11] An additional argument that Keynes used, for a time, against a return to the prewar parity was that the terms of trade had turned against Britain and Europe about 1900. He repeats this argument several times (2, pp. 5–6, 13–15; 19, pp. 125–7) using indexes of the prices of manufactured exports and agricultural imports to make his point. He concludes that population should be controlled to reduce food imports (19, p. 124). Sir William Beveridge criticized Keynes's conclusions in an address to the British Association and, in a letter to Keynes (ibid., pp. 137–8), pointed out that Keynes's conclusion about exports depended on his joining two series at 1900. If he continued the earlier series, his conclusion would not hold.

hand over . . . management to the possible weakness or ignorance of boards and governments . . . The present state of
affairs has allowed to the ignorance and frivolity of statesmen
an ample opportunity of bringing about ruinous consequences
in the economic field . . . A chief object of stabilizing the exchanges is to strap down ministers of finance. (ibid., pp. 135–
6)

Keynes's solution then and later is a managed currency: "Convertibility into gold will not alter the fact that the value of gold itself depends
on the policy of the central banks . . . The gold standard is already a
barbarous relic" (ibid., pp. 136–7). Concern is now with the stability
of business; there is no going back to a system that permits fluctuation
in employment and prices to maintain the exchange value with gold
(ibid., p. 140). While his ideas about monetary management changed
several times, he never gave up interest in a managed system, linked
to gold, with some type of adjustable exchange rate.

The solution proposed in the *Tract* is a managed system, loosely
linked to gold in the short run. Gold does not circulate but is held as
a reserve and used to stabilize the exchange rate in an emergency.
The gold price is not fixed once and for all; it changes in the long run
with the price index of a basket of commodities.[12] The aim of the system
is to achieve price stability. This meant, at the time, controlling the
quantity of money but adjusting the quantity to avoid transitory fluctuations in the exchange rate (ibid., p. 141).

Keynes rejected Irving Fisher's compensated dollar as "cut and
dried" (ibid., p. 148) and chose to rely on observed price changes in
a basket of commodities as the principal criterion guiding monetary
policy in the long run. The *Tract* is in the long tradition – vociferously
argued in recent years – of proposals to stabilize prices by using a price
rule to guide monetary policy. He recommended that the central bank
use data of employment, production, foreign trade, interest rates, and
other variables during business cycles to supplement price data, but
he did not wish to rely either on their unrestricted interpretation of
these data or on market forces. A firm decision must await experience
with the system. He proposed also that the Bank of England obtain
some of the benefits of the pre-1914 gold standard by announcing buying and selling prices for gold each week, along with the announcement

[12] Keynes's discussion of commodity standards, here and in the *Treatise*, makes no
reference to either Benjamin or Frank Graham. There is no doubt that he was (eventually?) aware of their contributions. In a 1943 letter to Benjamin Graham, he refers
to Graham as one of the pioneers of commodity proposals (26, p. 37). Also, his criticisms of the gold standard make no reference to the pioneering work of Jevons – work
that Keynes discussed later in his essay on Jevons (10, pp. 109–60).

of bank rate. The buying and selling prices were to be changed periodically based on the decision of the central bank about commodity prices. The spread between the buying and selling price would be as much as one percent, wider than under the prewar gold standard but narrower than his later proposals in the *Treatise* and after. Further, Keynes proposed that the Bank announce buying and selling prices for forward exchange.

To manage the system effectively, the Bank of England had to recognize whether gold movements represented a permanent change in the internal exchange rate of gold for commodities (domestic prices), or in the external exchange rate of gold for foreign currencies, or a temporary, seasonal, or random movement. Internal changes required a change in the gold price to maintain price stability; external changes required a change in bank rate to prevent a monetary expansion or contraction that would change internal prices. Temporary changes could be ignored or offset by expanding or contracting money. Keynes proposed that changes in the buying and selling price for forward exchange be used to hold the pound at a discount or premium and, thus, draw funds to or from foreign markets when this contributed to stability. He does not discuss how the central bank can set the gold price, the forward exchange rate, and the discount rate consistently and simultaneously. He presumes, without any discussion, that the three prices will be compatible and will be set so as to increase stability of both the price level and the exchange rate.

The details of Keynes's proposal are less important than two remarkable features. First, Keynes spends many pages of the *Tract* discussing risks, fluctuations, and errors of interpretation. He points repeatedly to the problem of extracting information capable of distinguishing between permanent and transitory changes. Yet, he makes no mention of these issues and shows no awareness of the problem when he proposes that the Bank of England seek to maintain price stability *and* reduce seasonal and other short-term fluctuations in the exchange rate.[13] He recognizes at one point that it "is not the *past* rise in prices but the *future* rise that has to be counteracted" (4, p. 148), but he does not mention that forecasting errors and expectations may make his system less stable than some of the alternatives he rejects.

Second, Keynes recognizes, and tries to solve, the problem of maintaining both internal and external stability. The Bank of England should

---

[13] When discussing the Federal Reserve, Keynes is alert to the political problems. The Federal Reserve's commitment to buy and sell gold keeps the gold price stable. This commitment may not be reliable. "We have not, as yet, sufficient experience as to the independence of the Federal Reserve System against the farmers, for example, or other compact interests possessing political influence" (4, p. 157).

aim for price stability. If the Federal Reserve aims for price stability also, the pound–dollar exchange rate will be stable[14]: "My recommendation does not involve more than a determination that, in the event of the Federal Reserve Board failing to keep dollar prices steady, sterling prices should not . . . plunge with them merely for the sake of maintaining a fixed parity of exchange" (4, p. 147). If these two major currencies pursue the common aim of domestic price stability, other countries can peg to one, or the other, or a mixture of the two, maintaining "reserves of gold at home and balances in London and New York to meet short-period fluctuations" (ibid., p. 160). Third countries, also, can make discretionary adjustments within the framework of rules for price and exchange rate stability.[15]

The *Tract* recognizes that stability is a public good. If the major countries maintain price stability, currency fluctuations will be damped. Third countries can import price stability by fixing their exchange rates to the exchange rates of "key" currencies and by using their limited discretion to adjust money and interest rates for domestic purposes. Keynes blamed monetary or price instability for the "triple evils of modern society" (19, p. 160). In the light of his later work the second of the three evils is particularly noteworthy – "disappointment of expectation and difficulty of laying plans ahead" (ibid.). Disappointment of expectations returns to prominence in the *General Theory*.

Keynes retained his interest in his early proposals for currency reform. Years later, after Britain left the gold standard, he returned to the ideas first advanced in the *Tract*. The preface to the German and Japanese editions of the *Treatise* speculates about rebuilding the monetary system along the lines suggested in the *Tract* and gives a preview of his later plan for a currency union. Gold has a role similar to its role in the *Tract*. Keynes talks of a common currency unit,

> the value of which would be kept stable within (say) 5 percent of the norm . . . in terms of a composite commodity . . . I conceive of the central banks of the new Union meeting from time to time to discuss a common policy towards bank rate, the volume of credit, the new issue market and the price of gold. (5, pp. xxi–xxii)

[14] This statement is hard to reconcile with Keynes's belief that business cycles are the result of real shocks, particularly alternating periods of optimism and pessimism about real returns to capital. Real shocks to investment affect the real exchange rate. If the central banks maintain expected price stability, all changes in expectations and productivity change real exchange rates, so the exchange rate moves with these shocks.
[15] Keynes received a warm, brief note from Alfred Marshall who agreed on the importance of reducing the role of gold in the monetary system (19, pp. 162–3).

"Notes on the Currency Question" (19, pp. 16–27), written for the Treasury after Britain left the gold standard in the fall of 1931, proposes a similar scheme using the commodity basket developed in the *Treatise* to set the price of gold.

The *Treatise*

The *Tract* emphasizes fluctuations and instability as factors affecting risk, but wages do not have a central role. The *Treatise* is very different. In the intervening years, Keynes had become much more concerned with employment, unemployment, and wages. In the *Treatise* (5, pp. 149–51), wage levels are determined by a combination of efficiency and effort. Efficiency wages are payments for piecework; hourly wages are payments for effort. Wage changes result from the autonomous behavior of workers or their unions or they are induced by changes in monetary policy. A country may inherit a wage level that is incompatible with its monetary position. When this occurs, or when there are autonomous wage changes, monetary policy can achieve internal price stability only by inducing compensating changes in wages and costs of production. To reduce wages that are too high for internal price stability, bank rate must rise. The rise in bank rate sets off a process that lowers investment relative to saving and reduces output and employment until wages fall to the level compatible with the exchange rate.[16] Unemployment increases during the adjustment. At one point (ibid., p. 264), Keynes describes the resulting unemployment as involuntary, but here involuntary unemployment is clearly cyclical and should not be confused with the involuntary unemployment of the *General Theory*.

Business cycles are mainly caused by real changes, including the actions of speculators on the stock exchange driven by expectations and mob psychology. Speculative changes on securities markets induce short-term changes in the relative prices of new investment and in the demand for money (5, pp. 224–7; 6, pp. 323–4).

Keynes recommends that the central bank respond to these fluctuations by changing the rate of interest until it exactly offsets the bullish or bearish sentiment. At times, the central bank must act boldly to saturate the demand for savings deposits or to reduce the supply (6,

---

[16] Keynes offers several versions of the dynamic process in closed and open economies. (See, e.g., 5, pp. 186–8, 197, 236–7.) As noted in the discussion of the model of the *Treatise* in Chapter 3 the dynamic implications for wages and output that Keynes discusses cannot be derived from the model. Output is given. The discussion in the text summarizes Keynes's beliefs as they are set out in the *Treatise*.

p. 332). He recognizes, in his phrase, that "exact balance may sometimes be . . . beyond the wits of man" (5, p. 227), but he never considers the possibility that the central bank's effort to offset shifts in asset demands can create an excess burden by introducing more variability into prices and incomes than it removes.

The *Tract* is concerned with price stability; the *Treatise* is uncertain about which price level to keep stable. A lengthy discussion of price standards concludes by dismissing the commodity price level and identifying two others that Keynes regards as more relevant for policy. One is the internal standard, which is now called the labor standard. It is a measure of the earnings or efficiency wages of labor. The other is the purchasing power standard, the price of goods and services traded internationally. When relative prices adjust to restore full equilibrium, all the measures or standards are compatible. Since the main concern of the *Treatise* is disequilibrium between prices and costs of production, the concern of monetary policy is to prevent or minimize fluctuations in costs relative to product prices.

The unambiguous commitment to price stability as a goal of the *Tract* becomes the more ambiguous "stability of money values" in the *Treatise*. This reflects Keynes's discussion of index numbers and his concern to develop policies that minimize the social cost of adjustment when wages adjust more slowly than prices and the values of financial assets.

A main criticism of the gold standard is that the social cost of the standard is excessive. Keynes's concern is not the resource cost. The excess burden is inherent in the standard. The proximate reason is that prices and interest rates do not adjust at the same speed. Efforts to expand demand by increasing money are more quickly reflected in interest rates than in prices and costs of production. An increase in money is followed by a speculative movement that produces a net capital outflow. Under gold standard rules, the Bank of England must respond to the capital movements by raising interest rates, so the expansionary policy is short-lived. In addition, banks sell bonds from their portfolios to make foreign loans, raising domestic long-term rates and reducing investment in domestic capital (21, p. 314).

After World War I, the British position was very different from either its own prewar position or the position of the United States (6, pp. 274–6). The existence of competitive financial centers in New York and Paris increased the likelihood that small changes in interest rates would induce large short-term capital movements. A relatively small stock of gold, after allowing for the reserves against note issues held in the Issue Department of the Bank of England, required the Bank to respond quickly to gold outflows by raising bank rate. Indirectly, the rise in bank rate lowered investment relative to saving and reduced real income. Further, Keynes was convinced that Britain had returned to the gold standard at a price that placed British costs (incomes) out of equilibrium with the levels of cost (incomes) in other countries on the gold standard. The result was sustained unemployment in the export industries. Attempts to increase investment by lowering interest rates produced an outflow of gold more quickly than a rise in domestic investment. The Bank was forced to respond to the outflow of gold by raising the rate of interest, so, again, the effort at expansion was short-lived.[17]

Keynes's argument and much of his criticism of the dynamics of the quantity theory in the *Treatise* derive from his recognition that asset markets adjust more quickly than the output market. The slower adjustment of output reflects the more gradual adjustment of costs of production, particularly wages. Differences in speeds of adjustment, though ignored by the traditional quantity theory, are critical for policy. To prevent a loss of gold, the central bank must stand ready to take action that increases unemployment. To prevent the price level effects of an inflow of gold, the bank must lower bank rate and encourage domestic expansion. In long-run adjustment, the economy achieves the position implied by the quantity theory but, along the way, these policy actions introduce variability and excess burdens that, Keynes believed, could be reduced by proper policies.

The problem was to find an international system compatible with expansion of domestic output, the stability of money values, and reduced uncertainty. Keynes reconsiders the standards discussed in the *Tract* from the perspective of the *Treatise* and also discusses a world central bank. He is clearer than in the *Tract* about his reasons for choosing a managed exchange rate in lieu of either rigidly fixed or freely fluctuating exchange rates. A fluctuating exchange rate, if properly managed to achieve long-run stability of money values, gives the central bank an opportunity to vary the exchange rate and the rate of interest so as to reduce fluctuations in employment.[18] By

---

[17] Here, too, we find Keynes developing an argument that reappears in the *General Theory* – the relevant rate of investment is the long-term rate. This rate responds very little to changes in Bank rate that are perceived to be transitory, so short-level expansionary policy is ineffective. The long-term rate appears to be "sticky," but the problem is that the decline in rates is not expected to persist.

[18] In the *General Theory*, Keynes amplifies the argument as the "element of scientific truth in mercantilist doctrine" (7, p. 335):

> In conditions in which the quantity of aggregate investment is determined by the profit motive alone, the opportunities for home investment will be governed, in the long run, by the domestic rate of interest; whilst the volume of foreign investment is necessarily determined by the size of the favourable balance of trade. Thus, in a society where there is no question of direct investment under the aegis of public authority, the economic objects, with which it is reasonable for the government to be preoccupied, are the domestic rate of interest and the balance of foreign trade. (ibid.)

applying appropriate doses of each at the right moment, there is much less risk of the loss of wealth and output due to the prevalence of general unemployment. For direct changes in the price of foreign-trade goods can be largely substituted for unemployment as the first link in the causal chain whereby external equilibrium is preserved and restored. Its disadvantage is to be found in the diminished mobility that it means (if that is a disadvantage) for foreign lending.

It is evident that no general answer can be given to the question where the balance of advantage lies. It depends partly on the relative importance of foreign-trade industries in our country's national conomy. But not entirely. For it also depends on whether the potential fluctuations in the volume of foreign lending, in the absence of the artificial check of sharp changes in the local rates of interest, are likely to be large relatively to those corresponding fluctuations in the amount of the foreign balance which can be brought about quickly and with a moderate change in the terms of trade. The answer to the last point is not unaffected by the tariff policy of the rest of the world – for a high degree of sensitiveness in the rate of foreign lending to small changes may be inconvenient, and even dangerous, if it is not accompanied by an equally high degree of sensitiveness in the response of foreign trade to small changes. (5, p. 326)

Here, Keynes recognizes that tariff policies in the rest of the world change the effective price elasticity of exports and, thus, alter the responses a country can expect from policies to maintain internal stability. There is nothing to suggest that Keynes recognized the possibility of retaliation or competitive devaluation at the time. His recommendation for an end to free trade, a few years later, also fails to consider losses from retaliation.

The *Treatise* analyzes tariffs (6, pp. 166–7) but does not recommend them. At the time, Keynes preferred restrictions that would "regulate the rate of foreign lending day by day" (ibid., p. 280). The aim of the restrictions was to reduce net capital outflow or even stimulate foreign investment in Britain.[19] He proposed two ways of reducing foreign

---

[19] Keynes's argument for restrictions on capital movements is based on his theory of international balance. The larger net foreign investment in Britain affects the trade account, not directly but by changing gold flows or interest rates. Keynes believed that the restrictions he proposed were a means of lowering long-term rates at home by reducing aggregate investment abroad. His analysis of the relation of the trade balance and its relation to net foreign investment is in the *Treatise* (5, pp. 296–300) and is summarized in Chapter 3 of this volume; Moggridge (1986, pp. 57–8) discusses the evolution of Keynes's views on capital movements in the 1920s and early 1930s.

lending. First, he wanted the Bank of England to have the power to disallow all dealing in fixed income foreign securities, and he favored a tax on income from outstanding securities held in Britain that did not have such approval (ibid., p. 281). Second, to reduce short-term capital movements, he wanted the Bank to have the power to change interest rates on foreign loans without an equivalent change in rates charged domestic borrowers (ibid., p. 285). Keynes recognized the difficulty in implementing an effective policy of this kind: "Credit is like water . . . it may be used for a multiplicity of purposes . . . and will remorselessly seek its own level over the whole field unless the parts of the field are rendered uncompromisingly watertight, which in the case of credit is scarcely possible" (ibid.).

To supplement these restrictions he repeated, in modified form, his earlier recommendation of wider gold points. He now favored a band of 2 percent, and he wanted the central bank to vary the difference between buying and selling prices as a means of attracting or discouraging gold flows (ibid., pp. 290–1). He expected that central banks would be able to change the premium or discount on the forward market and, in this way, widen or narrow the spread between domestic and foreign interest rates. To help them carry out the policy, he again urged the central bank to vary the forward market rates for sterling weekly. And, again, he did not consider how the central bank would choose the rate or whether his proposal moved toward or away from his objective of lower variability in prices or money values. He simply assumed that central bank operations would be stabilizing.

Although he recommended a domestically managed system as an improvement on the prewar gold standard, he did not regard it as an ideal. He preferred a world central bank and, in the last chapter of the *Treatise*, he offered some rules and procedures for a bank of this kind. These recommendations are not identical to his later plan for an International Clearing Union, but there are many similarities.

There are, in fact, two plans in the *Treatise*, a minimum and a maximum plan. Both represent Keynes's efforts to achieve two objectives of monetary management: the long-period objective of price stability (or gradual price increase) (ibid., pp. 350–3) and the avoidance of short-period fluctuations around the trend. Keynes argues (ibid., p. 349) that the economy can be made to work more efficiently if short-term fluctuations can be avoided, so the "expedient" (ibid.) choice of the long-period trend of prices is the particular trend that is least likely to require changes that disturb the equality between saving and investment.

Gold has a limited role in Keynes's proposal; it remains as a reserve for the world central bank. The price of gold is fixed but not constant.

He recommends a tabular standard to determine the price of gold.[20] The items in his proposed basket are sixty-two internationally traded commodities, mainly raw materials, food, and minerals. A principal advantage of this basket, according to Keynes, is that the prices change quickly in response to changes in investment (ibid., pp. 353–4). Action by the central bank to maintain the value of gold, relative to the commodity bundle, would also encourage a quick response to the business or trade cycle changes induced by changes in investment relative to saving.

Keynes envisages an activist world bank. His "maximum" plan (ibid., pp. 358–60) is for a supernational bank with central banks as members. Members deposit gold and receive supernational bank money (SBM). They can borrow from the supernational bank for three-month periods at a discount rate set by the bank. The size of discounts to any member is equal to a three-year average of the member's deposits, but this rule can be changed at the discretion of the supernational bank.

Each member central bank can hold reserves in gold or SBM. Members are required to accept SBM on the same terms as gold, and Keynes expressed his wish that all national moneys be exchangeable only for SBM.

Keynes offers his own critique. The supernational bank is not a panacea. He wondered whether any system based on fixed exchange rates can reduce fluctuations in a world with tariffs and fixed money wages. For the first time, he seems aware that one of his proposals for reform may not achieve his aim:

> What, then, is the reason for hesitating before we commit ourselves to such a system? Primarily a doubt whether it is wise to have a currency system with a much wider ambit than our banking system, our tariff system and our wage system. Can we afford to allow a disproportionate degree of mobility to a single element in an economic system which we leave extremely rigid in several other respects? (ibid., p. 299)

He gives other reasons for his skepticism. Countries are in different stages of development and have different attitudes toward gold (ibid., p. 301). The United States, with its large gold stock, has the advantage

---

[20] The idea of a tabular standard was not new. Fisher and Marshall, among others, had proposed tabular standards. In the *Tract* (4, p. 148) Keynes rejected the tabular standard because it did not damp short-period oscillations. In the analysis of the *Treatise*, with international commodity prices chosen as the standard, Keynes expected domestic prices and real wages to fluctuate around the standard.

of a domestic and international standard.[21] The same standard of value may not be ideal for every country (ibid., p. 302).

If the return to gold in the 1920s had been avoided, major countries might have moved toward independent national monetary systems with fluctuating exchange rates. Later, these national systems could have been joined into a managed international system (ibid., p. 302). Since these desirable developments did not occur, Keynes concludes: "The best *practical* objective might be the management of the value of gold by a supernational authority, with a number of national monetary systems clustering round it, each with discretion to vary the value of its local money in terms of gold within a range of (say) 2 percent" (ibid., p. 303, emphasis added). It is noteworthy that Keynes does not see a scheme, similar in some respects to his later proposal for a currency union, as the most desirable. He prefers to replace the gold standard, first, with a managed, domestic system and fluctuating exchange rates. Since fluctuating exchange rates are helpful in reducing unemployment but harmful to foreign lending (5, pp. 325–6), the domestic system is but a step toward a managed international system with an adjustable peg.[22]

Despite his reservations, he prefers the supernational bank to the then existing gold exchange standard, and he later described the arrangement as "ideal" (6, p. 358). A main reason is that the supernational bank can lend to debtor countries to offset fluctuations in output caused by the more rapid adjustment of the capital account and slower adjustment of the trade account:

> If English investors, not liking the outlook at home, fearing labour disputes or nervous about a change of government, begin to buy more American securities than before, why should it be supposed that this will be naturally balanced by increased British exports? For, of course, it will not. It will, in the first instance, set up a serious instability of the domestic credit sys-

---

[21] This is a reference to the fact that the United States, unlike the United Kingdom, did not have to follow the rules of the traditional gold standard, and the United States did not. To maintain domestic stability, the Federal Reserve produced a negative correlation between gold movements and the monetary base in the 1920s. Gold flows were too small relative to the U.S. stock to force the Federal Reserve to raise interest rates to prevent gold losses. Nurkse (1944) points out the United States was not the only country to deviate from the rules.

[22] Keynes does not give much space to the analysis of freely fluctuating exchange rates. I have two conjectures. First, he did not believe that the public, central banks, and governments were ready for the proposal (21, p. 26). Second, he probably believed that fluctuating rates increased variability and, by lowering foreign investment, reduced aggregate investment. He conjectured, at one point that "experience may show in the end that this is the best arrangment for everybody" (ibid.).

tem – the ultimate working out of which it is difficult or impossible to predict . . . If it were as easy to put wages up and down as it is to put bank rate up and down, well and good. But this is not the actual situation. A change in international financial conditions or in the wind and weather of speculative sentiment may alter the volume of foreign lending, if nothing is done to counteract it, by tens of millions in a few weeks. Yet there is no possibility of rapidly altering the balance of imports and exports to correspond. (ibid., p. 300)

Here Keynes gives up the views expressed in the *Tract* and moves toward the view of speculation as a source of instability that became a central theme of the *General Theory*. He brings together the idea of destabilizing speculation with the waves of optimism and pessimism that he regarded as a cause of fluctuations. The problem is that investors are influenced by short-term fluctuations. He speaks of the

half-unreasonable characteristics of the market which are the source of many of the troubles . . . if investors were capable of taking longer views, the fluctuations in the natural rate of interest would not be so great as they are. The real prospects do not suffer such large and quick changes as does the spirit of enterprise. The willingness to invest is stimulated and depressed by the immediate prospects. (ibid., p. 324)

This view, which appears near the end of the *Treatise*, may have been influenced by the movements of stock prices in New York in 1929 and 1930. Whatever its origin, it shows Keynes reaching the views that become a main theme of the *General Theory*.

Keynes considers various policies. He considers and rejects state control of investment (ibid., p. 335) except in extreme situations. He returned to this idea with greater enthusiasm in the *General Theory*. His argument in the *Treatise* again reveals suppositions about the types of policies likely to be followed by a government bureaucracy that are inconsistent with his criticisms of their past policies. Keynes was often unsparing in his criticisms of the governments, bankers, and central bankers who favored the return to the prewar gold price, demanded reparations at the Versailles conference, or maintained traditional policies against his advice. Yet, he imagined that during a slump the need might arise for "socialistic action by which some official body steps into the shoes which the feet of the entrepreneurs are too cold to occupy" (ibid.).[23]

---

[23] The "euthanasia of the rentier" in the *General Theory* also has an antecedent in the *Treatise*. One reason Keynes favors a tabular standard based on commodity prices

The proposal he favors as a means of reducing fluctuations is international lending and borrowing. Countries with current account deficits would borrow from the bank for up to three months in amounts based on the country's past deposits (ibid., p. 359). In this way, the bank would act as an intermediary, lending the balances accumulated by surplus countries to the deficit countries. Deficit countries would not be required to contract, or to contract as much, when faced with a short-term, seasonal or transitory, capital outflow. Surplus countries would relend reserves through the bank instead of increasing balances. As a result, prices and output would be more stable.

The supernational bank would also engage in open-market operations on its own initiative. Governments would have the right to prevent the purchase of their country's securities, but not the sale (ibid., pp. 359–60). Keynes does not explain the asymmetry, but a probable reason is that Keynes was more concerned about debtors who were reluctant to contract than about creditors unwilling to expand. Experience in the 1930s changed his view. He became more concerned about creditor countries that were unwilling to expand and put more emphasis on preventing deflationary policies than avoiding inflation.

The proposed supernational bank had some discretion about its operations but not about its aims. The bank had two main duties. The first was "to maintain, so far as possible, the stability of the value of gold (or SBM) in terms of a tabular standard . . . Its second duty should be avoidance, so far as possible, of general profit inflations and deflations of an international character" (ibid., p. 360).

In the *Treatise*, Keynes continued to believe in discretion limited by rules. The supernational bank had restricted authority, and the members who adhered to the system were restricted by their membership in the bank. The aims of the bank did not cover a panoply of objectives that would permit the managers to pick and choose. The bank's main purpose was to maintain stable prices and exchange rates.

From the *Treatise* to the currency union

The *General Theory* mainly discusses a closed economy, so reform of the international monetary system does not arise. During the 1930s,

instead of the price of labor services is that he expected such prices to fall relative to wages over time. He hoped this would permit a decline in the human effort required to pay interest on the debt: "The dead hand should not be allowed to grasp the fruits of improvements made long after the live body which once directed it has passed away" (6, p. 353). Keynes recognizes, however, that the loss of real value may be anticipated and included in the interest rate.

however, Keynes reconsidered international monetary reform in "The Means to Prosperity" (9, pp. 335–66), written in 1933. Also he participated in the discussions following Britain's departure from gold in 1931 and prior to the organization of the 1933 London conference on international monetary stabilization. In the *General Theory*, he expressed his views on monetary arrangements in the chapter on mercantilism. His comments and recommendations permit us to trace the development of his thought and the influence of the departure from gold, the worldwide depression, and the incomplete recovery.

Keynes was exuberant about Britain's departure from gold on September 21, 1931. He mentions a probable devaluation of 25 percent against gold and, at first, is optimistic about the effects on trade. He warns, however, that if many others follow, the principal effect will be a rise in the price of commodities.[24] He does not expect all countries to follow; France and the United States are mentioned as likely to remain on gold.

His attitude toward U.S. policy is set out clearly. It is of interest since it probably influenced his proposals for postwar arrangements:

> They have willed the destruction of their own export industries, and only they can take the steps necessary to restore them . . . The United States had, in effect, set the rest of us the problem of finding some way to do without her wheat, her copper, her cotton, and her motor cars. She set the problem and, as it had only one solution, that solution we have been compelled to find. (ibid., pp. 248–9)

The choice he sees is between a small gold bloc on one side and most of the world on the other or a reformed international system based on a "drastically reformed gold standard" (ibid.). Keynes clearly prefers the latter, but he does not describe what he has in mind.

A few weeks later, he is more explicit and shows that he continued to think along the lines of his proposal in the *Treatise*. The occasion is a request from the Treasury for his views about returning to gold. He is asked, specifically, what he meant by a "drastically reformed gold standard" (21, p. 1). Keynes responded by considering different proposals but recommended fixing the value of sterling in terms of the same sixty-two commodities he had used in his proposal in the *Treatise*. The value of the bundle should be raised to its 1929 value, consistent with a further devaluation of sterling to a dollar exchange rate of $3.50

---

[24] Capie, Mills, and Wood (1983) argue that the devaluation had very little effect on the price level and show that from September to December 1931 consumer prices rose about 1 percent. They argue that the devaluation was *not* a delayed response to overvaluation in 1925 but a result of the banking problems in central Europe.

(ibid., pp. 18, 24–6). Thereafter, the price of sterling should be fixed in relation to the bundle but "modified if necessary from time to time" when the value of gold, measured in terms of the bundle, changed materially (ibid., p. 26).[25]

In March 1933, Keynes wrote a series of articles for the *Times* that were republished as "The Means to Prosperity" (9, pp. 335–66). Most of his discussion concerns the domestic economy, but he also makes some proposals for recovery and reform of the international system.

Recovery requires higher world commodity prices. Keynes mentions several alternatives but concludes that simultaneous expansion of domestic expenditure is needed, and he proposes a world conference to address that problem, reparations, debts, and other topics (ibid., pp. 356–7).

His proposal for reform again calls for an increase in international reserves, based on gold. The reserves should be elastic, to be released when commodity prices are low and withdrawn when they are high. Keynes proposes a maximum of $5 billion of "paper gold" to be secured by gold bonds of participating countries. Countries would keep their currencies within 5 percent of their gold parity, but the parity would change, gradually, with the prices of international commodities (ibid., pp. 358–62).

The details differ from Keynes's earlier proposals, but we know that he regarded all three proposals as similar. The reason is that he was criticized as inconsistent and responded as follows:

> The proposal which I made . . . is substantially the same as that which I published in 1923 in Chapter 5 of my *Tract on Monetary Reform* before we returned to gold, and again in 1930 . . . My present proposal only differs from my previous proposals in that it is somewhat more cautious in establishing a link with gold. (21, p. 185)[26]

Despite the worldwide depression, Keynes's proposals for reform continued to call for discretionary policies constrained by fixed rules. And he continued to favor price stability after a rise in commodity prices to restore the 1929 price level.

---

[25] Keynes sent a copy of his memo to the Treasury to Montagu Norman, governor of the Bank of England. The response is curt, mentions "awkward" practical questions, and expresses doubt "that it is within the power of the Bank of England to prevent a decline in sterling" (21, p. 28).

[26] A German graduate student wrote to Keynes in the mid-1930s to sort out differences in Keynes's views given in the *Tract*, the *Treatise*, and the *Means to Prosperity*. Keynes's response indicates that he favored independent national systems with fluctuating exchange rates but also favored "practical measures" to achieve de facto stability within a margin of 10 percent of some parity. The practical measures include measures to control capital movements. (See Moggridge 1986, p. 66).

Keynes's proposal to issue $5 billion in paper gold would have raised the world gold stock by 23 percent, at the $20,67 gold price (Commission on the Role of Gold 1982, Vol. 1, pp. 196, 222). The rise would have been the equivalent of about ten years of production at the time. Keynes was, therefore, pleased when the United States returned to the gold standard at a price of $35 an ounce. The new price raised the value of the U.S. and the 1933 world gold stock by 69 percent, after all countries had revalued gold at the new price. Keynes saw it as part of an expansion program in the United States and predicted that the countries remaining in the gold bloc would ultimately abandon their fixed parities (21, pp. 311–12).

The chapter on mercantilism in the *General Theory* also rejects the unmanaged system, which he called laissez-faire. His discussion concerns a single country operating in a world without an international central bank or monetary authority. The main issue is whether a country's trade balance is self-adjusting or whether intervention by the central bank can produce a gain to the country that more than compensates for any loss arising from restrictions on comparative advantage (international division of labor) (7, pp. 333–4).

Keynes's argument turns on the "insufficiency of the inducements to new investment" (ibid., p. 335). In the absence of direct investment by government, investment – domestic and foreign (including accumulation of foreign exchange) – depends on the rate of interest and the trade balance. The rate of interest in an open economy depends on the stock of precious metals in wage units, so the balance of trade has both a direct and indirect effect on investment and domestic employment.

Keynes is no longer the unqualified partisan of free trade, but he does not make, or claim, a valid case for import restrictions in general or even in particular circumstances. On the contrary, he describes trade restrictions as "a treacherous instrument even for the attainment of its ostensible object, since private interest, administrative incompetence and the intrinsic difficulty of the task may divert it into producing results directly opposite to those intended" (ibid., p. 339). He introduces qualifications when making his argument and discusses retaliation. The main conclusion repeats an old theme: "The technique of bank rate coupled with a rigid parity of the foreign exchanges" rules out the possibility of maintaining a domestic rate of interest consistent with full employment (ibid.). Rigidly fixed exchange rates require changes in interest rates, and these changes introduce avoidable variability and uncertainty. Hence, the system is suboptimal.

Those who read Keynes as a proponent of trade restrictions find no support in the chapter on mercantilism. The correct idea of the mercantilists, he believed, is *not* the desirability of trade restrictions: "Contemporary experience in postwar Europe offers manifold examples of ill-conceived impediments on freedom which, designed to improve the favorable balance, had in fact a contrary tendency" (ibid., p. 338). The lesson to be learned is the need for an investment policy. Keynes, then, restates the main argument of the *General Theory:*

> The weight of my criticism is directed against the inadequacy of the *theoretical* foundations of the *laissez faire* doctrine . . . against the notion that the rate of interest and the volume of investment are self-adjusting at the optimum level, so that preoccupation with the balance of trade is a waste of time. (ibid., p. 339)

A few pages later, he explains that the economic problem could be reduced – and "an *optimum* level of domestic employment" achieved – without relying on trade restrictions (ibid., p. 349, emphasis added). The way to do so is to manage the rate of interest, without concern for international effects, and to institute a national investment program: "The simultaneous pursuit of these policies by all countries together . . . is capable of restoring economic health and strength internationally" (ibid.).

These passages suggest how much of the *Treatise* remained in Keynes's thoughts. His commitment to a managed system and his belief that all countries would gain from the establishment of an international monetary authority and by simultaneous expansion remain intact. He proposes neither rigidly fixed nor freely fluctuating exchange rates. Both systems impose excessive fluctuations on domestic economies, fluctuations and risks that are avoidable.

In the *Treatise*, Keynes argued that price fluctuations under the gold standard also imposed an excess burden on the economy. The emphasis there is on fluctuations in prices, profits, and employment. In the *General Theory*, Keynes extends the argument by claiming that if the fluctuations in employment and investment are damped, the rate of interest can be reduced and the level of income raised permanently. Indeed, he follows his discussion of mercantilism by repeating that the problem is the excess burden that raises private costs above the social cost: "The rate of interest is not self-adjusting at a level best suited to the *social* advantage" (ibid., p. 350, emphasis added).

The *General Theory* is silent elsewhere on the benefits attainable from a reconstituted, international monetary system. The beggar-thy-neighbor policies of the time must have made such speculations seem even more impractical than at the time of the *Treatise*. Nor does Keynes discuss how his proposal to reduce interest rates – possibly to zero – can be achieved by a single country acting alone. His postwar proposals give the answer. He favored a rigid system of exchange controls. We now know that he reached this conclusion no later than 1936. He wrote to L. F. Giblin in April of that year about the Australian pound, then pegged to the British pound: "I believe that most countries . . . will sooner or later have to have completely controlled exchanges in the sense that no transactions which do not arise out of current trade will be permissible except by license" (Keynes to L. F. Giblin, 22 April 1936, quoted in Moggridge 1986, pp. 58–9).[27]

The currency union

Planning for postwar monetary arrangements began as an effort to counter German plans for a "new order" in Europe. The Ministry of Information, in November 1940, sent Keynes some notes on postwar British economic policy and asked him to prepare a statement and broadcast to the Continent. The notes called for a return to the gold standard and were highly critical of the German proposals for a multilateral clearing system based on Schachtian policies.[28]

Keynes replied: "I am not the man to preach the beauties and merits of the pre-war gold standard" (25, p. 2). He was more favorable toward the principles on which the Germans based their proposal than toward a return to the interwar system. He described the latter as a system based on gold, high tariffs, and unemployment (ibid., p. 1).

New institutional arrangements were required, as the German proposals recognized (ibid., p. 2). The flaws in the German proposal arose from misapplication of the principles, not from the principles themselves. Keynes was skeptical about the Germans' intentions and their ability to develop a successful multilateral clearing arrangement. He expected the Germans to use the arrangement as exploitatively as Schacht had used interwar clearing arrangements. Britain would be more open in its dealings and, backed by the raw material production

---

[27] One possible explanation of the omission of exchange controls from the *General Theory* is that Keynes's statements about state direction of investment include control of foreign investment. This is entirely speculative. We know that Keynes advocated some controls in the *Treatise* and, as his letter to Giblin shows, he favored more stringent controls in the 1930s. At one point, he describes controls on foreign investment as a permanent necessity for Britain (19, p. 573). At another, he wants an embargo on foreign lending (ibid., pp. 572–3). In fact, Britain maintained some capital controls from 1929 to 1979 but did not retain the rigid controls that Keynes favored after World War II.

[28] The request was soon followed by a similar request from Lord Halifax, the British ambassador to the United States. Lüke (1985) compares Keynes's Clearing Union to Schacht's earlier plan.

of the empire, in a better position to offer a multilateral clearing arrangement that provided members with a wide range of goods and services (ibid., pp. 8, 12–13).

Keynes proposed that Britain offer to "open all our markets to every country . . . and give equal access for each to every source of raw material which we can control or influence, on the basis of exchanging goods for goods" (ibid., p. 12). Gold would remain as a central reserve, available for settlement, but capital movements would be restricted by a permanent system of exchange controls. The exchange of "goods for goods" did not mean a return to barter. Keynes wanted multilateral clearing of trade balances, with fixed exchange rates.[29] Countries within the bloc could use their balances to purchase from any other country within the bloc. If countries ran persistent surpluses, Keynes would require that the balance be spent in the deficit country (or countries) rather than encourage devaluation to adjust trade balances.

The aim of avoiding devaluation is consistent with Keynes's longstanding interest in price stability. His proposals seek to expand trade and "to interfere [with trade] as little as possible, provided a balance is maintained with the outside world as a whole" (25, p. 17). Since the countries within the bloc would only have dollars if they sold to the United States, discrimination against the United States would be necessary if the United States returned to its interwar policy of "maintaining an unbalanced creditor position" (ibid.). By controlling capital movements, Britain would become free to reduce interest rates.

In the *Tract* and the *Treatise*, Keynes proposed to reduce capital movements by widening the gold points and by central bank operations in the forward exchange market and by restricting or taxing foreign lending. In the *General Theory*, Keynes recognizes that businessmen observe persistent patterns of fluctuations and expect them to repeat. The risk of fluctuations is impounded in risk premiums, raising interest rates and reducing investment. Control of capital movements would dampen or remove these patterns, Keynes believed.

The early proposals for postwar reform are consistent with, and perhaps are based on, Keynes's conclusions in the chapter on mercantilism (7, Chapter 23) and his earlier writing. Changes reflect Keynes's concerns about Britain's position at the end of the war. He was convinced that, at the end of the war, Britain would be in a weak position relative to the United States and the Commonwealth. There would be large blocked balances from the sterling area on deposit in London, the result

---

[29] "The method of [exchange] depreciation is a bad method which one is driven to adopt failing something better . . . If the U.S.A. inflates more than we do, we might even *appreciate* sterling" (25, p. 17).

of wartime exchange controls. The balances represented a potential capital outflow if Britain removed the controls. A weakened economy with relatively large demands for food imports and an industrial structure damaged by war would be stretched to provide exports at a level that maintained the standard of living. A current account balance sufficient to reduce controls seemed improbable. If the United States remained in a net creditor position with high tariffs, the contractive influence of U.S. policy on the rest of the world would hamper world recovery in a fixed exchange rate system and make the task harder.[30] At the time, 1940, he was pessimistic about U.S. postwar policy, and he seems to have expected a return to the prewar policy – a creditor position with high degree of protection and agricultural subsidies.

The position taken by the United States was

> the outstanding economic problem of the post-war world . . . There are only three alternatives. Either that she becomes a reliable international lender, which is not very likely; or she imports more, which means a drastic revision of her tariff arrangements; or she seeks to export less, which means a drastic modification of her agricultural system. It is for her to choose. (27, p. 19)

A few months later, in September 1941, Keynes began to revise some of his views about the United States and to revamp his proposals for the postwar system. The origin of this change has been the subject of much discussion.[31] The new proposals gave the Americans "all they ask, provided they are really prepared to be truly internationally minded" (23, p. 209). This time he developed what he called, once again, an ideal scheme (25, p. 32), but he recognized that his proposal might be "too international or too Utopian" (ibid., p. 209).

The new proposal was required by a provision in the draft lend-lease agreement. The United States agreed to waive postwar repayment for

---

[30] Neither Keynes nor other officials proposed or, judging from Keynes's papers, discussed fluctuating exchange rates. In Britain, the alternatives were proposals like Keynes's earlier proposal based on bilateral agreements and clearing arrangements or the more autarchic system favored by Thomas Balogh and Joan Robinson.

[31] Haberler (1986, p. 422, n. 2) credits Lionel Robbins, Marcus Fleming, James Meade, and Redvers Opie for changing Keynes's views. Redvers Opie was in Washington representing the British government from 1940–6. He reports, in a personal letter, that during Keynes's visit in the United States from April to June 1941, "Keynes displayed such strong and dogmatic bilateralist views that I held up the dispatch of the telegram drafted by him and Sir Frederick Phillips . . . to Secretary Henry Morgenthau because of its condemnatory attitude to the multilateralism of the State Department." According to Opie, a change occurred in September: "In September 1941 . . . Lionel Robbins had written to say that Maynard was coming round to our (and the American) position in favor of multilateralism."

equipment and supplies furnished under lend-lease if the British agreed to eliminate trade "discrimination." The latter term was not well defined. Secretary Hull probably intended an extension of the most-favored-nation principle that had been the basis of his prewar trade policy. The British read the term as an attack on empire preference, the basis of their prewar policy and a frequent cause of friction between the two countries. Keynes saw the U.S. proposal as a restriction on the use of exchange controls.

Keynes had discussed the draft of the lend-lease agreement just prior to leaving the United States in July 1941. At a meeting with Dean Acheson, Keynes objected to the proposal in terms that Acheson describes as "strongly" (23, p. 176), and Keynes's own account supports him (23, pp. 171–2).[32] Keynes's proposal to Acheson offered nothing in return for the U.S. offer to forgive the war debt. Later in the summer, he warned against repeating that tactic on "grounds that it worked to Britain's disadvantage. If we make another derisory offer, we shall find the terms going up against us again" (ibid., p. 203).

Keynes's new proposal for a currency union became the basis from which Britain negotiated with the United States on the terms of postwar cooperation. The shift from the statist approach of his previous proposal, a major change in view, was to some degree a tactical shift to correct his earlier error.[33] His September 1941 draft (25, pp. 33–40) contains the main provisions used in the British government proposals of April 1943 (ibid., pp. 233–5). Many details changed; the proposal for adjustment became less specific; but the substance of the proposals adopted as a British White Paper is not very different from Keynes's 1941 draft, as Keynes and others recognized at the time (ibid., pp. 143, 236–7). The proposal is Keynes's mature view of the system he regarded as a workable, and possibly an ideal, monetary arrangement.

There are four main topics in the proposals for a clearing union or

---

[32] Keynes's discussion with Acheson seems to have disturbed British–American relations for a time and was the subject of discussion in London and Washington and an apology by Keynes (23, pp. 175–8, 207–10). Harrod (1951, p. 512) gives a different view, one that is not mentioned by Keynes. He claims that Keynes objected to the draft agreement on the grounds that the United States had not offered as much postwar cooperation on monetary arrangements as his talk with President Roosevelt had suggested. This objection was removed, however, when the U.S. proposal was expanded to include postwar cooperation in both trade and payments.

[33] Negotiating with the United States was difficult. The principal difficulty was inherent in the political system. Keynes warned his colleagues in the Treasury about the problem: "What our representatives say binds the British Government. What the State Department or the Treasury or the Departments of Commerce or Agriculture may initiate in the course of our conversations with them can and does bind no one. Thus every bargain can, and very likely will, be overthrown by Congress. It is one thing to make concessions for a definite *quid pro quo*, another one to make them for promises which evaporate in practice" (23, p. 211).

world central bank[34]: (1) the arrangements for producing and controlling the stock of international money, (2) arrangements for controlling the demand for money, (3) mechanisms for monetary adjustment, and (4) the effect of these proposals on internal and external stability. Keynes also discusses other economic issues, including tariffs, commercial policy, capital movements, commodity price stabilization, taxes, and reparations payments. These issues are not central to the design of a monetary arrangement, so I do not discuss any of them in depth. Of course, several of these issues influence the effectiveness and durability of any monetary arrangement.

The monetary system and the money stock

Keynes revived his proposal for a world central bank, now called the Clearing Bank, to reflect the importance placed on the principle of multilateral clearing. The Clearing Bank's assets were its reserves and loans to member central banks, its liabilities the deposits of central banks. As in Keynes's previous proposals, gold served as a reserve for the Clearing Bank and could either be coined or used by central banks to settle balances with other central banks. To inhibit countries from accumulating gold – the problem of liquidity preference discussed in the *General Theory* – Keynes restricted gold sales. Once gold was paid to the Clearing Bank, it could not be repurchased by either central banks or the public. Gold could be withdrawn only if it was distributed to the members (in proportion to their balances) at the discretion of the Clearing Bank's directors (25, pp. 85–6).

The bank had the right to issue its own liabilities, called *bancor*, for central banks to use in making payments to other central banks. Bancor was defined in relation to gold but could not be sold for gold. It was not redeemable. Keynes expected gold to increase confidence in bancor and in the proposed system, but he does not give an economic rationale or any explanation of the role of gold. Gold was not used to limit the stock of bancor.[35]

---

[34] The size of quotas, voting rights, and other political and administrative arrangements were important in the discussions and negotiations and for the working of the system, but they are not important for understanding Keynes's views on monetary reform, so I omit them.

[35] Some discussions of Keynes's proposal stress bancor and regard its elimination as a major defeat. Bancor is not in Keynes's original proposal. There is no monetary unit in the September 1941 draft. In the second draft, the monetary unit appears and is called *grammor*. Bancor is not mentioned until the third draft, December 1941. Keynes expressed regret at the loss of the medium of exchange in the Bretton Woods agreement, but he did not make a major effort to retain this part of his proposal (26, pp. 10–14).

The supply of bancor was made completely elastic up to a maximum for each country (ibid., pp. 140, 272). The Clearing Bank was permitted to expand bancor secularly in relation to a five- (later a three-) year moving average of world trade (ibid., pp. 35, 118). The short-term supply of bancor to each country was determined by the rules under which member central banks were permitted to borrow from the Clearing Bank.[36] Expansion of bancor, through overdrafts set in relation to each country's quota (subscription to the bank), was a right of membership and could not be restricted.[37] Keynes's desire to avoid the interwar problem of reserves held by surplus countries is behind this and other parts of the proposal. Early versions offered very specific proposals for regulating the behavior of debtors and creditors. He removed many of the details in response to criticism, but he never proposed a reserve requirement to fix the supply of bancor in relation to gold. The limitation on supply came from the rules setting a country's maximum indebtedness in relation to its quota. Keynes had argued in the 1920s against rigid restrictions on the stock of money under the gold standard, and he opposed gold reserve requirements for notes and deposits in the *Tract* and the *Treatise*. He intended to avoid a repetition of the prewar experience, so he was more concerned about keeping bancor in circulation and maintaining opportunities for expansion than in limiting the outstanding stock.

The demand for bancor

A main purpose of Keynes's proposal was to avoid the accumulation of inactive balances held in an individual country's reserves. Gold could not be demanded in exchange for bancor. Bancor served as a means of payment but not as a store of value. To assure that countries would not accumulate inactive bancor balances, Keynes wrote detailed rules requiring countries with large credit balances to revalue (25, p. 36), to give to the Clearing Bank (without compensation) the part of its balance defined as excess (ibid., p. 36), or later to pay interest on its excess holdings (ibid., p. 79).[38] These proposals did not survive in

---

[36] For a summary, see Moggridge (1986, pp. 76–7).

[37] Williamson (1983) estimates that, in 1945, the aggregate value of the overdrafts was $26 billion and the potential U.S. liability $23 billion. The latter is more than 50 percent of the U.S. monetary base at the time. In 1986 dollars, the aggregate value of the overdrafts proposed in 1945 exceeds $150 billion.

[38] Keynes is very clearly refighting the battle of the interwar period against the United States, but he is also providing against the demand for real balances that are held for speculative or precautionary purposes. Countries must be prevented, he believed, from holding gold and raising interest rates. This explains why his proposed rule is not symmetric. The Clearing Bank had the right to demand devaluation when a country's

negotiations with the United States, but the United States offered a so-called scarce currency clause as a substitute. This clause permitted restrictions on imports and other types of trade discrimination against a country with a credit balance so large that its currency was no longer available in exchange at the Clearing Bank.[39]

Keynes had no doubt about the importance of requiring adjustment by creditor countries as well as debtors. Accumulation of gold stocks by the United States, France, and others had made the interwar gold standard a deflationary system. Keynes's theory of money incorporates this idea. In the *General Theory*, people respond to uncertainty by holding money balances. The resulting increase in demand for real balances raises real interest rates and lowers real income and employment. A well-functioning monetary system can limit or reduce uncertainty about future monetary policy and, in this way, reduce fluctuations in the demand for precautionary balances. By removing this source of uncertainty, Keynes expected to increase trade (ibid., p. 75).

Monetary adjustment

Imbalances in trade between countries create excess supplies or demands for currencies. Unless all currencies are freely convertible, the imbalances restrict trade. Keynes did not favor a return to some type of gold standard with convertibility, and he regarded a return to the gold standard as undesirable and unlikely in the immediate postwar period. The only alternatives he discussed were autarky, bilateral exchange with state trading, and a return to the interwar system of currency blocs. These alternatives were distinctly inferior in his view (25, pp. 82, 154) to a system of multilateral clearing with most countries as participants. He told the House of Lords:

> The principal object can be explained in a single sentence: to provide that money earned by selling goods to one country can be spent on purchasing the products of any other country. In jargon, a system of multilateral clearing. In English, a universal currency valid for trade transactions in all the world. Everything else in the plan is ancillary to that. (ibid., p. 270)[40]

debt remained at 50 percent of its quota for a year, but a country was *required* to revalue if in surplus to the same extent. The rules for revaluation and devaluation reflect the view that devaluation should be permitted in the event of "fundamental disequilibrium," a main feature of the agreement.

[39] This was a major issue in the bilateral negotiations. In practice, the clause was never invoked.

[40] See, also, Keynes's letter to Montagu Norman (25, pp. 98–9). Later, he emphasized the creation of a medium of exchange or transaction money (ibid., p. 285).

Even in a multilateral system, countries can accumulate debts beyond their capacity to export. The functioning of the clearing arrangement required some means of adjusting the position of persistent debtors and creditors. The draft proposal gave the Clearing Bank authority to adjust the exchange values of member countries against bancor and, thus, against other currencies. In addition, countries had the right to change par values up to 5 percent when their credits or debts remained at 25 percent of the country's quota for a year.

Changes in par value were to be the principal means of adjustment. Keynes understood that countries could use trade restrictions or subsidies as an alternative to changes in parities. His rules are restrictive. After an initial period, members relinquished the right to use tariffs (in excess of 25 percent of value), import quotas, export subsidies, or barter agreements. The only exception Keynes permitted was the temporary use of protectionist measures by a country with a large, persistent, current account deficit (ibid., pp. 50–1).[41]

Internal and external stability

The Clearing Union was Keynes's last effort to propose a solution to the problems of internal and external stability. External stability was to be maintained by the system of fixed, but adjustable, exchange rates with multilateral clearing of trade balances. Internal stability received less attention, but there is no mistaking that a main purpose of the program is to reduce fluctuations and raise aggregate employment without producing inflation.

Keynes speculated, at times, that his proposed international monetary system had an inflationary bias (26, p. 33). In response to a comment to that effect from Jacob Viner, he wrote that he would not be surprised if the actual danger turned out to be an excess supply of international money (25, pp. 324–5). There is no indication that he favored worldwide inflationary policies, and he made many statements of opposition (ibid., pp. 104, 135–6, 168–9; 26, pp. 16, 37, 73), but he made no effort to avoid or reduce the inflationary bias. Perhaps the main reason is that he did not expect the United States to accept any proposal as expansive as his. The U.S. proposal was, indeed, more cautious, and Keynes's efforts were directed at expanding the size of quotas and borrowing rights.

The problem of price stability in a single country received more attention. Much earlier, Keynes had rejected his conclusion from the

---

[41] Keynes's plan permitted subsidies to domestic industry if offset by a countervailing levy on exports to bring the price to the world market price.

Tract that internal stability was achieved by stabilizing the price level, but he continued to oppose inflation in the *Treatise* and the *General Theory*. His only specific proposals to avoid inflation included in the discussions of his plan are management of the interest rate and an extension of wartime controls and rationing in the early postwar period (25, p. 105).

Keynes's interest in price stability remained. He favored devaluation only if efficiency wages increased relative to wages abroad. He was skeptical of the alleged advantages of devaluation in other cases, and he recognized that the "advantage . . . has been greatly diminished by the growing practice of linking money wage rates to the cost of living" (ibid., p. 107). In correspondence with Viner and others, he repeated his opposition to exchange rate changes during the transition (ibid., p. 102) and in general (ibid., p. 323). He preferred to "aim at as great stability as possible" (ibid.). Again, the only exception "is the movement of efficiency wages in one country out of step with . . . others. One needs flexibility of rates to meet that contingency and, apart from that contingency, one should generally speaking aim at stability" (ibid., p. 323).[42] Later, he extended the criterion for devaluation to include money costs of production, a somewhat broader measure (ibid., pp. 339–40). The United States objected that Keynes made no adjustment for nontraded goods and technical progress but did not press for specific criteria in the agreement (ibid., p. 340).

Keynes predicted that the postwar years would see "keen political discussions affecting the position of the wealthier classes and the treatment of private property" (ibid., p. 149). He expected these discussions to increase instability and induce capital flight, but he opposed any provision that would permit capital flight for political reasons or to avoid taxation (ibid., p. 212). He favored trade as free and unsubsidized as possible but wanted to restrict capital movements to those required to finance trade.

The objective of his proposed system of capital controls, fixed but adjustable exchange rates, and multilateral clearing was to damp the trade cycle, smooth exchange rates, and expand trade (ibid., pp. 149,

---

[42] Viner replied that he favored greater flexibility during the adjustment period at the end of the war and less flexibility thereafter. He warned that the wage criterion "accepts the business agent of the powerful trade unions as the ultimate and unlimited sovereign over monetary policy" (25, p. 329). This comment is similar to his comment on the *General Theory* (Viner 1936). Viner did not suggest a policy for controlling inflation. James Meade favored using a country's reserve position as a criterion for devaluation. Lionel Robbins was concerned that giving the fund responsibility for internal price stability would weaken the antiinflation forces. The fund would be a scapegoat (26, p. 66). Keynes appears to have shared Robbin's view and apparently "had benefit of hearing Mr. [Ernest] Bevin on this subject!" (ibid., p. 36).

155). He believed, or hoped, that the increased stability and expanded trade would reduce uncertainty and remove part of the excess burden that raised required private returns above the social cost of investment. Reducing uncertainty was the means of maintaining a higher level of effective demand, without inflation, and moving the economies of individual countries closer to the point at which the "demand for exports will always be equal to the supply, and gluts will not occur" (ibid., p. 155).

Conclusion

Keynes's major policy concern throughout his life was the development of rules for international monetary arrangements. No other policy issue received as much of his attention in books and articles throughout his professional career as well as in his memos and proposals for postwar planning at the end of his career.

How can we reconcile this lifetime concern about monetary arrangements with Keynes's expressed belief that the trade cycle and "involuntary" unemployment are real phenomena? One of Keynes's clearest answers is in a reply to a paper by Hayek advocating a commodity standard instead of Keynes's Clearing Union. Keynes offered two reasons.

The first is the claim that the " 'appropriate' quantity of money is a necessary condition of stable prices" (26, p. 31). The sufficient condition for price stability based on the *Treatise* is "the relation of money wages and other costs to efficiency" (ibid.). Second, gold or commodity standards can only maintain stable costs by creating unemployment. Keynes continued:

> The primary aim of an international currency scheme should be, therefore, to prevent not only those evils which result from a chronic shortage of international money due to the draining of gold into creditor countries but also those which follow from countries failing to maintain stability of domestic efficiency costs and moving out of step with one another in their national wage policies without having at their disposal any means of orderly adjustment. And if orderly adjustment is allowed, that is another way of saying that countries may be allowed by the scheme, which is not the case with the gold standard, to pursue, if they choose, different wage policies and, therefore, different price policies.
>
> Thus the more difficult task of an international currency

scheme, which will only be fully solved with the aid of experience, is to deal with the problem of members getting out of step in their domestic wage and credit policies. To meet this it can be provided that countries seriously out of step (whether too fast or too slow) may be asked in the first instance to reconsider their policies. But, if necessary (and it will be necessary, if efficiency wage rates move at materially different rates), exchange rates will have to be altered so as to reconcile a particular national policy to the average pace. If the initial exchange rates are fixed correctly, this is likely to be the only important disequilibrium for which a change in exchange rates is the appropriate remedy . . .

It is wiser to regard stability (or otherwise) of internal prices as a matter of internal policy or politics. Commodity standards which try to impose this from without will break down just as surely as the rigid gold standard. (ibid., pp. 32–3)

Keynes's response is related to the position he had developed earlier. Internal stability is a desirable goal of monetary arrangements (a position Keynes had taken in the *Tract*) but, as argued in the *Treatise*, it cannot be achieved in a fixed exchange rate system, based on gold or commodities, unless countries are willing to accept levels of unemployment and fluctuations in output that Keynes believed were avoidable. In his postwar plan, he abandoned the position he had taken in the *Treatise*, where he favored a tabular standard based on internationally traded goods, and again preferred stability of the domestic price level (ibid., p. 37). But, he retained the idea of fixed, but adjustable, exchange rates that he had favored since the *Tract*.

He treated price levels as directly related to money wage levels (as in the *General Theory*) and, in practice, more important for domestic stability. Short-term stability, in Keynes's view, required devaluation if efficiency wages rose relative to wages abroad. The problem of restraining wages was difficult and would be "hopelessly prejudiced if the trade unions believe that it is an international monetary convention which is at the bottom of the trouble" (ibid., pp. 36, see also pp. 39–40). Still, he did not favor so-called Keynesian policies to reduce unemployment by inflating the economy. His Phillips curve had a negative tilt. He wrote: "If money wages rise faster than efficiency, this aggravates the difficulty of maintaining full employment and, so far from being a condition of full employment, it is one of the main obstacles which a full employment policy has to overcome" (ibid., p. 37).

On the choice between precommitment and unlimited discretion, Keynes was mainly on the side of precommitment or rules and against activist "fine tuning" in international monetary affairs. Domestic policies were restricted by commitment to international rules, but there was more discretion about short-term actions. The stock of money must change to keep interest rates and exchange rates stable. As in all of Keynes's proposals, this involved discretion, but discretion was limited by rules. He wrote:

> In only one important respect must an international bank differ from the model suitable to a national bank within a closed system, namely that *more* must be settled by rules and by general principles agreed beforehand and less by day-to-day discretion. (25, pp. 73, emphasis added)

The rules of international monetary management embodied the principles that Keynes expected to reduce variability and instability and, as a consequence, raise investment, world output, employment, and standards of living. Four of these principles were main features of Keynes's International Clearing Union: (1) Countries with temporary deficits did not have to contract output and employment to maintain price and exchange rate stability. Instead, they were permitted to borrow under rules fixed in advance of the event. (2) If adjustment of exchange rates were required, the burden of adjustment would be shared between debtor and creditor countries, in accordance with rules for orderly adjustment. (3) The system was multilateral. Countries did not have to devalue or adjust because the pattern of trade left them with debts inside one currency bloc and credits in another. (4) Exchange rates were adjustable under fixed rules.

Keynes expected his proposal to economize on gold and foreign exchange holdings of central banks and to increase the stability of the domestic and world economy. Increased stability would lower the public's demand for idle money balances. As wealth shifted from gold, foreign exchange, and money balances to real capital, real interest rates would fall and investment would rise. Over time, the capital stock and per capita income would increase.

Throughout his life, Keynes was a proponent of price stability. He did not want to achieve price stability by varying output and employment. He claimed three advantages of the proposed international rules for domestic policy: (1) the external value of the currency conformed to its internal value, opposite to the gold standard; (2) interest rates could be reduced during recessions without fear of international capital movements; (3) the use of bank rate to induce monetary contraction, unemployment, and deflation was no longer required (26, p. 16).

Much has been written about Keynes's dissatisfaction with the Bretton Woods agreement and particularly about his disappointments at the first meeting of the member countries in Savannah, Georgia. There is nothing in his papers suggesting that his dissatisfaction persisted. He had always expected that the American proposals would dominate the final agreement. As early as April 1943, he commented that we shall "very likely accept their dress in the long run" (25, p. 268). He saw no reason for hasty compromises. An early agreement might cause the Americans to "run away from their own plan." He gave up his plan for an international medium of exchange, bancor, early in 1944 on the recommendation of many British negotiators, to avoid Congressional disapproval (ibid., pp. 405–6). By March 1943, he knew that Harry Dexter White's (American) plan permitted some free markets in foreign exchange and did not envisage creating a bank or a medium of exchange (ibid., pp. 220–25). Yet, a year later, he described the system as a new model of domestic policy and an international framework for full employment (26, p. 19). To Keynes, a framework for full employment meant that the difference between social and private costs of investment had been reduced to a negligible level.

The issues at Savannah were mainly organizational and political. Keynes opposed the creation of a large, permanent bureaucracy and the proposal to pay attractive salaries. He believed that the location of the headquarters in Washington, instead of New York, exposed the new organization to the pressures of domestic U.S. politics. He did not respect Fred Vinson, the new secretary of the U.S. Treasury (ibid., p. 217). He was disappointed to learn that the United States would not propose Harry White, who shared many of Keynes's views, as first managing director. He feared that the institution would be "run by gigantic American staffs, with the rest of us very much on the sidelines" (ibid.). But, he had always defended the plan that emerged from negotiations as the best available alternative, not as an ideal. Nothing that occurred at Savannah appears to have changed that view (ibid., pp. 220–34). His last, posthumously published paper is cautiously optimistic about prospects for the future under the new arrangments and the change from prewar U.S. policies (27, pp. 427–46; see also Moggridge 1986, p. 82, n. 17 which takes a similar view).

The alternatives Keynes envisioned were either resort to bilateral trade agreements and strict controls on trade and exchange or return to the interwar system of currency blocs, devaluations, and trade discrimination. He rejected the former completely on several occasions including a strong letter to the *Times*, written in response to Thomas Balogh.[43] Keynes disliked the interwar system and blamed the system

---

[43] Keynes's letter, dated May 18, 1944, refers to Balogh as a disciple of Dr. Schacht (26, pp. 8–9). The comment is odd in the light of his 1940 proposal and his comments on the German proposal. He was more polite, but no less firm, with Joan Robinson (ibid., pp. 132–3). The conclusion to Keynes's last paper, "Balance of Payments of the United States" (27, pp. 427–46) forcefully argues against systems of planning, import tariffs, and export subsidies.

for the high rates of unemployment in the 1920s and 1930s. A return to that system with Britain in a weaker position relative to the sterling bloc had no appeal. The new system, even if it was not Keynes's ideal, was in his words, "an international framework for the new ideas and the new techniques associated with the policy of *full employment*" (26, p. 19, emphasis added).

During the 1920s, Keynes's conviction grew that no system was capable of achieving internal and external stability, high employment, and freedom. He chose to sacrifice freedom and to be rid of laissez-faire. His wartime proposals for international exchange arrangements always include statements favoring exchange controls. The issue was not a main point in negotiation with the United States, not only because he regarded White's proposals for controls as more strict than his own but also because countries were free to adopt the restrictions on capital movements that they wished (25, p. 325).

The flavor of Keynes's views is given by his (repeated) statement that he did not think it would be necessary to use postal censorship after the war to enforce exchange controls (ibid., pp. 130, 325). He favored a permanent system of controls on all transactions into and out of the country. Open licenses would be issued for current trade, but remittance of interest and amortization would be limited, and purely private enterprise dealings in exchange would be prohibited (ibid., pp. 52, 212–13; 26, p. 131). Although he was certainly aware of the interwar experience of refugees, he would not permit "the flight of funds for political reasons or to evade domestic taxation or in anticipation of the owner turning refugee" (25, pp. 53, 87, 130).[44]

In the *Tract*, Keynes recognized that internal and external stability

---

[44] Exchange controls proved easier to recommend than to design. As late as August 1944, after the Bretton Woods agreement, Keynes and Dennis Robertson differed about the interpretation of the agreement. Both had participated actively in the conference, but they drew different interpretations of the obligation to sell foreign exchange to a holder of sterling who had received a payment on current account. The specific clause, Article 8 Section 2(a), said in part "no member shall . . . impose restrictions on the making of payments and transfers for current international transactions" (quoted in 26, p. 14). Robertson read this right as unrestricted as to the use of the proceeds and restricted only as to the currency that a central bank was obliged to offer. He interpreted the clause as requiring payment in the exporter's currency. Keynes read the section very differently. For him, there was no obligation to pay the exporter in his own currency. Doing so made "nonsense" of the exchange control provisions. The discussion of this section continued. Keynes eventually recognized an ambiguity, if not a mistake (26, pp. 114–15, 118–19, 124–7, 134–8). He wrote to White to explain the problem. According to Keynes's report, White expressed sympathy for Keynes's position but refused to accept Keynes's interpretation or to amend the agreement (26, pp. 148–9). After much more discussion and exchanges of letters (26, pp. 156–82), the British obtained an interpretation from Secretary Morgenthau. Keynes was not satisfied, but the issue was not pursued (ibid., pp. 183–5).

could be achieved without a loss of freedom. If each country used monetary policy to achieve domestic price stability and adopted adjustable exchange rates, relative price levels would be more stable. Greater stability of price levels would increase the stability of exchange rates and achieve a high degree of internal and external stability.

Keynes turned away from this proposal when he wrote the *Treatise* because he became convinced that monetary control is a necessary, but not a sufficient, condition for a stable price level. With sluggish adjustment of wages, changes in money affect employment and output. Freedom (laissez-faire) and the gold standard required each country to accept more variability in employment and prices than, Keynes believed, was required. His attention turned toward proposals for greater control and less freedom. He flirted with restrictions on foreign lending and later with tariffs. In the *General Theory*, he favored state direction of domestic investment as a means of reducing fluctuations in investment, output, and employment. In his plans for the postwar years, he extended the control to foreign investment.[45]

Keynes did not live to see the growth of per capita income in the first twenty-five postwar years under the modified version of his proposal. Possibly he would have given credit to the monetary and trade arrangements that he had proposed since the 1920s. Would such a claim be correct?

The Bretton Woods system did not work as Keynes had anticipated when he began work on the Clearing Union, and the problems that developed were not the ones he anticipated at the outset. The United States did not accumulate credit balances, absorbing gold or foreign exchange, as it had in the interwar period. Within a few years of the postwar reconstruction, the United States began to lose gold.[46] By the 1960s, U.S. domestic policy concerns and inflationary finance converted the system into an engine of world inflation. The arrangements gave insufficient incentive for the United States to supply price stability to the world and required collective action by others to discipline the United States. Here, too, incentives were weak and disincentives strong. Countries were reluctant to revalue so as to prevent inflation.

---

[45] An additional reason may have been to prevent capital from moving freely to less developed countries. This increased unemployment at home and, if continued, eventually lowered real incomes to the world level. Keynes spoke favorably about world development but did not want to either lower British standards or increase unemployment.

[46] Keynes is much closer to the mark in his last published paper where he is less convinced about a "dollar shortage" than some of his contemporaries. He believed that the United States "was becoming a high-living, high-cost country" (27, p. 444; see also pp. 485–6). He also believed that the United States had moved away from protectionism and other impediments to trade and payments adjustment (ibid., pp. 444–5).

The mechanisms to assure that both creditors and debtors had to adjust did not work to produce stabilizing adjustments.

Some of the flaws came from Keynes's proposal. He had long favored reliance on exchange rate adjustment to resolve persistent, so-called structural payments deficits and reliance on lending to adjust temporary deficits. He believed that the former arose from changes in relative costs of production, mainly from changes in efficiency wages.[47] The agreement provided no clear way to distinguish between persistent and transitory changes, so the decision to devalue or revalue was usually left to individual countries where it became involved in local and global political disagreements. To resolve disagreements about adjustment, the system relied on little parliaments, or groups of experts, instead of the judgment of the market place.

The effort to combine internal and external stability failed. Although by some measures, the system lasted for a quarter century, this is an overestimate of its success. Currency convertibility did not become official until the late 1950s. Within a decade, the system was on the edge of crisis with inflation rising and devaluations or revaluations common.[48]

In the *Tract*, Keynes placed much less emphasis on exchange rate stability and much more on domestic price stability. Exchange rates were to be kept stable by compatible domestic policies in major countries – Britain and the United States at the time. Domestic price stability in key countries reduced exchange rate fluctuations for those currencies and provided a monetary standard for third countries. Perhaps experience with competitive devaluations in the 1930s affected his judgment about the importance of exchange rate stability. We do not know. What seems clear is that the system based on his proposal provided neither the degree of price stability nor the exchange stability that Keynes wanted to achieve.

---

[47] This is a central idea of the *Treatise*.

[48] The idea continues in the European Monetary System, based on an adjustable peg with plans for a currency – the ECU; it continues in a different form in the discussion of target zones.

6

Other interpretations of the
General Theory

Five decades after its publication, the *General Theory* continues to arouse controversy about both its main message and its central hypotheses. Since many of the interpretations are firmly held by their expositors, the book remains subject to differing interpretations. The parties to these disputes often seem more interested in trading verbal blows than in resolving differences, so the differences remain. It does not seem likely that one interpretation is likely to emerge as the sole correct interpretation.

Much of the problem lies with Keynes. Readers as sympathetic as Seymour Harris long ago recognized that the book is difficult to read (Harris 1953, p. x). The same complaint has been made by others, for example, Johnson (1961, in Wood 2, p. 287) and Salant (1985, p. 1184). Keynes, the much praised stylist and maker of memorable phrases, was at his best when writing tracts like the *Economic Consequences of the Peace*, where precise analytic statements are less important for the reader's understanding of the main message than in the *Treatise* or the *General Theory*. Indeed, some of the difficulties of the latter book may arise from Keynes's attempt to use A. C. Pigou or classical economics as foils, much as he had used Clemenceau and Wilson in the *Economic Consequences of the Peace*, with the result that the criticisms of classical economics obscure both the central message and the close relation to his earlier work that seemed clear to Keynes (7, pp. xxi–xxii). Whatever the reason, the *General Theory* has been charged with ambiguity, lack of clarity, and even inconsistency since its earliest reviews (Pigou 1936, in Wood 2, pp. 21–3).

There is slight chance of resolving all differences about the interpretation of the *General Theory*, and it is neither my intention nor my purpose to try. The usefulness of my interpretation of the *General Theory* as the representation in economic theory terms of Keynes's principal beliefs from the 1920s does not depend on all other interpretations being completely wrong. Nor does it depend on finding a one-to-one relation between the *General Theory* and Keynes's policy statements. Keynes was capable of changing his mind, and he often did. What Schumpeter called his vision of society changed much less than his views about what should be done to improve a particular situation, and it is his vision of society that the *General Theory* was written to serve and to encourage others to accept.[1]

My view of the *General Theory* as an additional step beyond the *Treatise* is itself controversial. Leijonhufvud (1968) and Keynes (7, pp. xxi–xxii) are earlier statements of the close relation between the two. Patinkin (1975, in Wood 1, p. 504) sees a weaker relation, and many other readers interpret the *General Theory* in isolation from Keynes's earlier and later writing. My views of this issue are developed in earlier chapters, so this chapter concentrates on some of the alternative interpretations of the *General Theory* and does not treat the alternative interpretations of the *Treatise*, except in passing.

Although differences in interpretation abound, there are some broad agreements that, if not uniformly accepted, now seem to be widely shared. Salant (1985, p. 1180) expresses surprise "at the number of contributors who either deny, here [the Keynes Centenary at Cambridge] or elsewhere, that downward rigidity of wages is central to Keynes' conclusion." This is not a denial that Keynes mentions wage inflexibility; it simply accepts Keynes's 1939 statement (7, p. 400) that the main propositions of the *General Theory* do not depend on rigidity or inflexibility of the nominal wage. Also Salant (1985, p. 1181) shares my views (Meltzer 1981) that "The *General Theory* is not about the business cycle." Business cycles are mentioned, and Keynes (7, Chapter 22) sketches the application of his theory to the business or trade cycle, but as Salant notes "involuntary unemployment can persist" (ibid.).

Agreements are limited, however. Reference to the main propositions of the *General Theory* might suggest that there is agreement on what these propositions are. Alas, this is not so. For me, the main propositions are statements about "the forces which determine changes in the scale of output and employment" (7, p. xxii). As Keynes recognized, the level of output was fixed in the *Treatise* (ibid.). As soon as he recognized, or accepted, that output was fixed, he began to re-

---

[1] Chapter 2 restates his vision of society. Schumpeter relates the vision in the *General Theory* to the *Economic Consequences of the Peace* and mentions specifically "the vision of an economic process in which investment opportunity flags and saving habits nevertheless persist" (1946, in Wood 2, p. 62). I agree with this view but believe it is partial. Keynes's dislike of laissez-faire capitalism, his belief in the possibility of reducing variability and uncertainty, and so forth are part of his vision. Schumpeter's own view of Keynes's work is perhaps summarized by his statement: "What a *cordon bleu* to make such a sauce out of such scanty material!" (ibid.). On Keynes's social philosophy and its relation to all of his theoretical work, and particularly to the *General Theory*, see Lambert (1963). Moggridge and Howson (1974) trace the development of Keynes's policy views and show how theory and policy views changed while remaining consistent with Harrod's (1951) "presuppositions of Harvey Road" and Keynes's other beliefs.

work his analysis to determine the level of output at which equilibrium is achieved. The result was a theory that, he claimed on its opening page, was more general: "The postulates of the classical theory are applicable to a special case only . . . the situation which it assumes being a limiting point of the possible positions of equilibrium. Moreover, the characteristics of the special case . . . happen *not* to be those of the economic society in which we actually live" (ibid., p. 3, emphasis added). The postulate that had to be abandoned, he promptly noted, was the one that denied "involuntary unemployment" (ibid., pp. 16–17). Once this was done, output could remain in an equilibrium that was not optimal.

Abba Lerner (1936, in Wood 2, pp. 57–60) interprets involuntary unemployment as a long-run concept that arises in the *General Theory* because prices gradually adjust downward following a reduction in money wages. Others do not share this interpretation. As Alan Coddington notes (1983, p. 27), involuntary unemployment became identified with cyclical unemployment or with the "mass unemployment" (ibid., p. 25) of the 1930s. Since neither of these interpretations of "involuntary" unemployment makes sense in a standard model with flexible prices, several writers bring in the notion of wage rigidity during the business cycle to generate unemployment.[2] In recent versions of this interpretation, money wages adjust slowly because different groups of workers and employers sign multiyear contracts on different dates, and only part of the existing contracts is renegotiated each year.

Many, probably most, interpretations of the *General Theory* see the book as a statement about the short term. Fixity of the capital stock and even more Keynes's dictum in the *Tract* that in the long run we are all dead encourage this view. Vaizey (1969, in Wood 1, pp. 176–7) argues that Keynes's dictum is misinterpreted: "He sought to manage the economy so that short views were unnecessary" (ibid., p. 177).

---

[2] Coddington (1983, pp. 35–6, 48) quotes a number of prominent interpreters on the subject of involuntary unemployment without accepting their interpretations. Trygve Haavelmo describes unemployment as involuntary if it requires collective choice to remove it. Richard Kahn finds the concept of "no practical significance" but important conceptually! Robert Solow treats it as an empirical construct resulting from the failure of markets to clear in a time period long enough for macroeconomic policy to be effective. Don Patinkin (1965, pp. 313–14) interprets involuntary in choice theoretic terms. Involuntary unemployment means that workers are "off" the supply curves implied by maximizing behavior, subject to market prices and budget constraints, in a free, peacetime, democratic society. Of these four, and still other definitions discussed by Coddington, only Patinkin and Haavelmo mention the role of institutions, and they do not pursue this lead to study the effects of uncertainty and the institutions that augment or damp uncertainty. However, Patinkin explicitly avoids identifying involuntary unemployment with wage rigidity and notes (ibid., p. 643) that Keynes does not assume wage rigidity throughout.

Austin Robinson, on the other hand, sees Keynes as a political economist who sought to solve "immediate practical problem[s] in the application to government of the methods of economic analysis" (Robinson 1947, in Wood 1, p. 94).

Both interpretations can be correct. The apparent conflict between short- and long-term orientation is removed if we view Keynes as concerned both with institutional changes, as his lifetime interest in international monetary arrangements shows, and with current policy. When faced with a particular problem, he would advocate a policy for the particular circumstances even if his recommendation was inconsistent with his long-term goal. There are many examples, but perhaps the best known is Keynes's advocacy of protectionist measures in 1931. After a lifetime of opposition to protectionist measures and strong advocacy of free trade as an optimal or ideal policy, Keynes favored protection – particularly for Britain – to lower unemployment. Once the pound was devalued, he no longer advocated protectionist measures. Nor did he advocate protectionist measures about a decade later when he worked on postwar economic planning. Instead, he favored the more open system of trade that he had advocated in the *Treatise* and throughout the 1920s.

The concern for both current problems and for optimal long-term policy rules or procedures is a principal reason that one can find Keynes firmly positioned on different sides of the same issue. Keynes did not allow his firm beliefs about long-term policy rules, represented by his earlier proposals for international monetary reform in the *Tract*, the *Treatise*, or his proposals for postwar monetary reform, to deter him from advocating short-term measures when faced with a problem that, he believed, could be ameliorated.

Those who interpret the *General Theory* as a theory of the short-term position of the economy usually point to the fixed capital stock and population, assumed throughout. A variant sees the *General Theory* as "depression economics" – a blueprint for state fiscal action to increase activity and employment in a depression. Richard Kahn (1978, in Wood 1, p. 557) reads the *General Theory* that way. There can be no doubt that Keynes favored such action at times, but his advocacy predates the *General Theory*. His main ideas about fiscal stimulus were published as *Can Lloyd George Do It?* (9, pp. 86–125) shortly before he published the *Treatise*. The *General Theory* makes a few, but very few, references to countercyclical policy. The book's principal recommendation calls for state planning of investment; it is his attempt to provide the analytic foundation for the policies he proposed before he wrote the *Treatise* and the *General Theory*.

Keynes's views on state planning antedate his concern about the persistent unemployment of the 1930s. In "The End of Laissez Faire," (ibid., pp. 272–94), "Am I A Liberal?" (ibid., pp. 295–306), and other essays written in the mid-1920s, Keynes favored a new form of social organization, neither laissez-faire nor socialism. The problems, as Keynes saw them at the time, were uncertainty and ignorance:

> Many of the greatest economic evils of our time are the fruits of risk, uncertainty and ignorance. It is because particular individuals, fortunate in situation or in abilities, are able to take advantage of uncertainty and ignorance, and also because for the same reason big business is often a lottery, that great inequalities of wealth come about; and these same factors are *also the cause of unemployment of labour, or the disappointment of reasonable business expectations*, and of the impairment of efficiency and production. (ibid., pp. 291–2; emphasis added)

The emphasis on uncertainty and expectations, the reference to business as a lottery and the belief that uncertainty is a main cause of unemployment sound very much like the *General Theory*. The passage was written ten years earlier, however, long before the worldwide depression. Keynes's recommendations at the time, like his diagnosis, sound familiar to careful readers of the *General Theory*. He favored "deliberate control of currency and credit by a central institution" (ibid., p. 292) and planning of investment. Of investment, he wrote: "I do not think that these matters should be left entirely to the chances of private judgment and private profits, as they are at present" (ibid.).

At the other end of the spectrum of views are those who read the *General Theory* as an attack on capitalism. The passages that emphasize uncertainty and recommend planning, like Keynes's earlier criticisms of laissez-faire, form the basis for this interpretation. Although it is true that Keynes advocated investment planning, he never advocated state ownership, and he opposed socialism. In the 1920s, he had written:

> The abuses of this epoch in the realms of government are Fascism on the one side and Bolshevism on the other. Socialism offers no middle course, because it also is sprung from the presuppositions of the era of abundance, just as much as *laissez-faire* individualism and the free play of economic forces. (ibid., p. 304)

He did not change this view. As Harrod (1951, p. 350) notes, Keynes's policy views were formed by 1924 and changed little thereafter. In his last years, he remained an advocate of monetary and fiscal rules and investment planning.[3] There is no basis in Keynes's writings to sustain the interpretation that his criticism of laissez-faire led him to reject private ownership of the means of production.

This chapter summarizes and comments on some of the main interpretations of the *General Theory* under six headings. Since there is a vast literature, and my purpose is to compare the alternative interpretations to my own, I make no attempt at a comprehensive survey of the literature. Most often I choose selected representatives of each view. Some authors combine more than one interpretation. Others, whom I discuss with a particular group or those who subscribe to a particular interpretation, may differ on points that seem important to them.

Each interpretation emphasizes a distinct characteristic as the key to understanding Keynes's message. The six interpretations highlight the following: (1) wage rigidity, (2) intertemporal coordination failure, (3) high-interest elasticity of the demand for money and low-interest elasticity of investment, (4) irrational expectations and disequilibrium, (5) the denial of gross substitution between money and other assets, and (6) a miscellaneous grouping. Following this discussion, I consider, briefly, Keynes's short-term policies as illustrated by the relation between Keynes's policy views and those of Abba Lerner, an early and leading developer of the theory of "functional finance" or counter-cyclical fiscal action.

By suggesting that there are competing interpretations, I do not intend to suggest that they are all equally plausible or equally consistent with the *General Theory*. Consistency with the *General Theory* may not be the appropriate criterion. The aims of the interpreters differ. At least two types of interpretation are different enough to be distinguished. One, exemplified by Hansen (1953), tried to restate Keynes's argument and make it understandable. To do so, the interpretation may discard parts of the argument as unrelated and emphasize what they regard as Keynes's core argument. A second group, represented by writers as different as Leijonhufvud (1968) and Davidson (1978), accept that Keynes's argument is inadequate; his conclusions about involuntary unemployment (and other main propositions) do not follow from his analysis. These authors attempt to introduce new elements and to construct or reconstruct those parts of Keynes's argument that they regard as missing or defective. The first group asks what Keynes's argument was; the second presents what, the writers believe, it should have been. We now have available Keynes's comments and corre-

---

[3] See the discussion in Chapter 4 of Keynes's countercyclical fiscal policy proposals in his exchanges with James Meade and his monetary proposals in Chapter 5.

spondence; we can find evidence that he rejected some interpretations, disputed some points in others, and accepted or rejected particular arguments. We also have his comments on some of the early reviews of his book, so we know some of the interpretations that he accepted and some that he regarded as incorrect or incomplete. Although I do not seek the "true meaning," I use Keynes's comments to discard some misleading or incorrect interpretations. Where applicable, I use the model of the *General Theory* from Chapter 4 to criticize the alternative interpretations. The model is a modified IS–LM model. We now know that Keynes was willing to accept the IS–LM model with some qualifications, principally about expectations (14, pp. 79–81).

Rigid money wages

Many restatements and interpretations of the *General Theory* assign great importance to Keynes's assumption that money wages are rigid. Modigliani (1944) identifies the "Keynesian special case" with the condition that interest rates and money wages are at the minimum levels set by the liquidity trap and wage rigidity. Haberler (1946) and Hicks (1977, p. 81; 1982, pp. 319, 323) assume that money wages and perhaps the price level are fixed in the *General Theory*.[4] Schumpeter claims that Keynes "*wished* to secure his major results without appeal to the element of rigidity, just as he spurned the aid he might have derived from imperfections of competition" (1946, in Wood 1, pp. 65–66). He was unable to do so, according to Schumpeter, particularly in his discussion of underemployment. Brenner (1980, in Wood 2, pp. 412–13) interprets the *General Theory* as a theory in which there are long-term contracts for labor and financial assets. He believes that these contracts, particularly labor contracts, enhance price stability as Keynes (7, p. 239) claimed, but they produce short-term unemployment.

Harry Johnson (1961, in Wood 2, pp. 296–7) interprets Keynes's underemployment equilibrium as a consequence of rigid wages but recognizes, as have many others following Patinkin (1965), that the effect of falling prices on wealth restores equilibrium at full employment. Johnson interprets Keynesian unemployment as "a disequilibrium situation in which dynamic adjustment is proceeding very slowly" (p. 296). Further, he claims, Keynes used Marshall's periods to replace

---

[4] Hicks's interpretation of the main point of the *General Theory* changed several times. Coddington (1983, Chapter 5) traces some aspects of Hicks's changing views. Hicks's (1979) reply to an earlier version of Coddington's interpretation sketches some of the development of his own changing interpretations. Pursuit of these issues would take us far afield.

disequilibrium with short-period equilibrium analysis. Similarly, Coddington (1983, pp. 71–2) uses Hicks (1937) and Hicks (1967) to argue that the assumption of wage rigidity makes Keynes's theory a theory of short-run unemployment as compared to the long-run theory of the classical economists.

A problem with the short-run interpretation is that this view was standard long before Keynes and was used by Keynes long before the *General Theory*. Wage rigidity, if accepted as the main message, deprives the *General Theory* of its novel or revolutionary aspect. Wage rigidity or wage inflexibility was used as an explanation of unemployment as early as Thornton (1802) and was common among classical writers, including Pigou (1927), whose views Keynes criticized harshly.[5] Wages in Pigou (1927) are flexible only in long-run adjustment.

Keynes relied on wage inflexibility as an explanation of unemployment throughout the 1920s. In the "Economic Consequences of Mr. Churchill," he wrote about the problem of returning to the prewar parity:

> Our problem is to reduce money wages and, through them, the cost of living with the idea that, when the circle is complete, real wages will be as high, or nearly as high, as before. By what *modus operandi* does credit restriction attain this result?
>
> *In no other way than by the deliberate intensification of unemployment.* The object of credit restriction, in such a case, is to withdraw from employers the financial means to employ labour at the existing level of prices and wages. The policy can only attain its end by intensifying unemployment without limit, until the workers are ready to accept the necessary reduction of money wages under the pressure of hard facts. (9, p. 218)

As we have seen, wage (and cost) inflexibility has a major role in Keynes's discussion in the *Treatise*. There was no need to write the *General Theory* if short-run wage or cost inflexibility was the main point to be made.

Hicks (1974, pp. 61, 73), using a short-term interpretation, concludes that Keynes had no theory of money wage changes. Wages are simply fixed in the short run. Kahn (1978, p. 556) shares this view as does Tobin (1948, in Wood 2, p. 253). Later, Tobin (1983, p. 33) argues that wage fixity or stickiness does not arise from irrational money illusion or ad hoc assumption. His outline of Keynes's theory of nominal wages has money wages set in relation to money wages in other occupations.

---

[5] As sympathetic an interpreter as Alvin Hansen takes the same view. See Hansen (1953, p. 16) for additional citations to Pigou.

A rise in prices that lowers all real wages in proportion is more acceptable to wage earners than a reduction in money wages that is perceived as a fall in relative money wages.[6]

In my interpretation of the *General Theory*, money wages are set at the value expected to prevail in equilibrium. The money wage, on average, is equal to the wage expected in equilibrium. Wage changes were not large enough in noninflationary periods to change Keynes's beliefs, based on his observations, about the stability of money wages and the wage share.[7] In fact, the stability of money wages and expected money wages provide an anchor for prices in Keynes's analysis. This view appears in the *Treatise*, (5, p. 151–3) and reappears, with greater emphasis, in the *General Theory* (7, pp. 265, 269–71).

In the *General Theory*, Keynes relies on wage inflexibility to explain why output fluctuates around the equilibrium level. As Lerner (Colander 1972, pp. 7–12) among others has noted, Keynes argues against wage flexibility on two grounds.[8] First, a decline in money wages lowers prices by lowering costs of production. This is a medium-run or long-run argument. There is no basis for believing that Keynes thought prices would adjust instantly or in the short run; both the *General Theory* and the *Treatise* have the opposite perspective, and that perspective was standard. Second, reductions in money wages arouse expectations of further declines in wages and prices. Lerner notes that "the effects of *falling* wages and prices are the opposite of *lower* wages and prices" (Colander 1972, p. 12). Keynes assumes that wage expectations are extrapolative but that interest rate expectations are regressive. Interest rates can reach a floor from which everyone expects interest rates to *rise*, but expectations of falling wages typically give rise to expectations of a further fall. One of the defects in Keynes's argument is that the *General Theory* has no discussion of why the same

[6] Keynes used the relative wage hypothesis to explain why it was easier in a market economy to reduce all wages by inflation than by bargaining with individuals, groups, or unions. I believe Tobin puts excessive stress on Keynes's remark. Tobin also notes (1983, p. 34) that Keynes's analysis is incomplete in that there is no explanation of why workers choose idleness to lower wages. Tobin believes the gap can be filled by introducing increasing returns to scale and other elements of imperfect competition. Kalecki (1938), responding to Keynes's challenge to his research students, was the first to explore the effects of imperfect competition. Keynes (7, pp. 410–11) praises Kalecki's paper but describes the result as "no definite progress" toward an explanation of movements of money wages relative to other variables. Kaldor finds Kalecki's work "intellectually superior to Keynes's" (1986, p. 10, n. 17).

[7] Kahn (1978, in Wood 1, p. 556) reports the British data for the 1930s. In 1933, the money wage index had fallen at most 5 percent below its average for the mid-1920s despite a measured unemployment rate of 28 percent in 1932. Additional data supporting Keynes's belief are given later. (On the wage share, see 7, pp. 408–9.)

[8] I am indebted to David Colander for making the transcript of this interview and others available to me.

individuals hold different types of expectations in different markets. A possible reconciliation for some cases is that wages may reach a floor also (7, p. 265), but Keynes does not attempt to reconcile the different assumptions or even notice them.

Keynes's discussion of wage changes is ambiguous. Chapter 19 of the *General Theory*, which sets out to explain why workers cannot always reduce unemployment by lowering money wages, recognizes that the conclusion is not universal: "A reduction in money-wages is quite capable in certain circumstances of affording a stimulus to output, as the classical theory supposes"[9] (ibid., p. 257).

Keynes mentions several channels through which a fall of money wages increases employment. Two are of interest. In an open economy, a reduction of home money wages relative to money wages abroad increases employment if it is not offset by changes in tariffs and quotas. He dismisses this channel by assuming the economy is closed (ibid., p. 265). The second channel, a reduction of current money wages relative to expected future money wages, increases employment in two ways. The marginal efficiency of capital rises and, because money income is lower and firms have smaller wage bills, the community's liquidity preference declines, reducing the rate of interest. On the following page (ibid., p. 266) Keynes suggests that liquidity preference refers to the demand for money in wage units.

Keynes's analysis of wage changes can be developed using the model introduced in Chapter 4. The three equations for the output (IS), money (LM), and production-labor (SS) sectors are

$$\text{IS:} \quad Y/W = A(r, E; K) \tag{6.1}$$

$$\text{LM:} \quad Y/W = L(r, r^e(u); M/W) \tag{6.2}$$

$$\text{SS:} \quad p = Z(W, Y/W; K) \tag{6.3}$$

All symbols are as defined earlier. For given expectations of $r = r^e$ and $Y/W = E$ and for given values of W, M, and K, the three equations determine equilibrium values of Y/W, r, and p – real output in wage units, the rate of interest, and the price level, respectively. Figure 6.1 shows the underemployment equilibrium, Y_0/W_0, to the left of full employment equilibrium at Y^*/W^*.

The wage rate can change, but its expected value is given by con-

---

[9] Keynes states that Chapter 19 of the *General Theory* amplifies and explains his statement that wages are not equal to the marginal disutility of labor. In the light of the sentence in the text and the definition of full employment as maximal employment, it would have been clearer to say that wages are not always equal to the marginal disutility of labor.

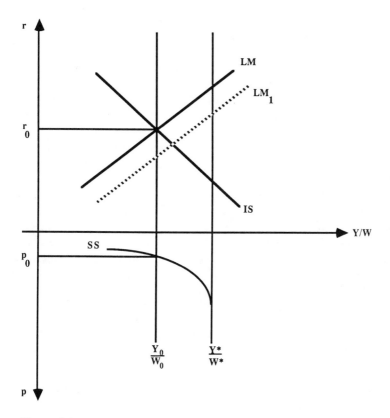

Figure 6.1

vention. Keynes defined conventions in terms of expectations (ibid., p. 152), so we may treat the equilibrium money wage as an expected value.[10] If W changes, but the change is not expected to persist, expected W remains unchanged.

The model shows that W affects p, but since p is dichotomous, there are no effects on real variables. A change in W also affects M/W, however. Money wage reductions increase the stock of real balances, shift LM to the right, and lower the rate of interest. Following a reduction in W, the equilibrium position of the output market is shown at the

---

[10] Keynes did not believe that we can calculate mathematical expectations, particularly for events that are distant in time. His discussion of the relation between conventions and expectations restates his view about mathematical expectations, then concludes: The "conventional method of calculation will be compatible with a considerable measure of continuity and stability in our affairs, *so long as we can rely on the maintenance of the convention*" (7, p. 152). In the material cited, Keynes is talking about the return on an investment, but the discussion is applicable to other conventions as well.

intersection of IS and the broken line LM_1 in Figure 6.1. Real output is higher, and interest rates are lower. The effect on the price level is ambiguous. The direct effect of wage reduction is a lower price level; SS shifts down (not shown); but the increase in output is accompanied by a rise of the price level, so the price level may rise or fall.

A major conclusion follows from the analysis of wage changes. Those who argue that wage reduction *maintains* stable employment at the full employment level must rest their argument on the effect of wage changes on interest rates and the demand for money: "The same reasons . . . which limit the efficacy of increases in the quantity of money as a means of increasing investment to the *optimum* figure, apply *mutatis mutandis* to wage reductions" (7, p. 266, emphasis added).[11] Keynes's emphasis on the effect of wage changes on real balances (in wage units) and interest rates is a new argument, as he insisted in correspondence with Haberler (29, p. 273). Previous discussion emphasized the effect on profits, as in his *Treatise*.

Keynes gives his reason for believing that money wage changes are no more reliable than changes in money for restoring full employment:

> Just as a moderate increase in the quantity of money may exert an inadequate influence over the long-term rate of interest, whilst an immoderate increase may offset its other advantages by its disturbing effect on confidence; so a moderate reduction in money-wages may prove inadequate, whilst an immoderate reduction might shatter confidence even if it were practicable. (7, pp. 266–7)

The implication of this statement is that no one knows the correct amount to change nominal money or nominal wages. Too large or too small a change in money balances (per wage unit) can cause rather than eliminate fluctuations. The principal reason that Keynes gives is that the effect on expectations, and therefore on investment, is destabilizing. Even gradual changes in money wages, he writes, "cause a great instability of prices, so violent as to make business calculations futile" (ibid., p. 269). Here, Keynes repeats the views about sustained (large) price changes expressed in the *Tract* and the *Economic Consequences of the Peace,* and he concludes that a flexible wage policy does not contribute to stability except in authoritarian societies where all wages can be changed simultaneously.

To achieve a permanent increase in output and employment, Keynes says, there must be a permanent change in spending and output or a

---

[11] Note that the reference is to the optimum level of investment, the full (maximum) employment position. He does not deny that actual output can increase.

permanent reduction in the expected rate of interest. Monetary and wage policy cannot produce a fall in the expected rate of interest but, in principle, wage policy can change expected output E. Keynes's argument becomes clear if we define E in terms of income payments:

$$E \equiv (W^e/W)N^e + r^e K \qquad (6.4)$$

From the IS curve [equation (6.1) and Figure 6.1], a sufficient increase in E raises Y/W to Y^*/W^*, the full employment equilibrium. To achieve this increase by wage policy, W must fall relative to W^e. The problem is not simply W but W^e. Here, Keynes's assumption about extrapolative expectations controls his conclusion. W can fall relative to W^e in the short run but not in the long run since there can be no long-run equilibrium with W less than W^e. Further, if W^e falls faster than W (or at the same rate), wage reduction reduces E (or leaves E unchanged).

Cyclical fluctuations in money wages cannot be relied on to increase the demand for investment. Keynes makes two arguments that are contradictory, as he clearly notes. First, as just discussed, a gradual reduction of money wages generates expectations of a further fall; entrepreneurs extrapolate, wait for the additional reduction, and delay investment. Second, if there is a general belief that the fall in money wages will not persist, wage reduction reduces short-term loans and interest rates more than long-term loans and rates (7, p. 263).

Keynes's main reason for dismissing wage reduction is that, in a market economy, wage reduction is gradual. The fall in money wages would be most effective if it were large and sudden but, he says, this does not occur in a system of free-wage bargaining. Since institutional arrangements prevent quick changes, "it would be much better that wages should be rigidly fixed and deemed incapable of material changes" (ibid., p. 265).[12] In this case $W = W^e$, but the price level is more stable and, Keynes conjectures, uncertainty is reduced, lowering r^e.

Short-term increases in output can occur at times. If W falls relative

---

[12] This statement should not be mistaken for a belief that wages should be fixed by government. Chapter 19 of the *General Theory* gives no justification for the so-called Keynesian policy of guideposts and guidelines. Keynes *prefers* rigid money wages as a policy to avoid the depressing effect of uncertainty about the trend of wages and to reduce fluctuations. Democratic governments cannot fix expected wages, so efforts to control actual wages do not have lasting effects and can increase instability. His belief that wage increases were slow to occur is a foundation for his argument that future profits are overestimated during expansions as well as his argument about costs, prices, and profits in the *Treatise*. His discussion, of course, pertains to an economy with price changes but no inflation. Introducing inflation does not change the basic problem of relating actual and expected wages and their rates of change.

to W^e and there is no anticipation of a further reduction, costs of production are lower than their long-term expected value. In equation (6.4), E rises with the decline in W relative to W^e. Keynes recognizes, however, that a reduction in W that gives rise to expectations of a further decline can lower W^e relative to W and reduce aggregate demand. In Figure 6.1, a reduction in E appears as a shift of IS to the left. This suggests, again, that the model summarizes Keynes's views.

It is difficult to find support in Keynes's analysis for the interpretation known as the Keynesian special case. The liquidity trap is not offered as the reason for failure or unreliability of money or wage policy to remove underemployment equilibrium. Wages are not fixed, and the influence of changes in the stock of money on prices and real wages is not denied in his analysis. The problem is that the change in real wages may be too large or too small to *maintain* full employment at a level that can persist only if investment is at an *optimum*. Price expectations are affected by changes in money and wages, and expectations are volatile, driven by the action of short-term speculators who are influenced by the policy changes and their guesses or beliefs about what is to follow.[13]

In an exchange of letters with Hubert Henderson (29, pp. 219–31) Keynes makes clear that he did not intend his theory to apply only to the short run. The discussion concerns the effect of a change in money, but it applies equally to a change in wages. After pointing out that in his view the quantity of money in wage units matters even when all relative prices have adjusted to a change in money, he notes that his response deals with

> what happens in the *long run*, i.e., after the lapse of a considerable period of time rather than in the long period in the technical sense . . . When relative prices are out of equilibrium, particularly the prices of durable goods and the wage unit, extra complications enter into the determination of the rate of interest. But I need *no essential modification* of my theory of liquidity preference, operating on the quantity of money in terms of wage units, when by the lapse of time these complications are supposed to have evaporated. (ibid., pp. 221–2, emphasis added)

Keynes does not prove that reducing money wages would fail to

---

[13] Keynes's recommendations for stable monetary policy differ markedly from the variable policies practiced in the United States, the United Kingdom, and elsewhere in recent years that are often described as "Keynesian" policies. See 7, p. 203 where Keynes strongly supports rules – policies "rooted in strong conviction, and promoted by an authority unlikely to be superseded."

reduce unemployment, nor does he claim to. His analysis, like much of the *General Theory* puts the rabbit, expectations, into the underemployment hat. By introducing expectations, he shows why the arguments of the writers he called classical economists – calling for wage reduction to reduce unemployment – were unlikely to produce the desired result. Their analysis, based on the relation of costs, prices, and profits was flawed, he believed. The analysis failed to take account of the effects on the rate of interest, particularly the long-term or expected rate. It is the effect on the rate of interest relative to the marginal efficiency of capital that determines whether wage reduction reduces involuntary unemployment in Keynes's analysis, not the relation between wages, prices, and profits. He rejects proposals for money wage reduction as unlikely to produce a permanent increase in employment. He adds, consistent with the relative wage hypothesis, that an agreement by trade unions to reduce money wages would be unlikely to be durable if nonunion wages remain unchanged. This, too, affects expectations.[14]

In the chapter, "Notes on the Trade Cycle," Keynes is explicit about the reasons cycles persist. Wages and wage adjustments are not the main focus. Once again, investment, the marginal efficiency of capital, and the stock of capital are at the center of the argument. He gives three reasons for the persistence of cycles. Once expectations change, time must pass before decay and obsolescence reduce the capital stock and, thereby, raise the marginal efficiency. Inventories of finished and semifinished goods are reduced during the recession, so for a time there is disinvestment in inventories. Investment in working capital or raw materials declines also. The only reference to wages in his discussion is a mention of current costs of production as a factor reinforcing the effect of declining current returns to investment. At the peak of the expansion, costs of production may be high relative to expected future costs, "a further reason for a fall in the marginal efficiency of capital" (7, p. 317).

---

[14] Keynes's reasons for departing from classical economics are not based on a belief in "money illusion." One of his clearest criticisms of classical economics is in his discussion of Ricardo (7, pp. 191–2). Here, Keynes distinguishes two interpretations of the idea that monetary policy is nugatory. One meaning is that the real rate of interest (and other real variables) is independent of the quantity of money. This, Keynes says, is correct: "His [Ricardo's] conclusion would hold" (ibid., p. 191). The second meaning of monetary policy is "the terms on which it will increase or decrease the quantity of money" (ibid.). A change in the terms on which money is offered – a change in the policy rule – affects the *equilibrium* position that the economy reaches: "Assuming flexible money-wages, the quantity of money as such is, indeed, nugatory in the long period; but the terms on which the monetary authority will change the quantity of money enters as a real determinant into the economic schemes" (ibid.). In modern terms, a regime change is not neutral. As Chapter 5 of this volume emphasizes, Keynes was intensely interested in the choice of regime throughout his life.

Keynes's more extensive discussion of short-term changes in real wages occurs early in his book (7, pp. 9–10). He suggested that studies be undertaken of the relation between real and money wages. Dunlop (1938) and Tarshis (1938) responded. Keynes (7, pp. 394–412) interpreted their evidence for Britain and the United States as showing (1) that real and money wages rise together and (2) that when money wages fall, real wages may rise or fall. The positive association when money wages rise is contrary to Keynes's proposition, and the lack of association when money wages fall furnishes no support.

Keynes did not accept the evidence as decisive, but his reply qualifies his earlier proposition in several ways. The most important, for present purposes, is his clarification of the relation of his statements about real wages in Chapters 2 and 19 of the *General Theory*. Chapter 2 discusses the relation between real wages and output when there are changes in aggregate demand. Chapter 19 allows money and real wages to change in response to changes in prices caused by forces other than the change in aggregate demand. The "rigidity" of wages, assumed explicitly in Chapter 3, and the relation between money and real wages, is, therefore, a partial equilibrium result. To properly investigate this relation, Keynes indicates, prices must be held constant, and hourly wages must be used instead of the weekly wages available to Dunlop and Tarshis (see also 29, p. 285). This argument suggests that the proper way to read many of Keynes's propositions about wages is as statements about general equilibrium, as in Figure 6.1, and not as statements about the properties of the labor market in isolation.

Keynes draws two very relevant conclusions from his model. The first is a tentative conclusion that "short-period changes in *real wages* are usually so small compared with the changes in other factors that we shall not go far wrong if we treat *real wages* as substantially constant in the short-period" (7, p. 403, emphasis added).[15] The second conclusion is even more striking. After pointing out that the relation between real and money wages in the *General Theory* is the traditional relation, based on the writings of Marshall and Pigou, Keynes adds[16]:

---

[15] The claim that real wages are constant appears to be a complete contradiction of the statements in Chapter 17 of the *General Theory* (7, pp. 229–33, espec. p. 232) explaining why interest rates do not fall enough to maintain full employment. The contradiction vanishes, however, if Chapter 17 is interpreted as a statement that the market economy fails to reach Keynes's full, i.e., maximal, employment because the market system cannot unaided remove the discrepency between private and social returns to capital. The same interpretation of full employment reconciles Keynes's discussion on p. 249 of the *General Theory* with his later views.

[16] Keynes cites Marshall's testimony in the late-nineteenth century before the Gold and Silver Commission and before the Indian Currency Commission. In the latter, Marshall relied on some evidence published by Bowley. Keynes (7, p. 398) extends Bowley's series and finds that the data after 1886 do not support the "traditional" interpretation

That I was an easy victim of the traditional conclusion because it fitted my theory is the opposite of the truth. For my own theory this conclusion was inconvenient, since it had a tendency to offset the influence of the main forces which I was discussing and made it necessary for me to introduce qualifications. . . . If . . . it proves right to adopt the contrary generalisation, it would be possible to simplify considerably the more complicated version of my fundamental explanation which I have expounded in my "General Theory." (ibid., pp. 400–1)

It is difficult to read these conclusions either as insisting on wage inflexibility or as evidence that rigidity of money wages is the central tenet on which the *General Theory* stands or falls. Although Keynes did not accept the evidence produced by Dunlop and Tarshis as sufficiently persuasive to change his opinion about cyclical changes in wages, he makes clear that the main conclusions of the *General Theory* do not depend on rigid money wages.[17]

Even in the *General Theory*, the assumption that wages are rigid is advanced as a working hypothesis not a firm conclusion. Keynes starts by noting that a fixed money wage "is introduced solely to facilitate the exposition. The essential character of the argument is the same whether or not money wages, etc., are liable to change" (ibid., p. 27). He repeats this idea when he makes "a provisional assumption of a rigidity of money-wages rather than of real wages . . . [to] bring our theory nearest to the facts" (ibid., p. 276). He cites the experience of 1924–34 as a reason for making the assumption. The language is cautious and tentative, and the assumption is introduced to contrast his theory of employment with Pigou's and to explain why, in Keynes's words, his theory is a general theory whereas the classical theory is "one equation short" (ibid., p. 276).

Sidney Weintraub frequently called attention to the relative stability of the wage share. Weintraub's (1978, Chapter 3) statistical analysis excludes government employees and measures the share of wages relative to gross business product. In Weintraub's view, prices are set by

on which he had relied. Keynes seems unaware of Henry Thornton (1802) who explained fluctuations in output by asserting that prices are more flexible than money wages.

[17] The issue remains not fully resolved, but recent work does not support Keynes's generalization. Recent work is summarized in Bils (1985). Bils finds that real hourly wages are procyclical, contrary to Keynes. He tries to reconcile his findings, using panel data, with the findings of earlier studies using aggregate data that show no consistent relation.

marking up costs using a constant markup over average productivity (output per man).

If the wage share is stable or constant, the money wage will generally not be constant unless nominal output is constant or unless prices fall proportionally as output rises. Keynes's views on the wage share are very clear. He described

> the stability of the proportion of the national dividend accruing to labour, irrespective apparently of the level of output as a whole and of the phase of the trade cycle . . . [as] one of the most surprising, yet best-established facts in the whole range of economic statistics, both for Great Britain and for the United States. (7, pp. 408–9)[18]

The comments on the wage share were made two to three years after the publication of the *General Theory*, so it is possible that the wage share would have received more attention, and countercyclical real wages less, if he had revised the *General Theory*. No firm conclusion can be drawn. What we know for certain is that he retreated from the position he had taken in the *General Theory* about cyclical changes in real wages without abandoning his theory. It is difficult to believe, therefore, that rigid money wages are the key point of his theory, particularly in the light of his statement that abandoning the assumption would simplify the exposition.

Coordination failure

Axel Leijonhufvud's book (1968) forcefully points out that the Keynesian model popularized in the textbooks is far removed from Keynes's theory. Keynesian theory, as described by Leijonhufvud, is economics without prices, the type of income–expenditure model later characterized by Coddington (1983) as "hydraulic Keynesianism."[19]

Leijonhufvud recognizes that the textbook income–expenditure

---

[18] Keynes presents data that suggest what he meant by stability. The ratios for Britain show a maximum of 43.0 and a minimum of 40.7 for the years 1911 and 1924–35. For the United States, data for 1919–34 have a maximum of 39.3 and a minimum of 34.9. A footnote cites some earlier data for 1880. Keynes concludes from these few sample points that the ratio remained stable for fifty-five years. Since these data are not adjusted for productivity growth, it is clear that he could not believe that money wages remained constant. Keynes's policy of eliminating the rentier by driving the real rate of interest to zero would change the ratio, so contrary to Weintraub the ratio should not be treated as a constant.

[19] One of Leijonhufvud's main contributions is his insistence on taking Keynes at his word by reading the *General Theory* as a further development of the ideas in the *Treatise* (1968, pp. 16–17).

model has no role for money (1968, p. 13), whereas the *General Theory* gives money an important role. Keynes's later comments and papers, as well as the *General Theory*, repeat many times that liquidity preference and the stock of money determine the rate of interest, so money cannot be ignored. Further, Leijonhufvud rejects interpretations based on wage rigidity, and he rejects explanations of depression that depend on monopolies, labor unions, and the like. These interpretations of involuntary unemployment imply that "if 'competition' could only be restored, 'automatic forces' would take care of the employment problem" (ibid., p. 37). Leijonhufvud notes that Keynes was critical of such explanations.

Robert Clower (1965, in Clower 1969) had earlier developed the "dual-decision" process that eliminates market clearing by eliminating Walras's auctioneer and the *tâtonnement* process. Without an auctioneer, Clower argues, the economic system may fail to find prices that clear all markets simultaneously. The auctioneer has the function of coordinating markets and assuring that quantities supplied and demanded are brought to equality. Without an auctioneer, this result cannot be assured. Decisions to sell labor are not coordinated with decisions to buy goods. As a result, decisions made on the labor market today can constrain future aggregate demand. Clower recognizes (1969, p. 290) that there is no evidence that Keynes had the dual-decision process in mind.

Leijonhufvud (1968, pp. 47–8) adopted Clower's interpretation and added two elements of his own. The first, on which he originally placed much emphasis, is quantity adjustment. At one point, he calls this Keynes's only major innovation (ibid., p. 24). Later (1983, p. 196) he changed his mind, regarding the emphasis on quantity adjustment as too mechanical, "an open invitation to fix-price rationing modelling" (ibid.). The second is related but distinct. Leijonhufvud interprets the *General Theory* as a dynamic theory of disequilibrium, although he recognizes that his interpretation is speculative (ibid., p. 43).[20] To bolster his explanation, he offers the confusing argument that Keynes's "model was static, but his theory was dynamic" (ibid., p. 36). The apparent meaning is that Keynes, following Marshall, compressed a dynamic problem into a static framework by using "periods" (ibid., p. 50).

The main point of Leijonhufvud's argument, however, is his explanation of what he calls effective demand failures. These failures arise

---

[20] Earlier, Smithies offered a similar interpretation (1951, in Wood 1, p. 276). Quantity adjustment outweighs price adjustment. The multiplier amplifies the adjustment, so small changes have large effects. Smithies emphasizes that there is no formal accelerator process.

in the *General Theory* for reasons that are given or restated in Leijonhufvud (1983). There are two main propositions. First, long-term expectations are "ill-behaved" (ibid., p. 185); they cannot be explained
by the model or models used to predict outcomes and to forecast future
events. Second, shocks to the system, including especially shifts in the
marginal efficiency of capital schedule create a disequilibrium at which
saving is not equal to investment. Since there is no auctioneer or co-
ordinator for the system as a whole, the economy fails to reach intertemporal equilibrium. In expansions investment exceeds (planned) saving; credit expansion provides investors with command over resources.
In contractions, planned saving exceeds investment; credit contraction
pushes (or holds) the system below the equilibrium (ibid., p. 193).

I accept the first proposition if it means either that long period expectations are not always consistent with the model or that there are
permanent shifts in the marginal efficiency schedule – the familiar alternation of waves of optimism and pessimism. The second proposition
is closer to the lengthy development of the business cycle in the *Treatise* than to the *General Theory*. Keynes may have had this role for
the banking system in mind, but if this is so he was reluctant to say
so and often suggested the opposite. His chapter on business cycles
assigns an important role to shifts in the marginal efficiency of capital
and in liquidity preference. People shift from desiring to hold capital
to desiring to hold money. Changes in the demands for money and
capital, not changes in the supply of bank credit, are at the center of
Keynes's argument (7, pp. 315–16).

Leijonhufvud's argument suggests that changes in interest rates and
the supply of bank credit could eliminate (or reduce) the problem. For
Keynes, there is no hint that a different policy by the banking system
could prevent the decline in investment. In fact, he expresses strong
doubt that there is a "practicable reduction in the rate of interest"
(ibid., p. 320) that would expand investment to full employment or
even to the average rate of employment. He concludes by restating his
view that "the duty of ordering the current volume of investment cannot safely be left in private hands" (ibid., p. 320). In other words,
Leijonhufvud's coordination problem is remediable but, for Keynes,
the remedy is to remove the divergence between private and social
cost by maintaining a higher and more stable average rate of investment. Keynes reaffirms this view in a familiar passage written to argue
against restrictions on credit expansion by raising interest rates in a
boom: "The remedy for the boom is not a higher rate of interest but
a lower rate of interest!" (ibid., p. 322).

Leijonhufvud emphasizes that everyone is not equally informed. He
tries to use differences in information to explain why a negative demand

shock results in unemployment of workers instead of money wage reduction. Once the reduction in employment occurs, consumption is affected. Buyers are constrained by the reduction in earned income, and the reduced demand triggers the multiplier, further reducing employment: "The unemployment that persists in the system *for this reason* Keynes called 'involuntary'" (Leijonhufvud 1983, p. 198).

This interpretation gives too much of a cyclical interpretation to involuntary unemployment and neglects the persistence, even permanence, of Keynes's average level of involuntary unemployment. Here, and elsewhere, Leijonhufvud ignores completely the difference between private and social cost of investment that I regard as the main reason that output and employment, on average, remain below their maximum values. Finally, although Keynes may have tried to develop ideas similar to those developed later by Clower and Leijonhufvud, as Leijonhufvud suggests (ibid., p. 198, n. 31), Keynes abandoned these efforts, so few, if any, signs of these arguments appear in his work.

Leijonhufvud's emphasis on differences in information as a reason for cyclical unemployment is a valuable insight. Market clearing models based on a representative, optimizing individual who knows whatever can be known (except about central bank policy) and who acts as if a Walrasian auctioneer coordinates all markets obstructs serious consideration of the searching, groping process by which people make decisions under uncertainty. Introducing costs of acquiring information seems a useful way to get price setting and quantity adjustment into the microfoundations of macrotheory. Whether or not Keynes had some of these ideas, he certainly did not develop them in the *General Theory*. Leijonhufvud's interpretation of Keynes should be seen as a possible research program that may eventually become a theory of fluctuations and unemployment. The theory may be called Keynesian, and it may provide the best statement of what Keynes would have had to say to reach some of his conclusions. There is no evidence that he developed these arguments in the *General Theory* or in the many exchanges that followed, and neither Leijonhufvud nor others claim that he did. We know that he explicitly rejects comparison with the Swedish economists on the grounds that he did not have a disequilibrium theory (14, p. 183).

Leijonhufvud misses what I regard as the main coordination failure stressed by Keynes. Private markets cannot reduce interest rates to the social minimum. Moral hazard, or moral risk in Keynes's terms, is a property of individual markets that can be reduced (or eliminated) by combining lenders and borrowers.

Two long-time students of Keynes's work accept key parts of Leijonhufvud's (1968) book, where Leijonhufvud (1983, p. 80) emphasizes quantity adjustment instead of price adjustment. Hicks (1982, p. 289 and elsewhere) urges that Keynes's theory must be treated as a dynamic theory with some prices held fixed by assumption. Hicks (1979, pp. 989, 992–3) repudiates his *Trade Cycle* (1950) as a ''narrowly Keynesian model'' and suggests that the central simplifications that form the basis of the *General Theory* are the use of fixed price markets for output and flexible price markets for financial assets. Harry Johnson (1976, in Wood 2, pp. 371, 378), following Leijonhufvud, points to quantity adjustment not wage rigidity as the major break with prior economic theory. On the other side, Grossman (1972) argues that Leijonhufvud's interpretation has little to do with Keynes's theory. Grossman (ibid., p. 28, n. 11) claims that prices, but not wages, adjust instantaneously in the *General Theory*.

In my interpretation of Keynes's theory, the response of the price level is given by the slope of the SS curve. The steeper the SS curve in Figure 6.1, the larger is the change in price level per unit change of output. Since the price level does not affect Y/W, r, E, r^e, or M/W, neither the absolute value of the price level nor its rate of change affects the stock-flow equilibrium position. Keynes makes use of this lack of relationship to simplify his analysis, as noted earlier. In the last half of the book, Keynes puts the elasticity of p with respect to Y/W between 0 and 1 until full employment is reached. There is no suggestion that the precise value is important, as required by Leijonhufvud's (1968) analysis and Hicks's interpretation.

Elasticity pessimism

Many interpretations of the *General Theory* emphasize Chapter 3, called ''The Principle of Effective Demand.'' This chapter appears in the early part of the book where Keynes holds wages and prices fixed. The chapter is written to present a summary or outline of the theory, not the theory itself (7, p. 27). Keynes also uses the chapter to introduce the notions of effective demand and aggregate demand, two ideas that, he points out, had not been part of traditional economic analysis (ibid., p. 32).[21] Aggregate demand is a schedule, and effective demand is the point at which the aggregate demand schedule intersects the aggregate supply function (ibid., p. 25). Keynes points out that the main point of his book is to determine where this point is. Chapter 3 also discusses

[21] Eshag (1963, pp. 106–7), who finds antecedents for most of Keynes's ideas in Marshall, credits Keynes with reviving the concept of aggregate demand found earlier in Malthus and Hobson.

his denial of Say's law and his conclusion that the economy can reach equilibrium at less than full employment.[22]

The unifying theme of the interpretations to be grouped under "elasticity pessimism" is that changes in interest rates have little effect on the economy. The reason is either that the interest elasticity of the demand for money is high while the interest elasticity of investment demand is low or that interest rates have reached a low level where they cease to have much influence. For some interpretations, the low-level liquidity trap is used to bolster the argument, but this is not uniformly true and is explicitly rejected by some writers. The common thread joining the interpretations is not, therefore, the liquidity trap. It is the belief that, for one reason or another, interest rates do not adjust enough (or fast enough) to restore equilibrium at full employment.

Hansen (1953) is one of many who bases much of his interpretation of the *General Theory* on Chapter 3. His *Guide to Keynes* sees the chapter as the key and presents the substance in terms of the now familiar Keynesian cross diagram where aggregate supply is given by the 45° line and aggregate demand is a function of employment (income). There are no prices, no interest rates, and no expectations. Later, Hansen (ibid., p. 84) minimizes the role of interest rates. Although he praises Chapter 12 on expectations as "brilliant" (ibid., p. 125), he does not tie the discussion of expectations into either investment or money in his presentation of Keynes's theory. And he describes some of Keynes's discussions of money, economic policy, and other ideas as inconsistent, wrong, puzzling, or fanciful (ibid., pp. 132, 155, 215, for example). Hansen misinterprets Keynes's statements about neutrality (7, pp. 266–7) of the equilibrium level of employment as statements about the elasticity of the demand for money.

Keynes, in contrast, brings expectations into his Chapter 3 (ibid., p. 24, n. 3), insists that the constancy of money wages and other costs is "a simplification with which we shall dispense later" (ibid., p. 27), and also mentions that interest rates and money must be brought into his theory (ibid., pp. 28, 32). A major difficulty with Hansen's interpretation is that he fails to show how the simplified model of Keynes's Chapter 3, which abstracts from these forces, is related to the complete model in which money, interest rates, prices, and expectations affect

---

[22] The description of full employment deserves emphasis. Keynes (7, p. 89) defines full employment as a *maximum* level of employment – the level at which the marginal disutility of labor equals the real wage. Some readers of my earlier article (Meltzer 1981) objected to my equating full employment with maximum employment and the equating of maximum with the (dynamic) production frontier, but I can find no other interpretation of this and similar statements.

aggregate demand, effective demand, and the equilibrium position. A valid interpretation of the *General Theory* should be consistent with more than the simplified, bare bones exposition.

Patinkin (1976) reaches a conclusion similar to Hansen's from a different starting point. Like Hansen, he summarizes Keynes's analysis in the 45° diagram (ibid., pp. 88, 106), but he offers a different explanation.[23] Patinkin finds "*the apex of the General Theory*" in Keynes's Chapter 19. He interprets the arguments of the chapter as a statement that flexible wage policy cannot maintain full employment. Adverse expectations start a decline that cumulates. Unemployment reduces money wages, increases the quantity of money in wage units, lowers the interest rate, and starts a cumulative process that restores full employment. Patinkin, then, invokes elasticity pessimism: "The essence of Keynes' argument . . . is that because of a relatively high interest elasticity of the demand for money interacting with a relatively low interest elasticity of demand for investment – both of whose effective magnitudes are very much influenced by the state of expectations – this automatic adjustment process is not very efficacious" (1976, p. 106). Although Patinkin (ibid., pp. 105–6) does not mention the price level, he summarizes his discussion in a diagram in which prices change as demand shifts along the aggregate supply curve. Once full employment output is reached, output is fixed.[24]

Patinkin interprets the *General Theory* as an analysis of an economy in dynamic disequilibrium (1965, pp. 323–4; 1976, p. 113). He recognizes that "dynamic analysis received scant attention . . . indeed it is barely adverted to outside of Chapter 3" (ibid., p. 86). He defends his

[23] Patinkin (1978, p. 139) also uses the familiar Keynesian cross to summarize the theory. Patinkin emphasizes the role of changes in output as an equilibrating device. Patinkin (1976, p. 118) recognizes some role for price changes, but these are discussed in passing to express doubt about Leijonhufvud's (1968) contention that Keynes's theory replaced price adjustment with quantity adjustment. I find it difficult to reconcile this passage with Patinkin's emphasis on quantity adjustment in his 1978 article. I have difficulty also reconciling Patinkin's use of the Keynesian cross with his explicit rejection of the diagram (1965, p. 339). Elsewhere (e.g., 1979), Patinkin develops an interpretation of the aggregate supply function and both there and in later writing continues a controversy about Keynes's aggregate supply function. The latter is not a central issue here.

[24] In the equations for demand, aggregate demand depends on real output, the rate of interest, and the state of long-term expectations (Patinkin 1976, pp. 105–6). A few pages later, Patinkin (p. 117) discusses the adjustment using a diagram drawn in the price–output plane, as noted in the preceding footnote. In an earlier discussion (Meltzer 1981), I was misled by the absence of prices in Patinkin's discussion of his Figure 10.1 and by the use of axes in this figure showing real magnitudes (in wage units). Patinkin (1976, pp. 90–1) notes that prices change as the economy moves along the aggregate supply curve of this diagram, and this is required to reach Keynes's conclusion that real wages fall as output rises. I regret this error of interpretation in my earlier work.

interpretation by pointing to two passages in the *General Theory*. In one of them Keynes discusses an economy whose money wage level and rate of interest are continuously falling, but "whose schedule of the marginal efficiency of capital is falling more rapidly than the rate of interest" (7, p. 173, quoted by Patinkin, 1976, p. 113). In the other, Patinkin (ibid., p. 113, n. 10), quotes Keynes's statement (7, p. 236) that "the rate of interest declines more slowly, as output increases, than the marginal efficiencies of capital-assets measured in terms of it." Neither interpretation concerns dynamic disequilibrium. The first appears as part of Keynes's discussion of qualifications to the proposition that an increase in the quantity of money can, under certain conditions, fail to lower the interest rate. The passage Patinkin quotes is part of a paragraph explaining why increases in money, at times, may not stimulate the economy and containing the oft-quoted passage about slippage between the cup and the lip. The second appears as part of Keynes's discussion in Chapter 17 explaining why an economy with money (an asset having a low elasticity of production and substitution) can reach equilibrium at less than full employment.[25]

The explanation of Patinkin's misinterpretation is his desire to explain persistent departures from full employment without relying on either rigid money wages or the liquidity trap (1976, p. 114). He recognizes that in equilibrium the rate of interest must remain constant, so if money wages are flexible, he believes a liquidity trap is required in a static model to hold the interest rate constant. Since he interprets the *General Theory* as a dynamic theory, and he neglects or minimizes the role of interest rate expectations in setting the level around which interest rates – particularly long-term rates – fluctuate, he can find no other way to explain why an economy with changing prices, wages, and interest rates experiences persistent unemployment. He falls back on sluggish, dynamic adjustment and, therefore, relies on elasticity pessimism, though he recognizes that Keynes does not make this argument (1965, p. 339; 1976, p. 86).

In fact, Keynes makes a very different argument with considerable emphasis on expectations and not much emphasis on sluggish ad-

---

[25] Later, Patinkin (1976, p. 140, n. 4) notes that Keynes wrote: " 'Short-period expectations are always fulfilled'." He interprets this correctly as a statement about short-period equilibrium, but he does not attempt to reconcile this statement with his conclusion about disequilibrium. Patinkin's interpretation of Keynes's underemployment equilibrium as a position of disequilibrium is a restatement of the position developed in Chapter 13 of Patinkin (1965, esp. pp. 323–4). Neither this chapter nor the following (Chapter 14) provides an adequate interpretation of short- and long-period expectations or of the effect of long-period expectations on investment, of investment on capital and, thus, on the suboptimal position of equilibrium. Rather, expectations enter (ibid., pp. 337–8) as part of Patinkin's discussion of disequilibrium.

justment as a general problem. What matters is the relation between actual and expected rates and the credibility of policy: "The [actual] short-term rate of interest is easily controlled by the monetary authority . . . But the long-term rate may be more recalcitrant when once it has fallen to a level which, on the basis of past experience and *present expectations* of *future* monetary policy, is considered 'unsafe' by representative opinion" (7, pp. 202–3, some emphasis added). The response to interest rates depends on expectations and on beliefs about the permanence of change: "A monetary policy which strikes public opinion as being experimental in character or easily liable to change may fail in its objective of greatly reducing the long-term rate of interest . . . The same policy . . . may prove easily successful if it appeals to public opinion as being reasonable and practicable and in the public interest" (ibid., p. 203). In modern terms, long-term rates cannot be reduced unless policy is credible and the lower rates are expected to persist. A credible, predictable monetary policy – a policy rule – can contribute by lowering the risk premium not by alternating unsystematically between expansion and contraction or by trying to stabilize income by raising interest rates to slow expansions (ibid., p. 322).

In the model summarized in Figure 6.1, the expected rate of interest is r_0. As long as this rate is unchanged, policy can do little to change the equilibrium position:

> *Any* level of interest which is accepted with sufficient conviction as *likely* to be durable *will* be durable; subject, of course, in a changing society to fluctuations for all kinds of reasons round the expected normal . . . If it is the prevailing opinion that the rate of interest is self-adjusting, . . . the failure of employment to obtain an optimum level [is] in no way associated, in the minds either of the public or of authority, with the prevalence of an inappropriate range of rates of interest. (ibid., pp. 203–4)

Patinkin's discussion of gradual adjustment (1976, pp. 102–7) treats Keynes's comparative statics propositions and speculations about the determination of the position of equilibrium as a discussion of cyclical dynamics. An example is found on page 103. Here, Patinkin begins by citing parts of Keynes's analysis of the formation of long-run expectations and the interrelation of interest rates, expectations, and the demands for capital and money. He then chides Keynes for failing at times to distinguish "precisely, if at all, between the results due to the properties of a given demand curve and those due to a shift in the curve itself" (ibid., p. 103). The illustrative example is a reference to Keynes's discussion (7, p. 172) of some circumstances in which the interest rate becomes relatively insensitive to changes in money (a near liquidity trap) and the effect of the "trap" on the stability of the (comparative statics) equilibrium position. Keynes's discussion is not at all concerned with dynamics in the section that Patinkin cites.

Keynes's discussion of fluctuations, (ibid., Chapter 22) starts by noting that the preceding chapters show "what determines the volume of employment at any time" (ibid., p. 313). I do not see how this can be read except as a statement about the equilibrium position, implying that previous chapters are mainly concerned with comparative statics and the determination of the equilibrium position. The discussion of fluctuations begins in the "late stages of the boom" (ibid., p. 315). The "predominant explanation of the crisis is . . . a sudden collapse of the marginal efficiency of capital" (ibid.). Keynes is not open to Patinkin's criticism. A footnote makes clear that the discussion concerns the schedule, not a movement along the schedule. Keynes then explains why business cycles last as long as they do and why their duration is relatively constant. His explanation highlights the role of the marginal efficiency schedule and expectations about future returns. In these pages, he recognizes the importance of a decline in interest rates but stresses the factors changing expectations. To quote, again:

> If a reduction in the rate of interest was capable of proving an effective remedy by itself, it might be possible to achieve a recovery without the elapse of any considerable interval of time and by means more or less directly under the control of the monetary authority. But, in fact, this is not usually the case; and it is not so easy to revive the marginal efficiency of capital, determined as it is, by the uncontrollable and disobedient psychology of the business world. (ibid., pp. 316–17)

Patinkin's discussion of the recovery does not emphasize the revival (change) in expectations. Instead, Patinkin relies on the interest elasticities of the investment schedule and the demand for money to explain why the interest rate does not quickly fall to the level required to restore full employment. His discussion fails to separate the shift in the investment schedule that Keynes expected to follow an eventual reduction in pessimism – a change in expectations – from the movement along the investment demand schedule induced by a cyclical decline in interest rates. (See Patinkin 1976, pp. 103–6.)[26]

[26] Patinkin's discussion (1976, pp. 105–6) starts from a position of full employment. A wave of adverse expectations lowers the demand function for investment. The economy slowly returns to Q, described as full employment output (sic), through a process in which money wages decline so that money per unit of wages rises. This rise in real money balances reduces interest rates and increases investment. The restoration of equilibrium at full employment by lowering interest rates is contrary to Keynes's repeated statements.

Patinkin's failure to grasp the main point of the *General Theory* is illustrated by his comment on Keynes's 1937 response to some of his critics in the *Quarterly Journal of Economics* (14, pp. 109–23). Patinkin dismisses (1976, pp. 141–42) Keynes's argument as partly a repetition of the *Treatise* and partly a commonplace. He fails to recognize the central role of expectations and uncertainty in Keynes's explanation of (1) the position of the demand curve for money and the quantity of equilibrium real balances; (2) the effect of this demand on the equilibrium rate of interest, the expected rate of interest and, therefore, the volume of investment; and (3) the direct effect of expectations on the marginal efficiency schedule and the volume of investment. Having discarded these major determinants of the position that Keynes described as underemployment equilibrium, Patinkin looks for dynamic elements that are not there. He replaces Keynes's clear statements in the *General Theory* and after that full employment is rarely achieved and does not persist with his own belief that there is a slow return, but nonetheless a return, to full employment. Figures 10.1 and 11.1 of Patinkin (ibid., pp. 106, 117) and the accompanying text show the adjustment process departing from, or returning to, the position of full employment. (See also Patinkin 1975, in Wood 1, p. 494.)

Hicks's first reaction to the *General Theory* (1936, reprinted in 1982, pp. 96–7) interprets Keynes's unemployment as partly secular. He explains secular unemployment by the absence of attractive investments at low rates of interest. Hicks explains that heightened risk encourages saving but reduces investment and contributes to an excess of saving over investment. A floor to the interest rate prevents restoration of equilibrium. This was a promising start, although there is no mention of the difference between private and social returns. At the time Hicks, along with many others, did not bring in the real balance effect to remove disequilibrium. Later, in the third of his lectures on the two triads, Hicks (1967, pp. 52–3) explained that he does not believe that the real balance effect is symmetric. Rising prices and falling real balances induce increases in reserve balances but, Hicks claims, the reverse is less certain. An increase in money will "make expansion possible; but it is not easy to see that it can be an effective agent for bringing it about" (ibid., p. 53).

Viner (1936, in Wood 2, pp. 85–98) offers an interpretation of Keynes's underemployment equilibrium that stresses the public's desire to hold money instead of capital, but he argues that Keynes is wrong: "Keynes has grossly exaggerated the extent to which liquidity preferences have operated in the past and are likely to operate in the future as a barrier to 'full' employment" (Viner 1936, in Wood 2, p. 89).

Viner's comment drew a response from Keynes:

There are passages which suggest that Professor Viner is thinking too much in the more familiar terms of the quantity of
money actually hoarded, and that he overlooks the emphasis
I seek to place on the rate of interest as being the inducement
not to hoard. It is precisely because the facilities for hoarding
are strictly limited that liquidity preference mainly operates by
increasing the rate of interest . . . When, as happens in a crisis,
liquidity preferences are sharply raised, this shows itself not
so much in increased hoards – for there is little, if any, more
cash which is hoardable than there was before – as in a sharp
rise in the rate of interest . . . A rise in the rate of interest is
a means *alternative* to an increase of hoards for satisfying an
increased liquidity preference. (14, pp. 110–11)[27]

Here, Keynes rejects the "low interest rate" interpretation of the
liquidity problem. Slow adjustment of interest rates is not mentioned.
The problem is that when people want to hold money, given the quantity of money, the rate of interest rises, and investment falls. If investment was relatively unresponsive to interest rates, the problem
would be of minor importance. In the *General Theory*, as in the *Treatise*, Keynes took the opposite view, as the preceding quotation shows.
Shifts from capital to money drive up the rate of interest. Further,
sustained high demand for real balances is achieved at the expense of
investment and, ultimately, of the capital stock and the level of income.
The response to Viner is not an afterthought. In the *General Theory*
(7, p. 203), Keynes comments on the importance of conventions and
expectations as determinants of the level around which interest rates
fluctuate, and he remarks:

But it [the interest rate] may fluctuate for *decades* about a level
which is chronically too high for full employment . . .
   The difficulties in the way of maintaining effective demand at
a level high enough to provide full employment, which ensue
from the association of a conventional and *fairly stable* long-
term rate of interest with a fickle and highly unstable marginal
efficiency of capital, should be, by now, obvious to the reader.
(ibid., p. 204; emphasis added)

Once again Keynes insists that the expected (long-term) rate is too high

---

[27] The juxtaposition of "cash" and liquidity preference blurs the distinction between
nominal and real balances. The use of "hoarding" to describe money holding is a
throwback to earlier confusions.

(above the social optimum) and the marginal efficiency schedule is highly variable or unstable.

Harrod (quoted in Leijonhufvud 1968, p. 14) writes that "Keynes always attached the utmost importance to low interest rates; he never ceased to preach them." But, Keynes replied to Durbin:

> There are many passages in the book devoted to proving that attacks on the rate of interest by themselves are likely to prove an inadequate solution except perhaps temporarily. I, therefore, advocate measures designed to increase the propensity to consume, and also public investment independent of the rate of interest. (29, p. 232)

Moggridge and Howson quote Keynes's 1937 articles in *The Times* opposing efforts to change the long-term rate: "The long-term rate of interest must be kept *continuously* as near as possible to what we believe to be the long-term optimum" (1974, in Wood 1, p. 462). Here, Keynes was influenced by the increase in defense expenditures and preparations for war, factors that would raise interest rates.[28]

A clearer passage, relating to elasticity pessimism, is Moggridge and Howson's quotation from a comment Keynes sent to Mordecai Ezekial in 1941:

> I am far from fully convinced by the recent thesis that interest rates play a small part in determining the role of investment . . . I am quite unconvinced that low interest rates cannot play an enormous part in *sustaining* investment at a given figure, and when there is a movement from a higher rate to a lower rate in allowing a greater scale of investment to proceed over a very much longer period than would otherwise be possible (ibid., p. 463).

These comments are inconsistent with the view that Keynes believed (1) low-interest rates are ineffective and (2) that the response of investment to interest rates is slow or small. Moggridge and Howson's summary of Keynes's changing views on monetary policy rejects elasticity pessimism and monetary impotence. They conclude that "Keynes always believed that monetary policy was an important weapon of economic policy, although its exact role varied with circumstances and with Keynes's views as to how a capitalist economy works" (ibid., p. 465).

---

[28] Keynes's comments on the level of interest rates are put in context by his statement that current (1937) interest rates were above the rates prevailing in the nineteenth century (14, p. 132). Keynes believed that the nineteenth century had been characterized by a rate of investment sufficient to absorb saving at (or near) full employment.

There are many other dissents to the interpretation I have called elasticity pessimism. Lerner (Colander 1972, p. 8; Lerner 1961, in Wood 2, pp. 302–6) dismisses the liquidity trap as an essential element of Keynes's theory. Lerner describes the "Keynesian special case" popularized by Hicks (1937), Modigliani (1944), and others as a "caricature" (Lerner 1961, p. 303). Hicks (1974, pp. 34–6) departs from his earlier interpretation by introducing a spectrum of rates. Keynes's aim, to lower long-term rates in the depression, was difficult to achieve if speculators did not expect the change to last. This correct restatement of part of Keynes's theory brings in expectations that, Keynes noted, are missing from Hicks's (1937) article.[29] Kaldor (1983, pp. 10–11) dismisses the neoclassical synthesis and the liquidity trap, but he rejects the view that the monetary authority can restore equilibrium by lowering interest rates. However, Samuelson (1946, in Wood 2, p. 194) and Tobin (1948, in Wood 2, p. 251) emphasize deficient aggregate demand and dismiss or minimize the role of the demand for money and interest rates.

Not all of the interpretations that rely on elasticity pessimism invoke the liquidity trap, as we have seen. More relevant evidence on Keynes's views on the role of interest rates comes from his writings before and after publication of the *General Theory*. In his 1931 Harris lectures in Chicago, he urged a reduction in interest rates, particularly long-term rates, and gave examples of the types of long-term investment that would be stimulated (13, pp. 365–6). The tone is optimistic. Keynes talks about "growing richer on the principle of compound interest" (ibid., p. 366). But, he notes that confidence (expectations) is important and, returning to a theme that runs from *The Economic Consequences of the Peace* to the *General Theory*, he expresses concern that in rich countries saving will rise faster than opportunities for investment (ibid., p. 367). In his 1937 Galton lecture, Keynes remains optimistic about future standards of living provided there is either a decline in the rate of saving or a permanent reduction in the long-term interest rate or both (14, p. 132–3). The notes prepared for his statement to the National Debt Inquiry in 1945 say:

> If, after the war, we need more saving to provide more investment, we have to reduce the rate of interest up to the point of full employment. Thereafter, the old rules apply[;] we have to raise the rate of interest to prevent inflation . . . The previous theory [the quantity theory] is what works in conditions of domestic full employments. (27, p. 390)

[29] Once there are multiple markets for distinct financial assets, a liquidity trap can be rejected. (See Brunner and Meltzer 1968.)

Each of these statements reflects his mature view that the (market) rate of interest should be held at the level consistent with full employment – the level he regarded as the social optimum. His 1945 statement, like his 1937 article, reflects concern about inflation and makes clear that he favored raising the market rate to prevent inflation.

These and many other passages do not show Keynes as a proponent of elasticity pessimism. He favored policies to reduce interest rates to the level at which investment would absorb saving at full employment. That rate, he believed, would bring interest rates to zero in a generation. This is the correct interpretation, I believe, of Keynes's statements favoring lower interest rates.

A remaining problem with interpretations that rely on elasticity pessimism is the narrow focus that it gives to the book. Experience since 1950 in Japan, Western Europe, and North America has been characterized by relatively short recessions and, until the 1980s, by much lower rates of unemployment than experienced in Britain during the interwar period. Interpretations of the *General Theory* based on elasticity pessimism can explain these changing circumstances within that framework only by invoking changes in the size of the elasticities, first an increase then a decrease. An explanation of this kind removes the content from the *General Theory*.

Irrational expectations

Another interpretation of the *General Theory* sees irrational expectations as the central idea. Coddington (1983, p. 87) writes: "The irrationality of long-run expectations was something vigorously propounded by Keynes in the *General Theory*, and constitutes his ground for seeing investment in fixed capital as the volatile destabilizing element in the economy." Hicks refers to the "wicked" Chapter 12 of the *General Theory* on long-term expectations as the root of the trouble: "One can grant that there exists an irrational element without contending that they are so irrational as to be random" (1969, p. 213).

The leading proponent of irrationality as the central feature of the *General Theory* is G. L. S. Shackle. Shackle had been a student of Hayek at the London School of Economics. Hayek's stress on uncertainty about the future, a central theme in his analysis of dynamics and in his arguments for the superiority of free markets over planned economies, may be the source of Shackle's views. Whatever the source, Shackle stressed uncertainty about the future and the irrationality of expectations in a series of books and papers over many years.

According to Shackle (1961, pp. 211, 218) Keynes was concerned only with short-period equilibrium analysis. He writes that Keynes "saw as the main theme of his book the commanding importance of uncertainty . . . and the nonsense it makes of pure 'rational calculation'" (ibid., p. 211).

In a later work, Shackle (1967, p. 129) takes a stronger position: "Keynes's whole theory of unemployment is ultimately the simple statement that, rational expectation being unattainable, we substitute for it first one and then another kind of irrational expectation." He speaks, of the "deliberate self-deception of business, in supposing its investment decisions to be founded on knowledge and to be rationally justifiable" (ibid., p. 132). And he attributes involuntary unemployment "to men's failure to secure, in good time, knowledge of each others' conditional intentions or potential reactions" (ibid., pp. 140–1).

Shackle finds the explanation for unemployment in the use (or holding) of money in a world of prevasive uncertainty. Money does not reduce the cost of bearing uncertainty. It "enlarges the hurtful power of uncertainty at the same time as it enormously facilitiates the beneficent power of specialization" (ibid., p. 137). The result is "general overproduction" (ibid., p. 136), a term that Keynes does *not* use to describe involuntary unemployment. Shackle then redefines involuntary unemployment as the result of a failure to obtain knowledge of the (separate) conditional intentions of savers and investors and to coordinate these intentions. He reaches the odd conclusion that this failure of coordination arises most readily in an economy using money (ibid., pp. 140–1).

Earlier, Shackle (1961a, in Wood 1, p. 330) explained this puzzling statement by pointing out that money permits the saver to refrain from investing in capital. But, Shackle does not carry the argument to the aggregate level. Instead, he rejects Keynes's argument and concludes that saving and investment are *identical* in the *General Theory*; they are "but two names for the same thing" (1961, p. 334).[30]

What Keynes says is less obscure. In an economy with money, people hold part of their wealth in real balances. As a result, the rate of interest is higher (than if they held less money), and investment is lower. Therefore, there is less capital, less output, and less employment for given wage rates and other conditions, such as tastes and productivity. Keynes concludes that "in the absence of money . . . the rates of interest would only reach equilibrium [at] . . . full employment" (7, p. 235). In other words, if people did not hold real balances, interest

---

[30] Keynes (14, p. 211) criticized Hawtrey for making this claim. Mr. Hawtrey thinks that saving and investment "are two different names for the same thing." Keynes went on to explain how Hawtrey had erred. It is surprising to see this claim repeated by Shackle in the 1960s after the lengthy discussion of this issue in the 1930s.

rates would be lower and investment higher. Nothing would prevent interest rates from reaching the full employment level.

This argument makes an invalid comparison between an economy with money and one without, and it suggests (but does not say) that the introduction of money lowers output and employment.[31] Without an assumption of this kind, the comparison has no meaning.

While Hansen finds the main point of the *General Theory* in Chapter 3 and Patinkin in Chapter 19, Shackle (1967, pp. 132, 152) finds the main point in Chapter 12 and in Keynes's 1937 paper in the *Quarterly Journal* (14, pp. 109–23). This tendency to choose one chapter as "the essential chapter" is peculiar. Although I share Shackle's view that expectations are an important element, Keynes gives no reason, in Chapter 12 or elsewhere, to accept Shackle's claim that rational calculation is impossible.

Keynes makes the opposite claim in the very chapter that Shackle is fond of citing:

> We should not conclude . . . that everything depends on waves of irrational psychology. On the contrary, the state of long-term expectation is often steady, and, even when it is not, the other factors exert their compensating effects. We are merely reminding ourselves that human decisions affecting the future, whether personal or political or economic, cannot depend on strict mathematical expectation, since the basis for making such calculations does not exist; and that it is our innate urge to activity which makes the wheels go round, our rational selves choosing between the alternatives as best we are able, calculating where we can, but often falling back for our motive on whim or sentiment or chance. (7, pp. 162–3)

The juxtaposition of rational decision with whim or chance and the claim that decisions are rational but not governed by mathematical expectation are familiar themes in Keynes's writing. A main point of Keynes's *Treatise on Probability* (JMK 8) is to explain how rational individuals form beliefs or make inferences about an uncertain future using subjective (nonobjective) probabilities. In the *General Theory* (7, p. 148), Keynes refers to his earlier work when he distinguishes between the expectations people hold and the confidence or certainty with which they are held. The distinction is important to him. In the *Treatise on Probability*, he insists that our knowledge of the truth of

---

[31] See Brunner and Meltzer (1971) for an analysis of the private and social gains from using a medium of exchange (money). Keynes does not address the question of whether the introduction of money lowers the equilibrium (social) rate of return.

a proposition is uncertain (8, pp. 3–4). The probability that we attribute to a *rational* belief is subjective (ibid., p. 19).

The *Treatise on Probability* applies probability to propositions not to events. A person has a degree of belief in the truth or falsity of a proposition. Early in the book (8, pp. 28, 30–31) he rejects Bentham's calculus by which people can make numerical comparisons of objective probabilities. The same idea reappears in his 1937 article where he rejects the Benthamite calculus as a guide to the future (14, pp. 114, 122). In both statements, Keynes should be interpreted as opposed to objective, measured probabilities about future events, not as opposed to the use of partial knowledge to make rational decisions about uncertain, future events.[32]

The view of uncertainty Keynes expresses in the *General Theory* and in his 1937 paper is not a novel idea developed at the time. A similar idea is in his 1910 paper on free trade[33] where he states his belief that the investor's decision is determined

> not by the net income which he will actually receive from his investment in the long-run, but by his expectations. These will often depend upon fashion, upon advertisement, or upon purely irrational waves of optimism or depression. Similarly by risk we must mean, not the real risk . . . but the risk as it is estimated, wisely or foolishly . . .
>
> Since the risk of which we must take account is the subjective risk, the feeling, that is to say, in the mind of the investor, its magnitude very largely depends upon the amount of relevant information regarding the investment that is easily accessible to him. (15, p. 46)

This early view reflects both the work that Keynes had done on probability theory and the influence of Marshall. Moggridge and Howson (1974, in Wood 1, p. 455) note that in 1921 Keynes "explained fluctuations in terms of the conventional [Marshallian] model of businessmen's errors of optimism and pessimism." Keynes's beliefs about

---

[32] See the introduction to the *Treatise on Probability* (8, pp. xv–xxii) by Richard Braithwaite and the discussion by Hishiyama (1969, in Wood 1, pp. 373–92). Braithwaite points out that Keynes's main reason for writing on probability theory was "to explain how a degree of belief could be rational" (8, p. xxi). Hishiyama (1969, pp. 382–4) suggests that the criticism of Benthamite probability is intended as a criticism of Pigou. Chapter 26 of the *Treatise on Probability* discusses the application of probability to ethical conduct. Keynes rejects Bentham's theory of conduct based on the calculation of probabilities of outcome. Unless one is certain, probabilities are not a guide to truth (8, p. 356). Keynes also criticizes G. E. Moore's discussion of this issue (8, pp. 341–2) despite the importance of Moore in forming Keynes's early views.

[33] Much of the *Treatise on Probability* was written between 1906 and 1911, although the book was not published until 1921 (8, p. xv).

the cause of shifts in investment and the role of expectations and uncertainty remained much the same in the 1930s. The marginal efficiency of capital schedule is a more formal statement of the hypothesis that investment depends on subjective evaluation of future outcomes. This schedule was at times "unruly," reflecting the alternation of investors' optimism and pessimism. The *General Theory* differed from Keynes's earlier work, however, by making the *equilibrium* level of income, around which fluctuations occur, depend on the degree of uncertainty, reflected in the demand to hold money instead of capital in portfolios. Keynes summarized his position this way:

> It is an outstanding characteristic of the economic system in which we live that, whilst it is subject to severe fluctuations in respect of output and employment, it is not violently unstable. Indeed, it seems capable of remaining in a chronic condition of sub-normal activity for a considerable period without any marked tendency either towards recovery or towards complete collapse. (7, p. 249)

On the following pages, Keynes lists the conditions that maintain this stable outcome.

Shackle appears to have misinterpreted what Keynes wrote. There is, without doubt, discussion of irrationality and chance in the *General Theory*, but these are not the dominant themes and, for Keynes, these themes do not begin in the *General Theory*. Keynes had, from the earliest days, believed that the future is uncertain, that probabilities are not measurable, and that uncertain and improbable are not different words for the same concept. He had rejected the Benthamite calculus thirty years earlier, and in its place he put his own view of subjective probability.

Keynes regarded his concept of uncertainty as essential to explain two features of a monetary economy. The first is why people hold money as an asset and the consequence of their decisions to hold wealth in that form. This problem is posed in the *Treatise*. His explanation in the *General Theory* is that the demand for "money as a store of wealth is a barometer of the degree of our own calculations and conventions concerning the future" (14, p. 116). This statement reflects Keynes's experience under the gold standard and his conclusion that a relatively high, persistent demand for gold (or governmental note issue) raises the rate of interest, reduces investment, and, by reducing the capital stock, lowers per capita income. The LM curve of Figure 6.1 intersects the IS curve to the left of full employment, and society remains in a suboptimal position as long as people's uncertainty about the future remains unchanged. Second is the effect of sudden changes in belief.

Here the waves of optimism and pessimism enter. People's beliefs change and from these changes follow changes in the rate of interest, the prices of capital assets, and the rate of investment. Keynes concludes his argument by noting that *if* objective probabilities could be assigned to future events, "the liquidity preference curve . . . [would be] both stable and very inelastic" (ibid., p. 119). There would be zero (or very small) demand for money as an asset, and "available resources would normally be employed" (ibid.). The LM curve of Figure 6.1 would intersect the IS curve at some point on the full employment line, Y^*/W^*. Say's law would hold, and the classical theory would be relevant.

Nothing in the quotation in the previous paragraph, taken from the 1937 article cited so frequently by Shackle, suggests that irrationality plays a dominant role. The economy that Keynes discusses is not at full employment equilibrium and cannot get there except temporarily because the level of investment is too small on average, and the capital stock is too low.

Gross substitution and finance

Currently, so-called post-Keynesians are the most active group emphasizing expectations and uncertainty as the driving force in the *General Theory*. The post-Keynesians combine this emphasis with intense concentration on their own choice of a favorite chapter, Chapter 17 – "The Essential Properties of Interest and Money" – and on the role of money in "finance."[34] In a book (Davidson 1978) and in a number of articles (Davidson 1980 and 1984 are representative), Paul Davidson has carried forward the arguments of Shackle, Joan Robinson and, others about the role of expectations and uncertainty (Davidson 1978, pp. xii, 7, 13), but he has insisted that it is in the relation between money and liquidity that one finds the revolutionary aspect of the *General Theory*. Keynes, according to Davidson, wanted to deny "the axiom of gross substitution as a building block" (Davidson 1980, p. 305) for analyzing the economy. Keynes's analysis in Chapter 17 "requires that the elasticity of substitution between all liquid assets including money . . . and producible (in the private sector) assets is zero or negligible . . . Nonproducible assets that can be used to store savings are not gross substitutes for producible assets in savers' portfolios" (1984, p. 567). Money yields a stream of services that Keynes calls a liquidity premium (7, p. 240). No other asset provides equivalent services.

---

[34] Hansen claims that the discussion of own rates of interest in Chapter 17 of the *General Theory* "is confused and is of no real importance" (1953, p. 160).

Keynes is explicit, at several places, that the "essential"properties of money are (1) a near-zero elasticity of substitution and (2) small elasticity of production (ibid., pp. 230–1; 14, p. 119). The problem is to interpret the role these assumptions take in his theory and what he meant by them. This problem is made easier by Keynes's letter to Townshend:

> I am rather inclined to associate risk premium with probability strictly speaking, and liquidity premium with what in my *Treatise on Probability* I called "weight." An essential distinction is that a risk premium is expected to be rewarded on the average by an increased return at the end of the period. A liquidity premium, on the other hand, is not even expected to be so rewarded. It is a payment, not for the expectation of increased tangible income at the end of the period but for an increased sense of comfort and confidence during the period. (29, pp. 293–4)

Weight is a measure of the uncertainty assigned to the probability that a hypothesis about some future event is true. Classical theory ignores uncertainty of this kind, so it ignores the demand for money to satisfy the liquidity yield – "the sense of comfort and confidence" that comes from holding money (in a noninflationary world) instead of *risky* assets. Keynes accepted that classical theory can accommodate a demand for inactive balances, so money can be held in portfolios. The important difference is that, in classical theory, the demand for inactive balances is inelastic with respect to the rate of interest. A decline in the transactions demand "has the effect of lowering the rate of interest by whatever extent is necessary to restore them [inactive balances] to their previous figure" (ibid., p. 258).[35]

Keynes gives the demand for money a clear and decisive influence on the position the economy reaches. When the degree of uncertainty changes, the demand for money (in wage units) changes. This shift in demand changes the rate of interest. If a higher degree of uncertainty persists, the expected interest rate rises. Investment is lower, the cap-

---

[35] Davidson, in a letter, dismisses Keynes's response to Townshend as an early attempt to treat the problem of stochastic processes. However, Keynes made the same point in his reply to Jacob Viner. He wrote:

> If . . . our knowledge of the future was calculable, and not subject to sudden changes, it might be justifiable to assume that the liquidity–preference curve was both stable and very inelastic. In this case a small decline in money income would lead to a large fall in the rate of interest, probably sufficient to raise output and employment to the full. (14, p. 119)

See also the footnote to the paragraph where Keynes restates the argument.

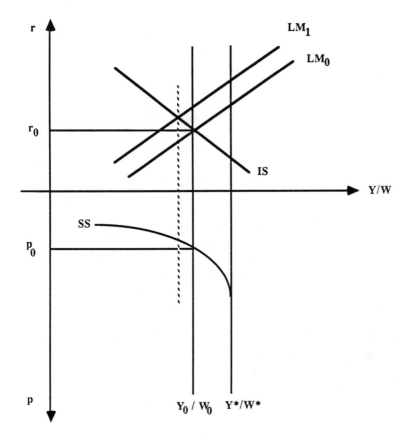

Figure 6.2

ital stock is eventually smaller, and expected income is lower than before.

Figure 6.2 shows equilibrium at Y_0/W_0, below the full employment level, Y^*/W^*. The economy remains in equilibrium as long as expectations are unchanged (and the capital stock is fixed); $r_0 = r_0^e$, $Y_0/W_0 = E$, and $p = p_0$ define the equilibrium. Changes in money perturb the system but, unless expectations change, the system returns to the underemployment equilibrium. Society is held in a suboptimal equilibrium by its beliefs.

Let the degree of uncertainty increase. Wealthowners now demand a larger liquidity premium to compensate for the increased uncertainty. Money provides this service, so equilibrium money holding (in wage units) increases. The LM curve shifts to the left, and the actual and expected rates of interest rise. The new equilibrium position is at a lower level of real income (in wage units), but it is an equilibrium conditioned on the new set of expectations. At the new equilibrium, investment is lower because interest rates are higher. Gradually, the capital stock falls with repercussions that, following Keynes, I ignore.

In a classical economy, according to Keynes, there is no uncertainty. The LM curve is farther to the right, and it is steeper; the demand for money is inelastic with respect to the rate of interest (ibid., p. 258). Changes in investment or consumption have larger effects on interest rates and smaller effects on real output. The economy fluctuates around a higher level of income. Output is higher and more stable. An economy of this kind would, of course, dominate Keynes's underemployment economy in a welfare sense; in Keynes's words, it would hold the optimal capital stock.

My interpretation of Keynes's statements about the essential properties of money can be summarized in the proposition that the public cannot drive the rate of interest down by producing money. A high price of wheat will encourage production and lower the price, but a high rate of interest does not stimulate production of nominal balances to drive down the interest rate. The adjustment must be made by a change in prices and money wages. Keynes gives a brief summary of his argument (7, p. 234). An increase in uncertainty raises the demand for money (liquidity). Labor cannot be employed to produce more (nominal) money, a proposition especially true of base money. There is no other commodity that can substitute for money in providing the liquidity service. Convention plays a large role in choosing the commodity used as money (ibid., p. 229): "It may be, for example, that gold will continue to fill this role in a country which has gone over to an inconvertible paper standard" (ibid.).

In Figure 6.2, an increased demand for money lowers the price level. Real wages rise, but money wages may fall. If money wages fall as the demand for money rises, the larger stock of real balances is achieved, at least in part, by a decline in money wages. A sufficient fall in money wages lowers the rate of interest by shifting the LM curve to the right. A fall in money wages also shifts the IS curve by changing expectations: "It is not possible to dispute on purely theoretical grounds that this reaction [the fall in money wages] might be capable of allowing an adequate decline in the money-rate of interest" (ibid., p. 232). Keynes is skeptical but, as in his discussion of money wage changes in Chapter 19 of the *General Theory*, he does not reach a firm conclusion.

This analysis of money or liquidity leads Keynes to a conclusion that is opposite to the conclusion reached in the neoclassical theory of money. To achieve optimality, recent neoclassical theory concludes that interest should be paid on money. Keynes concludes that the appropriate policy is to tax money balances so as to reduce money holding (ibid., p. 234). In my interpretation, the tax on money reduces the demand for liquidity services, shifts the LM curve to the right, reducing the market rate of interest, and permanently increasing the equilibrium level of real output. This achieves Keynes's result and is consistent with a main conclusion – perhaps the main conclusion – reached in Chapter 17:

> That the world after several millenia of steady individual sav-ing, is so poor as it is in accumulated capital-assets, is to be explained, in my opinion, neither by the improvident pro-pensities of mankind, nor even by the destruction of war, but by the high liquidity – premiums formerly attaching to own-ership of land and now attaching to money. (ibid., p. 242)[36]

This interpretation treats liquidity in much the same way that Fried-man (1969) treats the nonpecuniary return to money holding. To para-phrase Keynes (7, p. 240), the liquidity yield is the nonpecuniary return in safety or confidence that the money holder receives. Keynes wants to eliminate the return by taxing money balances; Friedman favors eliminating the return by satiating the demand for cash balances held for liquidity.

Keynes's discussion of liquidity differs from the interpretation of liquidity in Hicks (1974, pp. 38–9, 43, 57) where time has an important role. Hicks talks of "things which are unknown now, but will become known in time" (ibid., p. 39). Keynes, like Hicks, emphasizes that investors must look ahead. As long as the degree of uncertainty about the future remains unchanged, however, the passage of time has no effect on the demand for money. Short-term investments have more certain returns than long-term investments, but the difference in returns remains fixed on average. Keynes even assumes that short-term ex-pectations are fulfilled, but this does not remove the liquidity premium or eliminate the demand for money as an asset.[37]

---

[36] Keynes points out that money loses the attribute of liquidity if its future supply under-goes sharp changes (7, p. 241, n. 1). This statement is similar to his views about the destructive character of inflation and deflation written in the 1920s and contrary to the views of those like Kaldor (1982) who dismiss monetary changes as irrelevant.

[37] Tobin (1969, pp. 25–6) restates one part of Keynes's position when he states that the distinguishing characteristic of money is that its rate of interest is fixed by law or convention. He shows that the effects of changes in government debt and money on real returns depend on this convention. The zero rate of interest on money in Tobin (1969) follows from the assumption that the marginal product of money is zero. This dismisses Keynes's strictures about uncertainty. As noted in Brunner and Meltzer (1971), the assumption of zero or constant marginal productivity of money should have little appeal to economists. Keynes would not have accepted Tobin's assumption that

In addition to his concern for liquidity, Davidson also stresses the "finance motive" for holding money. He refers to this motive as the "Rosetta stone" of interest theory (Davidson 1978, p. 30). The issue about finance arose in Keynes's exchanges with Ohlin (and others) about saving, investment, and the theory of interest.[38] Keynes's statement in the *General Theory* that saving and investment are equal set off a lengthy, not very fruitful, discussion. In the course of the discussion, Ohlin pointed out that an increase in planned investment takes time to produce income, and therefore the saving that finances the investment lags behind the investment. Keynes accepted that some technique must be used "to bridge the gap between the time when the *decision* to invest is taken and the time when the correlative investment and saving actually occur" (14, p. 201). He then mentions several ways in which firms can finance planned activities, including investment, during the period in which plans are executed. One way is to accumulate a cash balance: "Let us call this advance provision of cash the 'finance' required by the current decisions to invest" (ibid.). Keynes makes a very similar argument in "Mr. Keynes on 'Finance'" (ibid., pp. 229–33).

This set off discussion of the "finance motive" for holding money. One of the participants was E. S. Shaw, who wrote to Keynes in the spring of 1938. In his reply Keynes explained that his use of the concept of "finance" was an attempt to express his ideas in a manner more compatible with the statements of his critics:

> "I do not consider that the concept of 'finance' makes any really significant change in my previous theory . . . [Finance] is no more than a type of active balance . . . I attached an importance to it in my article ["Alternative Theory of the Rate of Interest" 14, pp. 201–15] because . . . it provided a bridge between my way of talking and the way of those who discuss the supply of loans and credits etc. . . . . [Finance is] one of the

the marginal value of money services is constant at zero (or any other value). He speaks of a varying premium (7, p. 240). Grandmont and Laroque (1976) show that in a model with fiat money as the only store of value, an economy with exogenously fixed wages reaches temporary equilibrium at less than full employment. When wages reach their lower bound, labor is rationed by quantity not by price. Although their model has equilibrium at less than full employment, it seems far removed from Keynes's permanent underemployment equilibrium.

[38] Kahn (1984, p. 162) also regards the "finance" motive as important. Its importance arises, he claims, because it introduces availability of funds as a determinant of interest rates. Keynes had introduced availability in the *Treatise*, where he denies its importance for the United States. I do not see how Kahn can reconcile his interpretation with Keynes's statement in the text that follows. Further, Keynes says very little about credit availability and credit rationing. The most extensive passage is his discussion of the so-called fringe of unsatisfied borrowers in the *Treatise* (6, pp. 326–9). His later writings neither develop nor extend the argument.

sources of demand for liquid funds arising out of an increase in activity. But, alas, I have only driven them into more tergiversations. I am really driving at something extremely plain and simple. (29, p. 282)

So much for the importance of finance in Keynes's theory.[39]

Davidson's misplaced emphasis and misinterpretation leads him to recommend "a direct and permanent incomes policy" (1978, p. 362). This interpretation, shared by many post-Keynesians, finds no support in Keynes's writings. In the *Treatise* and the *General Theory*, Keynes argued that the price *level* cannot be stable in a noninflationary world, unless wages and costs of production are stable. In a state of persistently rising prices – "true inflation" (7, p. 303) – Keynes's theory is not applicable, as he recognized. Aggregate demand is beyond the point of full employment.[40]

---

[39] The reference to his critics refers to those who continued to insist that the interest rate is determined by flows of loanable funds or by flows of saving and investment. Principal among these critics were Dennis Robertson and Bertil Ohlin. Davidson, in an unpublished comment on this section, calls attention to Keynes's statement: "I should not have previously overlooked this point [finance motive], since it is the coping stone of the liquidity theory of the rate of interest" (14, p. 220). Keynes adds that an increase in planned activity raises interest rates in much the same way as an increase in actual activity. The reference to a "coping stone" seems to make the finance motive more important than Keynes's letter to Shaw suggests. Keynes returned to the subject in his 1939 review of a report on capital formation (ibid., pp. 278–85). There, Keynes acknowledges his error in the *General Theory* but advises the authors of the report to pay attention to the amount invested ("devoted to the acquisition of capital goods") and not to the means by which they are temporarily financed, a matter of secondary importance (ibid., p. 284). Unlike many later economists, Keynes also distinguishes between money and bonds. He sees no relation between the maturity of debt issues and the rate of inflation. In his words:

> It does not make the slightest difference to inflation whether they finance it [government spending] by Treasury bills or irredeemable securities. The idea that Treasury bill financing is what you call "credit expansion" and, therefore, dangerous and that an identical expenditure financed otherwise is not, is a baseless superstition. (21, p. 562)

[40] As Hicks (1983, p. 19) recognizes, by means of "incomes policies and treaties with trade unions . . . inflationary pressure may be temporarily checked . . . they offer no prospect of the longer-term stability, some degree of confidence in which has become a necessity for real recovery." Kahn (1978, p. 561) writes that Keynes did not have a solution to the problem of inflation in an economy close to full employment. Colander (1972, p. 7) reports Lerner's comment that Keynes in 1935 did not understand that inflation was likely to occur if aggregate demand was kept at full employment. Harrod reports on his search for Keynes's views on cost-push inflation:

> I have searched through his writings very carefully, . . . for the purpose of discovering anything he had to say about what we call "cost-push inflation" where the inflation is due to unions asking for, and being given, wage increases which, on the average, are in excess of the productivity increase of labour . . . I could only find one short passage in Keynes, just a couple of sentences, where he said, "Of course the wage earners might demand more and get more" and of course this would be a cause of inflation independent of those which he had been describing in his book. But he adds that "this is not a thing that is likely to occur often." (1972, p. 9)

Some other views

Richard Kahn was one of the young economists at Cambridge in the 1930s most closely associated with Keynes. He helped to convince Keynes that income was fixed in the *Treatise*, thereby accelerating Keynes's return to the development of the ideas he had tried to express in the *Treatise*. Kahn's article on the multiplier (Kahn 1931) had an important influence on the development of Keynes's theory. He served as critic, commentator, and close associate throughout Keynes's life.

In his Mattioli lectures, Kahn refers to the "disastrous misinterpretations of Keynes's teaching" (1984, p. xvii). Kahn is critical not only of the interpretations but of the book itself.

In Kahn's view, there are two major achievements – the theory of effective demand and the theory of investment, particularly recognition of the role of risk, uncertainty, and expectations (ibid., p. 142). Kahn refers to Chapter 11 of the *General Theory* on investment as "the most important" but also "one of the most confused" (ibid., p. 145).[41] The confusion stems from the comparison of the risk-free rate of interest to an uncertain stream of income (ibid., pp. 146–7). Here, Kahn simply disregards Keynes's discussion of the risk premiums in interest rates in Chapter 11 of the *General Theory*.

Kahn finds the distinction between precautionary and speculative balances "very blurred" (ibid., p. 138) and the definition of unemployment too complicated (ibid., p. 120). Keynes's treatment of the distinction between his theory and classical theory is "unnecessarily complex" (ibid.). In Kahn's view, Keynes did not clearly state what it was that made the theory general until the preface to the French edition in 1939.

Throughout, Kahn emphasizes the importance of expectations, but he does not adopt Shackle's view that decisions are irrational. Kahn criticizes Hicks's (1937) IS–LM model for neglecting expectations. He cites Keynes's criticism (14, pp. 79–81) and describes as "tragic" Keynes's failure to make a public protest when textbook versions of IS–LM began to appear (Kahn 1984, p. 160).

Kaldor (1983, pp. 13–15) believes that Keynes erred by neglecting increasing returns to scale. To him full employment equilibrium "is an artificial creation, the consequence of the artificial assumption of constant returns to scale in all industries . . . Once the artificial assumption . . . is abandoned, a Walrasian equilibrium with market-clearing prices

---

[41] Kahn's review of Malinvaud's lectures on unemployment (Kahn 1983) is highly critical of Malinvaud's representation of Keynes. A particularly sharp criticism is the treatment of investment and neglect of uncertainty and expectations. (See Kahn 1983, pp. 219, 226–8.)

in every market becomes a mirage" (ibid., p. 13). Kaldor dismisses the idea that Keynes's theory is a theory of disequilibrium dynamics or of "inverted velocities of price and quantity adjustments" (ibid.). The main proposition of the *General Theory* is that normally production is limited by effective demand, so the level of employment can be permanently increased by state action (ibid., p. 2).

Tobin's (1983) comment on Kaldor rejects irrational money illusion and other ad hoc explanations of wage rigidity. He doubts that the existence of involuntary unemployment can be proved and dismisses the issue. For him, the operational issue is that "inertia in nominal wage and price paths last long enough for unemployment to be a serious social problem and a costly economic waste" (ibid., p. 33).

Tobin appears to replace Keynes's underemployment equilibrium with slow adjustment. Slow adjustment arises because workers bargain for nominal wages in decentralized markets. Like Keynes, Tobin emphasizes the importance of relative wages. An economywide rise in prices that reduces all wages proportionately is more acceptable than the same reduction if it occurs locally (ibid.). To complete his wage theory, Tobin argues, Keynes requires increasing returns to scale, but he makes clear that Keynes did not make this assumption (ibid., p. 34).[42]

In his reply to Tobin, Kaldor (citing Chapter 19 of the *General Theory*) points out that "Keynes never assumed wage rigidity" and did not emphasize downward inflexibility of money wages (Kaldor 1983, p. 46). He points out that Keynes relied on pure competition: "Joan [Robinson] often told him that she tried to interest Keynes in imperfect competition for many years, and its relevance to the problem of the insufficiency of effective demand – but she never succeeded" (ibid., p. 47). In Colander (1972, p. 16), Lerner makes a similar argument.[43]

Short-term policy

My interpretation of Keynes's policy views sees Keynes as a proponent of discretionary action constrained by well-defined policy rules. The monetary rules he favored changed, as developed in Chapter 5 of this

---

[42] Tobin (1977) discusses four "central propositions" of the *General Theory*. His emphasis here, as elsewhere, is on sluggish adjustment of wages and prices, "especially, slowly to excess supply" (Tobin 1977, p. 459). Tobin also notes that investment depends on long-run profit expectations and risk: "These are not simple predictable functions of current and recent economic events" (ibid., p. 460).

[43] Keynes (14, p. 190) rejected imperfect competition when Ohlin suggested this explanation of unemployment.

volume, but at each state in the development of his thinking, there are rules for monetary policy. Keynes's postwar fiscal policy proposals, discussed in Chapter 4, aim at stabilizing the rate of investment at a permanently higher level. In contrast to Meade, who favored the use of fiscal policy to change private consumption, Keynes preferred a formula of the type later described as built-in flexibility (27, pp. 206–8).

In a section called "Misconceptions about the *General Theory*," Kahn (1984, pp. 158–9) notes that the *General Theory* advocates deficit finance in only one place and only if other means fail. Keynes's preferred postwar fiscal policy had two main features: (1) a steady rate of state-planned capital spending for two-thirds to three-fourths of the total investment (27, p. 322) and (2) changes in the social security taxes paid by firms to encourage investment during a recession. Tax reductions were to be automatic. When unemployment reached 8 percent, tax rates came down; when unemployment returned to 5 percent – "the minimum practicable rate" (ibid., p. 208) – tax rates were to return to their long-term value.

Keynes opposed countercyclical policies to change interest rates (ibid., p. 377), arguing along the lines of the *General Theory*. He was skeptical both about the ability to change the long-term rate for a short period and about the effectiveness of changing short-term rates. This is consistent with his view that interest rates should be kept low enough to encourage a steady rate of investment.

Keynes's notes for his statement to the 1945 National Debt Inquiry (ibid., pp. 388–96) generally favors stable policies with market interest rates held at the full employment level unless there is inflation (ibid., p. 390). His summary of the theoretical argument is familiar and contains several references to uncertainty. Contrary to Hansen (1953, pp. 147–8), Keynes sees the interest rate determined by saving, investment, the demand for money, and the money stock. The intertemporal aspect is present also in Keynes's statement that "we want to encourage prudence in the sense of distributing income through a man's life" (27, p. 395).

Keynes's summary (ibid., pp. 396–400) assigns a role to debt management in countercyclical policy, but it is a modest role. He remarks that changes in the

> complex of interest rates, with a view to controlling the trade cycle and to offset inflationary or deflationary trends, should not be precluded, but should affect the shorter-term, rather than the longer-term, issues, and should be regarded as secondary to the technique of rationing the volume rather than altering the terms of credit. (ibid., p. 397)

Additional evidence about Keynes's policy views comes from Abba Lerner's papers. Colander (1984) summarizes some relevant points. Three separate events suggest that Keynes learned about the countercyclical policies associated with fiscal "fine tuning," or functional finance, from Lerner. At first, he rejected the ideas, but he later accepted them as correct and praised Lerner and his work. There is no evidence that he accepted functional finance as a basis for policy, however.

The first event is a lecture Keynes gave at the Federal Reserve during a visit to Washington in 1943 or 1944.[44] At the informal lecture, Keynes expressed concern that, after the war, an excess of saving would cause a depression. Lerner reports:

> When I pointed out that the government could always induce enough spending by incurring deficits to increase incomes, he at first objected that this would only cause "even more saving" and then denounced as "humbug" my suggestion that the deficits required to induce enough total spending could always be financed by increasing the national debt. (1983, p. 437)

The second event occurred in 1943 after Keynes read Lerner's paper "Functional Finance and the Federal Debt" (Lerner 1983, pp. 297–310). He wrote to Meade recommending the paper and accepting the argument. Then he added, "but heaven help anyone who tries to put it across" (Colander 1984, p. 1574; JMK, 27, p. 320). The letter supports my interpretation that Keynes did not see the *General Theory* as an argument for the short-run policies often called "Keynesian."[*]

After Keynes read Lerner's *The Economics of Control,* he wrote to Lerner praising the book, describing several chapters on functional finance as "very original and grand stuff" (Colander 1984, p. 1574).[45] In his letter, Keynes proposed to hold a seminar at the British Treasury on functional finance. Keynes clearly did not take credit for the development of these ideas, as this third event shows. He also praised

---

[44] Memories differ about the date. Lerner (1983, pp. 394–437) uses 1944, but Hansen uses 1943. For Hansen's views, see Colander (1972, pp. 23, 25); Domar also recalls 1943; see Colander (1983, pp. 5–6). Hansen's account of the incident is vague, but Domar and Lerner give similar accounts and both use the word "humbug" to describe Keynes's response to Lerner's proposal. Keynes's letter to Meade, mentioned in the next paragraph of the text, suggests that 1943 is the correct date. Moggridge, in a personal note, reports that Meade's diary for the 1943 trip with Keynes does not mention the seminar.

[45] Moggridge cites Keynes's view on functional finance as "an idea and not a policy; part of one's apparatus of thought but not, except highly diluted under a considerable clothing of qualification, an apparatus of action" (1976, p. 24). The proposed seminar on functional finance is known as the National Debt Inquiry. The inquiry was held in 1945. (Keynes's contributions are in 27, pp. 388–414.)

Lerner to Alvin Hansen and indicated that Lerner should be brought back to Cambridge (Colander 1972, p. 24).

The three events are consistent with Keynes's postwar policy recommendations. They support my interpretation of the *General Theory* as a theory that reflects Keynes's long-standing view of the desirability of institutional changes to replace laissez-faire capitalism with the set of institutional arrangements that Keynes had favored since the 1920s. They are much less consistent – or inconsistent – with those interpretations that see the *General Theory* as the basis for short-term discretionary fiscal policy (or monetary policy) to offset fluctuations in employment.

Joan Robinson (1979) briefly describes Keynes's attitude and comments on Keynes's views about full employment and discretionary policies. She writes:

> In fact Maynard Keynes himself was somewhat skeptical about the possibility of achieving *permanent* full employment. When he dined in Washington with his converts, he told Austin Robinson next day: I was the only non-Keynesian there. It was his British disciples, rather than he, who drafted the white paper in 1944 which proclaimed that it is the responsibility of government to maintain a high and stable level of employment. Keynes said: you can promise to be good but you cannot promise to be clever. (p. 27)

Keynes recommended fiscal expansion before he wrote the *General Theory*. His popular writings, urging expansionist policies, were written in the late 1920s or early 1930s with unemployment high and persistent and the economy far from a position he could regard as full employment. At the time, the monetary policy rules and procedures differed from those that Keynes favored. But even in his 1931 Harris lectures, where he favors public investment to raise business profits, he remarks that he hesitates "to depend too much in practice on this method alone unaided by others" (13, p. 364). The Harris lectures put greater emphasis on monetary measures to drive down the long-term rate of interest than on fiscal measures (ibid., p. 366).

At the height of the depression in 1933, Keynes wrote *The Means to Prosperity* (9, pp. 335–66). He proposed government spending on capital improvements, tax reduction, and other reforms. His proposed increase in government spending was £100 million (ibid., p. 365), which he soon after reduced to £60 million (21, p. 181). At the time (1933), central government spending was about £770 million and GNP was approximately £4.4 billion, so his revised proposal called for an increase equal to about 8 percent of government spending and 1.4 percent of GNP (Mitchell 1976, pp. 702, and 790). Assuming a multiplier of $1\frac{1}{2}$ or $1\frac{1}{4}$, the values Keynes used as safe estimates instead of the value of 2, which he preferred (21, p. 176), the proposal would have raised government spending from 17.5 to 18.5 percent of GNP when the adjustment was completed. The £60 billion increase would have restored government spending to the 1932 level (Mitchell 1976, p. 702).

The depression proposals can reasonably be regarded as cautious. Keynes is, in fact, more cautious than at first appears. In response to his critics, he wrote:

> We should not refrain from good schemes because they will take some time to mature or because the expenditure they involve *will be spread over several years*. I advocate this, not only because slow maturity is a characteristic of many of the best proposals but because . . . abnormal unemployment, though not on the present scale, may be a chronic problem with us for several years to come. I do not believe that we shall regret five years hence that works started today will be still, in some instances, uncompleted. (21, pp. 181–2, emphasis added)

In this passage, Keynes makes clear that he intended his program to provide a permanent (or sustained) level of investment expenditure, not temporary relief.[46]

Conclusion

There are many interpretations of the *General Theory* and major differences between interpreters about the meaning of the book and its

[46] To avoid misunderstanding, let me restate that I do *not* claim that Keynes opposed public works or public spending. My claim is that his proposals are consistent with his position in the 1920s. He favored more investment, and more steady investment, planned by the state. In the depression, he favored a permanent increase in investment in housing, roads, railroads, and other forms of capital. These were usually not intended to be countercyclical fiscal responses. They were intended to raise the level of investment permanently. There are exceptions, however. One of the clearest is in his 1937 series in the *Times* (21, pp. 384–95), where despite unemployment near 12 percent, Keynes talks about retarding "certain types of investment, so as to keep our most easily available ammunition in hand for when it is more required" (ibid., p. 387). The articles make clear that Keynes opposed a rise in the rate of interest: "The long-term rate of interest must be kept *continuously* as near as possible to what we believe to be the long-term optimum" (ibid., p. 389). The main point is that the increased expenditure for war production was a threat to stability. Keynes was concerned, at the time, with avoiding a boom so as to avoid a succeeding slump (ibid., pp. 390–1).

central message. After fifty years of discussion, there is little reason to expect that one interpretation will become *the* accepted interpretation, with the others discarded. Nonetheless, there are substantial differences in the degree to which the different interpretations find support in Keynes's writings in the *General Theory* and after.

Some ideas are repeated more often than others. A leading graduate textbook discusses the standard (sic) Keynesian model and its characteristic features. Sargent presents a model, then writes: "The *essential* difference between the classical model and the Keynesian model is the absence from the latter of the classical labor supply curve combined with the labor market equilibrium condition" (1979, p. 49). Not a word is said about uncertainty or expectations, issues to which Keynes devoted much attention and which he emphasized in his 1937 restatement.

Moggridge (1976) comments on two myths that have developed around the *General Theory*. The first views Keynes's predecessors and contemporaries

> as concentrating on wage cuts and rejecting counter-cyclical public works policy . . . The second myth . . . saw Keynes in the *General Theory* simply making special assumptions of rigid wages and a liquidity trap and thus made it possible to accommodate him as a special case in the consensus over economic theory. This myth still dominates most undergraduate textbooks. (ibid., pp. 177–8)

Much of what has been written about the *General Theory* is partial and selective. Some of this is inevitable, given the large amount of Keynes's writing. I have been struck, however – as I believe this chapter brings out – by the considerable extent to which authors have gone to single out specific chapters and dismiss, neglect, or disregard large parts of the book. There is no basis in Keynes's later work for dismissing major parts of the book and concentrating on a single chapter or ignoring the interpretations Keynes gave in the discussion that followed publication. One passage from that discussion is worth quoting at length:

> This that I offer is, therefore, a theory of why output and employment are so liable to fluctuation. It does not offer a ready-made remedy as to how to avoid these fluctuations and to maintain output at a steady *optimum* level. But it is, properly speaking, a theory of employment because it explains *why*, in any given circumstances, employment is what it is. Naturally I am

interested not only in the diagnosis, but also in the cure; and many pages of my book are devoted to the latter. But I consider that my suggestions for a cure . . . are not meant to be definitive . . . But my main reasons for departing from the traditional theory go much deeper than this. They are of a highly general character and are meant to be *definitive*.

I sum up, therefore, *the main grounds* of my departure as follows:

(1) The orthodox theory assumes that we have a knowledge of the future of a kind quite different from that which we actually possess . . . In a system in which the level of money income is capable of fluctuating, the orthodox theory is one equation short of what is required to give a solution. Undoubtedly the reason why the orthodox system has failed to discover this discrepancy is because it has always tacitly assumed that income *is* given, namely at the level corresponding to the employment of all the available resources. In other words it is tacitly assuming that the monetary policy is such as to maintain the rate of interest at that level which is compatible with full employment . . .

(2) The orthodox theory would by now have discovered the above defect, if it had not ignored the need for a theory of the supply and demand of output as a whole (14, 1973, pp. 121–3, some emphasis added).

In these few paragraphs, Keynes restates his main differences with classical theory. Specifically, Keynes emphasizes:

1. The relation of his policy conclusions to his *General Theory*.
2. His concern with *two* issues, avoiding fluctuations and maintaining the *optimum* level of output.
3. That his theory is a theory of the demand and supply of output not just the demand for output; that the classical theory is "one equation short."
4. That classical economists assume that the monetary authority keeps the rate of interest at the (natural) rate compatible with full employment; in Keynes's words: "For every rate of interest there is a level of employment for which that rate is the 'natural' rate, in the sense that the system will be in equilibrium" (7, p. 242).
5. That the neglect of uncertainty not only makes the classical theory of interest incomplete but prevents

classical economists from recognizing that an equation is missing; the missing equation determines the actual position of equilibrium.

6. That his reasons for rejecting classical theory are, in his words, "definitive."

This summary statement and similar statements that Keynes made repeatedly are the basis for my interpretation of the *General Theory*. There is no mention here of wage rigidity, dynamics, the relative rates of price and output adjustment, disequilibrium, absence of substitution, irrational behavior, or other special features emphasized in the several alternative interpretations discussed here. The elements that Keynes emphasizes are that output is below the optimum level and that a principal reason is the presence of uncertainty.

Keynes believed, and said repeatedly, that the average level of output fluctuates around a (stable) level that is less than the maximum attainable. In Keynes's words, "we oscillate . . . round an intermediate position appreciably below full employment" (7, p. 254). The difference between the maximum and the average level, measured in employment units, is "involuntary unemployment." Keynes understood that employment is a real variable, so he did not rely on changes in money, money wages, or any other nominal value to increase *equilibrium* employment.[47] He believed that society could increase equilibrium employment by increasing the stock of capital. This required a higher level of investment until the capital stock reached a social optimum. Keynes did not believe that investment could reach the level consistent with the *optimum* capital stock and the *optimum* level of income under prevailing institutional arrangements. Under existing arrangements, Keynes thought, the degree of uncertainty about the future was not at a minimum. A main reason he gave, at length in Chapter 12 of the *General Theory*, is the volatility of expectations about future prices and market conditions. He favored some form of state intervention to plan or direct investment. The precise form of the intervention was not fully worked out or, as in the quotation, "not definitive."

The important role given to the optimum capital stock reflects the importance of supply – specifically the supply of output – in Keynes's

---

[47] In the *General Theory* he distinguished between anticipated and unanticipated changes: "If it (the change in the value of money) is not foreseen, there will be no effect on current affairs, whilst, if it is foreseen, the price of existing goods will be forthwith so adjusted that the advantages of holding money and of holding goods are again equalized" (7, p. 142). It is difficult to read these passages and hold to the view that Keynes's equilibrium at less than full employment depends on misperceptions or money illusion.

theory. Keynes's main criticism of the classical theory is that the theory does not provide an explanation of the level of output except in the limiting case of full employment. This failure of the classical theory is a direct consequence of the classical assumption that equilibrium output is identical to *maximum* output, whereas Keynes believed that maximum output can be achieved only when society holds the optimum capital stock.

Full employment has a precise definition in the *General Theory* and in Keynes's later writings. Full employment is "a situation in which aggregate employment is inelastic in response to an increase in the effective demand for its output" (ibid., p. 26). He wrote to Hicks: "If I were writing again, I should indeed feel disposed to define full employment as being reached at the same moment at which the supply of output in general becomes inelastic" (14, p. 71). Then, he added: "A great part of my theory ceases to be required when the supply of output as a whole is inelastic" (ibid.). Generally, as in these quotations, Keynes believed that equilibrium employment was less than full employment, as he defined the term. The difference is involuntary unemployment.

The three preceding paragraphs are a brief restatement of my interpretation of the main argument of the *General Theory*. They do not capture all of the argument. I do not discuss here the relation of the rate of interest, the marginal efficiency of capital, the demand for money, and expectations, topics that Keynes emphasized repeatedly in his letters to Robertson, Hawtrey, Ohlin, and many others in some major papers published after the *General Theory* and in the book itself.

Any brief discussion of a book such as the *General Theory* runs the risk that brevity will be mistaken for oversimplification. My purpose in writing a succinct summary here is not to supplant my longer discussion but to bring out some principal differences between my interpretation and some others.

While preparing this chapter, I read or reread some of the vast literature that has grown up around Keynes and the *General Theory*. I have been pleased to find others who share, at least in part, my interpretation of the *General Theory* as the restatement, using economic analysis, of beliefs Keynes had held for a decade or more.

Schumpeter is one of these. He describes two elements in any comprehensive theory of society. The first he calls the theorist's vision – what the theorist uses to understand the state of society; the second is the technique used to conceptualize the theorist's vision: "In the *Economic Consequences of the Peace* we find nothing of the theoretical apparatus of the *General Theory*. But we find the whole of the vision of things social and economic of which that apparatus is the technical complement. The *General Theory* is the final result of a long struggle *to make that vision of our age analytically operative"* (Schumpeter 1946, p. 56).[48]

[48] A similar view is expressed by Smithies (1972, p. 427).

7

Conclusion

A main theme of this book is that the *General Theory* put into the language of economics beliefs that Keynes held in the 1920s. The beliefs concerned progress, the role of the state in achieving progress, the importance of investment for progress, and the harmful effect of uncertainty on investment and progress.

As early as 1924, Keynes gave a lecture at Oxford "The End of Laissez-Faire." What I have called the main themes are there, not hidden as afterthoughts in a wide-ranging essay but as main ideas:

> Many of the greatest economic evils of our time are the *fruits of risk, uncertainty, and ignorance*. It is because particular individuals . . . are able to take advantage of uncertainty and ignorance, and also because for the same reason big *business is often a lottery*, that great inequalities of wealth come about; and these same factors are also *the cause of the unemployment* of labour, or *the disappointment of reasonable business expectations*, and of the impairment of efficiency and production . . .
>
> I believe that some coordinated act of intelligent judgment is required as to the *scale* on which it is desirable that the community as a whole should save, the scale on which these savings should go abroad in the form of foreign investments, and whether the present organization of the investment market distributes savings along the *most rationally productive channels*. I do not think that these matters should be left entirely to the chances of private judgment and private profits, as they are at present. (9, pp. 291–2, emphasis added)

Keynes was an economist, one of the greatest, and his criticism of classical theory is an economist's criticism. He believed he had detected a flaw in the system of resource allocation, that he had found a divergence between private and social cost that could be removed. The problem was not general. Keynes did not complain about the markets for consumption goods. Problems arose in the market for investment goods. There, Keynes claimed to find two related problems. Both were consistent with his long-standing belief, exemplified by the preceding quotation, that there was excessive uncertainty. The first we may call Keynes–Knight uncertainty – in modern terms, we cannot assign a meaningful, prior probability to some events. The second is that there is double counting of the premium for bearing uncertainty; the borrower requires a rate of return on the project that compensates for the uncertainty; lenders increase the loan rate to cover the cost. Consequently, investment fails to rise, on average, to the social optimum. The capital stock is less than optimal, and real incomes are below the attainable maximum.

Individuals face this premium for uncertainty but, Keynes believed, society does not. Keynes treats society as analogous to an individual with infinite life. In contrast to risk-average individuals, society can avoid the borrowers' and the lenders' risk of default and therefore make investments that individuals do not make. The risk, which Keynes called moral risk and we now call moral hazard, is, on his argument, an avoidable risk. Freed of this risk, society would achieve a higher capital stock and a higher standard of living.

Details aside, the core of Keynes's argument is that in a society with the optimum capital stock, the social rate of interest is zero. All productive opportunities are realized. The decisions of risk-averse private individuals cannot achieve the social optimum. Hence, there is an ineradicable difference between private and social returns if investment is left to private decisions.

This is the argument for which Keynes had been searching in the *Treatise*. Many of the elements that Keynes regarded as important appear in the *Treatise*. There is excessive variability of prices, a real theory of the business cycle based on expectations – waves of optimism and pessimism – emphasis on the primacy of investment, and a stock-flow analysis of interest rate determination. The key to progress and stability is investment; saving has a more passive role, and increases in saving are not a means of increasing investment. By reducing sales and profits, increases in saving have the opposite effect. In the *Treatise*, Keynes introduces a demand for assets in place of the more or less well-behaved velocity of classical economics and his own *Tract*. People can choose to hold liquid assets instead of real capital, thereby affecting the interest rate and investment.

The key difference, after the *Treatise*, is Keynes's discovery that output does not fluctuate around the optimal level. Output is not given, as in classical theory, but depends on social institutions, anticipations, and policy arrangements. Hence, output can be changed and standards of living increased by proper policies.

The change in view is reflected in the policy recommendations that

Keynes drew from his work. In the *Tract* and the *Treatise*, Keynes proposes changes in monetary institutions to reduce price variability. In the *General Theory*, the main proposal is for the state to act as the director of investment to smooth the flow of investment so as to reduce uncertainty and increase the capital stock and the level of output.

My interpretation ties together much that is puzzling in standard interpretations that concentrate on short-run fluctuations in employment or the level of unemployment and neglect the long-term effects on "progress" and living standards. Contrary to Hansen (1953) and many others who followed him, Keynes's discussions of variability of stock prices, of expectations and uncertainty, of the properties of money and interest rates in Chapter 17 of the *General Theory*, and the views on mercantilism and policy with which he ends the book are not passing thoughts or unrelated speculation. They are an integral part of his argument and his search for a policy consistent with the *General Theory*.

"The philosophy toward which the General Theory leads" is, not by accident, the philosophy that its author had expressed ten years earlier. Although Keynes recognized that many of his views were compatible with socialism, there were important differences. First, Keynes distrusted the socialists. "Am I A Liberal?" explains that the socialists would not be led by the intellectual elite who, Keynes believed, could be expected to place public interest ahead of class or personal interests (9, p. 297). Hence, they could not be relied upon to choose policies that, on Keynes's analysis, were socially optimal. Experience with the Labour government in the early 1930s confirmed Keynes's belief that a Labour government would not seek to produce Keynes's vision of the social optimum. Second, Keynes favored policies to increase investment, not consumption. He believed that income redistribution from rich to poor would increase consumption and reduce saving. Hence, he held ambivalent views about income redistribution. He clearly favored lower profits and interest rates and, more generally, lower returns to capital. But, he favored policies to lower these returns by increasing the capital stock to the point at which capital ceased to command a return above its cost of production.

An alternative interpretation

By emphasizing the divergence between private and social cost and the optimum capital stock, have I neglected Keynes's major achievement?[1] Many see his work as primarily concerned with the develop-

---

[1] This is not a hypothetical question. I have met this question many times, particularly with respect to Chapter 4 in this volume.

ment of a theory of short-run fluctuations and policies for reducing fluctuations. I do not deny that he was concerned with these issues, but the basis or foundation of the alternative interpretation suggesting that these topics were his main concern in the *General Theory* seems weak. There are three reasons.

First, from an analytic point of view, the emphasis on Keynes's theory of employment or unemployment has not been fruitful. More than fifty years have passed since the publication of the *General Theory*. Keynes's suggestions about the theory of labor supply, or the various interpretations of that theory, have not produced an empirically successful theory of the labor market or of unemployment. The conjecture that unemployment could be caused by the rigidity of money wages is an old idea. Keynes did not claim to have originated the conjecture, and he did not have to write a book to present an idea that was well known. Further, the rigid wage conjecture as a key to fluctuations is not consistent with most postwar data; real wages have not systematically fallen during expansions and increased in contractions.

Reading Keynes's arguments of the 1920s shows how much of the rigid wage conjecture was part of his discussion of the costs of returning to gold in 1925. In fact, the conflict between relative and absolute wage reduction, part of Keynes's argument in the *General Theory*, is clearly brought out in his earlier statement.

> Our export industries are suffering because they are the *first* to be asked to accept the 10 percent reduction. If *every one* was accepting a similar reduction at this time, the cost of living would fall, so that the lower money wage would represent nearly the same real wage as before . . .
>
> Those who are attacked first are found with a depression of their standard of life, because the cost of living will not fall until all the others have been successfully attacked too . . . Nor can the classes, which are first subjected to a reduction of money wages, be guaranteed that this will be compensated later by a corresponding fall in the cost of living, and will not accrue to the benefit of some other class. Therefore, they are bound to resist so long as they can . . .
>
> I see no reason why, with good management, real wages need be reduced on the average . . .
>
> If Mr. Churchill had restored gold by fixing the parity lower than the pre-war figure, or if he had waited until our money values are adjusted to the pre-war parity, then these particular arguments would have no force . . . For he was committing himself to force down money wages and all money values, without any idea how it was to be done. (9, pp. 211–12)

Keynes then analyzes the reason the error was made. The main mistake was a failure to recognize that the equality of prices of internationally traded goods in the United States and the United Kingdom did not imply that wages in the export industries had adjusted. Even more, the adjustment of wages in the export industries, should it occur, would not imply that wages in other industries, particularly what he calls the sheltered sectors, would be adjusted to the new level. A correct analysis would have emphasized the difficulties of obtaining wage and price adjustment. Keynes then sets out the argument that Churchill's advisors should have made.

> Money wages, the cost of living, and the prices which we are asking for our exports have not adjusted themselves to the improvement in the exchange, which the *expectation of your restoring the gold standard*, in accordance with your repeated declarations, has already brought about. They are about 10 percent too high. If, therefore, you fix the exchange at this gold parity, you must either gamble on a rise in gold prices abroad, which will induce foreigners to pay a higher gold price for our exports, or you are committing yourself to a policy of forcing down money wages and the cost of living to the necessary extent.
>
> We must warn you that the latter policy is not easy. It is certain to involve unemployment and industrial disputes. (ibid., p. 214, emphasis added)

Second, by 1928, before completing the *Treatise*, Keynes had the main ideas that became his theory of aggregate demand. There is no need for careful interpretations. Keynes is explicit about the idea that became the multiplier, the role of investment, and the importance of anticipations and their relation to demand.

> Generally speaking, the indirect employment which schemes of capital expenditure would entail is far larger than the direct employment . . . the greater part of the employment they would provide would be spread far and wide over the industries of the country. But the fact that the indirect employment would be spread far and wide does not mean that it is in the least doubtful or illusory . . .
>
> The fact that many work people who are now unemployed would be receiving wages instead of unemployment pay would mean an increase in effective purchasing power which would give a general stimulus to trade. Moreover, the greater trade activity would make for further trade activity; for the forces

of prosperity, like those of trade depression, work with a cumulative effect . . . In the economic world, "coming events cast their shadow before," and the knowledge that large schemes of work were being undertaken would give an immediate fillip to the whole trade and industry of the country. (ibid. p. 106–7)[2]

Although it is true that Keynes did not have the precise formulation of the short-run theory of effective demand in 1928, it is also true that he was not much concerned with precise formulation once the point was clear. To draw the conclusion that increased government spending for investment would raise aggregate demand by a multiple of the initial spending, he did not require more precision than he had achieved. The main idea was clearly formulated before he completed the *Treatise*.

Nor did Keynes need the *General Theory* to argue for fiscal stimulus. He made these arguments (with Henderson) to support Lloyd George's campaign in 1929, as shown by the material just quoted. Indeed, Keynes's main arguments for fiscal stimulus to raise income during the depression antedate the *General Theory*. There is only one mention of public works spending in that book and much less emphasis on expansionist policy after the book was published. This is difficult to explain if the main point of the *General Theory* is to establish that government can manage aggregate demand by changing public works spending or taxes.

Keynes's wartime memos show that he did not favor the discretionary policies to manage short-term changes in aggregate demand that are called Keynesian. He favored preannounced rules with built-in flexibility and opposed James Meade's efforts to introduce so-called Keynesian policies. This was neither a new departure nor a recantation. His fiscal proposals in the late 1920s and early 1930s were modest proposals to raise the level of aggregate demand to full employment over several years by maintaining a higher level of investment. Nor did he favor manipulation of interest rates or countercyclical interest rate policy. His main proposal in the *General Theory* and after is to *maintain* interest rates at a level below the average of the recent past. His main aims were to reduce variability and uncertainty and to lower interest rates permanently to the level of the marginal social product of capital and ultimately to zero.

Third, the interpretation of the *General Theory* as a theory of demand management of short-term fluctuations or of the special problem of the

---

[2] Robinson (1985, p. 86) comments on this passage by reporting that "R. F. Kahn went off for his summer holiday with this in his rucksack. . . He came back with his analysis of what became known as the multiplier."

1930s depression is so well entrenched that few read what Keynes said about his aim: "This book has evolved into what is *primarily* a study of the forces which determine changes in the *scale* of output and employment as a whole" (7, p. xxi, emphasis added). To an economist trained in Marshallian analysis, the study of changes in the scale of output is a study of the factors affecting the long-run stock of capital available to firms, in this case to firms in the aggregate.

Keynes was concerned with the problems of unemployment and output. The *General Theory* attacks these problems by proposing a means of permanently changing the scale of output. Keynes interpreted classical theory, specifically Say's law, as a statement that increases in investment must come at the expense of consumption. Scale is fixed. Output is given. This same argument, called in the particular instance the Treasury view, had been used against Keynes's efforts to increase output both when he supported Lloyd George's program and after.

Whether or not one accepts the argument that Keynes's principal concern is to reduce the divergence between private and social returns to investment and increase the scale of output by reducing uncertainty, there can be no doubt that the argument is present and that it leads to the main policy conclusion in the *General Theory*. Concentration on short-run aggregate demand management has obscured the principal message. The problem, as I see it, is not to establish whether Keynes may have favored short-term demand management on occasion. What is surprising is how much has been built on the statements that can be found and how much of his argument and his conclusion about long-term policy has been neglected.

Short-term fiscal policy has not proven to be an effective tool of stabilization. There are many reasons, but in practice, perhaps most important for many countries has been the effects of expansive policies on prices and international trade and payments. Attempts to lower unemployment by short-term policy adjustment have been followed by rising prices and capital outflow or currency depreciation. Countries have responded, sooner or later, to these consequences by changing policy, slowing the growth of aggregate demand, and often inducing recessions. This experience has led several countries to reduce their earlier reliance on short-term policy changes and adopt so-called medium-term strategies to increase stability.

The usual explanation of the unwanted consequences of fiscal policy has been that fiscal policy has been inflexible. Governments have delayed fiscal changes until the "proper" time for change had passed. Government spending proved to be easier to increase than to reduce. Legislatures were more willing to reduce than to increase tax rates, and even the reductions were often delayed. Whatever merit these arguments may have, they are partial. On average, economists have not produced forecasts sufficiently accurate to distinguish between booms and recessions one quarter or one year ahead.[3] Policies based on forecasts are therefore likely to be poorly timed, inconsistent, and as a result, suboptimal (Kydland and Prescott 1977).

Keynes would not have been surprised at many of these problems. His consideration of Tinbergen's work left Keynes unconvinced about the methods advocated by Tinbergen, particularly the use of econometric models for policy and forecasting (14, pp. 285–9, 306–18). He did not develop his theory as the basis for short-term policy adjustment. Indeed, he did not believe econmic theory could be used successfully for that end.

Where Keynes went wrong

There are many critiques of Keynes's major works. He acknowledged the flaws of the *Treatise*. He acknowledged, also, that his treatment of the labor market in the *General Theory* was not satisfactory and needed revision. Reliance on a wage lag was criticized early by Dunlop and Tarshis and has failed to find empirical support. The *General Theory* has only one market-determined rate of interest, a serious omission if the theory is concerned with short-term changes. The analytic structure is unclear, and this lack of clarity has led to continuing controversy about the supply of output, the role of wealth, and other issues. Capital accumulation and time are neglected, so the underlying dynamics remain obscure, and most of the dynamic theory remains to be completed. Efforts to do so have not been uniformly successful, so the focus of these efforts has shifted repeatedly, recently by introducing imperfect competition, a proposition Keynes rejected explicitly.

One of the most serious analytic flaws, on my interpretation, is that his theory does not explain unemployment. The divergence between social and private cost, which leads to a suboptimal capital stock, explains why per capita income is below potential. It does not explain why the forces that reduce income also cause unemployment. If the failure of wages to fall is made part of the theory – by introducing downward wage rigidity – the theory becomes open to the charge of mixing short- and long-term considerations in a peculiar and unattractive way, as Pigou (1936) noted. Further, downward wage rigidity is hardly a theory of the scale of employment, the problem Keynes set out to explain.

---

[3] Meltzer (1987) finds that this finding applies to all forecasting methods currently in use – econometric models, judgment, or time series analysis.

A second serious flaw is Keynes's treatment of expectations. Here, Keynes is better than many of his contemporaries, particularly Hicks (1937), who neglected expectations even when Keynes insisted on their importance. But, Keynes's treatment of expectations is cavalier. Expectations shift from regressive to extrapolative as required for his argument, and he made no effort to explain how very different beliefs about future interest rates and prices (or wages) could be reconciled.

A third flaw is puzzling. Keynes carefully analyzed the effects of inflation on average cash balance in the *Tract*. If the problem of a suboptimal capital stock arises because the public desires to hold more than the socially optimal stock of real balances, inflation is a possible means of permanently lowering cash balances. Although Keynes discusses explicit taxes on cash balances, he never seems to have connected these two pieces of analysis.

These criticisms pertain to the analytic structure, the models Keynes used to reach his conclusions. A different set of criticisms concern the vision of the world toward which his analytic work and his policies led. How well does his vision correspond to experience in the fifty years that followed? Was the vision coherent? Was it correct?

There are four major flaws, I believe. First is the omission of open-economy aspects in the *General Theory*. Second is the failure to treat the inflationary consequences of the policies he espoused and of the Bretton Woods system to which he contributed so much. Third is his judgment or belief that state direction of investment would lower the social return-to-capital to zero, or some minimum level, by increasing the stock of capital until capital is no longer scarce. Fourth is his neglect of, or willingness to sacrifice, freedom.

Keynes's neglect of the open-economy aspects of the policies recommended in the *General Theory* is inexplicable. Few economists have given more time and attention to these issues. One of Keynes's main criticisms of the interwar gold standard in Britain was that expansive policies were followed by a loss of gold, so they could not be sustained. Yet, much the same criticism can be made of British policies after World War II. Efforts at domestic expansion were often followed by so-called payments crises, with increases in interest rates used to attract foreign capital and to slow inflation.

Neglect of the open-economy aspects leaves the *General Theory* incomplete. It is unlikely that Keynes intended his analysis to apply to the world economy. There was no central world authority to carry out his investment program. His concern was Britain, and perhaps other countries like Britain, which suffered from the policies of the interwar period and more generally were not at an optimum. For a single country acting alone, Keynes's policies of increasing investment (or government) spending and keeping interest rates low could not be sustained. France under Mitterand is only the most recent example of the failure of these policies in a single country under a fixed (or adjustable) exchange rate. Risk premiums are not eliminated, as Keynes expected, and interest rates do not fall. Instead, a capital outflow usually brings the expansive policies to an end, at least temporarily. Keynes's analysis recognized that experience of this kind would affect expectations and thus the risk premium and the rate of private investment.

Earlier, I speculated that Keynes would have resolved this problem by introducing exchange controls to restrict the capital outflow or reduce its magnitude. The puzzle is then changed to why the the *General Theory* fails to mention this important feature. Policymakers in many countries must have been misled when their application of expansive policies resulted in a capital outflow and the perceived need to shift to more restrictive policies. Further, French experience in the early 1980s suggests that imposition of exchange controls cannot be relied upon to avoid a sizeable capital outflow. France was forced to choose between repeated devaluations and a policy more closely harmonized with the policies of its principal trading partners.

These experiences suggest that Keynes's basic idea applied by a single country is incorrect. Countries have not been able to reduce instability or provide greater certainty by pursuing expansive policies out of step with their neighbors. Countries that have been relatively successful in raising wealth and income, such as Germany in the 1950s and 1960s or Japan from the 1950s to the 1980s, relied mainly on private investment and, for Germany, generally allowed the interest rate or exchange rate to adjust to keep inflation from increasing to the world average or above.

Keynes was neither oblivious to nor unconcerned about the effects of inflation. He opposed inflation throughout his life and did not advocate trading more inflation for less unemployment. On the contrary, he did not fall into the error of assuming that real variables such as output or unemployment could be changed permanently by inflation.

Many of Keynes's students and followers conclude that Keynes's theory had no implications about the appropriate response to inflation. Kahn (1978, reprinted in Wood 1, p. 561), Lerner (in Colander 1972), and Robinson (1985, p. 97) make this claim. Harrod tells us the probable meaning of these criticisms: "I have searched through his [Keynes's] writings very carefully . . . for the purpose of discovering anything he had to say about what we call 'cost push inflation' . . . I could find only one short passage . . . but I have not put down the page reference . . ." (1972, p. 9).

The reason the references are hard to find is that Keynes always regarded inflation – or true inflation in the language of the *General Theory* – as a monetary problem, not as a problem of cost push by trade unions or businessmen. Inflation began at or near the point at which aggregate demand reached full (maximum) employment output (7, p. 296). Keynes laid the basis for misunderstanding, however, by making the price level depend on the money wage rate in the aggregate supply function. He did not insist that the wage rate was subject to autonomous shocks from the trade unions.[4] This step was taken by his students and followers, some of whom wanted to deny any connection between monetary expansion and inflation. (See, e.g., Kaldor 1982.)

Keynes had opposed inflation in the 1920s and frequently expressed hostility to inflation. Howson (1973, in Wood 1, p. 447) shows that Keynes in 1942, on rereading his 1920 anti-inflation recommendations, thought that his earlier views were correct. He had not changed his opinion that to stop inflation, the government had to rely on restrictive monetary policy until the danger of inflation had passed.[5]

Nevertheless, Keynes took the lead in developing an international monetary system with a bias toward inflation. Keynes's role is clear. He had advocated a stronger bias than the one that emerged, and he had proposed penalties for countries that accumulated reserve balances or failed to expand. These features of the Bretton Woods system and of Keynes's proposal reflected the interwar experience. The United States had accumulated gold reserves, raised tariffs in 1922 and again in 1929, and sterilized gold inflows after the mid-1930s. France had accumulated gold after the 1927 stabilization and failed to expand. Keynes, White, and many others wanted to avoid a repetition of that experience.

When the United States chose to follow inflationary policies, particularly after the mid-1960s, the capital outflow from the United States expanded the stock of world reserves. The increase in world reserves set off a widespread inflation, affecting all developed countries. Countries could have avoided inflation by revaluing their currencies against the dollar but failed to do so. The Bretton Woods system, the extant version of Keynes's postwar plan, collapsed.

I believe experience has shown Keynes's idea to be wrong. The Bretton Woods system did not maintain stability and reduce uncertainty. If we date the true beginning of the system in the late 1950s, when currency convertibility was restored, the Bretton Woods system

[4] He made wage changes discontinuous *responses* to changes in effective demand. He explained the discontinuity by invoking workers' psychology (anticipations) and trade union behavior (7, pp. 301–2).
[5] Robinson (1985, pp. 93–4) summarizes his wartime views.

lasted less than fifteen years. This probably overstates its contribution to stability. The closing of the U.S. gold window in 1971 was one step in a series of events. By 1968 at the latest, accumulation of gold by private holders and almost continuous discussion of international monetary reform suggest that the strains on the system were widely recognized. Uncertainty about its future was widespread.

Probably the major failure, certainly the one most relevant for Keynes's basic views, is the failure of many programs of investment management to reduce uncertainty and stimulate the progress that Keynes sought. The failure occurred at two levels. In developed countries, government policies often encouraged consumption and did not work to sustain a higher average rate of investment. The variability of investment in housing, an active concern of government in many countries, has been noted frequently. Fiscal restraint in many countries often meant reductions of public investment or reductions of support for private investment. To control budget deficits or government spending, governments were less inclined to reduce transfers and more inclined to reduce defense spending or nondefense capital outlays. The investment tax credit in the United States, intended to encourage investment, was started and ended seven times in two decades with uncertain effects on the timing of investment spending. In both developed and developing countries, public investment projects were often wasteful and unproductive. Prestige projects such as national airlines or supersonic commercial aircraft, highways in the Amazon, or development or expansion of steel capacity are a few of the many examples of projects that did little to further Keynes's goal of raising per capita income or achieving a more efficient allocation of a country's resources.

Keynes's error with respect to investment planning is a surprising failure to understand or foresee the way in which the political process would operate. It is surprising for two reasons. First, Keynes had considerable experience with government bureaucracies. Although he was highly successful in influencing decisions in his late years, his experience prior to World War II was very different. His campaigns against the return to gold at the prewar parity and against the Treasury view are two of his best known failures to persuade governments to change course. There are many others. Second, Keynes's criticism of the Labour Party written during the 1920s emphasizes the difficulties of control of the party agenda and its actions by the knowledgeable, intellectual leaders of the party – people such as himself:

> I do not believe that the intellectual elements in the Labour
> Party will ever exercise adequate control; too much will always

be decided by those who do not know *at all* what they are talking about; and if – which is not unlikely – the control of the party is seized by an autocratic inner ring, this control will be exercised in the interests of the extreme left wing – the section of the Labour Party which I shall designate the party of catastrophe. (9, p. 297)

Were these problems unique to the Labour Party? Keynes seems to have been convinced that he and others like him could control the agenda and its implementation by other (nonsocialist) parties. He must have recognized that Labour would achieve power, that, at some time, the "party of catastrophe" would control the agenda, and that his program would be pushed aside, replaced by a program chosen by "those who do not know at all what they are doing." How could his program bring stability or achieve an economic optimum if at times it would be run by people who did not share his objectives?

The usual attempt at explanation invokes the "presuppositions of Harvey Road" at this point. This suggests that Keynes remained a Victorian patrician who believed to the end that Britain could be run by an intellectual elite. This is at best a partial explanation. Keynes tells us that he retained many of his early beliefs late in his life, but the same is true of many people. We know that he was surprised and displeased to learn at the Savannah conference that the International Monetary Fund would be run by a large, well-paid bureaucracy. He had hoped that intellectuals, including himself and others like him, would influence the development and that Harry White would serve as managing director. This suggests that he did not foresee, at least in this instance, the administrative and political consequences of his proposals. Yet, he was very much aware of the influence of competing pressure groups and sectional interests in the United States. Did he fail to recognize that these pressures and interests, often reflected in votes, were at work in Britain and elsewhere? Did he fail to see that pressures for income redistribution, not disinterested intellectuals, would have a large role in the policymaking process?

Keynes never resolved the conflict between the goal of raising living standards by increasing efficiency and stability and the means of achieving the goal. He criticized governments for not choosing policies to reduce uncertainty, but his proposals increased opportunities for behaving in the ways he criticized and offered no incentive to behave otherwise. Further, he favored policy rules but did not reject discretion. An early statement reflects his ambivalence:

The State must never neglect the importance of so acting in ordinary matters as to promote certainty and security in business. But when great decisions are to be made, the State is a sovereign body of which the purpose is to promote the greatest good of the whole. When, therefore, we enter the realm of State action, *everything* is to be considered and weighed on its merits. (4, pp. 56–7)

We know that Keynes was not blind to the conflict over the direction and aims of public policy. He wrote to Hayek about *The Road to Serfdom* expressing his broad agreement with Hayek's moral and philosophical position: "I find myself in agreement with virtually the whole of it; and not only in agreement with it, but in deeply moved agreement" (27, p. 385). Keynes went on to argue that with increased wealth economic sacrifices to secure noneconomic benefits had become affordable. Keynes also praised Hayek's discussion of the profit motive and even criticized him for not putting more emphasis on the role of profits. Keynes then turned to the role of planning and expressed his preference for more planning and his conviction that planning is often more efficient. Then he added:

The planning should take place in a community in which as many people as possible, both leaders and followers, wholly share your own moral position. Moderate planning will be safe if those carrying it out are rightly orientated in their own minds and hearts to the moral issue. This is already true of some of them. But the curse is that there is also an important section who could almost be said to want planning not in order to enjoy its fruits but because morally they hold ideas exactly the opposite of yours, and wish to serve not God but the devil . . .

What we need is the restoration of right moral thinking – a return to proper moral values in our social philosophy. (ibid., p. 387)

Much the same theme reappears at the end of Keynes's last published paper, "The Balance of Payments of the United States." There and in his speech to the House of Lords in favor of the Bretton Woods agreement, he spoke of the "attempt to use what we have learnt from modern experience and modern analysis, not to defeat, but to implement the wisdom of Adam Smith" (ibid., p. 445).

These sentences have been read by some as a change of view, a retreat from his earlier positions. I do not think that Keynes believed that he had sacrificed freedom and enterprise for planning. He believed he had found a way to reconcile state direction, higher living standards, increased efficiency, and economic freedom for consumers. Robinson writes:

In his heart Keynes was just as committed to "freedom" as any neoclassic. When it came to drafting the last chapter of the *General Theory* he produced a version that was all on that side of the question. He sent it to me saying: "I know this won't do. It is just how it welled up" (or words to that effect) . . . The last chapter was redrafted. (1985, p. 84)

If Keynes's sympathies lay with freedom, his policies often sacrificed freedom. In addition to state direction of investment, he favored a cartel to help the Lancashire producers in the 1920s, commodity price stabilization schemes in the 1930s and 1940s, and capital restrictions and eventually rigid exchange controls. He changed his position on tariffs when he became convinced that they would ameliorate the unemployment problem in the early 1930s. I believe he was capable of convincing himself that the restrictions he proposed were beneficial socially and therefore justifiable.

The "presuppositions of Harvey Road" entered not as a fixed philosophy but as a belief that an intellectual elite could make the proper choices in a democratic society for that society. Keynes does not ponder why society would delegate so much authority to a small, non-elected group.

Where Keynes was right

The period from the early 1950s to the 1970s is a period of major progress in Keynes's meaning of progress. Standards of living rose for more people and in more different countries than in any previous period for which we have records. This is true not just in the trivial sense that world population is higher now than in the past. It would remain true, I believe, if adjustment is made for the change in population. Countries as different as Mexico, Brazil, Korea, Hong Kong, and Taiwan as well as Japan, and most of Western Europe experienced sustained development with only a few brief interruptions. The contrast with the 1920s and 1930s is striking.

Stability as measured by the relative length of peacetime recessions and expansions in the United States increased also. The National Bureau method of measurement shows that during the interwar period expansions lasted twenty-six months on average, whereas contractions averaged twenty months. This is similar to the record under the gold standard and during the nineteenth century. Postwar, peacetime expansions averaged thirty-four months and contractions eleven months, the latter nearly 50 percent shorter than peacetime recessions during the interwar period.[6]

The increased stability appears to be a general phenomenon affecting many countries. The reasons for the increased stability are not entirely clear. Tariff barriers were reduced under GATT rules and international agreements. Transport and communication costs declined, lowering the costs of trading, and expanding trade. The increased size of government gave the so-called built-in fiscal stabilizers larger scope. The product mix changed; the relative importance of agriculture declined and the relative importance of services increased in the developed countries. Keynes would almost certainly have added the policy arrangements under the Bretton Woods agreement that provided loans from surplus to deficit countries. These arrangements provided that deficit countries were not required to contract fully. They could borrow to maintain domestic spending, production, and imports. Surplus countries loaned part of their accumulation instead of adding to their gold reserves.

Keynes's argument seems correct. The problem is that if the Bretton Woods arrangement enhanced stability, stability should have declined after 1971, when the Bretton Woods arrangement ended. Limited evidence does not suggest that this occurred generally. Several countries appear to have less variability of prices and output after 1971 or 1973 than before (Meltzer 1985, 1986a,b). This evidence is not conclusive; it is more relevant for the role of Bretton Woods than for Keynes's argument. The reason is that deficit countries continued to borrow and surplus countries continued to lend, often through intermediaries, after 1973. Japan, Taiwan, Germany, and some of the oil-producing countries became large net creditors while the United States, Brazil, Mexico, and Argentina became large net debtors, but the world economy continued to expand.

Keynes's conjecture about the importance of institutions – rules – appears to have been correct. Much of the world experienced increased stability and increased growth of output and per capita consumption after World War II. The comparative experience is even more striking. Differences between East and West Germany, North and South Korea, and Taiwan or Hong Kong and mainland China show that countries with similar culture, language, and traditions can have very different rates of increase in consumption and production so that after a generation living standards are very different. The differences appear to be related to the choice of institutions and policy rules, as Keynes believed.

[6] National Bureau measurement of expansions and contractions is based on movements of a number of series and are thus not subject to the criticism of unemployment measures in Romer (1986).

Further, Keynes believed that the market system operating under proper rules would show that Marxism was an obsolete and inferior system. I believe this is the correct reading of his statement about the "wisdom of Adam Smith," his comments to Hayek, and his criticisms of Marxism. Forty years of postwar experience suggest that, here too, Keynes was correct.

Keynes believed that the central problem of coordination arose because prevailing institutional arrangements prevented the rate of interest from falling to the social marginal efficiency of capital. He blamed uncertainty about the long-term future and stubbornly held anticipations that the future would be similar to the past. To Keynes, this meant that recoveries were characterized by brief and short-lived expansions that did not last. On average, private demand remained below socially optimal demand.

Keynes saw that the solution to this problem was a change in the rules to remove, or reduce, the obstacles to progress, that is, rules to encourage investment and higher living standards. I believe that he chose the wrong policy rules. The important message of his book, however, is not the particular recommendation he made about the cure but the diagnosis of the problem.[7]

It is not surprising that Keynes found much to admire and praise in Hayek's writing about society and the importance of rules and that he disagreed mainly about the choice of rules. A key passage from Hayek's *The Constitution of Liberty* could have been written by Keynes:

> Man learns by the disappointment of expectations. Needless to say, we ought not to increase the unpredictability of events by foolish human institutions. So far as possible, our aim should be to improve human institutions so as to increase the chances of correct foresight. (1960, p. 30)

What happened?

> The lesson given to mankind by every age, and always disregarded – that speculative philosophy, which to the superficial appears a thing so remote from the business or life and the outward interests of men, is in reality the thing on earth which most influences them, and in the long run overbears any in-

---

[7] Colleagues in his own country were not much interested in rules. They read his message as a plea for frequent, discretionary changes. They gained less than most of their neighbors, and their real incomes declined relative to their neighbors.

fluences save those it must itself obey. (Mill 1875, p. 330, quoted by Hayek 1960, pp. 112–13)

Keynes's version of this idea – that in the long-run, "the world is ruled by little else" (7, p. 383) than the ideas of philosophers and economists – has been more true for him than for many other economists. Yet, if my interpretation is correct, the ideas that survived and influenced "civil servants and politicians and even agitators" (ibid., p. 384) were not the ideas he emphasized but the interpretation of those ideas by others.

What became known as Keynesian policy concentrated on the narrow issue of what could be achieved in the next quarter or semester and what could be done now to change that outcome. The importance of rules to increase stability and reduce uncertainty that appears repeatedly in Keynes's work in the 1920s and 1930s disappeared from discussion.[8]

A complete explanation of the development of Keynesian economics from Keynes's theory requires detailed study that I have not attempted. Four reasons would, I believe, be part of a complete explanation.

First, the *General Theory* is ambiguous and subject to different interpretations. This point seems so obvious that it requires little elaboration. One need only point to the many different interpretations. As shown in Chapter 6 of this volume, even a small sample covers a wide range. Ambiguity alone cannot explain, however, why the theme that I believe is most important in his life's work receives the least attention or no attention at all.

Second, Hicks (1937) developed an easily manipulated model. Hicks's work was followed by other models such as the Metzler (1951) and Patinkin (1965) versions of Keynes's theory. These models facilitated major advances in the formal structure of economics and the replicability of its implications by thousands of economists. The models enabled generations of economists to present the main ideas in the form of a few equations that could be reproduced in textbooks and taught to the millions of students that studied macroeconomics. Models of this kind eliminate a certain kind of ambiguity from arguments; it is often possible to see from the algebra how a particular conclusion is reached or why it differs from earlier work. Models, even simple algebraic models such as those of Hicks, provide a type of discipline that is attractive. The Hicks (1937), Metzler (1951), and Patinkin (1965)

---

[8] Examples I have not emphasized hitherto include "Economic Possibilities for Our Grandchildren" (9, pp. 321–32) and "Some Economic Consequences of a Declining Population" (14, pp. 124–33).

models of Keynes or the textbook versions of these models were substituted for the original, however.

Third, Hicks's model and many of the textbook treatments of Keynesian economics offered a theory that seemed to explain unemployment and business cycles and to offer a remedy. Here was a way to show the cause of recessions and depressions – declines in private investment – and the solution – substitution of public for private spending. Although a few critics, notably Clark Warburton and Milton Friedman, soon insisted that these explanations did not fit the facts, the bulk of the profession rejected these criticisms for a time. The attraction of at least being able to tame the business cycle and to influence events was a powerful siren.

Fourth, the manipulation of a few variables such as spending and taxes to improve welfare and redistribute income appealed to many planners and social reformers. Many of Keynes's students and followers encouraged this interpretation. The opportunity to redistribute income and to increase governmental control of the economy and of the distribution of income also appealed to parts of the political spectrum, particularly the recipients of grants, subventions, and subsidies.

The design of rules or institutions that reduce uncertainty and instability is far more demanding than the manipulation of government spending in the quasi-mechanical way emphasized in the popular versions of Keynesian economics. After many attempts to forecast and control spending, we know that the apparent simplicity is misleading; the quasi-mechanical models – whether expressed in a few or a few hundred equations – have proved to be an unreliable guide to the future. We now understand much better why this is likely to remain true. The challenge to economists is to build on that understanding to devise rules and develop institutions that reduce risk to the minimum in a world subject to real and nominal shocks that differ in magnitude and duration.

References

Abbeglen, J. C. and Stalk, G. Jr. 1985. *Kaisha, the Japanese Corporation.* New York: Basic Books.

Alchian, A. A. 1969. Information costs, pricing and resource unemployment. *Western Economic Journal,* 7 (June), pp. 109–28.

1977. Why money. *Journal of Money, Credit and Banking,* 9 (February), pp. 133–40.

Baumol, W. J. 1952. The transactions demand for cash: an inventory theoretic approach. *Quarterly Journal of Economics,* 66 (November), pp. 545–6.

Benjamin, D. and Kochin, L. 1979. Searching for an explanation of unemployment in interwar Britain. *Journal of Political Economy,* 87 (June), pp. 441–78.

Beveridge, W. 1936. An analysis of unemployment: part I. *Economica N.S.,* 3 (November), pp. 22–43.

Bils, M. J. 1985. Real wages over the business cycle: evidence from panel data. *Journal of Political Economy,* 93 (August), pp. 666–89.

Bodkin, R. G. 1969. Real wages and cyclical variations in employment: a reexamination of the evidence. *Canadian Journal of Economics,* 2 (August), pp. 353–74.

Bomhoff, E. J. 1983. *Monetary Uncertainty.* Amsterdam: North-Holland.

Brenner, R. 1980. The role of nominal wage contracts in Keynes' General Theory. *History of Political Economy,* 12 (Winter), pp. 582–7; reprinted in Wood 2, pp. 410–15.

Brunner, K. and Meltzer, A. H. (1968). Liquidity traps for money, bank credit and interest rates. *Journal of Political Economy,* 76 (January–February), pp. 1–38.

1971. The uses of money: money in the theory of an exchange economy. *American Economic Review,* 61 (December), pp. 784–805.

Brunner, K., Cukierman, A., and Meltzer, A. H. 1983. Money and economic activity, inventories and business cycles. *Journal of Monetary Economics,* 11, pp. 467–92.

Cagan, P. 1966. *Changes in the Cyclical Behavior of Interest Rates.* New York: National Bureau of Economic Research, Occasional Paper 100.

Capie, R., Mills, T. C. and Wood, G. E. 1982. Was the war loan conversion operation a success? Centre for Banking, City University (London), Discussion Paper 5, multilithed.

1983. What happened in 1931? Centre for Banking, City University (London), multilithed.

322

Capie, F. and Webber, A. 1985. *A Monetary History of the United Kingdom, 1870–1982, Vol. 1 Data, Sources and Methods*. London: Allen & Unwin.

Clark, C. 1977. The "golden" age of the great economists. *Encounter*, 49 (June), pp. 80–90.

Clower, R. W. 1965. The Keynesian counter-revolution: a theoretical appraisal, in F. H. Hahn and F. P. R. Brechling (eds.) *Theory of Interest Rates*. London: Macmillan; reprinted in R. Clower (ed.) *Monetary Theory: Selected Readings*. Baltimore: Penguin, 1969.

Coddington, A. 1983. *Keynesian Economics: The Search for First Principles*. London: Allen & Unwin.

Colander, D. 1972. The development of Keynesian economics: an interview with Abba Lerner and Alvin Hansen, multilithed, Middlebury, Vermont.

1983. An interview with Evsey Domar, multilithed, Middlebury, Vermont.

1984. Was Keynes a Keynesian or a Lernerian? *Journal of Economic Literature*, 22 December, pp. 1572–5.

Commission on the Role of Gold in the Domestic and International Monetary Systems, 1982. *Report to the Congress*. Washington, D.C.: U.S. Treasury Department.

Cooter, R. and Rapaport, P. 1984. Were the ordinalists wrong about welfare economics? *Journal Economic Literature*, 22 (June), pp. 507–30.

Corry, B. 1978. Keynes in the history of economic thought: some reflections, in A. P. Thirlwall (ed.) *Keynes and Laissez Faire*. New York: Holmes and Meier, pp. 3–34.

Cukierman, A. 1984. *Inflation, Stagflation, Relative Prices and Imperfect Information*. Cambridge: Cambridge University Press.

Davidson, P. 1978. *Money and the Real World*, 2nd ed., London: Macmillan.

1980. The dual-faceted nature of the Keynesian revolution: money and money wages in unemployment and production flow prices. *Journal Post-Keynesian Economics*, 2 (Spring), pp. 291–307.

1984. Reviving Keynes's revolution. *Journal of Post-Keynesian Economics*, 6 (Summer), pp. 561–75.

DeGrauwe, P., Janssens, M., and Leliaert, H. unpublished. Real exchange rate variability during 1920–1926 and 1973–1982. Unpublished, Louvain.

Dunlop, J. T. 1938. The movement of real and money wage rates. *Economic Journal*, 48 (September), pp. 413–34.

Eshag, E. 1963. *From Marshall to Keynes*. Oxford: Blackwell.

Fetter, F. 1977. Lenin, Keynes and inflation. *Economica* (February), pp. 77–80.

Fischer, S. and Merton, R. C. 1984. Macroeconomics and finance: the role of the stock market. Carnegie-Rochester Conference Series on Public Policy, 21 (Autumn), pp. 57–108.

Fisher, I. 1911. *The Purchasing Power of Money*, 2d. ed. New York: Macmillan.

Friedman, M. 1957. *A Theory of the Consumption Function*. Princeton: Princeton University Press for the National Bureau of Economic Research.

1962. *Price Theory: A Provisional Text*. Chicago: Aldine.

1968. The role of monetary policy. *American Economic Review*, 58 (March), pp. 1–17.

1969. The optimum quantity of money, in M. Friedman (ed.), *The Optimum Quantity of Money and Other Essays*. Chicago: Aldine.

Friedman, M. and Schwartz, A. J. 1963a. Money and business cycles. *Review of Economics and Statistics*, 45 (February), pp. 32–64.

1963b. *A Monetary History of the United States 1867–1960*. Princeton: Princeton University Press for the National Bureau of Economic Research.

1982. *Monetary Trends in the United States and the United Kingdom*. Chicago: University of Chicago Press for the National Bureau of Economic Research.

Gertler, M. and Grinols, E. 1982. Monetary randomness and investment. *Journal of Monetary Economics*, 10 (September), 239–58.

Grandmont, J. M. and Laroque, G. 1976. On temporary Keynesian equilibrium. *Review of Economic Studies*, 43 (February), pp. 53–67.

Grossman, H. I. 1972. Was Keynes a "Keynesian?" *Journal of Economic Literature*, 10 (March), pp. 26–30.

Haberler G. 1946. *Prosperity and Depression*, 3rd ed. Geneva: League of Nations.

1962. The general theory after ten years, in R. Lekachman (ed.), *Keynes General Theory*. New York: Norton.

1986. Reflections on Hayek's business cycle theory. *Cato Journal*, 6 (Fall), pp. 421–35.

Hamilton, E. J. 1929. American treasure and the rise of capitalism (1500–1700). *Economica*, November.

Hansen, A. H. 1953. *A Guide to Keynes*. New York: McGraw-Hill.

Harcourt, G. C. (ed.) 1985. *Keynes and His Contemporaries*. New York: St. Martin's.

Harris, S. E. 1953. Preface in Hansen, A. H., *A Guide to Keynes*. New York: McGraw-Hill.

Harrod, R. F. 1951. *The Life of John Maynard Keynes*. New York: Harcourt Brace.

1972. Keynes's theory and its application, in D. Moggridge (ed.), *Keynes: Aspects of the Man and His Work*. New York: St. Martin's Press, pp. 1–12.

Hayek, F. A. 1931. Reflections on the pure theory of money of Mr. J. M. Keynes. *Economica*, 3 (August), pp. 270–95.

1960. *The Constitution of Liberty*. Chicago: University of Chicago Press.

Hicks, J. R. 1936. Mr. Keynes' theory of employment, *Economic Journal*, 46 (June), pp. 238–53.

1937. Mr. Keynes and the "classics": a suggested interpretation, *Econometrica*, 5 (April), pp. 147–59.

1950. *A Contribution to the Theory of the Trade Cycle*. Oxford: Clarendon Press.

1967. The "classics" again, in Hicks, J. R., *Critical Essays in Monetary Theory*. Oxford: Clarendon Press.

1969. Automatists, Hawtreyans, and Keynesians. *Journal of Money, Credit and Banking*, 1 (August), pp. 307–17.

1974. *The Crisis in Keynesian Economics*. New York: Basic Books.

1977. *Economic Perspectives: Further Essays on Money and Growth*. Oxford: Clarendon Press.

1979. On Coddington's interpretation: a reply. *Journal of Economic Literature*, 17 (September), pp. 989–95.

1982. *Money, Interest and Wages, Vol. II Collected Essays on Economic Theory*. Cambridge: Harvard Press.

1983. A skeptical follower. *The Economist*, June 18, pp. 17–19.

Hishiyama, I. 1969. The logic of uncertainty according to J. M. Keynes. *Kyoto University Economic Review*, 39 (April), pp. 22–44; reprinted in Wood 1, pp. 373–92.

Howson, S. 1973. A "Dear Money Man?": Keynes on Monetary Policy, 1920. *Economic Journal*, (June) 83, pp. 456–64; reprinted in Wood 1, pp. 442–50.

Hutchinson, T. W. 1978. *On Revolutions and Progress in Economic Knowledge*. Cambridge: Cambridge University Press.

Jordan, J. 1983. On the efficient markets hypothesis. *Econometrica*, 51 (September), pp. 1325–43.

Johnson, H. G. 1961. The *General Theory* after twenty-five years. *American Economic Review*, 51 (May), pp. 1–25; reprinted in Wood 2, pp. 286–300.

1976. Keynes General Theory: revolution or war of independence? *Canadian Journal of Economics*, 9 (November), pp. 580–94; reprinted in Wood 2, pp. 367–380.

Kahn, R. F. 1931. The relation of home investment to unemployment. *Economic Journal*, 41 (June), pp. 173–98.

1978. Some aspects of the development of Keynes's thought. *Journal of Economic Literature*, 16 (June), pp. 545–59; reprinted in Wood 1, pp. 546–63.

1983. Malinvaud on Keynes, in J. Eatwell and M. Milgate (eds.), *Keynes's Economics and the Theory of Value and Distribution*. Oxford, pp. 214–28.

1984. *The Making of Keynes' General Theory*. The Raffaele Mattioli Lectures. Cambridge: Cambridge University Press.

Kaldor, N. 1982. *The Scourge of Monetarism*. Oxford: Oxford University Press.

1983. Keynesian economics after fifty years, in D. Worswick and J. Trevithick (eds.), *Keynes and the Modern World*. Cambridge: Cambridge University Press, pp. 1–27.

1986. Recollections of an economist. *Banca Nazionale del Lavoro Quarterly Review* (March), pp. 3–26.

Kalecki, M. 1938. The determinants of distribution of national income. *Econometrica*, 6 (April), pp. 97–112.

Keynes, J. M. 1936. Art and the state – I. *The Listener* (August 26); reprinted in D. Moggridge (ed.), *Keynes: Aspects of the Man and His Work*. New York: St. Martin's Press 1974, pp. 33–9.

(1913–1946). *The Collected Writings of John Maynard Keynes*,

Vol. 1 *Indian Currency and Finance* (1913). London: Macmillan and St. Martin's Press for the Royal Economic Society, 1971.

Vol. 2 *The Economic Consequences of the Peace* (1919). London: Macmillan and St. Martin's Press for the Royal Economic Society, 1971.

Vol. 3 *A Revision of the Treaty* (1922). London: Macmillan and St. Martin's Press for the Royal Economic Society, 1971.

Vol. 4 *A Tract on Monetary Reform* (1923). London: Macmillan and St. Martin's Press for the Royal Economic Society, 1971.

Vol. 5 *A Treatise on Money, 1 The Pure Theory of Money* (1930). London: Macmillan and St. Martin's Press for the Royal Economic Society, 1971.

Vol. 6 *A Treatise on Money, 2 The Applied Theory of Money* (1930). London: Macmillan and Cambridge University Press for the Royal Economic Society, 1971.

Vol. 7 *The General Theory of Employment, Interest and Money* (1936). London: Macmillan and St. Martin's Press for the Royal Economic Society, 1973.

Vol. 8 *A Treatise on Probability* (1921). London: St. Martin's Press for the Royal Economic Society, 1973.

Vol. 9 *Essays in Persuasion* (full texts with additional essays) (1931). London: Macmillan and St. Martin's Press for the Royal Economic Society, 1972.

Vol. 10 *Essays in Biography* (full texts with additional biographical writing) (1933). London: Macmillan and St. Martin's Press, 1972.

Vol. 11 *Economic Articles and Correspondence* (various). D. Moggridge (ed.). London: Macmillan and Cambridge University Press for the Royal Economic Society, 1983.

Vol. 12 *Economic Articles and Correspondence* (investment and editorial). London: Macmillan and Cambridge University Press for the Royal Economic Society, 1983.

Vol. 13 *The General Theory and After: Part I, Preparation*. D. Moggridge (ed.). London: Macmillan and St. Martin's Press for the Royal Economic Society, 1973.

Vol. 14 *The General Theory and After: Part II, Defence and Development*. D. Moggridge (ed.). London: Macmillan and St. Martin's Press for the Royal Economic Society, 1973.

Vol. 15 *Activities 1906–14: India and Cambridge*. E. Johnson (ed.). London: Macmillan and St. Martin's Press for the Royal Economic Society, 1971.

Vol. 16 *Activities 1914–19: The Treasury and Versailles*. E. Johnson (ed.). London: Macmillan and St. Martin's Press, 1971.

Vol. 17 *Activities 1920–2: Treaty Revision and Reconstruction*. E. Johnson (ed.). London: Macmillan and Cambridge University Press, 1977.

Vol. 19 *Activities 1924–9: The Return to Gold and Industrial Policy*. D. Moggridge (ed.). London: Macmillan and Cambridge University Press for the Royal Economic Society, 1981.

Vol. 20 *Activities 1929–31: Rethinking Employment and Unemployment Policies*. D. Moggridge (ed.). London: Macmillan and Cambridge University Press for the Royal Economic Society, 1981.

Vol. 21 *Activities 1931–9: World Crises and Policies in Britain and America.* D. Moggridge (ed.). London: Macmillan and Cambridge University Press for the Royal Economic Society, 1982.

Vol. 23 *Activities 1940–3: External War Finance.* D. Moggridge (ed.). London: Macmillan and Cambridge University Press for the Royal Economic Society, 1979.

Vol. 25 *Activities 1940–4: Shaping the Post-War World: The Clearing Union.* D. Moggridge (ed.). London: Macmillan and Cambridge University Press for the Royal Economic Society, 1980.

Vol. 26 *Activities 1943–6: Shaping the Post-War World: Bretton Woods and Reparations.* D. Moggridge, (ed.). London: Macmillan and Cambridge University Press for the Royal Economic Society, 1980.

Vol. 27 *Activites 1940–6: Shaping the Post-War World: Employment and Commodities.* D. Moggridge (ed.). London: Macmillan and Cambridge University Press for the Royal Economic Society, 1980.

Vol. 29 *The General Theory and After: A Supplement (to Volumes 13 and 14).* D. Moggridge (ed.). London: Macmillan and Cambridge University Press for the Royal Economic Society, 1979.

Knight, F. H. 1921. *Risk, Uncertainty and Profit.* Boston: Houghton Mifflin.

Kravis, I., Heston, A., and Summers, R. 1978. Real GDP per capita for more than one hundred countries. *Economic Journal*, 88 (June), pp. 215–42.

Kydland, F. and Prescott, E. C. 1977. Rules rather than discretion: the inconsistency of optimal plans. *Journal of Political Economy*, 85, pp. 473–92.

Lambert, P. 1963. The social philosophy of John Maynard Keynes. *Annals of Collective Economy*, 34 (October–December), pp. 483–515; reprinted in Wood 1, pp. 342–72.

Lange, O. 1942. Say's law: a restatement and criticism, in O. Lange, S. McIntyre, and T. Yntema (eds.), *Studies in Mathematical Economics and Econometrics in Memory of Henry Schultz.* Chicago: University of Chicago Press.

Leijonhufvud, A. 1968. *On Keynesian Economics and the Economics of Keynes.* New York: Oxford.

1983. What would Keynes have thought of rational expectations? in D. Worswick and J. Trevithick (eds.), *Keynes and the Modern World.* Cambridge: Cambridge University Press, pp. 179–205.

Lerner, A. P. 1936. Mr. Keynes' *General Theory of Employment, Interest and Money. International Labour Review*, 34 (October), pp. 435–54; reprinted in Wood 2, pp. 55–70, 1983.

1961. *The General Theory after twenty-five years*: Discussion. *American Economic Review*, 51 (May); reprinted in Wood 2, pp. 302–6.

1983. *Selected Economic Writings of Abba P. Lerner*, D. Colander (ed.). New York: New York University Press.

Lucas, R. E., Jr. 1972. Expectations and the neutrality of money. *Journal of Economic Theory*, 4 (June), pp. 103–24.

Lüke, R. 1985. The Schact and the Keynes plans. *Banca Nazionale del Lavoro Quarterly Review*, 152 (March), pp. 65–76.

Mantoux, E. 1946. *The Carthaginian Peace or the Economic Consequences of Mr. Keynes*. London: Oxford University Press.

Marshall, A. 1920. *Principles of Economics*, 8th ed. New York: Macmillan.

1923. *Money Credit and Commerce*. London: Macmillan.

Marshall, A. and Marshall, M. P. 1879. *The Economics of Industry*. London: Macmillan.

Mascaro, A. and Meltzer, A. H. 1983. Long- and short-term interest rates in a risky world. *Journal of Monetary Economics*, 12 (November), pp. 485–518.

Matthews, K. G. P. 1985. Unemployment in interwar Britain: An equilibrium approach. Working paper 8501, University of Liverpool.

Meltzer, A. H. 1981. *Keynes's General Theory*: A different interpretation. *Journal of Economic Literature*, 19 (March), pp. 34–64.

1983. Interpreting Keynes. *Journal of Economic Literature*, 21 (March), pp. 66–78.

1985. Variability of prices, output and money under fixed and fluctuating exchange rates: an empirical study of monetary regimens in Japan and the United States. *Bank of Japan Monetary and Economic Studies*, 3 (December), pp. 1–46.

1986a. Some evidence on the comparative uncertainty experienced under different monetary regimens, in C. Campbell and W. R. Dougan (eds.), *Alternative Monetary Regimes*. Baltimore: Johns Hopkins, pp. 122–53.

1986b. Size, persistence and interrelation of nominal and real shocks. *Journal of Monetary Economics*, 17 (January), pp. 161–94.

1987. Limits of short-run stabilization policy. *Economic Inquiry*, 25 (January), pp. 1–13.

Metzler, L. A. 1951. Wealth, saving and the rate of interest. *Journal of Political Economy*, 59 (April), pp. 93–116.

Mill, J. S. 1875. Bentham. *London and Westminster Review* (1838); reprinted in J. S. Mill (ed.), *Dissertations and Discussions*, I, 3rd. ed. London, as quoted by Hayek (1960).

Mitchell, B. R. 1976. *European Historical Statistics, 1750–1970*. New York: Columbia University Press.

Modigliani, F. 1944. Liquidity preference and the theory of interest and money. *Econometrica*, 12 (January), pp. 45–88.

Moggridge, D. E. 1972. Keynes the economist, in D. E. Moggridge (ed.), *Keynes: Aspects of the Man and His Work*. New York: St. Martin's Press, pp. 53–74.

1976. *John Maynard Keynes*. New York: Penguin.

1986. Keynes and the international monetary system 1909–46, in J. Cohen and G. C. Harcourt (eds.), *International Monetary Problems and Supply-side Economics*. London: Macmillan.

Moggridge, D. E. and Howson, S. 1974. Keynes on monetary policy, 1910–1946. *Oxford Economic Papers*, 26 (July), pp. 226–47; reprinted in Wood 1, 451–71.

Nurkse, R. 1944. *International Currency Experience: Lessons of the Interwar Experience*. Princeton: League of Nations.

Patinkin, D. 1965. *Money, Interest and Prices*, 2nd ed. New York: Harper & Row.

1975. The collected writings of John Maynard Keynes: from the *Tract* to the *General Theory*. *Economic Journal*, 85 (June), pp. 249–71; reprinted in Wood 1, pp. 487–509.

1976. *Keynes' Monetary Thought*. Durham: Duke University Press.

1978. On the relation between Keynesian economics and the Stockholm school. *Scandinavian Journal of Economics*, 80, pp. 135–43.

1979. A study of Keynes' theory of effective demand. *Economic Inquiry*, 17 (April), pp. 155–76.

Pigou, A. C. 1927. *Industrial Fluctuations*. London: Macmillan.

1936. Mr. J. M. Keynes' *General Theory of Employment, Interest and Money, Economica*. 3 (May), pp. 115–32; reprinted in Wood 2, pp. 18–31.

Ramsey, F. P. 1928. A mathematical theory of saving. *Economic Journal*, 38 (December), pp. 543–59.

Robertson, D. H. 1915. *A Study of Industrial Fluctuations*. London: King.

1926. *Banking Policy and the Price Level*. London: King, 3rd impression, 1932.

1931. Mr. Keynes' theory of money. *Economic Journal*, 41 (September), pp. 395–411.

Robinson, E. A. G. 1947. John Maynard Keynes 1883–1946. *Economic Journal*, 57 (March), pp. 1–68; reprinted in Wood 1, pp. 86–143.

Robinson, J. 1979. Has Keynes failed? *Annals of Public and Cooperative Economy*, 50 (Jaunary–March), pp. 27–9.

1985. (with Wilkinson, F.) Ideology and logic, in F. Vicarelli (ed.), *Keynes's Relevance Today*. Philadelphia: University of Pennsylvania Press, pp. 73–98.

Romer, C. 1986. Spurious volatility in historical unemployment data. *Journal of Political Economy*, 94 (February) pp. 1–37.

St. Etienne, C. 1984. *The Great Depression*. Stanford: Hoover Institution Press.

Salant, W. S. 1985. Keynes and the modern world: a review article. *Journal of Economic Literature*, 23 (September), pp. 1176–85.

Samuelson, P. A. 1946. Lord Keynes and *The General Theory. Econometrica*, 14 (July), pp. 187–200; reprinted in Wood 2, pp. 190–202.

Sargent, T. 1979. *Macroeconomic Theory*. New York: Academic Press.

Schumpeter, J. A. 1946. John Maynard Keynes 1883–1946. *American Economic Review*, 36 (September), pp. 495–518; reprinted in Wood 1, pp. 51–72.

Shackle, G. L. S. 1961a. Keynes and the nature of human affairs. *Weltwirtschaftliches Archiv*, 87, pp. 93–107; reprinted in Wood 1, pp. 329–341.

1961b. Recent theories concerning the nature and role of interest. *Economic Journal*, 71 (June), pp. 209–54.

1967. *The Years of High Theory*. Cambridge: Cambridge University Press.

Shiller, R. J. 1981. Do stock prices move too much to be justified by subsequent changes in dividends? *American Economic Review*, 71, (June), pp. 421–36.

Skidelsky, R. 1983. *John Maynard Keynes I. Hopes Betrayed 1883–1920*. London: Macmillan.

Smithies, A. 1951. Reflections on the work and influence of John Maynard Keynes. *Quarterly Journal of Economics*, 65, (November), pp. 578–601; reprinted in Wood 1, pp. 267–86.

1972. Keynes revisited. *Quarterly Journal of Economics*, 86 (August), pp. 463–75; reprinted in Wood 1, pp. 416–27.

Smithin, J. N. 1985. The definition of involuntary unemployment in Keynes' general theory: a note. *History of Political Economy*, 17, pp. 219–22.

Tarshis, L. 1938. Real wages in the United States and Great Britain. *Canadian Journal of Economics*, 4 (August), pp. 362–76.

Tatom, J. 1985. Interest rate variability and economic performance: further evidence. *Journal of Political Economy*, 93 (October), pp. 1008–18.

Thornton, H. 1802. *An Enquiry into the Nature and Effects of the Paper Credit on Great Britain*, reprints of *Economic Classics*. New York: Kelley, 1965.

Tobin, J. 1948. The fallacies of Lord Keynes' general theory: comment. *Quarterly Journal of Economics*, 62 (November), pp. 763–70; reprinted in Wood 2, pp. 250–6.

1958. Liquidity preference as behavior towards risk. *Review of Economic Studies*, 25 (February), pp. 65–86.

1969. A general equilibrium approach to monetary theory. *Journal of Money, Credit and Banking*, 1 (February), pp. 15–29.

1977. How dead is Keynes? *Economic Inquiry*, 15 (October), pp. 459–68.

1983. Comment [on N. Kaldor, Keynesian economics after fifty years], in D. Worswick and J. Trevithick (eds.), *Keynes and the Modern World*. Cambridge: Cambridge University Press, pp. 28–36.

Tobin, J. and Buiter, W. 1976. Long-run effects of fiscal and monetary policy on aggregate demand, in J. Stein (ed.), *Monetarism*. Amsterdam: North Holland, pp. 273–309.

Vaizey, J. 1969. Keynes. *Irish Banking Review* (June), pp. 10–19; reprinted in Wood 1, pp. 169–81, 1983.

Viner, J. 1936. Mr. Keynes on the causes of unemployment. *Quarterly Journal of Economics*, 51 (November), pp. 147–67; reprinted in Wood 2, pp. 85–98.

Weintraub, S. 1978. *Capitalism's Inflation and Unemployment Crisis*. Reading, Mass: Addison-Wesley.

Williamson, J. 1983. Keynes and the international economic order, in D. Worswick and J. Trevithick (eds.), *Keynes and the Modern World*. Cambridge: Cambridge University Press, pp. 87–112.

Wilson, T. 1983. Comment on Angodike-Dune, Dennis Robertson and Keynes' *General Theory*, in G. C. Harcourt (ed.), *Keynes and His Contemporaries*. New York: St. Martin's pp. 124–8.

Wood, J. C. (ed.) 1983. *John Maynard Keynes, Critical Assessments*, Vols 1–4. London: Croom and Helm.

Index

331